MW00579923

FALLS OF THE OHIO RIVER

Florida Museum of Natural History: Ripley P. Bullen Series

FALLS
of the Ohio River

Archaeology of Native American Settlement

EDITED BY

David Pollack, Anne Tobbe Bader,
and Justin N. Carlson

University of Florida Press

Gainesville

Copyright 2021 by David Pollack, Anne Tobbe Bader, and Justin N. Carlson
All rights reserved
Published in the United States of America

26 25 24 23 22 21   6 5 4 3 2 1

Library of Congress Cataloging-in-Publication Data
Names: Pollack, David, 1951– editor. | Bader, Anne Tobbe, editor. |
    Carlson, Justin N., editor.
Title: Falls of the Ohio River : archaeology of Native American settlement
    / edited by David Pollack, Anne Tobbe Bader, and Justin N. Carlson.
Other titles: Ripley P. Bullen series.
Description: Gainesville : University of Florida Press, [2021] | Series:
    Florida Museum of Natural History: Ripley P. Bullen series | Includes
    bibliographical references and index.
Identifiers: LCCN 2020045487 (print) | LCCN 2020045488 (ebook) | ISBN
    9781683402039 (hardback) | ISBN 9781683402381 (pdf)
Subjects: LCSH: Indians of North America—Ohio River Valley—Antiquities. |
    Indians of North America—Kentucky—Louisville—Antiquities. |
    Louisville (Ky.)—History. | Ohio River Valley—History.
Classification: LCC E78.O4 .F35 2021 (print) | LCC E78.O4 (ebook) | DDC
    977—dc23
LC record available at https://lccn.loc.gov/2020045487
LC ebook record available at https://lccn.loc.gov/2020045488

UF PRESS

**UNIVERSITY
OF FLORIDA**

University of Florida Press
2046 NE Waldo Road
Suite 2100
Gainesville, FL 32609
http://upress.ufl.edu

DEDICATED TO THE MEMORY OF MICHAEL W. FRENCH
A cherished friend, a valued colleague, and a loving family man.
He had an inquisitive mind, a huge heart, and a ready laugh.
He will be greatly missed.

Contents

Figures

Tables

Preface

In 2017, archaeologists from Indiana and Kentucky, some of whom had more than fifty years of experience working in the Falls region, gathered to share data and findings. This gave all present an opportunity for researchers to present their findings on their latest data and interpretations, and to interact with others interested in the archaeology of the Falls region. The focus was a thirty-five-kilometer-radius area surrounding the natural Falls of the Ohio River, located near downtown Louisville, Kentucky. This radius extends to the mouth of the Salt River in Hardin County, and encompasses all or large portions of six counties in Kentucky and Indiana. The subject area includes the Falls of the Ohio River and a surrounding catchment that incorporates four major environmental provinces. These include the dissected uplands of the Outer Bluegrass/Muscatatuck Regional Slope with its numerous streams, the Knobs/Norman Upland, the karstic Mississippian Plateau/Mitchell Plain, and the spring-fed central lacustrine wetlands of the Scottsville Lowlands. Within these provinces, significant environmental settings include the Ohio River floodplain and the dissected valleys of the Floyd's Fork and Salt River drainages.

Known as the "Gateway to the South," the Falls region was a place of convergence for multiple ethnic groups and entrepreneurs. The same was undoubtedly the case prior to European-American settlement—since archaeological research conducted in the Ohio valley suggests that for at least twelve thousand years the Falls of the Ohio River has been an important landscape feature and the Falls region has represented an interaction or boundary zone, separating Native American groups living downstream from those living upstream. For the purposes of the volume we viewed the Falls region as a dynamic interaction zone in which broader regional trends converged, mixed, and perhaps conflicted—resulting in distinct local signatures and patterns that changed over time.

The Louisville Bridges Project involved the construction of two new bridges across the Ohio River: one downtown and one to the east of Louisville. The primary objective of the project was to alleviate downtown traffic congestion. To offset adverse impacts to significant archaeological resources from the construction of both bridges and associated access roads, the Kentucky Transportation Cabinet/Federal Highway Administration funded a survey and investigation of rockshelter sites in the Floyds Fork drainage of eastern Jefferson and Bullitt Counties. In addition to supporting archaeological research in the Falls region, the sponsoring agencies also provided funds for a gathering on the archaeology of the Falls region. Chapter 3 of this volume is a direct result of the study funded by the Kentucky Transportation Cabinet.

Though archaeological fieldwork has been undertaken in this area for more than one hundred years, no one had ever attempted to prepare a regional synthesis. Some of the objectives of these informal discussions were to determine how Native American utilization of the Falls region changed over time; to identify aspects of Archaic, Woodland, and Mississippian lifeways and settlement patterns that served to distinguish those living in the Falls region from their neighbors; to determine the extent to which the archaeological record of the Falls region reflects inter-regional interaction; to identify the extent to which the Falls of the Ohio River was a social boundary; and to contextualize developments in the Falls region relative to those documented in neighboring regions. The result of these discussions is this volume.

The editors of this volume would like to take this opportunity to thank all of the contributors to this volume for all of their hard work and their patience as we undertook the editing process. We also would like to thank those archaeologists from Indiana and Kentucky who shared their time and data, in addition to the two outside reviewers. Your insights greatly enriched the chapters included in this volume.

We also would like to thank the staff of the Kentucky Heritage Council. Finally, we would like to acknowledge the support of the Kentucky Transportation Cabinet/Federal Highway Administration for funding additional work in the Falls region, and encouraging the publication of this volume. We also would like to thank Susan Neumeyer and Daniel Davis of the Division of Environmental Analysis for their support, encouragement, and patience.

1

Introduction

ANNE TOBBE BADER, DAVID POLLACK, AND JUSTIN N. CARLSON

Throughout history, the Falls of the Ohio River has been described both as an idyllic environmental wonder and as a terrifying force of nature (Figure 1.1). This distinctive natural feature was a focal point for cultural development for thousands of years. To the early native peoples, it undoubtedly was imbued with a special symbolic significance. During early historic times, the Falls figured prominently in the navigation lore of the Ohio River. Historical accounts of early travelers are filled with romantic and perhaps exaggerated personal experiences with the Falls.

> Here, the magnificence of the scene, the grandeur of the falls, the unceasing brawl of the cataract, and the beauty of the surrounding prospect, all contribute to render the place truly delightful. . . .
>
> Ashe 1909:21, from Rush 1994:245

> . . . the view of the Falls from the city . . . is one of beauty and romance. They are occasioned by a parapet of limestone extending quite across the stream, which is here about 1 mile in width; and when the water is low the whole chain sparkles with bubbling foam-bells. When the stream is full the descent is hardly perceptible but for the increased rapidity of the current, which varies from 10 to 14 miles an hour. Owing to the height of the freshet, this was the case when we descended them, and there was a wild air or romance about the dark rushing waters. . . .
>
> Flagg 1906 from Thwaites 1904–1907, Vol. 46, pgs. 48–51

Prior to the opening of the Louisville and Portland Canal in 1830, the Falls of the Ohio River presented the single most serious impediment to river navigation between Pittsburgh and New Orleans, a corridor of more than one thousand five hundred kilometers. At the Falls, the Ohio River is diverted

Figure 1.1. The Falls of the Ohio River, 1922. Caufield and Shook Collection (CS 044303). University of Louisville Archives & Special Collections, University of Louisville. http://louisville.edu/library/archives.

into one of three main channels or chutes, each with its own set of rapids. During periods of high water, boats could pass safely over the Falls of the Ohio River with the help of a licensed and experienced Falls pilot.

> They are a terrible place to pass through when the water is as low as now. For the first time I had a dread of wrecking our boat. The rocks are so cragy [sic], the channil [sic] so crooked, and the water so furious and rapid that it requires the utmost care and dexterity to avoid the danger. There are several islands in the Falls and a large island and several sand bars below and riffles for two miles below, so that indeed there is four miles of rapid and difficulty; but the pilot only conducted us the first two and we came safe over the others.
>
> Rodney, edited by Smith and Swick 1997

Rather than a single vertical drop, the Falls of the Ohio River is better characterized as a four-kilometers-long series of low, cascading rapids, dropping more than eight meters along its course. At the widest part of the rapids, the river is nearly one and a half kilometers across. Mallott describes the Falls as follows:

Where the Ohio River crosses the Scottsburg Lowland [see below], the valley is open and several miles in width, and is quite in contrast to the narrow valley and high rocky bluffs either up or down the river from the lowland. Yet it is in this broad portion of the river valley across the lowland that the only stretch of bed-rock is to be seen entirely across the channel [of the Ohio River], and over which occurs the "Falls of the Ohio" where a descent of about 23 feet is made in little over 2 miles.

Mallott 1922:91

As described by Levi (1921):

... the river made a great bend and tossed and tumbled and leaped and roared as it rushed over its rocky bed or glided in and about of the five wooded islands: Towhead, Goose Island, Corn Island, Rock Island, and Sand Island.

During most of the year, the Ohio River was too low for boats to pass over the Falls of the Ohio. This necessitated crews to portage boats, passengers, and goods around the rapids. As a result, the Falls of the Ohio River was largely responsible for the growth of Louisville in Kentucky as well as Jeffersonville and Clarksville in southern Indiana, as businesses sprung up to support the burgeoning cities. Aptly dubbed the "Gateway to the South," the Falls of the Ohio River became a place of convergence for entrepreneurs, traders, and travelers, and it became a place where peoples of many different ethnicities and national origins came together.

The same was undoubtedly the case prior to European-American settlement. Christopher Gist, in his journals of the 1750s, noted that Native Americans knew how to pass safely through the Falls of the Ohio River in their canoes and taught the French traders in the 1600s the safest passageway (Pirtle 1910; Olliges 2015:3,30). He also noted that the currents were strongest on the northwest side and in this area flowed over several ledges (Darlington 1893:59). There are references in Gist's journals to the Falls of the Ohio River as an important Native American landmark and meeting place (Darlington 1893). Gist also mentions the region's salt licks, in Bullitt and Oldham counties (Darlington 1893:130). Native Americans would have arrived at the Falls region by boat or along overland trails. These trails often followed earlier buffalo traces. One such trace crossed a horizontal bed of limestone that stretches nearly the width of the Ohio River just upstream from the Falls. During periods of seasonal low water, crossing was not difficult, and numerous historical accounts tell of people walking across the river with little trouble (Schultz 1810). Extending from the Cumberland Gap to the plains, the buffalo trace at the Falls of the Ohio River connected Native American groups moving overland from the southeast to the northwest. Thus, not only was the Falls of the Ohio River a meeting place for groups moving up and down the Ohio River, but also it was a meeting place for those who followed overland trails.

Archaeological research conducted in the Ohio valley for more than one hundred years has demonstrated that prior to European-American visits, the Falls of the Ohio River was an important landscape feature for more than twelve thousand years. Initially it may have been a place to visit and acquire high-quality chert, but over the millennia its significance on the landscape was dynamic. Often the Falls of the Ohio River formed a boundary zone between Native American groups living downstream from those living upstream. At other times, it was a dynamic interaction zone in which broader trends converged and blended, resulting in a local identity with distinct signatures and patterns that changed over time. By employing the notion of historicity, supplemented with ideas concerning social boundaries and identity, this volume's contributors contextualize the Falls of the Ohio River within these local and broader regional trends.

Historicity, Social Boundaries, and Identity

Societies and ecosystems are not static or unilineal during their long and dynamic histories (Crumley 1994; Winterhalder 1994). Thus, the notion of historicity, which recognizes that cultural developments occur in times of specific interweaving social, political, and environmental conditions, is an important starting point for archaeological inquiry (Balée 2006; Crumley 1994). Sociocultural and ecological constructs of previous events, relationships, and decisions by various actors create legacies that can influence environments and societies long after settlements have been abandoned (Winterhalder 1994; Sassaman 2010). An awareness of a local historicity allows researchers to better model and understand complex cultural developments (Balée 2006; Crumley 1994; Winterhalder 1994). Historicity accounts for dynamic processes that occur on various chronological scales (Green and Perlman 1985; Sassaman 2010). The vestiges of past processes are patterned in the archaeological record in any given region (Green and Perlman 1985). Holistic examination of a variety of archaeological and environmental datasets allows for in-depth and meaningful discussions about the lifeways of groups during specific chronological eras (Crumley et al. 2018).

Humans and the local environment are not disconnected, but rather intertwined, mutually acting upon each other to varying degrees (McGlade 1999:460). Though archaeologists often consider human adaptations to shifting climatic conditions, they also must recognize that humans have altered local environments often in relation to historically specific economic, social, and political circumstances (Håkansson and Widgren 2014). As Rossen and Turner note in Chapter 10, plant domestication was often the result of human creativity in the manipulation and enhancement of the environment (niche construction). In some instances, the imprints of these modifications persisted for only a few seasons (e.g., burning a field or overharvesting plants or animals), while in other cases, their signatures are still etched upon the landscape today (e.g., construction of a platform mound and associated borrow pit that may today be a pond) (Young and Fowler 2000). Some of these actions had the potential to degrade or enhance resources, while others were inconsequential (Balée 2006; Crumley 1994; Crumley et al. 2018; Håkansson and Widgren 2014; Thompson 2013). Modifications to the local environment that survive into succeeding periods may influence actions or choices of later groups (Beneš and Zveleil 1999:74; Fairclough 1999:120).

Examples of Native American impacts on environments seen in the archaeological record of eastern North America are the construction of earthen mounds (Sherwood and Kidder 2011); river mussel discard leading to the formation of deep and expansive shell middens (Marquardt and Watson 2005; see Chapter 4); forest disturbance to promote nut-bearing tree species (Gardner 1997; Munson 1986; Wagner 2005); plant domestication (Smith 2006; see Chapter 10); and the clearing and maintaining of land for agricultural fields (Campbell 1985; Peres and Ledford 2016). One way of clearing land was through burning. For instance, the Big Barrens grasslands encountered by early European settlers in south-central Kentucky were, in part, promoted by Native American land burning perhaps as early as the Archaic period to create habitats for animals and plants (Baskin et al. 1994; Carlson 2019a). Central Kentucky was known historically as the land of cane and clover in large part due to clearing of agricultural fields by Fort Ancient farmers (Campbell 1985), and the cane breaks observed in the Falls region were likely a result of Native American clearing of land for settlements and crops (The Draper Manuscripts, as quoted in Hammon 1978:153). In the Cumberland Plateau, increased charcoal frequencies in pond sediments correspond with archaeological evidence of early plant domestication during the Archaic and Woodland periods (Delcourt et al. 1998).

These modifications occurred in a complex web of socioecological variables and were tied to organizational structures within societies that were aimed at investments in their surrounding landscapes (Håkansson and Widgren 2014). Through consideration of these investments and commitments to landscapes, archaeologists can understand how people become anchored to a place and establish their lives in that location. The Falls region is a distinct landscape that attracted human occupation for many millennia, and the archaeological record reflects how humans interacted with the local environment and neighboring groups through the decisions they made. These decisions were based on the willingness to invest in creating strong daily lives in the region. Decisions changed based on what was socially, politically, economically, or ecologically important at different times, and this is apparent in the archaeological record of the Falls region.

How then do archaeologists acknowledge complex human and environmental histories, while also understanding the dynamism of spatial patterning of people on the landscape? Through an examination of social boundaries, one can gain insights into how people organized themselves on the landscape. The more closed the boundary, the less the social interaction (see Chapters 10 and 11). Boundary maintenance would be reflected in the archaeological record by regional differences in material culture, settlement and subsistence patterns, and social and political organization.

When boundaries are more permeable there is greater interaction between neighboring groups (Feuer 2016; see Chapter 12). Along more permeable cultural boundary zones we often see new relationships develop. Through an examination of these relationships archaeologists can "account for and describe complex cultural trends, [provide a] measure of explanation for these trends, and . . . situate them in a wider anthropological context that permits some discussion of their occurrence and recurrence and thus their historically contingent causes" (Martindale 2009:83). Individuals and social groups at cultural boundaries are often involved in complex webs of economic, political, social, and cultural ties that link them to assimilated objects and practices (Dietler 1998, 2010; Martindale 2009). People use these objects and practices for their own political agendas and assign new meanings to borrowed cultural elements according to their own cosmologies, political relations, and cultural perceptions (Dietler 1998:299). Through their daily decision-making, they become agents of change by constructing new forms of social identity at cultural boundaries.

The relationships between people become manifest through material culture in patterned ways in the archaeological record. Changes in material culture also may be used to express one's social identity. How individuals see themselves and others, and how they relate to broader groups, may be expressed in how they decorate bone pins, the types of bannerstones they make, or how they decorate their ceramic vessels (Diaz-Andreu et al. 2005:1; Peeples 2011:2; see Chapters 6 and 11). Social identity involves a sense of belonging to a place and a group that can be distinguished from other groups. Individuals, during the course of a lifetime, can have multiple identities constructed through interaction, informed by history, culturally mediated, and acquired through agency (Barth 1969; Calhoun 1995; Díaz-Andreu et al. 2005; Emberling 1997; Jenkins 2008; Jones 2002; Peeples 2011).

With a highly recognizable landmark surrounded by distinct environmental zones ranging from floodplains to wetlands to upland ridgetops, the Falls region provides an opportunity to examine the interplay of societal and environmental changes/interactions on a distinct landscape over several millennia. By focusing on a regional historicity, the establishment and maintenance of social boundaries, and changing social identities, the chapters in this volume examine the complex human-human and human-environmental interactions that took place in the Falls region for more than twelve thousand years (Balée 2006; Crumley 1994; Crumley et al. 2018).

Environmental Setting

The Falls of the Ohio River lies within a rich and diverse landscape. Encompassing all or large portions of six counties, the Falls region includes Jefferson, parts of Bullitt and Oldham in Kentucky, and Clark, Floyd, and portions of Harrison in Indiana (Figure 1.2). Each, except for Bullitt, has extensive frontage along the Ohio River; Bullitt contains the Salt River, a major tributary of the Ohio.

The Falls region can be described as a broad flat peneplain that lies between the foot of the Muscatatuck regional slope to the east and the Knobstone Hill Escarpment to the west (Ray 1974:10) (Figure 1.3). The Muscatatuck regional slope is a gently west dipping bedrock that descends a distance of forty kilometers from an altitude of nearly two hundred seventy meters at its east margin to merge with the Scottsburg Lowland one hundred fifty meters in elevation along the Ohio River at the Falls of the Ohio River (Figure 1.3). The north-south aligned lowland is more extensive north of the Ohio River, but intrudes south into Kentucky. It was formed on a belt of limestones, shales, and siltstones that easily erode. To the west, the Knobs rise from the lowland to form the western boundary of the Falls region. The

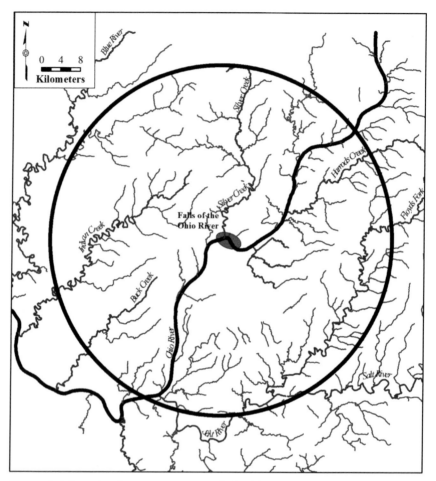

Figure 1.2. Falls region drainage system. Note lack of drainage to the south of the Falls of the Ohio River.

numerous small, isolated, and erosional remnants of the Knobs persist in the lowlands and were preferred locations for Native American habitation (see Chapter 4).

Two predominant stream systems cross the Scottsburg Lowland and flow through deep valleys of the Knobstone-Muldraugh Hill escarpment. These are the Muscatatuck-East Fork of the White River in the northern portion of the lowland, and the Ohio-Salt River system south of the Ohio River. Small tributaries to these major rivers flow across the lowlands in the general north-south axis (Ray 1974:10). Tributaries to the south of the Ohio River include Beargrass Creek, Floyds Fork, and Pond Creek. North of the

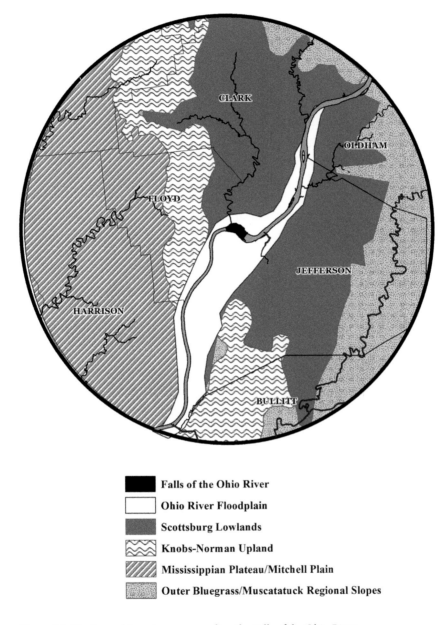

Falls of the Ohio River

Ohio River Floodplain

Scottsburg Lowlands

Knobs-Norman Upland

Mississippian Plateau/Mitchell Plain

Outer Bluegrass/Muscatatuck Regional Slopes

Figure 1.3. Physiographic regions surrounding the Falls of the Ohio River.

Ohio River, Silver Creek, Mill Creek, Indian Creek, and tributaries of the Blue River drain Clark and Floyd counties.

The Falls region lies at the northern extremity of what is known as the Constricted Ohio River valley (Ray 1974). The gorge-like shape of the valley widens to about eight kilometers at the Falls of the Ohio River. The expansive floodplain south of the Ohio River is the broadest open track of bottomlands upstream from the mouth of the Green River, some one hundred sixty kilometers to the southwest. At the Falls of the Ohio River, the river is dominated by a floodplain swell-and-swale topography with discontinuous linear terraces adjoining steep uplands. Upstream from the Falls of the Ohio River, the valley remains relatively wide for about seventy-five kilometers.

Historically, the broad floodplain south of the Falls was poorly drained, consisting of wet and marshy conditions. According to early accounts, central Jefferson County was once peppered with numerous ponds and marshes. The presence of so many ponds created a wetland-like environment that attracted Archaic hunters and gatherers (see Chapter 4). According to Casseday (1852:51), a "map of the city as it was sixty or even thirty years ago, would present somewhat the appearance of an archipelago, a sea full of little islands." Taylor (1933) adds:

> Ponds of one sort or another were once a very conspicuous feature of the topography of the city. They were everywhere and some of the better known of these ponds persisted until fairly recent years . . . I have often heard it said, although I have never had the experience, that one could skate with few interruptions, from the "Junction" clear across to the river, by following the chain of ponds and runs to the south of the city.

The Falls region is further characterized by a convergence of the four major environmental zones. These zones, mirrored on the Kentucky and Indiana sides of the river, are the dissected karstic uplands of the Outer Bluegrass/Muscatatuck Regional Slope with its low-to-moderate relief and broad valleys; the hilly Knobs/Norman Upland that encircles the Falls region to the west and south, and is characterized by flat-topped narrow divides, steep slopes, deep V-shaped valleys, and poor soils; the karstic Mississippian Plateau/Mitchell Plain, a karstic plateau with low relief and numerous sinkholes, sinking streams, streamless valleys, springs, and caverns; and the Scottsburg Lowland, the low, flat, spring-fed, lacustrine wetwoods (McGrain and Currens 1978; Kentucky Geological Survey http://www.uky.edu/KGS/geoky/regionbluegrass.htm; Mallott 1922; Indiana Geological Survey https://igs.indiana.edu/Surficial/Landscapes.cfm). Through these zones flows the Ohio River with its own distinctive natural resources.

This mosaic of proximal habitats provided unusually rich floral and faunal resources to the native inhabitants of the area. In view of the thickness of some Archaic shell middens, mussel beds were extensively exploited by Native Americans residing in the Falls region. For much of its course, the Ohio River flows through limestone-rich bedrock that provides favorable conditions for shellfish. Within this region, numerous mussel species once occupied a variety of microenvironments, including shallow flats, deeper calm pools, and narrow crevices in the rock of fast-moving currents (Goodrich 1929). In 1820, there were more than sixty-eight identifiable freshwater mussel species in the Ohio River (Rafinesque 1824). By as early as 1885, with the construction of locks and dams, in addition to overharvesting and pollution, critical habitat for shellfish had significantly degraded and resulted in a loss of mussel habitat (Goodrich 1929:13; Taylor 1989:188; Williams 1882:17). Still, even by the late 1800s, numerous mussel species persisted in large numbers.

The Falls region also boasts an abundance and variety of high-quality raw materials for making chipped stone tools, including in particular Muldraugh and Wyandotte cherts. The chert of the Muldraugh Member of the Lower Mississippian Borden Formation is found on slopes but is also present on some ridgetops. This chert-rich landscape, with high-quality Muldraugh and Wyandotte cherts widely available below the Falls of the Ohio River, appears to have influenced Early Archaic group movement into and across the region's landscape (see Chapter 2). For much of the Middle and Late Archaic, however, as groups settled into the region and increased their exploitation of upland resources during the Holocene Climatic Optimum, they devoted less effort to seeking out higher-quality cherts, relying instead on more locally available, lesser-quality Muldraugh chert (see Chapters 3 and 4). By the Terminal Archaic and continuing into the Early and Middle Woodland subperiods, there was a renewed interest in high-quality Wyandotte chert, which was used not only to manufacture projectile points but also to create ritual items for exchange with other groups on a regional scale (see Chapters 8 and 9). By the end of the Late Woodland subperiod and continuing into the Mississippian period, local flint knappers again focused greater attention on Middle to Upper Devonian Boyle Formation cherts that can be found in the alluvial deposits of the Ohio River and its tributaries.

Summary of Chapters/What Is to Come

By the beginning of the Early Archaic, the Falls region had become a focal point on the landscape and would remain so for the following twelve thousand years (Figures 1.4–1.7). The Falls of the Ohio River was a landmark that would have been readily recognized and easy to locate by Native Americans. As such, it would have been a convenient meeting place. Without this feature, native populations may never have aggregated at this location to the extent that they did.

Though the Falls region was undoubtedly used by Paleoindian hunters and gatherers, to date no Paleoindian sites have been excavated in this area. Paleoindian use of the region is reflected in the recovery of fluted projectile points (e.g., Clovis, Cumberland, and even Folsom-like examples) and the later un-fluted points (Agate Basin, Beaver Lake, Hardaway, Dalton, and Quad) (Harrell 2005). Numerous examples of these points have been found as isolates or within Archaic contexts from high terraces overlooking the Ohio River valley (Seeman 1975), river crossings, upland karstic areas, prominent overlooks near high-volume springs, rockshelters and caves (Bader et al. 2018; Carlson and Pollack 2019), and low marshy areas with salt and mineral deposits (Collins and Driskell 1979:1027). The materials from which these artifacts were made include local sources, but nonlocal cherts are well represented, reflecting the transient nature of Paleoindian use of the Falls region.

It is possible that intact Paleoindian sites are present in deeply buried sites along the Ohio River floodplain. For instance, at the Longworth-Gick site in southwestern Jefferson County, chipped stone debris was recovered from a depth of four meters below the Kirk and Palmer zones, though no associated diagnostics were recovered and recovery was complicated by depth, leading to investigation only through coring (Collins 1979a). The remains of Pleistocene megafauna are not uncommon finds in the Falls region. Though most have been from deeply (ca. twelve meters) buried deposits in the Ohio River alluvium and gravels, they also have been found in more shallow contexts in the uplands of the Bluegrass region to the east, and in the shallow caves and rockshelters in the dissected tributary valleys of the Salt River.

The chapters in this volume have synthesized the cultural history of the Falls region. Underpinned by historicity, social boundaries, and social identity, they recast the Falls region as a stage for processes of sociocultural and socioenvironmental interaction. The patterns observed in the archaeological record represent the impressions of manifold historical events that played out over several thousand years. Thus, whether during the Archaic,

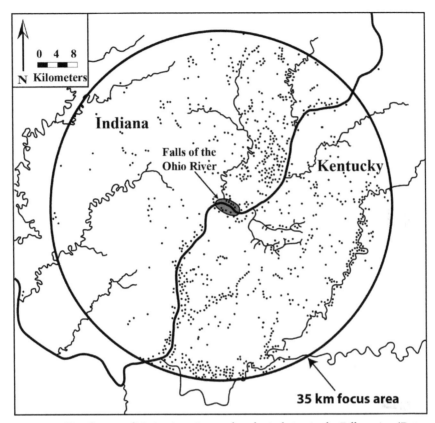

Figure 1.4. Distribution of Native American archaeological sites in the Falls region (Data provided by the Kentucky Office of State Archaeology and Indiana Division of Archaeology and Historic Preservation-SHAARD).

Woodland, or Mississippian periods, the Falls region would have been a dynamic interaction zone, subject to historically particular developments that are fluid, ever-changing, and constantly renegotiated, based on cultural preferences and needs; group and individual identities; and shifting environmental conditions. The resulting sociocultural and socioenvironmental relationships have chronological and spatial dimensions that are influenced by internal and external forces. This volume reflects the authors' consideration of the innumerable variables, environmental and cultural, that played a role in the everyday lives of those who lived in the Falls region over several millennia.

Following this introduction, Russell Stafford (Chapter 2), through an examination of projectile point styles, suggests that by Early Archaic times the Falls region was a significant cultural boundary zone. But rather than

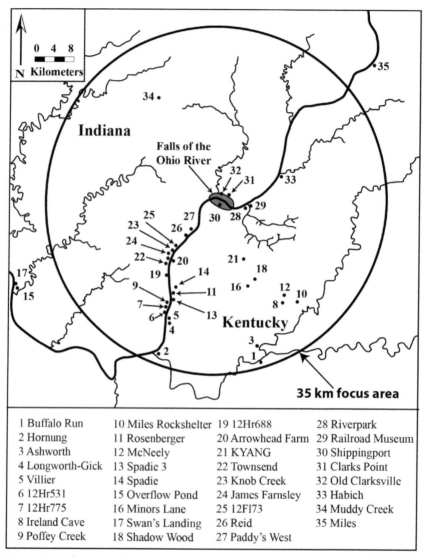

1 Buffalo Run	10 Miles Rockshelter	19 12Hr688	28 Riverpark
2 Hornung	11 Rosenberger	20 Arrowhead Farm	29 Railroad Museum
3 Ashworth	12 McNeely	21 KYANG	30 Shippingport
4 Longworth-Gick	13 Spadie 3	22 Townsend	31 Clarks Point
5 Villier	14 Spadie	23 Knob Creek	32 Old Clarksville
6 12Hr531	15 Overflow Pond	24 James Farnsley	33 Habich
7 12Hr775	16 Minors Lane	25 12Fl73	34 Muddy Creek
8 Ireland Cave	17 Swan's Landing	26 Reid	35 Miles
9 Poffey Creek	18 Shadow Wood	27 Paddy's West	

Figure 1.5. Archaic period sites mentioned in text.

an east-west boundary marker, affinities were with groups to the north and south. This is reflected by the presence of both Thebes projectile points, a type more common to the north of the Ohio River, and Kirk projectile points, a type more common at sites to the south of the Ohio River. The presence of a Pine Tree Kirk variety, however, is suggestive of a distinctive style zone that is not present in other areas of the southeast United States. Stafford also identifies a great deal of diversity in Early Archaic mobility

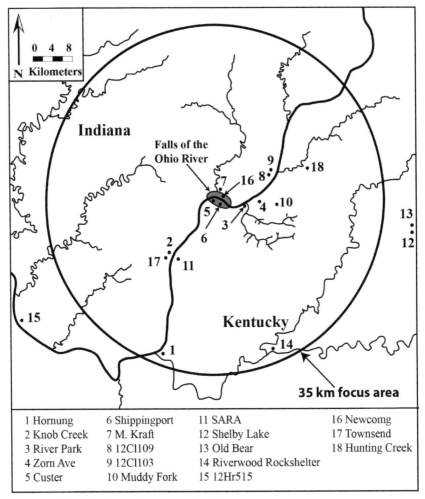

1 Hornung	6 Shippingport	11 SARA	16 Newcomg
2 Knob Creek	7 M. Kraft	12 Shelby Lake	17 Townsend
3 River Park	8 12Cl109	13 Old Bear	18 Hunting Creek
4 Zorn Ave	9 12Cl103	14 Riverwood Rockshelter	
5 Custer	10 Muddy Fork	15 12Hr515	

Figure 1.6. Woodland period sites mentioned in text.

patterns, landscape use, stone tool production, and chert procurement strategies. Clearly, by Early Archaic times, Native Americans were repeatedly visiting the Falls region on their seasonal rounds to exploit the region's high-quality chert resources.

In Chapter 3, Justin Carlson, Greg Maggard, Gary Stinchcomb, and Claiborne Sea examine Middle Archaic human-environmental relationships and shifting resource procurement and settlement strategies. They argue that the warming and drying trends of the Middle Holocene resulted in the frequent, short-term residential moves of local hunter-gatherers who

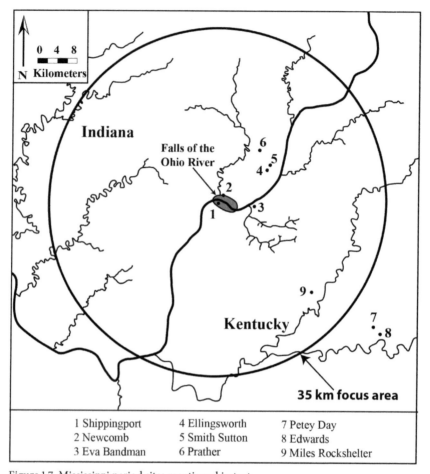

1 Shippingport	4 Ellingsworth	7 Petey Day
2 Newcomb	5 Smith Sutton	8 Edwards
3 Eva Bandman	6 Prather	9 Miles Rockshelter

Figure 1.7. Mississippi period sites mentioned in text.

sought to take advantage of increased upland nut mast and large deer populations. The seasonal rounds of Middle Archaic hunter-gatherers involved continued use of floodplains supplemented with increased use of upland caves and rockshelters. Sedimentation histories documented at both lowland and upland sites suggest that the drier conditions of the Middle Holocene resulted in significant upslope erosion and downhill accumulation. They also note that as groups settled into the region, projectile point styles such as Knob Creek Stemmed and Middle Archaic Corner Notched reflect a local social identity. These changes in settlement patterns and projectile point styles are correlated with a shift from an emphasis on high-quality Wyandotte chert, to poorer quality cherts located near upland camps.

In Chapter 4, Anne Bader notes that with the introduction of Matanzas projectile points (ca. 4300 BCE), those residing in the Falls region had greater affinities with those living to the west in the lower Ohio valley. Throughout the Scottsburg phase (4300 to 3400 BCE), hunter-gatherers living in the Falls region situated themselves in strategic locations, such as atop knolls beside wetlands, at the confluences of streams, and along river terraces within easy access to mussel shoals. With a long-term vested interest in these places, many became persistent places on the landscape. In addition, the association of cemeteries with many of these sites may reflect the development of corporate group boundaries within the Falls region, with certain locales designated as appropriate places to bury the dead.

In Chapter 5, Duane Simpson and Stephen Mocas consider the relationship between stratified alluvial deposits and the archaeological record at the RiverPark site. Through their examination of mobility patterns in the Falls region, they argue that the amount of time Late Archaic groups stayed at any one site during their seasonal rounds was highly variable, with some sites being occupied multiple times within a single year. At the RiverPark site there was a change in mortuary practices toward the end of the Late Archaic from discrete cemeteries and habitation areas, to individuals being interred within habitation areas. In either case, during revisits, residents would have remembered ancestors buried at the site. By so doing, they were leaving their mark on the physical landscape and building social memories surrounding that landscape.

In Chapter 6, Rick Burdin argues that large features with associated postholes documented at the Overflow Pond and Spadie 3 sites represent the remains of early Late Archaic houses. Burdin goes on to suggest that these more substantial structures represent changing hunter-gatherer social organization associated with increased sedentism within the Falls region. The building of structures implies greater investments associated with territorial demarcation and smaller home ranges. With more permanent settlements and decreased mobility, individuals and groups would have made efforts to communicate their social affiliations and status to others. This led to distinctive bannerstone styles that reflected social boundedness and identity within the Falls region, and to bone pin styles that signaled ties to those living to the west in the lower Ohio River valley.

In Chapter 7, through an analysis of a forearm cache recovered from Site 12Fl73, Christopher Schmidt examines the social impact of what he refers to as "trophy taking": the intentional placement of isolated elements from other individuals with the dead. In contextualizing the Site 12Fl73 cache relative to other known examples of trophy taking, he suggests that Middle and Late Archaic mortuary practices may have been dominated by a cosmology that required the collection and burial of certain human body parts (see also Chapter 4 and Chapter 5). In addition, the economic resources of the Falls region, coupled with an increasing use of symbols and stylizations to communicate group membership and group identity, besides the territoriality implied by cemeteries, may have formed a nexus whereby trophy taking became a legitimized sociocultural phenomenon.

In Chapter 8, Stephen Mocas and Duane Simpson consider the late Archaic Riverton and the Terminal Archaic Buck Creek phases. Late Archaic and Terminal Archaic settlements reflect a continuation of earlier Archaic patterns, with an intensification of the exploitation of nut resources and an increased reliance on starchy seed plants of the Eastern Agricultural Complex (EAC). By the Terminal Archaic, there is a shift from the use of river gravels and other local sources to manufacture projectile points to a preference for high-quality Wyandotte and St. Louis cherts. This shift in chert use is associated with the production of Turkey-tail cache blades manufactured from Wyandotte chert. The widespread distribution of Turkey-tail points is suggestive of the participation of those living in the Falls region in broader rituals of the Eastern Woodlands that may presage those of later Adena and Hopewell groups.

In Chapter 9, Stephen Mocas summarizes trends in Early, Middle, and Late Woodland material culture, settlement patterns, subsistence patterns, and mortuary practices. Throughout the Woodland period the Falls region appears to have been a border area, with material culture similarities suggestive of greater interaction with groups to the east than to the west of the Falls region. For the Early and Middle Woodland subperiods, Mocas suggests a seasonal settlement system similar to that of the Late Archaic, but with floodplain sites being occupied more intensively and for longer periods of time, coupled with an increased reliance on starchy and oily seeded plants and a decline in nut consumption. An increase in house size and the presence of large storage pits reflect a greater investment in place. The mining of Wyandotte chert for the production of blanks for extra-regional exchange continued to be important to the local economy. By Late Woodland times, however, there was less demand for Wyandotte chert. There also is evidence of seasonal rounds, with a greater focus on floodplain localities in the summer and the upland rockshelters and ridgetops during the winter.

In Chapter 10, Jack Rossen and Jocelyn Turner highlight trends in Native American plant use in the Falls region. Archaic and Woodland patterns parallel those in other regions, with an initial heavy reliance on nuts and wild plants giving way to a greater reliance on native cultigens by the Woodland period. By 1000 CE, as Rossen and Turner suggest, Mississippian groups living at and downstream from the Falls region, and Fort Ancient groups living upstream from the Falls region, had different plant subsistence strategies. Mississippian groups appear to have maintained a reliance on nuts and native cultigens as they increased their consumption of maize. In comparison, as Fort Ancient groups increased their consumption of maize, they decreased their reliance on nuts and native cultigens. Unlike Mississippian groups, Fort Ancient peoples incorporated beans as part of their diet by at least 1200 CE. After 1300 CE the Mississippian/Fort Ancient plant-use boundary appears to have been more permeable.

For the purposes of this volume, the Mississippian occupation of the Falls region was divided into early and late subdivisions. The early Mississippian subdivision extends from 1000–1300 CE, and the late Mississippian subdivision extends from 1300–1450 CE. For the early Mississippian subdivision, Robert McCullough and Cheryl Ann Munson note that the Prather polity was situated on the northeastern boundary of the Mississippian world (Chapter 11). They also suggest that the Prather polity was a result of interaction with larger Mississippian polities to the west, such as Cahokia. This interaction led to the establishment of a mound center. As with the plant use noted by Rossen and Turner, the material culture recovered from early Mississippian sites in the Falls region is suggestive of a rigid Mississippian/Fort Ancient boundary.

In Chapter 12, Michael French and David Pollack examine the late Mississippian occupation of the Falls region, which followed the collapse of the Prather polity and lasted until 1450 CE. French and Pollack argue that ceramic production is a learned behavior and is tied to the social identity of a person or a group. They note strong similarities between Falls region and Angel ceramic vessel form and decoration, which, they suggest, points to continued interaction with downriver polities following the demise of the Prather polity and reflects a reaffirmation of their Mississippian social identity. The large number of Fort Ancient ceramics recovered from some late Mississippian sites reflects the presence of Fort Ancient households within these settlements. This supports the notion of a more permeable boundary at this time, as reflected in plant food consumption.

In Chapter 13, David Pollack, Anne Bader, Justin Carlson, and Richard Jefferies characterize trends in the changing cultural landscape of the Falls region. They note that the chapters included in this volume demonstrate that for more than twelve thousand years, the Falls of the Ohio River was a focal point on the social landscape. As such, it was at times a crossroads, a social interaction zone, and a frontier or boundary. From a historical eco-logical perspective, over time, groups living in the Falls region constantly negotiated changing social and environmental conditions.

ACKNOWLEDGMENTS

The authors would like to express their appreciation to Mr. Paul Olliges of the Falls of the Ohio State Park and Mr. Jim Holmberg of the Filson Club Historical Society for providing a comprehensive compilation of historical eyewitness accounts of the Falls of the Ohio River from the Library and Special Collections of the Society. This paper was compiled in 2015 by Mr. Olliges and was entitled "Falls Rapids Eyewitnesses"; it was the source of many of the historical quotes contained in this chapter. Many thanks as well to Dr. Tim Sullivan for many hours of hard work drafting the figures for this chapter.

2

Early Archaic Dating, Chert Use, and Settlement Mobility in the Falls Region

C. RUSSELL STAFFORD

As with later Native Americans, the rapids at the Falls of the Ohio River was undoubtedly a well-known place on the landscape for Early Archaic hunter-gatherers during the early Holocene, and, based on the rich archaeological record (see Jefferies 2008), it appears that resources, including high-quality tool stone, consistently attracted hunter-gatherers to this area. The purpose of this chapter is to review the Early Archaic (8000–6000 BCE) archaeological record in the Falls of the Ohio region by focusing on excavation data recovered from three sites with buried occupations: James Farnsley (12Hr520) (Stafford and Cantin 2009a), Swan's Landing (12Hr304) (Mocas and Smith 1995; Smith 1986), and Longworth-Gick (15Jf243) (Collins 1979a) (Figure 1.5). I also discuss several additional archaeological sites where more limited investigations have encountered buried Early Archaic remains in the Ohio River floodplain, including the Townsend site (12Hr482) (Mocas 2008), the Poffey Creek site (12Hr403) (Stafford and Cantin 1992), and the Duke Energy Gallagher Pipeline project (12Hr688, Hr689, 12Hr775, 12Hr531) (Cantin and Stafford 2012). From the excavated sites, there are at least twelve separate Early Archaic occupations associated with 22 radiocarbon dates. This sample of the Early Archaic time horizon will be used to evaluate chronological issues, stone raw material use, style boundaries, and variability in settlement mobility in the Falls region.

MIDDLE OHIO RIVER GEOMORPHIC HISTORY

Since most of the available data comes from buried site contexts, it is essential to briefly summarize the geomorphic history of the Ohio River below the Falls of the Ohio River. During the Wisconsin epoch, large quantities of coarse sand and gravel outwash were deposited in the Ohio valley trench (Gray 1984). Late Wisconsin episodes of river downcutting created two high terraces at an elevation of 135 m above mean sea level (amsl) or greater below the Falls of the Ohio River (Gray 1984). The Ohio River channel meandered extensively during the Holocene (Gray 1984; Stafford 2004), producing a ridge and swale topography in most bottom reaches of the valley. The ridges are typically the product of compound channel side bars and point bars resulting from Ohio thalweg channel meandering (Gray 1984; Stafford 2004). Stafford (2004) proposed that soil orders could be used to estimate Holocene floodplain landform age and found that Alfisols are strongly correlated with early to middle Holocene landforms in the floodplain and can be used to predict the location of Early Archaic and early Middle Archaic buried sites (Stafford 2004).

The stratigraphy and dating at the Caesars Archaeological Project (CAP) provide a baseline record of the development of the Holocene floodplain (Stafford 2004). CAP is located at the downriver end of Knob Creek bottom about seventeen kilometers below the Falls. Figure 2.1 shows a cross-section of the Holocene deposits at CAP based on both excavation and drilling records (Stafford 2004). The Holocene alluvial sequence is about ten meters thick, which is typical in the floodplain in this reach of the river. Based on a series of radiocarbon ages from CAP, the river channel was on the west side of the valley in this segment during the early Holocene with fine-grained point bar sediments deposited by 9500 BCE (Stafford 2004). Deposition waned by about 6900 BCE, and a soil began developing at the surface of this landform. The Alfisol soil mapped in this location is consistent with this early Holocene age (Stafford 2004). Subsequently the Ohio River channel meandered to the east and reached its current location by 6400 BCE (Stafford 2004). The current levee at CAP stabilized by about 2500 BCE, although there was a resumption of overbank deposition during the historic period, creating a thin capping veneer.

The early Holocene terrace surface is at 132.7 m amsl at CAP, which is several feet higher than the current Ohio River levee (<131.8 m amsl) and about five meters above the Knob Creek floodplain that flanks the terrace escarpment. This CAP terrace is traceable along the western valley margin as far upriver as the mouth of Knob Creek to at least twenty kilometers downriver in Rosewood Bottom (Stafford and De Rego 2012). It varies in elevation from 132.8 m amsl at Knob Creek to 131.5 m amsl in Rosewood Bottom. An Alfisol, characterized by a highly weathered B horizon, is consistently mapped on this terrace surface. Based on studies to date we have

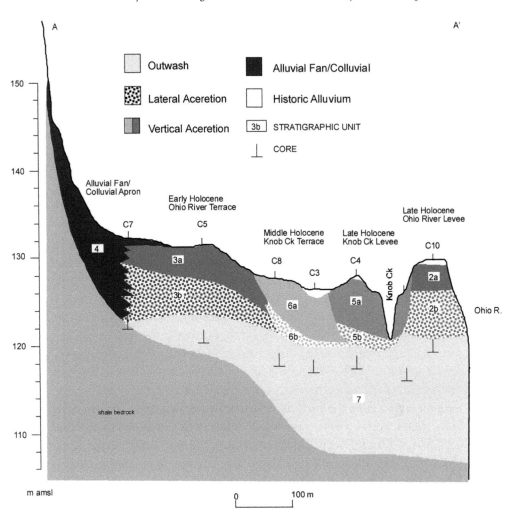

Figure 2.1. Schematic cross-section of deposits at the Caesars Archaeological Project.

informally named this landform the Rosewood Terrace, although others have simply referred to it as the high floodplain (Boulding 1995).

The terrace is often flanked by a deep paleochannel swale (6 m) that is very apparent upriver from CAP in Knob Creek bottom (Scholl 2008) and in Rosewood Bottom (De Rego 2012), as well as other reach segments. Limited coring (Stafford and Cantin 2010; De Rego 2012) indicates that this swale is a partial fragment of the early Holocene Ohio River channel that did not completely backfill, because channel meandering was impeded by high elevation late Wisconsin gravel bars as it meandered from west to east (De Rego 2012; Stafford and De Rego 2012). The Holocene Ohio River was largely incapable of moving glacial gravels, and thus there were relatively sudden shifts in channel location leaving deep swales that contained wetlands. Geomorphological investigation thus far indicates that the meandering channel pattern of the Ohio River was established early on (pre-Holocene) and that floodplain paludal environments remained largely unchanged in character over the last ten thousand years.

FALLS EARLY ARCHAIC CHRONOLOGY

As previously noted, there are 22 Early Archaic radiocarbon ages available from the Falls region (BCE dates are the calibrated median probability; Calib 7.1). Figure 2.2 is a schematic representation of the stratigraphy at the Longworth-Gick, Swan's Landing, James Farnsley, and Townsend sites showing the typical thickness of the Holocene alluvium in this area. The majority of the dates are from the Farnsley site stratigraphic sequence, which spans the period from more than 10,000 to 7300 BCE. The earliest cluster of dates is from what has been termed the Early Side Notched component, which is buried up to five meters below the surface of the Rosewood Terrace. Samples from this zone cluster around 9500 BCE; that is, the samples cluster around the late Wisconsin/Holocene boundary. All of these dates are derived from surface hearth features. Only four diagnostic projectile points were recovered from the Early Side Notched zone (and two nondiagnostic base fragments). Two of these points are associated with a hearth dated to 7694 BCE (9955±86 RCYBP) at about five meters below surface in point bar sediments. Both are reworked but have close affinities to the Thebes cluster (Figure 2.3A). One of the other points more closely aligns with the Kirk Corner Notched Small type (see Stafford 2009:294–96). The fourth point looks like a stemmed type, but the original base (see Stafford 2009:298) of a previously notched point was broken and reworked into its current form. The blade shape and retouching are consistent with St. Charles technology (see Stafford 2009).

Charcoal was scarce in the Thebes/St. Charles zone, so only a single date from a surface hearth is available (8770 BCE; 9490±60 RCYBP) (Figures 2.2 and 2.4). Its sigma overlaps with the dates from the Kirk zone at the top of the sequence. The Thebes workshop to the west, higher on the landform, lacked charred remains, and no associated radiocarbon dates are available for this zone. Two sediment samples associated with the workshop were run using optically stimulated luminescence dating (Feathers 2007), yielding an average calendar date of 8220 BCE (10,500±424 cal BP). Although the standard error is large, in calendar years, the date is consistent with the

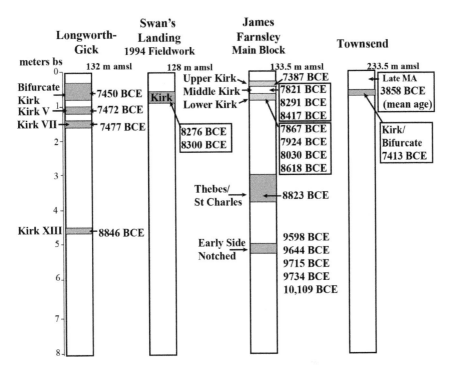

Figure 2.2. Schematic sections of buried Early Archaic sites in the Falls region (BCE ages are the calibrated mean probability).

one radiocarbon age from the Main Block. Thebes points (including classic keyhole form; Figure 2.3B) and St. Charles points were recovered from the Main Block and Workshop.

The Kirk zone was divided into three subzones (Lower, Middle, and Upper) based on changes in debris density and feature depths. There were no culturally sterile deposits separating the subzones. The seven dates from the Lower and Middle Kirk zones range from 8610 to 7752 BCE, but they overlap considerably. Four Kirk Corner Notched Cluster subtypes were identified in the more than 2,100 points associated with the Kirk zone. The subtypes in order of frequency are Pine Tree, Kirk Large, Kirk Small, and Stilwell (Figure 2.3). Although Pine Tree points (Figure 2.3C) are typically seen as reworked or resharpened Kirk Corner Notched points, most Pine Trees at Farnsley were originally manufactured in that form and represent a distinctive style (Cantin 2009). In the first three subtypes there are no stratigraphic trends in frequency by depth. Stilwell points (Figure 2.3F), however, are most prevalent in the Upper Kirk subzone and a significantly later date of 7374 BCE (8320±80 RCYBP) is associated with this zone.

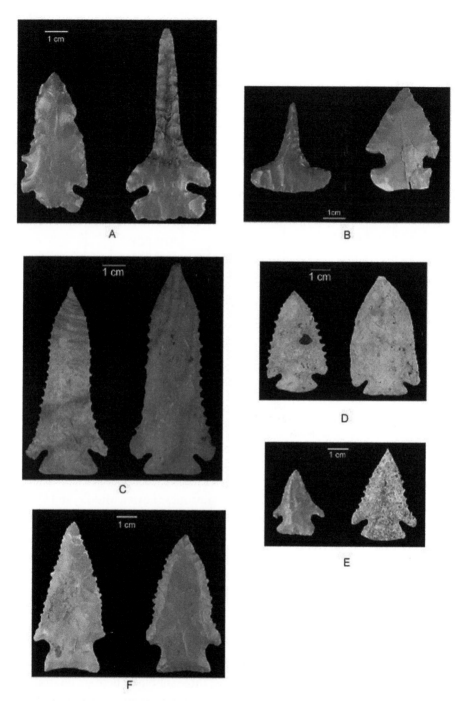

Figure 2.3. Early Archaic projectile points from the Farnsley site (12Hr520): *a*, Early Side Notched; *b*, Thebes Cluster; *c*, Kirk Corner Notched Pine Tree; *d*, Kirk Corner Notched Large; *e*, Kirk Corner Notched Small; *f*, Stilwell.

Calibrated Age Ranges

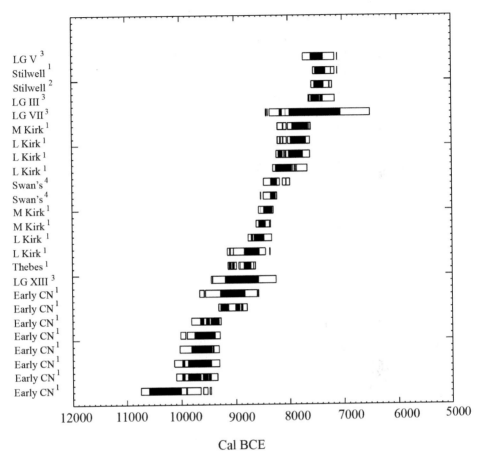

Figure 2.4. Calib 7.04 one and two sigma block plot of Early Archaic radiocarbon ages in calendar years BCE (outlier Early Side Notched date (Beta152942) not included and split sample average from feature F313 used): 1) Farnsley, 2) Townsend, 3) Longworth-Gick, 4) Swan's Landing.

The adjacent Townsend site is characterized by a thick late Middle Archaic rock-filled midden that overlays a significant Early Archaic occupation. Although mixing is present, this zone contains all of the Kirk subtypes found at Farnsley. Like the Upper Kirk subzone, Stilwell points are also present, as well as MacCorkle bifurcates. A pit feature from this Early Archaic zone yielded a date of 7413 BCE (8360±80 RCYBP) (Mocas 2008), consistent with these later point types and with the age from the Upper Kirk at Farnsley. Light density occupations are present at a greater depth at

Townsend, but no diagnostic artifacts were recovered from this zone. Nor were any radiocarbon samples obtained.

Although Swan's Landing in western Harrison County has long been known by collectors, professional investigations have been limited to a few units (Smith 1986; Mocas and Smith 1995). The initial excavations at Swan's Landing in the 1980s resulted in radiocarbon ages that were outside the expected dates for Kirk occupations, and contamination (coal) was suspected. Excavations from the 1994 field season produced samples with radiocarbon dates within the predicted range at 7000+ BCE (Mocas and Smith 1995) (Figures 2.2 and 2.4). Kirk Corner Notched points, including the Pine Tree variety, were recovered in association with these dates, although the point sample is small. The radiocarbon samples come from a thick but shallowly buried cultural deposit (<1 m below surface) on the high floodplain surface (Mocas and Smith 1995), equivalent to the Rosewood Terrace. The Kirk deposits also slope toward the current river channel, where they are more deeply buried (3 m below surface) and stratified with at least two separate zones. Overall the Swan's Landing ages fall well within the date range of the Lower and Upper Kirk components at the James Farnsley site (see Figure 2.4).

The Longworth-Gick site, located in southwest Jefferson County, Kentucky, was one of several sites where major excavations were conducted during the 1970s (Collins 1979a). A very thick (7.5 m) stratigraphic sequence of Early Archaic occupations was encountered at the site (Figure 2.2). Single radiocarbon dates were obtained from four different Early Archaic zones. The oldest date is 8846 BCE (9490±230 RCYBP) (Collins 1979a:579) (Figures 2.2 and 2.4). It was obtained from Zone XIII at a depth of 4.5 m below surface. A single small Kirk-like point was recovered from this zone (Collins 1979a; cf., French 1998). It is superficially similar to the Kirk Small point from the Early Side Notched zone at Farnsley.

Two zones from which Kirk Corner Notched points were recovered yielded very similar radiocarbon ages of about 7455 BCE (8400±86 RCYBP), substantially younger than the dates from the Kirk zones at Farnsley and Swan's Landing. At the top of the stratigraphic sequence is a thick deposit (Zone III) of artifacts and features where Kirk Corner Notched and a variety of bifurcates were recovered, including MacCorkle, LeCroy, and Kanawha (Collins 1979a). This mix of point styles is similar to the Early Archaic occupation at the Townsend site and to a certain extent (although lacking bifurcates) to the Upper Kirk zone at the Farnsley site. The radiocarbon date from the Kirk/Bifurcate zone at Longworth-Gick of 7458 BCE (8420±110

RCYBP) is consistent with the late Kirk dates at Townsend and Farnsley. Radiocarbon ages in the 8000 BCE range typically have wide probability distributions as seen in Figure 2.4, but the available ages form a largely cohesive cluster.

Figure 2.4 is a Calib 7.04 (Stuiver et al. 2017) block plot of 22 radiocarbon samples from the Falls region that helps us to better visualize the relationship between the Early Archaic occupations. It is apparent that the dating of Early Archaic sites in the Falls region provides some of the earliest known radiocarbon ages and point samples from the Midsouth or Midwest. Dates and points from Farnsley, and potentially the Longworth-Gick Zone XIII occupation, span the poorly known late Wisconsin-early Holocene boundary. Radiocarbon ages in the 9500 BCE range typically have wide probability distributions as seen in Figure 2.4, but the available ages form a largely cohesive cluster. Thebes Cluster points are, in particular, poorly dated even though it is not unusual to recover them in surface surveys (Stafford et al. 1988; Justice 1987). Radiocarbon ages from Twin Ditch (Morrow 1996) and Graham Cave (Klippel 1971) far to the west provide the only other Thebes Cluster dates. In addition, the small Kirk-like forms from the Early Side Notched zone and Longworth-Gick Zone XIII fall into this boundary period, suggesting a contemporaneous association of early Thebes and Kirk Corner Notched points.

The Kirk Corner Notched Cluster dates at Farnsley and Swan's Landing are consistent with radiocarbon ages from the Tennessee River valley (Chapman 1976) and elsewhere in the southeast ranging from ca. 7400 to 6700 BCE. Longworth-Gick ages from Zone V and Zone VII are more difficult to assess given the wide probability distributions (especially the Zone VII age), but they do overlap at two sigma with the Swan's Landing and Middle and Lower Kirk ages at Farnsley.

The late dates from the Early Archaic at Farnsley, Townsend, and Zone III at Longworth-Gick are consistent with point styles considered later in the Early Archaic sequence, like MacCorkle, other smaller bifurcates, and Stilwell. The presence of Kirk Corner Notched large and small varieties in these contexts may be seen as problematic by some, given the late ages compared to classic Kirk Corner Notched in the Southeast. Slowing depositional rates at these sites might account for this mixing, but the lack of buried A horizon development reflecting a stable surface makes this explanation less tenable. Furthermore, there is some evidence that the generic Kirk Corner Notched style persists even after 6900 BCE into the early Middle Archaic (Stafford 2004; Stafford and Cantin 2009a; see also Chapter 3).

EARLY ARCHAIC POINT CLUSTERS AND STYLISTIC BOUNDARIES

The two major Early Archaic point clusters represented in the Falls region are Thebes and Kirk Corner Notched. These two clusters have different geographic distributions across the Midwest and Southeast, although they do overlap. Thebes Cluster (Thebes/St. Charles) points are commonly found in surface contexts across Ohio, Indiana, Illinois, and Missouri (Justice 1987). In the few excavated contexts like Graham Cave, Twin Ditch, and Farnsley, Thebes and St. Charles points co-occur, although St. Charles points are thought to have a wider distribution than Thebes, insofar as they also occur across much of southeastern United States (Justice 1987:54). In general, however, the Thebes Cluster appears to be a more northern and Midwestern point style (that is, north of the Ohio River valley). The origins of the Thebes Cluster are hinted at by the deep excavations at the James Farnsley site. Two of the points from the Early Side Notched zone, discussed earlier, have clear affinities to the Thebes Cluster, even though they have been extensively reworked. These Early Side Notched zone dates suggest that the Thebes Cluster has its origins during (or possibly earlier than) the late Wisconsin/Holocene boundary. In the Falls region, this may be the equivalent to Dalton given its apparent absence from, or at least rarity in, this area (Jefferies 2008:82).

As seen in the large collection of Kirk Corner Notched Cluster points from the Farnsley site and other excavated Kirk sites, there is a wide range of variation in this cluster that probably accounts for its identification over most of the eastern United States (Justice 1987). The Kirk Corner Notched Cluster, although found over a wide geographic area, is primarily a Southeastern-centered style being most common in Kentucky, Alabama, Georgia, and the Carolinas (Justice 1987:72). It is also a common type in the Falls region, as evidenced by the sites discussed in this chapter.

It is clear that Kirk Cluster points and associated stone tool production borrows heavily from Dalton technology (Cantin 2009; Stafford and Cantin 2009a). As documented by Cantin (2009), the distinctive serial serration on Pine Tree points is identical to the technology that was used during the Dalton period to serrate point blades (Bradley 1997). In addition, the technomorphology of the large number of adzes recovered from the Kirk zone at Farnsley is essentially the same as that of the Dalton adzes (Cantin 2009). Sassaman (2010:31; see also Justice 1987:43) argues that there is a lineal connection between Dalton, Hardaway Side Notched, and later Early Archaic notched point styles. As noted previously, the Early Side Notched zone at Farnsley contains a point that falls morphologically into this sequence in association with the 8000+ BCE range. The small Kirk-like point from the Early Side Notched zone is distinguishable from the Kirk Corner Notched Small variety from the later Kirk zone at the site. The flaking pattern on the blade lacks the pressure retouch typically found on later Kirk Corner Notched Small points. It is a single point, however, so it is unclear if this technological difference is a clear marker of the earliest Kirk Cluster points. Nevertheless, it places the small Kirk-like points at the late Wisconsin/Holocene boundary, suggesting that both Thebes and Kirks have very early roots in the Falls region.

In the later Kirk zone, the Pine Tree subcluster is distinctive as a type that may represent a style zone in the Falls region. Although Pine Trees are distributed throughout the Southeast, they are usually a minor component of the Kirk Corner Notched Cluster samples from these sites (Cantin 2009) and are usually characterized as resharpened Kirk Corner Notched Large (Justice 1987:80). At Farnsley, they are the most common subtype and the retouch is technologically distinctive. This type of Pine Tree also occurs at Swan's Landing (Cantin 2009) and Ashworth Rockshelter (DiBlasi 1981). They do not appear to be present in the Kirk zones at Longworth-Gick, however (Collins 1979a; French 1998). Overall the data suggests that there is a distinctive Pine Tree style zone in the Falls region. Clearly, the Falls region and the Ohio River in general comprise a significant culture boundary zone even in the early Holocene.

EARLY ARCHAIC SITE STRUCTURE AND FUNCTION

The Early Archaic is typically viewed as a period of high residential mobility, as hunter-gatherers adjusted to early Holocene environments and postglacial rivers. Some of the Early Archaic occupations at CAP are consistent with this pattern, but there is significant variation in the archaeological record of the Falls region.

The data from the Early Side Notched zone was obtained largely by blading and exposing features, supplemented with hand excavation of small areas. The dominant feature type is large surface hearths. Debitage density is the lowest of all of the occupations, and very few tools (n=57) were recovered. Large blade-like retouched flakes and unifaces (reminiscent of Paleoindian) are more common than bifaces (Stafford 2009) in this zone. Most of the debitage is Muldraugh (62.0 percent), but this is the lowest percentage of any of the Early Archaic occupations at the site. Wyandotte (33.0 percent) is more common than in any other component, suggesting that Wyandotte tools were being reworked or resharpened.

Similar to the lithic assemblage, charcoal density is very low in this zone, with twice as much wood charcoal as charred nutshell. Black walnut is the most common nut type, followed by hazelnut. Thick-shelled hickory nutshell is present in low frequency but is moderately ubiquitous (23 percent) (Schroeder 2007:184). The wood analysis (Schroeder 2007:182) indicates that nonresinous coniferous wood is present in every feature in this zone. The species represented are most likely red cedar or eastern hemlock given the site setting (Schroeder 2007:182). Although these species were found historically in southern Indiana, coniferous wood is not present in any of the later Early Archaic occupations at Farnsley or at nearby Townsend. The next most ubiquitous wood is oak, followed by cottonwood/bigtooth aspen and elm/hackberry; that is, there are bluff slope and mesic bottomland forest species historically found in this area (Schroeder 2007:18). Oak and elm/hackberry are the most common wood species in all of the later Early Archaic occupations. If firewood selection is species "indifferent" and therefore a representative sample of the species that are present, as proposed by Asch and Asch (1986), then this data may suggest a shift in early Holocene forest composition (cf., Schroeder 2007:185–86).

Lithic scatters are the most common feature associated with the St. Charles/Thebes zone in the Main Block. Only one surface hearth on the lower slope of the bank was exposed. Three shale scatters were also found, but their function is unknown (no evidence of heating/burning). Debitage density is low but almost two times higher than in the lower Early Side Notched zone. Tools are scarce (n=38) and were mostly manufactured from Wyandotte chert. Tool types include bifaces, cores, a chopper, an adze, and a side scraper (Stafford 2009). The debitage, however, is overwhelmingly Muldraugh chert (98.0 percent), equal to the percentage in the Thebes workshop. This similarity suggests that the two occupations are connected.

The Thebes lithic workshop is to the west of the Main Block and is more shallowly buried than the St. Charles/Thebes zone due to surfaces sloping toward the Ohio River channel. A series of mini blocks exposed all of this occupation. It is characterized by well-defined lithic scatters (n=7) consisting of "piles" of debitage associated with raw material blocks (some of which were tested), polyhedral cores, broken stage one bifaces, and hammerstones. Ninety-eight percent of the debitage and 90.0 percent of the chipped stone tools are manufactured from Muldraugh chert. There are no surface hearths, and charcoal is virtually absent. This occupation appears to be exclusively the result of initial tool reduction after the procurement of raw materials from the nearby bluffs. The lack of heating facilities and low tool diversity suggests a very short-term occupation associated with the logistical procurement of tool stone and the roughing out of bifaces for later completion elsewhere. The similar Muldraugh debitage percentage in Main Block Thebes/St. Charles, along with a high frequency of Wyandotte tool disposal, suggests that some exhausted Wyandotte tools were being replaced with Muldraugh equivalents initially formed at the workshop.

As with the Early Side Notched zone, charcoal density is very low in the Main Block Thebes/St Charles (no charcoal was recovered in the Thebes workshop), and wood makes up 99.8 percent of all charcoal (Schroeder 2007:187 does not believe this is due to preservation). Black walnut was the only nutshell present in samples.

The Lower and Middle Kirk zones represent vastly different types of occupations, which are most strikingly characterized by an inordinately large amount of debitage and high tool densities. Features also are present in greater numbers and variety. There are, however, marked differences between the two zones. Surface hearths are common in both zones, but lithic scatters are notably more common in the Middle than in the Lower Kirk zone. In addition, a unique feature referred to as an oxidized ring is found exclusively in the Lower Kirk zone. Typically, these features are small pits with in situ oxidation at the rim and commonly have charcoal zones (some of which are charred bark) near the pit base. These features may be smudge pits, but whatever task they reflect, they indicate a unique activity not associated with the Middle Kirk zone.

The amount of debitage and tools are greater in the Middle Kirk zone than in the Lower Kirk zone. The average debitage density in the Middle Kirk zone is more than twice that of the Lower Kirk zone. Similarly, more than 2.8 times as many tools were discarded in the Middle Kirk zone relative to the Lower Kirk zone. Muldraugh chert dominates both debitage collections at 79.0 percent (Middle) and 74.0 percent (Lower). The majority of tools in each zone are made of Muldraugh chert (Middle: 58.0 percent; Lower: 56.0 percent) but Wyandotte chert accounts for about a quarter of the tools (Middle: 26.0 percent; Lower: 29.0 percent). Some tool types in both zones favor specific types of raw material. Endscrapers are mostly (80.0 percent) manufactured from Wyandotte chert, while adzes are predominantly made from poor-quality Muldraugh chert (94.0 percent), indicating functionally specific tool stone requirements.

The focus of the Middle Kirk zone appears to have been lithic tool reduction given the high debitage densities, large number of discarded tools (over one thousand points for example), and discrete knapping episodes reflected in definable lithic scatters (identified despite the level of "background noise" of debitage recovered in units). Although there is less debitage and fewer tools, lithic reduction is still important in the Lower Kirk zone. The greater variety of features and the unique oxidized rings, however, suggest that a wider range of tasks were associated with this zone. These differences in material culture and feature type are indicative of Early Archaic settlement diversity and use of the Falls region.

Wood charcoal makes up the majority of the samples in the Lower Kirk zone, but is less than fifty percent of the charcoal in the Middle Kirk zone, suggesting that nut processing was potentially more important in that occupation. In the Lower Kirk zone, black walnut is the highest frequency nut type, with hazelnut commonly occurring in features but in low frequency. Hickory is less common, and acorn is present in trace amounts. In the Middle Kirk zone, black walnut is still the taxon with the highest frequency, but hazelnut is also common. Hickory is again third in abundance and ubiquity.

Along the bank of the Ohio River paleochannel is another unique feature. It consists of a dense deposit of debitage, tools, and charcoal draped over the channel bank. This feature originates near the top of the bank slope, extends more than twelve meters toward the river channel, and is present along the entire length of the main block, although it is denser at the south end. Tool density and debitage density in the trash deposit are equal to that in the Middle Kirk zone. So, it appears that during the Middle Kirk occupation substantial quantities of lithic debris were cast down the bank of the river. The charcoal in the deposit, however, is more likely from the Lower Kirk zone and the associated oxidized ring pits. Biface fragments recovered from the secondary deposit were refitted with bifaces from both the Middle and Lower Kirk zones, indicating that trash removal took place during both occupations. A hearth feature on the bank that directly underlies the trash dates to 8720 BCE (9420±100 RCYBP), indicating that the deposit began forming shortly after the earliest Kirk occupations at the site. In the Kirk secondary deposit there is half as much nutshell as in the Middle Kirk, and hickory nutshell appears in greater frequency than black walnut nutshell.

Only nine features (hearths and lithic scatters) are associated with the Upper Kirk zone. Debitage density is relatively low in this zone. In fact, it is six times less than the Middle Kirk zone and half as dense on average as the Lower Kirk zone. Tool density is equally low compared to the other zones. The proportion of Muldraugh and Wyandotte debitage, including chipped stone tools, is similar, however. This occupation may be an extension of the Early Archaic component at the nearby Townsend site, since both are shallowly buried below the same terrace surface and are approximately the same age. The Upper Kirk zone is more typical of the light density sites, for surface hearths are common elsewhere during the Early Archaic.

As noted, an occupation similar to the Upper Kirk zone is present at the nearby Townsend site (Mocas 2008). The Townsend Early Archaic component is on the edge of the Rosewood Terrace escarpment. The dated zone immediately underlies the late Middle Archaic rock-filled midden at the surface of the terrace. Although there has been considerable mixing of the two deposits, it is possible to separate the Early Archaic materials from the later cultural remains (see Mocas 2008). Three surface hearths form an arc with refuse scatters at either end (Mocas 2008:183). They consist of a scatter of debitage and a tool cache. A small refuse pit feature also has been exposed. Points are the most common tool type, followed by bifaces, utilized flakes, unifaces, and scrapers (Mocas 2008:103). Chert debitage from units, although predominantly Muldraugh (63.0 percent), did contain a high percentage of Allen's Creek (16.0 percent) flakes. Wyandotte is the most common chert type recovered from features (63.0 percent).

Overall charcoal density and the nutshell-to-wood ratio is low, especially compared to the overlying late Middle Archaic rock midden. The mix of nut species is comparable to the Farnsley Early Archaic samples (Schroeder 2007:198). Hickory and black walnut are common in units, and hazelnut and acorn predominate in the single feature exposed (Schroeder 2007).

Overall there is a great deal of diversity in the Farnsley Early Archaic occupations that appears to represent distinctive mobility patterns, landscape use, stone tool production, and chert procurement. The archaeobotanical remains are reminiscent of other Early Archaic sites (Asch and Asch 1985b:103–5), where the low nutshell-to-wood ratio suggests that nuts were less important in the diet compared to the late Middle Archaic and Late Archaic (Stafford et al. 2000). At the same time the variety of nut species and the predominance of black walnut and the consistent presence of hazelnut in all the occupations stand in contrast to the rock-filled middens of the late Middle Archaic where hickory is quite common, almost to the exclusion of all other taxa (Stafford et al. 2000). The Early Archaic botanical record at Farnsley is in keeping with the idea that early Holocene hunter-gatherers were using an encounter foraging strategy where nuts were one of a number of resources that they collected as they encountered them on the landscape rather than the central focus of foraging, as indicated by hickory nut bulk processing seen at late Middle Archaic rock-filled midden sites (Asch and Asch 1985b:103–5; Stafford et al. 2000).

Rosewood Terrace Early Archaic Sites

The Duke Energy Gallagher Pipeline Project right-of-way crossed thirty kilometers of Ohio River floodplain from the Gallagher Power Station south of New Albany to Rosewood Bottom (Cantin and Stafford 2012). Although the project was cancelled before archaeological investigations were completed, 144 trenches were excavated to an average depth of about two meters below surface in a sample of the areas that had been determined to have high buried site potential (Stafford and Cantin 2010). The 36 buried sites documented in these areas ranged in age from Early Archaic through Mississippian (Cantin and Stafford 2012). The Rosewood Terrace was sampled extensively, and three buried Early Archaic Kirk occupations were identified.

At Site 12Hr688/689, a series of six trenches were excavated in a mix of colluvial slope and Early Holocene alluvium underlying the Rosewood Terrace (Cantin and Stafford 2012). In Trench 138, a scatter of debitage (n=42) was mapped in the profile between 110–40 cm below surface and a lithic concentration was defined (Feature 21) in the same zone. Sixty-seven flakes, three bifaces, two cores, five utilized flakes, and a chopper were recovered from the feature. Although the majority (59.0 percent) of the flakes recovered were Muldraugh chert, St. Louis makes up slightly more than twenty percent of the debitage, followed by Wyandotte and Allen's Creek. The cores and two of the bifaces also were made from St. Louis chert. Overall there is a noteworthy amount of chert diversity at this site. Although no diagnostic Early Archaic artifacts were recovered from Trench 138, a Kirk Corner Notched point base (Wyandotte) was recovered from the equivalent stratigraphic context at 130 cm below surface from Trench 141 (Site 12Hr689) located nearby on the Rosewood Terrace.

Site 12Hr775 is associated with a small, steep colluvial fan in Poffey Creek Bottom. A single trench (T215) encountered a scatter of lithic debris between 150 and 185 cm below surface. Two concentrations of debitage were defined as features. A Kirk Corner Notched Small projectile point made from Allen's Creek chert was recovered at 160 cm below surface. Several cores (all Muldraugh), a Stage 3 biface (Muldraugh), and a hammerstone also were recovered (Cantin and Stafford 2012). The features appear to represent individual knapping episodes. The vast majority of debitage is Muldraugh, although a few Wyandotte and Allen's Creek flakes/shatter are present. The Early Archaic occupation is contained within Early Holocene Ohio River alluvium associated with the Rosewood Terrace. This deposit underlies gravelly colluvium associated with the fan. Lack of soil development in the fan deposits indicates a Historic period origin.

Site 12Hr531 (Cantin and Stafford 2012) spans five trenches (240 m) excavated into the Rosewood Terrace near Eversole Creek. Two zones of lithic debris (n=50) occurred between 90 and 140 cm below surface in the three northern trenches. Three surface hearths were noted in the profile wall of T233. A Kirk point blade (Wyandotte) was recovered at 90 cm below surface. A core (Allen's Creek) and a biface (Muldraugh) also were recovered. A Kirk-like adze was recovered from the plowzone. Unlike the previous two sites, Allen's Creek chert is more common than Muldraugh in the flake debris associated with the Kirk component. This suggests a nearby source for the former chert type (Allen's Creek chert co-occurs with Muldraugh, but is usually less abundant).

A buried Early Archaic occupation also was encountered at the nearby Poffey Creek site (Stafford and Cantin 1992). At this site, two trenches were excavated below the high Wisconsin Terrace on the most interior Ohio River ridge (Rosewood Terrace), one of which exposed an Early Archaic occupation at 2.25 m below surface. Unit excavation in Trench 1 recovered debitage (n=156), a biface, and a Thebes point (Wyandotte) from this lower occupation (a late Middle Archaic zone was present to a depth of 70 cm below surface). The Thebes point is not from a secure context, insofar as it was recovered during overburden removal in the lower part of the trench, but a potlid flake from the hand excavated unit in this lower zone is refitted with the fire-damaged pot-lidded point, making it highly likely that it is from this lower occupation. The percentage of Muldraugh debitage (68.0 percent) recovered at the site was lower in comparison to the typical Kirk component near Muldraugh outcrops. On the other hand, relatively large amounts of Wyandotte (26.0 percent) were recovered, which is comparable to the Early Side Notched zone at the Farnsley Site.

The deposition of Ohio River alluvium on the western side of the valley trench from Knob Creek to Rosewood Bottom begins during the critical late Wisconsin/Early Holocene boundary before 8000 BCE. It is evident, based on the data gathered so far, that Early Holocene hunter-gatherers were frequently camping on the banks of this early channel and exploiting resources, including the abundant tool stone materials available in the nearby bluffs. There would seem to be a close tie between this tool stone source and the abundance of sites associated with the Rosewood Terrace.

The Chert Landscape and Early Archaic Mobility Patterns

The two cherts most readily available to Early Archaic hunter-gatherers below the Falls of the Ohio were Muldraugh and Allen's Creek, both occurring in the bluffs immediately adjacent to the Rosewood Terrace (Figure 2.5). These cherts are from the Mississippian system that occurs in the Floyds Knob limestone. They outcrop near or at the bluff crest. According to Cantin et al. (2007), Allen's Creek appears to be stratigraphically above the Muldraugh bed and may be eroded away in some locations with only residuum currently present near CAP. As one might expect from a relatively coarse grain fossiliferous chert, the knapping quality typically varies from poor to medium (Cantin et al. 2007).

At least near CAP, Muldraugh appears to be more common with beds extending several hundred meters and as thick as 30 cm along the bluffs. Residuum blocks as large as 50 cm also were observed by Cantin et al. (2007:379). Muldraugh chert quality ranges from poor to high, with the latter exhibiting a waxy luster and a fine-grained matrix. Some of the highest quality Muldraugh chert was observed in the outcrop adjacent to the Farnsley site (Cantin et al. 2007:379).

A tabular variety of the fossiliferous St. Louis chert (Figure 2.5) also was identified in lag deposits in the headwater forks of Buck Creek immediately to the west of CAP (6 km) (Cantin et al. 2007:390). Although high-quality St. Louis chert is found regionally in Kentucky and southern Illinois, this variety is typically poor quality with only fair conchoidal fracture.

The second most common chert recovered from CAP Early Archaic occupations is Wyandotte, which outcrops extensively in western Harrison County and across the river in Kentucky some 30 km away. It occurs in nodules and tabular form in chert-bearing horizons 2–4 m thick in the Ste. Genevieve limestone (Mississippian System) (Bassett and Powell 1984:243). Cortex is usually well-developed on nodules unlike the tabular forms of chert just described. Due to its lack of flaws, cryptocrystalline structure, and homogeneity, it has unsurpassed knapping qualities (Tankersley 1985). Although other chert types occur at CAP, these four types comprise the vast majority of the debitage and tools.

Given the ubiquity of Muldraugh chert in the bluff immediately adjacent to the Rosewood Terrace, it is not surprising that it is usually the dominant chert type represented in the Early Archaic debitage. However, as seen in Table 2.1, there is considerable variability among the occupations, despite the fact that Muldraugh is the closest high-quality chert. The highest percentages of Muldraugh debitage are associated with the Farnsley Thebes lithic workshop, and contemporaneous and nearby Thebes/St Charles occupation near the river bank. At one of the Poffey Creek Bottom localities, Site 12Hr775, Muldraugh also is in the 90 percent range. At the other end of the spectrum are the Early Side Notched component at Farnsley and the

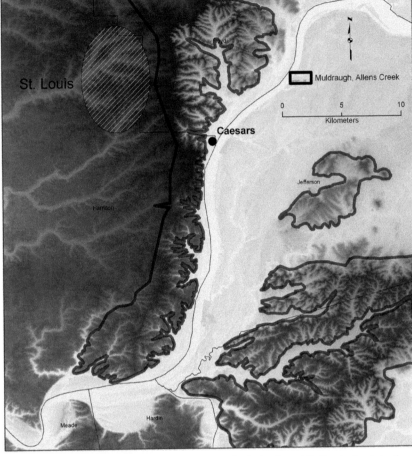

Figure 2.5. Map of the distribution Muldraugh/Allen's Creek and St. Louis cherts in the Falls region (modified from Cantin et al. 2006).

Thebes component at Poffey Creek with much higher percentages of Wyandotte debitage, suggesting more on-site refurbishing of tools made from this chert type. Sites 12Hr531 and 12Hr689 are unusual in that they have significant amounts of Allen's Creek and St. Louis chert debitage, respectively. This variability in raw material utilization is probably the product of a number of factors, including immediate and future tool kit needs, patterns of movement where hunter-gatherers are either following the river or approaching from the interior uplands (for example, encountering St. Louis chert in the headwaters of interior upland streams), and simple variation in the availability of material along the bluff line (Muldraugh vs. Allen's Creek).

Table 2.1. Rosewood Terrace occupation chert types

Occupations	Muldraugh	Wyandotte	Allen's Creek	Other
Hr481 Upper EA	62.8%	10.5%	15.9%	10.8%
Hr520 Upper Kirk	76.7%	9.1%	5.6%	8.5%
Hr520 Middle Kirk	79.2%	5.3%	3.4%	12.1%
Hr520 Lower Kirk	74.3%	9.2%	8.3%	8.2%
Hr520 Thebes	98.6%	0.8%	0.6%	0.0%
Hr520 Main Block St. Charles/ Thebes	98.5%	1.5%	0.0%	0.0%
Hr520 Early Side Notched	62.5%	33.0%	4.3%	0.2%
Hr688/689	59.0%	10.0%	10.0%	21.0%[a]
Hr775	90.0%	10.0%	0.0%	0.0%
Hr531	43.0%	2.0%	53.0%	2.0%
Hr403 (Poffey Creek)	68.0%	26.0%	6.0%	0.0%

[a] St. Louis.

The Rosewood Terrace is a relatively continuous landform in this segment of the valley below the Falls. There are many places on this feature that are seemingly identical in terms of floodplain or chert resources, meaning that camp relocations over time by mobile early Holocene hunter-gatherers would not have been constrained to particular places and would not necessarily result in the reuse of previous locations. Most of the occupations discussed here reflect short-term camps with limited reoccupation that fit a pattern of mobility that Binford (1982) has referred to as leap-frog camp relocation.

The Lower and Middle Kirk deposits are noticeably different, however. Exceptionally high densities of lithic debris in association with features are concentrated in a narrow band along the terrace escarpment no longer than sixty meters. Undoubtedly, this record represents repeated reoccupation of this precise location over time. Although many locations on the levee would seem suitable, this place is a point on the landscape much like a rockshelter. The Lower and Middle Kirk occupations are reminiscent of point-to-point movement, whereby hunter-gatherers move from one relatively rare location to another. Such moves may be many times the foraging radius of a group (Binford 1982:10).

The frequency of lithic debitage and tools in the Lower and Middle Kirk occupations indicates the importance of tool production and maintenance at this location. Although Muldraugh chert can be procured from many locations adjacent to the Rosewood Terrace, it does vary from poor to high quality. Reconnaissance of the bluff at CAP has located a high-quality source of material within two hundred meters of the Farnsley site (Cantin et al. 2007; Stafford and Cantin 1996). Although there may have been other unknown resources concentrated at this place, availability of high-quality chert at a potentially rare point source may be the factor that led to the long-term reuse of this place on the landscape during the Middle and Lower Kirk occupations.

Do the Middle and Lower Kirk occupations represent more than reoccupied residential camps? The secondary trash deposit composed of debitage, tools, and charcoal indicates that enough trash was being generated by the occupants to require its removal from the primary camp area, resulting in disposal on the river bank. A number of factors could account for the high debris depositional rate. For example, if this were an aggregation camp (Anderson and Hanson 1988), then higher amounts of debris would likely be produced within a short period of time, necessitating trash cleanup. However, the limited size of the site could not have accommodated a large group. The proposed size of macroband aggregation camps (Anderson and Hanson 1988; Robinson et al. 2009; Seeman 1994) is presumably several orders of magnitude larger (hectares in size) than the space used at the Farnsley site (ca. twelve hundred square meters maximum).

More likely, the Lower and Middle Kirk occupations represent frequently reoccupied residential camps where "gearing up" activities were predominant, resulting in the discard of significant numbers of tools and the generation of large quantities of lithic debris. Tool production and repair, or refurbishing in the Lower and Middle Kirk occupations, was probably carried out in a specific season when these activities were not competing with subsistence tasks (in the fall or in the winter) (Binford 1979). The quantities of discarded tools suggest complete replacement of tool kits, regardless of condition, because high-quality tool stone was so readily available.

Ultimately, this may not be an entirely satisfying explanation, however, given the extraordinary magnitude of the debris densities in these deposits compared to other Kirk sites. It is worth considering that although the availability of high-quality raw material may have led to the initial establishment of a camp at this location, repeated reuse over time may lie in cultural motives that assigned meaning to this location on the Early Archaic cultural landscape.

SUMMARY AND CONCLUSION

The Falls region is well known for its rich archaeological record and the Early Archaic is no exception. Well-dated occupations extend back to the late Wisconsin/early Holocene boundary and indicate the deep roots of Native American cultures associated with the Thebes and Kirk point traditions. As it clearly was for later Native cultures, it is likely that the Falls region served as a boundary zone for more northerly (Thebes) and southerly (Kirk) groups, which both appear to be using the area by the end of the late Wisconsin and at the beginning of the Holocene. Moreover, the common occurrence of the distinct Pine Tree Kirk points at Farnsley and their presence at Swan's Landing suggest that a distinctive style zone may exist for Kirk Corner Notched in the Falls region that is not present in other areas of the southeast United States.

The Falls region is a landscape rich in chert, and high-quality Wyandotte and Muldraugh cherts were widely available below the Falls of the Ohio River. For projectile points and some other tools (e.g., endscrapers), Wyandotte was the preferred tool stone during the Early Archaic, although if the high-quality variety of Muldraugh was available, it was often used as well. The importance of acquiring high-quality raw material for many of their implements appears to have influenced Early Archaic group movements across the landscape.

It is clear that there is significant variation in the types of settlements in the Falls region that reflects a more complex pattern of early Holocene hunter-gatherer mobility than has been typically acknowledged. Certainly, Early Archaic hunter-gatherers were highly mobile, but the pattern of early Holocene landscape use was at least partially structured by the availability of high-quality lithic material, whereby in some cases groups were tethered to specific locations on the landscape in portions of the seasonal round. This pattern may be documented at both Farnsley (Muldraugh) and Swan's Landing (Wyandotte). This is a pattern that is not exclusive to the Falls region, but it has been observed across much of eastern North America among early Holocene hunter-gatherers and has its origins in the Paleoindian period (see Seeman 1994).

Given the importance of the availability of raw materials for stone tools to Early Archaic hunter-gatherers, it is not surprising to find that sites dating to this period are plentiful along the Rosewood Terrace. The early Holocene Ohio River below the Falls of the Ohio River was located on the western side of the valley. The overbank deposits that formed as the river channel moved to the east systematically buried Early Archaic occupations, sometimes well below the surface as the floodplain formed that became the Rosewood Terrace. We can expect to find many other well-preserved sites that will yield significant information about this period in the future.

ACKNOWLEDGMENTS

This chapter benefited from many lengthy discussions about the Early Archaic with Mark Cantin and Steve Mocas. I would also like to thank David Pollack, Anne Bader, Justin Carlson, and Mark Seeman for their comments on an earlier version of this chapter.

3

Middle Archaic Lifeways and the Holocene Climatic Optimum in the Falls Region

JUSTIN N. CARLSON, GREG J. MAGGARD, GARY E. STINCHCOMB,
AND CLAIBORNE DANIEL SEA

For much of the Middle Archaic (6000–4300 BCE), hunter-gatherers living in the Falls region retained lifeways similar to those of their Early Archaic predecessors (Jefferies 2008, 2009; Stafford and Cantin 2009a; see Chapter 2). However, as the regional effects of the Holocene Climatic Optimum or Hypsithermal Climatic Interval (ca. 7000–2200 BCE) became established, the Falls and surrounding regions experienced conditions that were, at that point, unprecedented in Native American history (Walker et al. 2012). The era was characterized by higher temperatures, reduced rainfall, and more open vegetation structure (Delcourt 1979; Driese et al. 2005; Klippel and Parmalee 1982; Wilkins et al. 1991). Studies undertaken throughout the eastern United States have generated a more fine-grained record that demonstrates that multi-centurial warm and dry cycles occurred (Driese et al. 2008; Driese et al. 2017; Kocis 2011; Stinchcomb et al. 2013). Sustained up-hill erosion and downhill accumulation, apparently associated with climatic fluctuations, also occurred (Ahler 1993, 1998; Carlson 2019a; Carlson and Pollack 2019; Butzer 1978; Hajic 1990; Springer et al. 2010).

Responding to Middle Holocene environmental conditions, Middle Archaic hunter-gatherers living in the Falls region remained highly mobile and dispersed their activities across multiple physiographic settings. In addition to establishing short-term encampments adjacent to the Ohio River, they also increasingly frequented rockshelters and caves in upland settings. Both lowland and upland localities were incorporated into task-oriented trips, in which groups procured and processed nut mast to a greater degree than in the Early Archaic. Resultant nutshell debris may have also been used as fuel (Anderson 1996; Carlson 2019a; Carlson and Pollack 2019; Homsey-Messer

2015; Schroeder 2007; Stafford 1994; see Chapter 2). Increased Middle Archaic harvesting of nut mast in the early portion of the Middle Archaic may indicate a transitional stage from residential foraging to logistical collecting lifeways that were prominent by the late Middle Archaic (Homsey-Messer 2015; Stafford et al. 2000; see Chapter 4).

Although Middle Archaic sites are underrepresented in the archaeological record of the Falls region, excavations undertaken at a number of sites have generated new data. This chapter draws on four sites that contain significant Middle Archaic components and associated radiocarbon dates (Table 3.1). Of these, two are floodplain sites on the Indiana side of the Ohio River, Knob Creek (12Hr484) (Stafford and Cantin 2009a) and Paddy's West (12Fl46) (Smith and Mocas 1995). The other two are upland sites, Ireland Cave (15Jf839) (Carlson and Pollack 2019) and McNeely Lake Cave (15Jf200) (Carlson 2019b; Granger 1985). Both are located in the highly dissected Knobs region of Kentucky. The Middle Archaic components identified at these sites are roughly contemporaneous (Stafford and Cantin 2009a).

Human-environmental interaction throughout the Middle Archaic consisted of a series of spatially and temporally specific dynamic feedbacks and adjustments. While Middle Archaic hunter-gatherers reacted to the Holocene Climatic Optimum, they also transformed landforms and ecosystems, inadvertently and purposefully, through their daily activities (Balée 2006; Crumley 1994; Crumley et al. 2018; Håkansson and Widgren 2014; Sassaman 2010; Thompson 2013; Winterhalder 1994). In this chapter, we examine Middle Archaic material culture, subsistence practices, settlement patterns, and soil geomorphological histories in alluvial and upland karstic settings to discuss the interplay of social and environmental factors that resulted in settlement strategies and resource procurement in the Falls region.

MATERIAL CULTURE

For the most part, early Middle Archaic material culture in the Falls region reflects a continuation of Early Archaic technological traditions, supplemented with new distinct local styles. Despite their long and continued use as diagnostic temporal markers, projectile point typologies are generally insufficient as indicators of anything other than broad-scale temporal change (Andrefsky 1998; Odell 2000). This limitation is especially evident in the archaeological record of transitional subperiods—like the Early to Middle Archaic—that are characterized by subtle or poorly defined shifts in human lifeways and behavior (Anderson 1996; Jefferies 2008). The early Middle Archaic in the Falls region represents just such an example in which

Table 3.1. Radiocarbon dates for Middle Archaic sites in the Falls region mentioned in the text

Site/Lab No.	rcybp	2 Sigma Cal BP	Median Cal BCE
Ireland Cave (15Jf839)[a]			
ISGS-A3187	6815±25	5736–5656	5698
ISGS-A3188	6725±25	5704–5570	5640
ISGS-A3189	6450±20	5474–5373	5420
ISGS-A3192	6335±20	5365–5228	5317
ISGS-A3186	6195±25	5220–5053	5134
ISGS-A3190	6165±20	5210–5049	5128
ISGS-A3191	5390±20	4328–4180	4278
ISGS-A3194	5380±20	4327–4227	4258
ISGS-A3185	5320±20	4234–4052	4136
McNeely Lake (15Jf200)[a]			
D-AMS 015563	6984±33	5979–5770	5870
D-AMS 015561	6264±33	5318–5079	5258
Knob Creek (12Hr484)[b]			
ISGS-4955	7220±70	6229–5985	6094
ISGS-4954	7220±70	6229–5985	6094
ISGS-4953	7110±80	6204–5800	5984
ISGS-4980	7170±70	6215–5907	6043
Oxford A-0265	6942±60	5979–5719	5825
Oxford A-0264	6872±56	5883–5657	5759
ISGS-4981	6840±70	5876–5626	5729
ISGS-4996	6780±80	5839–5546	5683
ISGS-4994	6740±90	5796–5486	5652
ISGS-4960	6730±80	5751–5489	5644
Beta-115654	6700±70	5722–5494	5619
ISGS-4973	6670±70	5705–5484	5591
ISGS-4995	6270±70	5461–5035	5243
Beta-113983	5830±90	4903–4464	4687
Paddy's West (Site 12Fl46)[c]			
ISGS-2483	6530±70	5613–5363	5494
ISGS-2480	6620±120	5733–5337	5558

Note: All dates have been calibrated using the online platform of Calib 7.1 (Stuiver et al. 2017).
[a] Carlson and Pollack 2019.
[b] Stafford and Cantin 2009a.
[c] Smith and Mocas 1995.

Figure 3.1. Knob Creek Stemmed projectile points from the Knob Creek site.

a change in our temporal framework (the transition from Early to Middle) was traditionally assumed to be reflected in the morphological attributes of the associated projectile points (e.g., the replacement of corner notching by stemmed forms).

At the Knob Creek site, Stafford and Cantin (2009a) recognized a new projectile point type (Knob Creek Stemmed; n=57) associated with clearly defined and well-dated early Middle Archaic deposits (Figure 3.1). Morphologically, Knob Creek Stemmed points are small with a short (and sometimes wide) stem in relation to the blade. Shoulders range from weak to barbed, and basal edges can range from straight to concave. Stafford and Cantin (2009a) have suggested that this style may be an offshoot of the Early Archaic bifurcated tradition, since many have concave bases and are similar in form and size. Indeed, Knob Creek points share affinities, such as concave bases, with Early Archaic Kirk Stemmed and LeCroy cluster points (Justice 1987; Stafford and Cantin 2009a), and are morphologically similar to the early Middle Archaic Stanly Stemmed point type. Yet Knob Creek points can be distinguished from Stanly Stemmed types because they are smaller and younger by several hundred years (Stafford and Cantin 2009a). One of the most important characteristics of Knob Creek points is variation in the form (e.g., corner notched or stemmed varieties) that they can exhibit. Knob Creek Stemmed points are also present at Ireland Cave (n=4) and McNeely Lake Cave (n=6) in association with early Middle Archaic dates, but this type is not present at Paddy's West (Carlson 2019b; Carlson and Sea 2019; Smith and Mocas 1995).

At Paddy's West, eight corner notched projectile points exhibited traits similar to those of the Early Archaic Kirk Corner Notched type, such as corner notching, pronounced or barbed shoulders, ground basal elements, broad blades, wide necks, and random, wide, percussion-thinning flakes across the blade (Justice 1987; Smith and Mocas 1995). Charcoal samples from associated features returned calibrated medians of 5558 and 5494 BCE, placing them in the early Middle Archaic subperiod (Smith and Mocas 1995) (Table 3.1). The association of Middle Archaic dates with Early Archaic-like points led Smith and Mocas (1995) to conclude either contamination of the charcoal or "fortuitous" association. Based on their work at the

Figure 3.2. Kirk Corner Notched points (*two upper left top row*) and Middle Archaic Corner Notched points (*two upper right top row and bottom row*) from Ireland Cave.

nearby Knob Creek site, which resulted in the recovery of similar points in association with Knob Creek Stemmed points, Stafford and Cantin (2009a) reclassified these points as Middle Archaic Corner Notched to distinguish them from the earlier Kirk Corner Notched points. Likewise, Middle Archaic Corner Notched points were found in association with Knob Creek Stemmed points at Ireland Cave (Figure 3.2) (Carlson and Sea 2019). Based on the data, Knob Creek Stemmed and Middle Archaic Corner Notched points are considered to be representative of the early Middle Archaic in the Falls region (Stafford and Cantin 2009a).

During the late Middle Archaic, by ca. 5000 BCE, these point styles give way to the Middle Archaic Side Notched Cluster, which includes Raddatz, Graham Cave, Big Sandy II, and Godar types (Jefferies 2008). These types were recovered at Knob Creek, Ireland Cave, and McNeely Lake Cave (Figure 3.3).

Figure 3.3. Raddatz Side Notched projectile points from Ireland Cave.

In addition to projectile points, other tools recovered from Middle Archaic sites are bifaces and unifacial technologies including endscrapers, side scrapers, retouched flakes, and utilized flakes. At both Knob Creek and Ireland Cave, unifacial tools predominate (Carlson and Sea 2019; Stafford and Mocas 2008). Limited information is available on the early Middle Archaic shell and bone tool industry.

Middle Archaic strategies in chert selection and procurement for tool production differ from those seen during the Early Archaic in the Falls region (see Chapter 2). While Early Archaic hunter-gatherers seem to have aggregated around high-quality cherts such as Wyandotte, Middle Archaic groups focused less on positioning themselves in relation to these high-quality lithic resources and utilized readily available local cherts to a greater extent. Because chert resources are so abundant in the Falls region, no site is limited to one particular type. In Middle Archaic lithic assemblages, the overwhelming majority of cherts used came from areas in close proximity to sites, such as Ireland Cave and Knob Creek (Carlson and Pollack 2019; Carlson and Sea 2019; Kepferle 1972, 1974; Stafford and Mocas 2008).

By the late Middle Archaic, formalized ground stone tools, such as grooved axes and pestles, became part of lithic assemblages (Jefferies 2008). Pestles and mortars have been argued to be evidence of more intensive bulk processing activities centered around nut crops (Moore and Dekle 2010). The advent of ground stone tool technologies, such as grooved axes, seems to coincide with early anthropogenic environments in Kentucky (Carlson 2019a; Wagner 2005).

Subsistence

In the Falls region, nutshell occurs in higher frequencies in the Middle Archaic archaeological record relative to the Early Archaic. Inhabitants primarily ate nuts, with the most common being hickory, followed by much smaller amounts of black walnut and trace amounts of acorn and hazelnut. In addition to nut mast, they consumed fleshy fruits such as grape, oily seeded plants such as sunflower, maygrass, and chenopod, and starchy plants such as smartweed. All lacked evidence of domestication (Rossen 2019; Schroeder 2007).

Although Middle Holocene paleoclimate data in the Falls region is scarce, a number of regional proxies shed light on the likely conditions. Sediment cores from ponds in Kentucky, Missouri, and Tennessee show that during this time desiccation occurred, while tree species common in temperate, mesic environments were replaced by an open mosaic of drought-tolerant oak, hickory, and chestnut species, and were fragmented by grassland eco-systems, including barrens and prairies along the margins of the Prairie Peninsula (Carlson 2019a; Delcourt 1979; Driese et al. 2017; King and Allen 1977; McMillan and Klippel 1981; Wilkins et al. 1991).

Similar trends have been documented throughout much of the mid-continent. Based on her work at Dust Cave, Stanfield-Worley Bluff Shelter, and Russell Cave in Alabama, in addition to Modoc Rockshelter in Illi-nois, Homsey-Messer (2015) noted that Middle Archaic hunter-gatherers increasingly utilized caves and rockshelters, and they actively processed nut mast gathered from upland tree-stands. The xeric conditions in the uplands may have promoted drought-tolerant nut mast species, resulting in a greater reliance on hickory relative to black walnut and perhaps a greater reliance on silviculture. In addition to its value as a food source, nutshell may have also been a source of fuel for fires, and oil may have been extracted from nuts through boiling (Carmody 2009; Gardner 1997; Moore and Dekle 2010; Munson 1986; Stafford 1994; Stafford et al. 2000).

A very small assemblage was recovered for the faunal record from Knob Creek. At the site, early Middle Archaic hunter-gatherers procured fresh-water drum, white-tailed deer, and turtles, though it is unclear whether the turtles were aquatic or terrestrial. This led researchers to suggest that both aquatic and terrestrial species were procured and that these groups may have fished often. Mussel shell was absent (Stafford and Mocas 2008). The faunal assemblage from Ireland Cave was much larger than that from Knob Creek, perhaps partially because of better preservation. At Ireland Cave, and at nearby upland rockshelters, Manzano (2019) noted that Middle Ar-chaic inhabitants focused their diet primarily on small mammals and deer. In addition, they ate birds, terrestrial and aquatic turtles, fish, and mussels. By the late Middle Archaic at the Bluegrass site in southwestern Indiana, groups focused on small mammals, deer, and nuts. This work led Stafford (1994; Stafford et al. 2000) to suggest that during the Middle Holocene, the drier conditions promoted resource-rich ecosystems in upland settings that attracted hunter-gatherer groups, in addition to resources located in the wetlands.

SETTLEMENT PATTERNS

From the data at hand, it appears that in the Falls region, early Middle Ar-chaic hunter-gatherers used all aspects of the landscape rather than aggre-gating in particular locations, such as floodplain or wetland settings, as is evident in this region by the late Middle Archaic (see Chapter 4). Knob

Creek and Paddy's West are located in the floodplain of Knob Creek near where it empties into the Ohio River. Ireland Cave and McNeely Lake Cave are in the Knobs region and overlook the upper portions of Floyds Fork, a tributary of the Salt River, which empties into the Ohio River. The entrances of these caves are restricted areas for activities on the landform. This more dispersed settlement pattern may be related to the environmental effects of the Holocene Climatic Optimum. At this time, resource availability may have been patchy, requiring dispersed settlement strategies. Localities may have been used briefly as part of seasonal rounds in which resources available at these times were procured.

At Knob Creek small activity areas are scattered along the levee parallel to the Ohio River. Based on this distribution of features, Stafford and Mocas (2008) argued that mobile hunter-gatherers placed residential camps along the river to exploit different resources. The spatial distribution of surface hearths and activity areas at Knob Creek is suggestive of short, ephemeral occupations by highly mobile groups (Stafford and Mocas 2008). Within camps the most common features are shallow surface hearths, and this feature type accounts for just over eighty-one percent of the 167 Middle Archaic features at the Knob Creek site (Stafford and Mocas 2008). Likewise, at Ireland Cave, small surface hearths predominate. These hearths contain thin masses of burned sediment, which are sometimes surrounded by scattered thermally altered rocks and disaggregated burned sediment (Carlson and Pollack 2019). Such hearths, which require little preparation, may be indicative of the amount of time groups would use these camps. This pattern of reuse is reflected in the thick midden deposits documented at this site and at several other rockshelter/cave sites in the Floyds Fork drainage (Carlson and Pollack 2019).

Based on the large quantities of nut remains recovered from these sites, it may be inferred that a common use of these features was to process nut mast. In many cases nut residue and associated wood removed from the hearths was thrown to the side as thin discard lenses and as middens filled with nutshells, documented within both the Ireland Cave and Knob Creek deposits (Carlson and Pollack 2019; Stafford and Mocas 2008). This seems to indicate that though there was minimal effort in hearth creation, these features were cleaned and prepared for subsequent immediate processing of nut mast. This could indicate a focused effort to quickly process such resources. It is notable that at both Knob Creek and Ireland Cave, prepared basin-shaped formal hearths are relatively rare. Pits are present, but not common at the open sites (Stafford and Mocas 2008), suggesting that storage was a low priority.

If a shift toward nut mast procurement occurred during the Middle Archaic, then it is possible that hunter-gatherers altered their settlement-subsistence strategies toward what Homsey-Messer (2015) terms "low" residential mobility, a transitional category between the "high" residential mobility of the Early Archaic and the reduced mobility of the logistical collecting strategies that characterized the late Middle Archaic (Jefferies 2008; Stafford 1994; Stafford et al. 2000).

The data from the Falls region and elsewhere suggest that drought-tolerant upland resources played an integral role in forager subsistence strategies for much of the Middle Archaic. In the Falls region, hunter-gatherers appear to have responded to mid-Holocene warming by increasing their utilization of upland xeric-tolerant resources, such as nut mast, leading to resource procurement strategies that were foundational for the advent of logistical collecting strategies of the late Middle Archaic/early Late Archaic (see Chapter 4).

MIDDLE HOLOCENE SEDIMENTATION HISTORY

One of the arguments for why there are so few Middle Archaic sites documented in the Falls region is that they are deeply buried. In fact, as the sites discussed in this chapter indicate, deep burial of archaeological deposits by alluvium and colluvium occurred during the Middle Holocene (Carlson and Pollack 2019; Stafford 2004; Stafford and Mocas 2008). High amounts of sedimentation seen throughout the mid-continent during this time have been argued to be an indicator of changing climatic conditions during the Holocene Climatic Optimum (Ahler 1993, 1998; Butzer 1978; Carlson 2019a; Carlson and Pollack 2019; Hajic 1990; Springer et al. 2010; Styles 1985).

The more open vegetation structure associated with the Middle Holocene Climatic Optimum may have caused significant erosion from upslope locations. Because the limestone outcrop that contains Ireland Cave acted as a catchment for sediment, it represents a good example of increased erosion of upland areas during the Middle Archaic (Figure 3.4). Using zone depths and AMS radiocarbon dates, it was possible to statistically model sedimentation throughout the occupational history of the site (see Blaauw and Christen 2011) (Figure 3.5). The results show a steep sedimentation slope (0.09 cm yr^{-1}) during the Middle Archaic, primarily between 5600–4000 BCE, suggesting consistent sedimentation. Open canopy with moisture variability and frequent droughts were plausible mechanisms that would have increased erosion in upland settings. Sedimentation slowed after 4000 BCE (0.01 cm yr^{-1}), which is potentially related to stabilization of the landform as

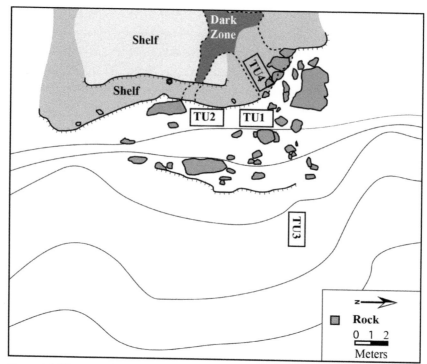

Figure 3.4. Planview of Ireland Cave showing excavations.

conditions ameliorated, forest canopy closed, and soil formation began to outpace soil erosion. Soil geomorphological analyses, including magnetic susceptibility, loss-on-ignition, and soil micromorphology mirror the sediment accumulation rate data (Carlson and Pollack 2019).

Similar changes in soil/sediment histories have been noted to the south at Crumps Sink in Kentucky (Carlson 2019a), Anderson Pond in Tennessee (Driese et al. 2017), and Buckeye Creek Cave in West Virginia (Springer et al. 2010). The inferred sedimentation rates from Koster, Napoleon Hollow, and Modoc Rockshelter in Illinois also suggest that the uplands were subjected to erosion throughout the Middle Holocene and that the transfer of sediment to the adjacent lowlands was enhanced (Ahler 1993, 1998; Butzer 1978; Hajic 1990; Springer et al. 2010; Styles 1985).

With such extensive erosion occurring in the uplands during the Middle Holocene, Middle Archaic sites in the lowlands can be expected to be deeply buried, as is the case at Knob Creek, where deposits assigned to this subperiod were buried beneath 2–3.5 m of sediment (Stafford 2004, 2009). In addition to being deeply buried, archaeological "thinning," the result of relatively short, ephemeral occupations that were frequently covered with

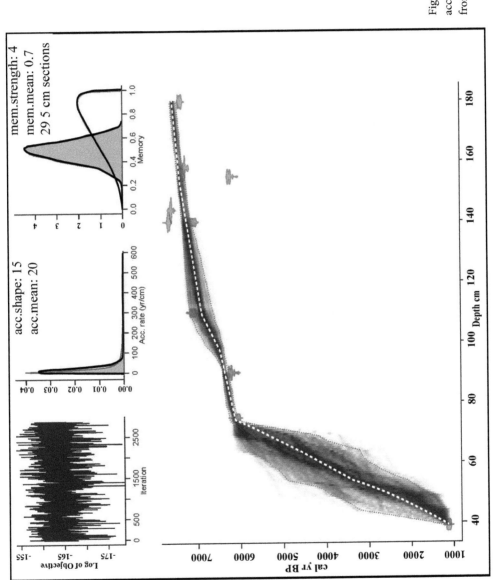

Figure 3.5. Sediment accumulation rates from Ireland Cave.

sediment, may have contributed to the low visibility of Middle Archaic components. Over time, even if reoccupations were frequent, they would appear diffuse and spread out in the vertical stratigraphic record by geomorphological processes, rendering them less concentrated and more difficult to identify.

Conclusions

The recognition of the Knob Creek Stemmed and Middle Archaic Corner Notched points distinct to the Falls region reflects the development of a local social identity. This social identity is indicative of continued technological traditions from earlier times, but is anchored to this region. Along with changes in material culture, in response to changing climatic conditions Middle Archaic hunter-gatherer groups in the Falls region altered their resource extraction and mobility strategies. The warming and drying trends of the Middle Holocene resulted in dispersed settlement patterns and frequent, residential moves that sought to take advantage of local nut mast and deer populations in lowland and upland settings. Efforts were made to undertake task-oriented trips to procure and process nut mast.

Middle Archaic hunter-gatherer groups frequented upland caves and rockshelters to a greater extent than Early Archaic groups. Drier conditions led to increased erosion and colluvial deposition. As populations grew in the Falls region and climatic conditions stabilized (decreased upland erosion), wetland resources took on increased importance, and groups modified their settlement and subsistence patterns to better exploit and perhaps to better protect those resources (see Chapter 4).

Acknowledgments

The authors would like to thank Susan Neumeyer of the Kentucky Transportation Cabinet and John Swintowsky of Louisville-Metro Parks for their help and cooperation. Hayward Wilkirson photographed projectile points and prepared the map of Ireland Cave. Russell Stafford provided the image of Knob Creek points from the Knob Creek site. The authors also would like to thank Mark Seeman and the other outside reviewer for their comments on an earlier version of this chapter.

4

The Late Middle/Early Late Archaic in the Falls Region

ANNE TOBBE BADER

By ca. 4300 BCE and continuing for nine hundred years, the continued dry conditions of the Hypsithermal Climatic Interval led hunter-gatherer groups living in the Falls region to aggregate in large settlements (base camps) along the floodplains and terraces of the Ohio River, in part to harvest the mussels associated with nearby shoals and, in and around the wetlands, to exploit the rich aquatic resources of these interior lowlands (Brown and Vierra 1983:167; Jefferies 2008:123; Jefferies and Lynch 1983). High-quality chert outcrops may have initially drawn groups to the Falls region (see Chapter 2), but it was the region's environmental diversity that kept them there and, during the Hypsithermal, led to some localities becoming favored destinations throughout the latter part of the Middle Archaic and the beginning of the Late Archaic.

Sites of this period have historically been assigned to the Old Clarksville phase in Kentucky or to the early French Lick phase in Indiana (Munson and Cook 1980:721–40; Granger 1985, 1988; Stafford and Cantin 2009a). To reflect its unique position in both states, this period is referred to herein as the Scottsburg phase, on account of its association with the Scottsburg Lowlands in which the sites are located or which the sites overlook. The distribution of Scottsburg phase settlements after 4300 BCE is suggestive of both year-round and seasonal exploitation of the region's natural diversity, with an intensive use of local resources. While some sites are characterized by thick dirt/rock middens, shell middens, diverse artifact assemblages, a variety of feature types, and cemeteries, these attributes are not shared by every large settlement. Variation in settlement organization and use may reflect a site's function within the regional settlement system. At some sites, internal site structure appears to have been organized into distinct habitation loci, activity areas, and burial precincts. The association of cemeteries with some, but not all, of the intensively occupied camps may reflect the development of corporate group boundaries within the Falls region, with certain locales designated as appropriate places to bury the dead.

Modification of key landscape features after 4300 BCE reflects an increase in the long-term investment in some localities as base camps. Once established, some of these localities continued to be used throughout the Woodland and into the Mississippian period, fitting the definition of these as "persistent places" as described by Moore and Thompson (2012), following Schlanger (1992:97). In their view, a persistent place is one that is proximal to a concentration of resources, which have natural or cultural features that "structure" reuse or that promote reoccupation (Thompson 2010:218), being created through "practice" over a long period of time through revisitation (Thompson 2010:218; Moore and Thompson 2012). One such natural resource is Duck Springs at the KYANG site, with its large, deep, permanent twin pools. Likewise, Claassen (2015:213) notes that it is likely not a coincidence that the Falls of the Ohio itself, with its dense concentrations of fossil beds, is associated with numerous shell-bearing burial sites, suggesting the incorporation of fossils in rituals and beliefs as a reason to repeatedly visit the Falls. KYANG also represents a site created through "practice," defined by Littleton and Allen (2007) as the continued use of a location for burial, which was by its nature "structured" for its reuse as a cemetery. Within the Falls region, Scottsburg phase cemeteries were commonly situated on naturally high prominences within central low wetlands. The height of these knolls may have been augmented by intentional midden deposition. Other examples of landscape modification in the Falls region include the formation of shell mounds on the floodplain terraces and the establishment of permanent stone fish weirs at the shallows within the Ohio River. Some of the latter were still visible prior to the impoundment of the river. As a group, these sites over time became enduring features on the landscape (Thompson 2010:218).

The varying intensity of utilization of post–4300 BCE Middle Archaic sites in the Falls region is consistent with the diversity of the environment and the mosaic of seasonally dependent resources in this region. At this time, settlements were often situated at key vantage points on the landscape or at the juncture of two or more environmental zones to take advantage of critical resources. Such strategic places included the head of the rapids at the Falls of the Ohio River, the convergence of major streams, the prominent and commanding elevated knolls amid the wetlands, and the proximity to locally rich chert resources, springs, and mussel shoals. The larger settlements often contain dense middens with an abundance of fire-cracked rock and mussel shell, side notched projectile points, a variety of groundstone objects, and—at sites with adequate preservation—large faunal assemblages and a highly developed and diversified bone and antler artifact industry. The emergence of formal cemeteries after 4300 BCE reflects a distinctive suite of mortuary behaviors, including the extensive use of red ochre and evidence of ritual behavior involving fire. Dog burials also are present at some sites.

In the remainder of this chapter, Scottsburg phase material culture, settlement/subsistence patterns, site structure, and mortuary behavior are characterized. The intent is to highlight the importance of place within the Scottsburg settlement system.

MATERIAL CULTURES

The Scottsburg phase spans the Middle-Late Archaic transition in the Falls region. As a group these sites are associated with the production of Matanzas and related projectile points (Salt River Side Notched) (Janzen 2016) over an approximate nine-hundred-year period between 4300–3400 BCE (Figure 4.1 and Table 4.1).

In addition to shallow side notched Matanzas points, chipped stone tool assemblages of the Scottsburg phase contain large amounts of Brewerton Eared projectile points (Figure 4.1). At most sites, forty percent or more of the Matanzas points were recycled as hafted scrapers, and many are totally exhausted to the haft (Figure 4.1). This recycling of broken projectiles into scrapers has been noted at contemporary sites throughout much of the Midwest and Midsouth (Cook 1976; Jefferies 1990; Stallings 1996, 2001; Stallings et al. 2008:218).

Nearly all Matanzas points were made from locally available materials, of which Muldraugh chert was the material most frequently used (McElrath and Evans 2006; Stallings et al. 2008:217). Cobble chert and other local bedrock fossiliferous varieties were also used to varying degrees; the percentages of chert types utilized at a given location appear to be directly related to the proximity of the site to the source (Granger et al. 1981). Nearly all examples made from Muldraugh chert exhibit thermal treatment, a practice that is not typical with Muldraugh use in the later Archaic. The predominance of Matanzas projectile points in local site assemblages suggests that those living in the Falls region tended to interact more with groups downriver and to the west in southern Indiana and southern Illinois (McElrath and Evans 2006) than with groups living in the middle Ohio River valley, where this point type is not as common.

Figure 4.1. Matanzas projectiles (*upper row*); reworked into hafted scrapers (*middle row*); exhausted specimens (*bottom row*). A (Miles Rockshelter); B (Hornung); C (Lone Hill).

Groundstone tools include both full and three-quarter grooved axes of various styles. Pestles are made not only from hardstone igneous rock but also commonly from hematite, a much-used local resource. Large elongated rolling pins and large pitted stones have also been recovered from the Falls sites. The frequency of occurrence of these implements indicates both a reliance on plant resources and a less mobile lifestyle. The recurring use of specific locations with respect to these artifacts forms a component of the site furniture that was commonly "stored" in features at sites for later reuse, being too heavy to transport from camp to camp.

A local social identity in the Falls region at this time may be reflected in stylistic attributes of bannerstones characterized by a flaring rectangular

Table 4.1. Relevant late Middle/early Late Archaic radiocarbon dates

Site Name/No./Lab No.	rcybp	2 Sigma Cal BCE	Median Cal BCE	Reference
ASHWORTH 15BU136				
R.L.-1552	5020±270	4440–3099	3818	DiBlasi 1981
BUFFALO RUN 15BU463				
Beta-292045	4690±40	3628–3367	3456	Wetzel et al. 2017
Beta-370485	4890±40	3766–3634	3676	
Beta-287976	5250±50	4230–3968	4073	
LONE HILL 15JF10/15JF562				
Beta-222434	4790±40	3540–3630	3569	Bader 2007
HORNUNG 15JF60				
UGa-390	5085±85	4043–3666	3869	Janzen 1977a
UGa-401	5100±75	4040–3709	3878	
M-2460	4900±200	4226–3104	3688	
M-2464	5000±200	4312–3364	3803	
M-2461	5220±230	4529–3525	4040	
D-AMS 025787	4708±29	3340–3025	3457	
D-AMS 025788	4642±29	3514–3359	3460	
KYANG 15JF267				
Beta-29627	5010±80	3958–3655	3807	Bader and Granger 1989
D-AMS 004896	5188±32	4043–3956	3993	Personal communication, Mocas 2017
D-AMS 004895	5023±32	3942–3710	3838	
RAILWAY MUSEUM 15JF630				
Beta-70350	4780±80	3700–3370	3556	Anslinger et al. 1994
Beta-70351	4720±70	3636–3369	3507	
MUDDY FORK 12CL199				
D-AMS 005829	5387±28	4333–4077	4265	French et al. 2015
D-AMS 005836	5296±28	4231–4042	4132	
D-AMS 005837	5224±28	4220–3966	4017	
REID 12FL1				
UGa-309	5480±90	4494–4054	4325	Janzen 1977a
D-AMS 025786	5304±26	4182–4042	4134	
TOWNSEND 12HR481				
ISGS-5024	5360±70	4339–4003	4189	Stafford and Cantin 2009a
ISGS-5017	5100±70	4038–3711	3877	
ISGS-5020	5020±70	3959–3662	3819	
ISGS-5018	4990±70	3944–3655	3782	

(*continued*)

Table 4.1—*Continued*

Site Name/No./Lab No.	rcybp	2 Sigma Cal BCE	Median Cal BCE	Reference
Miles Rockshelter 15Jf671				
D-AMS 015568	4431±26	3323–2929	3066	Bader et al. 2018
D-AMS 015571	5208±28	4048–3964	4010	
Ireland Cave 15JF839				
ISGS-A3191	5390±20	4328–4180	4278	Carlson and Pollack 2019
ISGS-A3194	5380±20	4327–4227	4258	
ISGS-A3185	5320±20	4234–4052	4136	
McNeely Lake Cave 15JF200				
D-AMS 015562	4749±28	3635–3382	3571	Carlson 2019b

Note: Calibration derived from the CALIB program version 7.1 (Stuiver et al. 2017).

shape and a concave end (Rick Burdin, personal communication 2018; see Chapter 6). These finely ground artifacts have been found at Lone Hill (15Jf10), Old Clarksville (12Cl1), and Minor's Lane (15Jf36).

The bone tool assemblages reflect a broad range of procurement and domestic activities, as well as personal adornment. Bone projectiles, awls, scrapers or beamers, needles, fishhooks, and much more have been recovered in large numbers, perhaps preserved by the presence of shell in the trash middens (Bader 1992). Antler artifacts include two forms of atlatl hooks, atlatl handles, reamed projectile points, as well as flaking tools and pierced palmate sections of antler often referred to as "wrenches" or "shaft straighteners." The breadth and expertise in bone and antler technology is exceptional and may be partially due to excellent preservation brought about by association with shell deposits. The bone and antler assemblages, furthermore, may reflect diagnostic cultural differences insofar as several distinctive technologies have been recognized in some tool classes, such as fishhook production (Janzen 2008).

As with Matanzas projectile points, decorative motifs engraved on bone pins point to increased interaction with downriver groups. The distinctive geometric motifs associated with these pins are remarkably like those found at contemporary sites in southern Indiana and southern Illinois (Jefferies 1997; see Chapter 6) (Figure 4.2). On the other hand, several decorated bone implements found at Old Clarksville, Hornung, and KYANG may indicate a more local phenomenon in the use of curvilinear designs and punctations in the bone (Figure 4.2). An increase in personal ornamentation is further seen in burnished and polished tubular bird bone beads, large polished

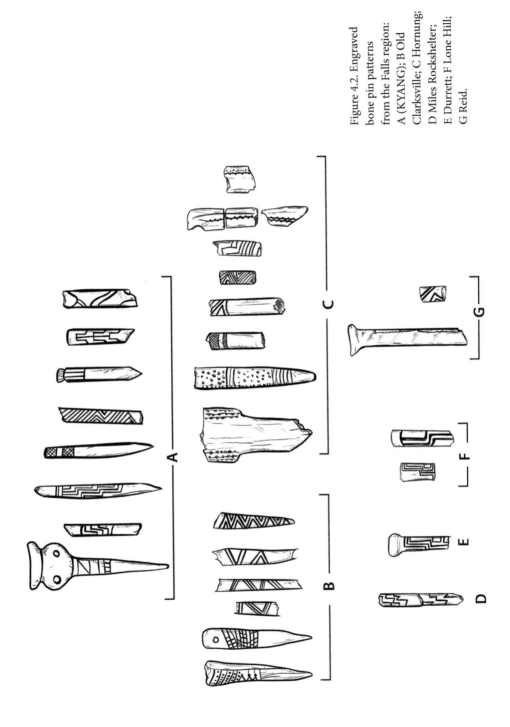

Figure 4.2. Engraved bone pin patterns from the Falls region: A (KYANG); B Old Clarksville; C Hornung; D Miles Rockshelter; E Durrett; F Lone Hill; G Reid.

tubular cannel coal beads, shell beads, as well as necklaces of perforated canine and other teeth.

Settlement/Subsistence Patterns

Site types vary during the Scottsburg phase in the Falls region, ranging from substantial habitation locales in riverine and interior wetlands to small hunting camps or specialized activity sites associated with upland contexts. The more intensively occupied sites have often been classified as base camps. For the purposes of this chapter, a base camp is defined as one that was intensively occupied multi-seasonally, for several months of the year, or for much of the year. These sites contain evidence of a variety of feature types associated with diverse domestic activities, including cooking, storage, and refuse, and often include distinct specialized activity areas (see Chapter 5 for an alternative interpretation). Structures also may have been present (Chapter 6). Significantly, at sites with a mortuary component, segregation of burial areas or cemeteries is noted, with interment occurring on elevated landscape features within or adjacent to wetland areas. In the burial precincts within these sites, features appear to be primarily associated with mortuary ritual, with few related to habitation. This is especially evident at KYANG (15Jf267), where the burial area, situated at the top of a small knoll, is located approximately thirty to forty meters from the residential portion of the site (Bader and Granger 1989; Stallings et al. 2013). A similar pattern is noted for shell midden sites in the middle Green River valley (Marquardt and Watson 2005:111–13).

During the Scottsburg phase, groups hunted and consumed a variety of mammalian species, with an emphasis on whitetail deer, supplemented with a variety of small mammals. In the central lacustrine area, faunal assemblages reflect an aquatic or marsh-oriented subsistence pattern characterized by gathering freshwater mussels and obtaining fish that prefer standing bodies of water (Hill 1974; Redman 2007:217; Thibadeau 1972). Drumfish was the most utilized fish species, insofar as they frequented the mussel beds exploited by late Middle/early Late Archaic gatherers. Although these fish could often be captured by hand or by spear in the shallow shoals, the numerous bone fishhooks and stone netsinkers found in large numbers at sites like Hornung and Old Clarksville are evidence of other forms of fishing.

Botanical data reflects the consumption of a variety of wild plants. However, nutshell is the predominant plant species recovered from most sites, accounting for over seventy percent of the botanic remains at some sites, such as KYANG (Stallings et al. 2013:107). Black walnut, hickory, acorn, butternut, and hazelnut are ubiquitous in features and middens. The use of other wild plants is evidenced by the presence of grape, blackberry/raspberry, chokecherry, arrowroot, sumac, wild beans, in addition to starchy and oily seeds, such as maygrass, chenopod, marshelder, and sunflower (French et al. 2015:298; Moeller 2007; Stafford and Mocas 2008:133; Stallings et al. 2013:107; Turner 2017). Scottsburg phase groups also utilized gourds and squash, in addition to wetland plants, such as bulrush and pondweed. Pokeberry was likely used as a dye. Several of these plants were later domesticated, namely gourd, squash, maygrass, chenopod, and sunflower.

Based on an examination of the distribution of late Middle/early Late Archaic sites, Janzen (1977a; see also Jefferies 2008; Muller 1986) noted that base camps were commonly located at the juncture of two or more resource-rich environmental zones (see Chapter 1). These different environmental settings provided a rich and varied suite of resources in a relatively constricted area, resulting in the reduction of seasonal movement (Janzen 1977a). This logistic pattern of mobility and resource procurement allowed groups to occupy a base camp for much of the year, with forays to nearby zones to procure needed resources that were then brought back to camp for processing and consumption (Granger 1988; Granger et al. 1981; Jefferies 2008:151; Munson and Cook 1980). Among the resources they would have exploited are the numerous quarries of Muldraugh chert in the uplands of the adjacent Knobs. Hematite and limonite also were obtained from the Knobs for the manufacture of pestles. Forays to other locations included those areas near the extensive mussel beds of the Ohio River and the plant and animal resources of the interior wetlands. Specific mussel beds were likely harvested only for several consecutive years or on a rotating annual basis to avoid overexploitation, since it could take up to five years for a heavily harvested bed to replenish (Bader 1988). Nearby caves and rockshelters (e.g., Miles (15Kf671), Ashworth (15Bu136), Ireland (15Jf839), and McNeely Lake (15Jf200) in the dissected uplands also would have been visited. These sites are characterized by small shallow hearths and midden deposits consistent with seasonal hunting and plant-collecting camps.

The Townsend site (12Hr481) is a good example of a base camp that was likely occupied during multiple seasons (Stafford and Cantin 2009a:303). Features at this site consisted primarily of refuse scatters and pits, surface hearths, and basin hearths (Stafford and Mocas 2008:51). The spatial distribution of features is suggestive of a variety of activity areas associated with cooking, nut processing, mussel steaming, tool manufacture and maintenance, woodworking, and, to a lesser extent, mortuary activities. The recovered artifact assemblage is large and diverse, consistent with a broad range

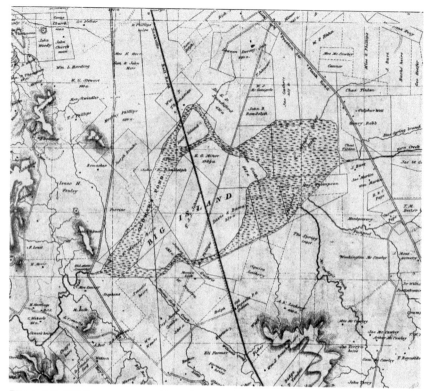

Figure 4.3. G.T. Bergmann map, 1858, showing the historic lake, springs, and knolls within the Wetwoods.

of activities. The high nut densities at the Townsend site suggest that the residents' economy was strongly oriented toward nut utilization. The Buffalo Run (15Bu463) site in Bullitt County also contained numerous pits of diverse function and specialized activity areas, such as a communal cooking area with shallow roasting pits possibly for processing of fish, and large deep pits with dense nutshell content (Wetzel et al. 2017).

Scottsburg phase sites south of the Ohio River in Kentucky are strongly associated with the interior Scottsburg Lowlands as opposed to the riverine settings. The Scottsburg Lowlands abut the Knobs to the south. This large lacustrine lowland, known locally as the "Wetwoods," lacks surface drainage (Chapter 1). It was once a large spring-fed inland lake and marshland that comprised much of central Jefferson County (Figure 4.3). Within this low-lying area, a broad, shallow lake was present well into the late nineteenth century. The area may well have been wet during the Middle Archaic and Late Archaic because it is underlain with New Albany shale that is impervious to drainage, resulting in standing or ponding water. The water from the

Figure 4.4. August 16, 1953, image of the Lone Hill Site. Credit© Courier Journal-USA TODAY NETWORK.

central ponds exited in a southwesterly direction into Pond Creek, which then emptied into the Salt River not far from its junction with the Ohio River, forming a natural corridor from the river into the interior. The Hornung site is located at this key juncture. In addition to numerous springs, expansive salt licks are associated with this lowlands area. Many small knolls and high points, which are erosional remnants, are present within and around the wetlands, and most contain evidence of Scottsburg phase occupation. The most prominent of these was Lone Hill. Destroyed in the 1960s, Lone Hill was a massive 17 m tall and 91 m long hill that figured large on the landscape within the surrounding flat marshlands (Bader 2007) (Figure 4.4). At the base of the hill, along a 23 m wide trench, were hundreds of human burials associated with extensive red ochre amid a black earth midden scattered with shell (Burnett 1963; Janzen 1968). This feature was occupied for thousands of years and was almost certainly a meaningful place throughout the past, but especially during late Middle Archaic and Late Archaic times.

SHELL MIDDENS

In the Falls region, mussel shell collecting peaks ca. 3800 BCE. As with shell midden sites in the Green River region of Kentucky, the stratigraphy at the shell-bearing sites begins with a shell-free "pre-midden" zone, overlaid by a moderate to dense layer of shell, which was overlaid by a zone containing sparse shell or no shell (Hensley 1991; Marquardt and Watson 2005). Comparisons between the observed frequencies of shell between the lower and upper strata at both KYANG and Hornung show clearly that mussel collecting was more important during the Scottsburg phase occupation than during subsequent use of these sites (Figure 4.5). The general absence of

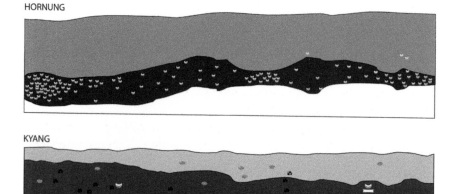

HORNUNG

KYANG

1 FT   ➍ SHELL   ⬤ FIRE CRACKED ROCK   ✸ FIRED CLAY   ✎ BONE

Figure 4.5. Differences in shell frequency in upper and lower components at Hornung (*top*) and KYANG (*bottom*).

shell in the later component, along with changes in projectile point forms, suggests a shift in subsistence strategies, perhaps one that was increasingly focused on plants.

Some shell-bearing middens can be several meters thick, as seen at the Reid site (12Fl1) (Janzen 2016), while others contain only small concentrations of shell. With the exception of the dense shell middens, such as that documented at Reid, the shell is generally not continuous across the site, but is often mounded or irregularly distributed within the black earth midden, as is the case at KYANG and Hornung. Considerable discussion has occurred regarding the nature of the shell midden deposits at these sites (see Hensley 1991; Marquardt and Watson 2005:110–15 for summaries). Some researchers see these deposits as an indication of either increasing sedentism or a series of occupations, which consist of accumulating habitation debris deposited as part of the annual subsistence cycle (Milner and Jefferies 1998). It has been suggested that habitation midden may have been deliberately spread across a slight natural elevation on the landform to increase its height and to elevate it further from seasonally wet conditions (Marquardt and Watson 2005:114). Others interpret the shell middens to have been intentionally created, often due to their natural topographic attributes, as formal "monuments" or cemeteries to bury the dead (Claassen 1992, 2015:23). At these locations, groups may have come together periodically for feasting and ritual. Thompson (2010:220) takes an alternative view and suggests that these sites may represent various combinations of groups and events. On the one hand, supporting evidence for the habitation hypothesis is suggested by the dense content of domestic debris intermixed with the shell in the middens that appears to exceed the amount that would have accumulated by feasting alone. On the other hand, arguments against the habitation hypothesis include the lack of structural features at these sites, in addition to the association of burials and shell mounding.

Whether the shell deposits reflect the accumulation of habitation and domestic debris, or they were dedicated to specific ritual or burial activities, it appears that there was segregation between the two functions at sites in the Falls region. This is seen, for instance, at the KYANG site where a portion of the site contains a large number of burials but with virtually no features, such as hearths, storage/refuse pits, structures, or specialized tool production areas that could be associated with day-to-day living (see more below). This has been noted at shell mounds in the Green River region (Hensley 1991; Claassen 1992). In contrast, however, approximately forty meters to the southwest of the nearest known grave at the KYANG site, a concentration of features was found that revealed evidence of domestic function. A series of eleven closely spaced features appear to have been used for cooking or for storage (Stallings et al. 2013). This segregation between mundane and ritual space has also been noted at the Hornung shell mound, RiverPark (15Jf597/598) and at the Shadow Wood site (15Jf674) (Kreinbrink 2008:89). Downriver, in Spencer County, Indiana, the Meyer site (12Sp1032) excavations revealed a site structure that is very similar to that of KYANG.

Mortuary Patterns

While isolated burials from earlier periods are often found in natural locations such as rockshelters, caves, river terraces, and knoll tops (Claassen 2015:23), at some point locales emerged as established cemeteries and sacred places. Claassen (2015:23) holds that these are not merely associated with natural features but were "created" and enhanced as sacred burial grounds. Primary mortuary sites in the Scottsburg phase include Old Clarksville, Clark's Point (12Cl3), Lone Hill, KYANG (Bader and Granger 1989), Hornung, and the earliest component at RiverPark (Simpson and Mocas 2017) (see Chapter 5). The cemeteries tend to be situated on naturally high points on the landscape overlooking wetlands or a river valley (Jefferies 2008:280). The establishment of cemeteries indicates not only a certain degree of sedentism (Charles and Buikstra 1983; Mires 1991:128), but also the favored use of specific locales to bury the dead. The association of many of these cemeteries with accretional midden deposits atop natural high points may be the precursor of the burial mounds of the Woodland period. As with large burial mounds (Clay 1991:32–33), late Middle Archaic cemeteries may have demarcated corporate group boundaries within the Falls region, and as in the case of the Falls of the Ohio River, were important landscape features.

At sites such as KYANG and Hornung, individuals of this period were interred within pits excavated in the culturally sterile clay below the midden, as was also noted in the Green River region (Hensley 1991:90). The body was arranged in a moderately to tightly flexed position, and based on the proximity of the extremities to one another as well as the testimony of ethnohistorical accounts, the extremities may sometimes have been tied and the body wrapped with skins, a blanket, or a robe (Joutel 1906 as cited in Howard 1981:150; Collett 1878; Voegelin 1944:243). Some graves also contained jumbled or neatly stacked bones of multiple individuals, suggesting that these individuals died elsewhere, with the remains brought to the cemetery during the annual residential cycle. Grave pits containing the disarticulated remains of multiple individuals also have been documented. Other graves contain isolated skeletal elements, such as the skull, which could reflect the taking of trophies (see Chapter 7). Evidence of what appear to have been violent deaths is apparent at some sites. The use of red ochre in burials is significant (see Chapter 5). Noting an ochre-stained grinding slab, Smith and Mocas (1995:350) suggest that hematite may have been processed for ochre and may have been used in mortuary ceremonialism at Site 12FL148 in Floyd County.

Scottsburg phase burials documented in the Falls region are generally intact and not disturbed by subsequent interments. Likewise, while later Archaic burials occasionally intruded into the Matanzas phase middens, they did not commonly disturb the interments associated with the Scottsburg phase occupation. It thus appears likely that throughout the use of these cemeteries, those who interred their loved ones in the cemetery were aware of the locations of the previous graves. This suggests that they may have been marked, perhaps by wooden poles (Logansport Telegraph, October 21, 1837; Collett 1878). The tight clustering of radiocarbon dates at KYANG is very similar to that obtained from the Meyer site in Spencer County, Indiana (Bader 2017) and reflects a relatively short utilization of both cemeteries, for perhaps no more than two or three generations, by an extended family group.

Mortuary ritual behavior at these cemeteries appears to have involved the use of fire. Evidence in support of this suggestion comes from the direct association of one or more small (30 cm in diameter) smudge pits associated with most of the burials (Bader 2011, 2017). These features were located near the head and feet, knees, and elbows of the deceased. Based on ethnographic accounts (see Bader 2011; Voegelin 1944; Voegelin and Voegelin 1939), these small charcoal concentrations may be evidence of ritual "watch fires" that were kept burning throughout the night for perhaps three to four days of the burial observance. Other mortuary rituals consisted of offerings of mussel shells and the covering of parts of the body with red ochre. This was especially evident at the Meyer site in southern Indiana (Bader 2011, 2017).

At these sites, there appears to have been equal access to the cemeteries, with individuals of all ages and genders represented. Grave goods, though not common, were non-specific to age or gender, reflecting that the criteria for inclusion were unrelated to achievement. Items placed with the burials include canine necklaces and pendants, turtle carapaces, bone awls and needles, paired rodent mandibles, and other polished bone (Federal Register 2013). The placement of bone pins around the interred individual may be related to the securing of burial robes.

Analyses of the KYANG site burials offer the only insights into the health of the late Middle and early Late Archaic residents of the Falls region. A study performed in the 1980s on the more complete skeletons found evidence of malnutrition in individuals of all ages in the form of tooth hypoplasias and Harris lines (Haskell et al. 1985:96; Saunders 1986). Osteoarthritis and ear exostoses (which may be associated with shell fishing) also have been identified. Periodontal disease and abscesses due to extreme dental attrition have been noted in numerous individuals. Although several fractures have been noted, few exhibited healing or infection (Saunders 1986), meaning that the individuals may not always have survived their injuries. In sum, though the KYANG population was generally healthy, those interred at this site experienced periodic illnesses, trauma, and malnutrition (Haskell et al. 1985:97; Saunders 1986).

CONCLUSIONS

During the late Middle/early Late Archaic, the Scottsburg phase exhibits greater affinities with groups living in the lower Ohio valley relative to those living upstream in the middle Ohio valley. These affinities are reflected by a shared core of common elements, imposed on local material culture and adaptations. Many of these elements are shared with the Shell Mound Archaic of the Green River region, while others align more with the French Lick phase of southern Indiana and the Helton phase of Illinois (Jefferies and Lynch 1983; Jefferies 1997). The elements common to the region include a preference for Matanzas projectile points, the presence of components with shell deposition, and aggregated burial populations (cemeteries). The shared use of engraved bone pin designs with sites to the southwest reflects this interaction, while certain bone artifact engravings appear to be more unique to the immediate Falls area. Likewise, bannerstone styles may indicate a more local Falls identity. In general, however, the Falls region represents the northeastern frontier of the Scottsburg phase. This boundary was not likely sharp and clearly defined, but permeable, reflecting continued interaction of groups that came together at this major landmark. It is precisely in these border zones that ethnic and social identity is most important (Bader 2005a). As noted by Feuer (2018:37), all societies "recognize boundaries that separate or distinguish them from other groups." This interaction was not always without conflict (see Chapter 7), and resource competition may have been a factor.

While the late Middle Archaic in the Falls region began as a continuation of earlier Archaic patterns of short-term encampments (see Chapter 3), it ended with a growing investment in specific places on the landscape. A trend toward reduced mobility and increased sedentism is indicated during the later Middle Archaic and into the early Late Archaic. During this time, the local settlement system appears to be consistent with a pattern of reduced mobility and logistical resource procurement.

As elsewhere, Scottsburg phase base camps are often found in riverine environmental contexts. Many of these sites were located near the confluences of the Ohio River and its major tributaries, such as the Salt River, to take advantage of major mussel beds. Other base camps were situated to take advantage of significant inland springs and expansive shallow inland wetlands, in addition to numerous salt licks. In general, these base camps are characterized by thick middens, many of which contain dense quantities of mussel shell, diverse artifact assemblages, and a range of feature types related to both domestic life and mortuary rituals. The placement of large and small camps in proximity to multiple natural resources or environmental settings is characteristic of the Scottsburg phase in the Falls region. Collectively, the varying intensity of utilization of these sites is consistent with the diversity of the environment and a mosaic of seasonally dependent resources.

Site selection reflects an interplay of both natural and cultural features on the landscape that became imbued with special meaning. As stated by Barrett (1999:27), meaning "is not simply produced or stated: it must be recognized through a practical understanding of the world and its interpretation." He further says that to inhabit the land—to gain an understanding—one must observe and make sense of the landscape, that is, to interpret it. An understanding of the landscape draws upon previous experiences in order to recognize appropriate actions that may be required. Modifications to the land are done knowledgeably and reflect that understanding (Barrett 1999:26).

The Scottsburg phase occupation at the Falls ends with a gradual transition from shallow side notched to longer stemmed projectiles, decreased recycling of points into hafted endscrapers, marked reduction in the thermal pretreatment of Muldraugh chert, cessation in the production of the distinctive Midwestern decorative bone implements, changes in mortuary behavior, and settlement shifts, especially as related to the duration of occupation of major settlements (see Chapter 5). The exploitation of mussels drops out of the spectrum of critical or valued resources. The fact that rock-earth middens continued to accumulate over the shell-bearing deposits at favored sites speaks to the longstanding importance of these localities as persistent places, perhaps places of a sacred reality, on the landscape.

ACKNOWLEDGMENTS

The author would like to acknowledge and recognize the work of those who excavated in the Falls of the Ohio area in the past, beginning with E.Y. Guernsey in the 1930s. More recently, during the late 1960s and throughout the 1970s, significant excavations have been done by Dr. Joseph E. Granger and Dr. Donald E. Janzen. Their efforts laid the groundwork for our current understanding of the area's Native American history. The author would also like to acknowledge the assistance and lively debates with Stephen T. Mocas, Duane B. Simpson, and Michael W. French. Finally, the editorial suggestions by Dr. David Pollack and Dr. Justin N. Carlson, as well as our outside reviewers, are greatly appreciated. Graphic support by Dr. Tim Sullivan and Ms. Leigh A. Stein was essential.

5

The Late Archaic in the Falls Region

A RiverPark Site Perspective

DUANE B. SIMPSON AND STEPHEN T. MOCAS

The Late Archaic in the Falls region dates from approximately 4200–1400 BCE. Sites dating to this subperiod are found in large numbers in every environmental and physiographic setting, representing the most significant settlement expansion throughout the entirety of the Native American occupation of this region. Sites range in size from extremely large, spanning as much as a kilometer in length, to smaller occupations that appear to represent specialized encampments. Within the Falls region, a majority of the largest sites tend to be associated with mid-channel islands or extensive side-channel bars that were high points along the floodplain and among the most favored locations for occupation throughout the Late Archaic (Simpson and Scholl 2014).

Some researchers (e.g., Jefferies 2008; Jefferies et al. 2005; Meadows and Bair 2000; Stafford and Cantin 2009a; Vickery 2008; Winters 1969) have suggested that relative to the Early and Middle Archaic subperiods, the presence of large Late Archaic "base camps" reflects an increase in the regional population, with population levels peaking toward the end of the Late Archaic. The data from RiverPark, however, suggests that these large sites actually represent a palimpsest of smaller and varied occupations over an extended period of time rather than large, multi-seasonal "base camps" (see also Boisvert 1986; Collins and Driskell 1979). Based upon the development sequence documented at RiverPark, it is possible that few, if any, "base camps" are present in the Falls region. Rather, large, complex Late Archaic sites represent "preferred camps" that grew in size incrementally for a specific array of economic reasons, such as nut processing or fishing, but were used differently over time. The cyclical reuse of these preferred localities and the establishment of cemeteries within them led to their establishment as important persistent places on the landscape. The shifts observed within certain aspects of a site's occupational history, such as mortuary traditions, appear to reflect broad cultural changes that occurred within the Falls region.

The stratified nature of the deposits documented at the RiverPark site provide a rare opportunity to evaluate how Late Archaic sites in the Falls region developed. It is the authors' opinion that RiverPark's development is consistent with the broad trends under which the majority of Late Archaic sites in the Falls region formed, and thus the site can be used to understand and to interpret Late Archaic settlement patterns in this region. While those patterns could be shown to be highly varied and dynamic from an individual occupational perspective at RiverPark, broad cultural trends have been noted that document consistent change over time, indicating that native groups living in the Falls region were intertwined with broad cultural trends and adaptations affecting the entirety of the Eastern Woodlands.

In this chapter, the three sites (15Jf596, 15Jf597, and 15Jf598) that comprise the RiverPark complex are used to examine how large Late Archaic sites in the Falls region developed and to interpret cultural changes that took place. These sites are located along a narrow section of Ohio River terraces 2.4 km northeast of downtown Louisville and 5.1 km upstream from the Falls of the Ohio River. Together, they represent a contiguous scatter of features and midden deposits. Given the distribution of the archaeological materials, these three sites are collectively referred to as RiverPark as a means of facilitating the discussion.

Investigation of RiverPark in 2007 resulted in the identification of 426 Late Archaic features, 57 burial pits, and stratified midden deposits (Simpson and Mocas 2017). All were documented within approximately 1.5 m of stratified soil deposits. Together they provide a detailed record of change throughout the latter half of the Late Archaic (3500–2100 BCE) (Table 5.1).

In the following sections, a brief review of previous Late Archaic research in the Falls region is presented. This is followed by a description of the River-Park site and its environmental setting. Four distinct aspects of RiverPark's archaeological record are examined: material culture, mortuary traditions, subsistence, and settlement patterns. These aspects of the archaeological record are used to interpret the site's Late Archaic occupational history and to relate the occupation of this site to Late Archaic use of the broader Falls region.

Table 5.1. Radiocarbon dates obtained from RiverPark

Lab No.	Provenience	Stratum[a]	Material	(rcybp)[b]	2 Sigma cal (BCE)[c]	Component
D-AMS002082	F84A	Ab_2	nutshell	3795±31	2338–2137	late LA
D-AMS001647	B56–59,74	Ab_2	nutshell	3849±31	2457–2206	late LA
D-AMS001645	F192	Ab_2/Bw_2	nutshell	4196±26	2890–2679	middle LA
D-AMS001644	F212	BC_1	nutshell	4374±28	3008–2910	middle LA
D-AMS001636	F173	BA	nutshell	4493±30	3347–3092	early LA
D-AMS001634	F59	BA	nutshell	4602±30	3500–3137	early LA

[a] Refer to Figure 5.2 for stratum and feature locations.
[b] Radiocarbon years before present (rcybp)—uncalibrated.
[c] Calibration with Calib 7.10 program using intcal13 (Stuiver et al. 2017). All dates are AMS.

PREVIOUS LATE ARCHAIC RESEARCH IN THE FALLS REGION

Investigations of Late Archaic sites in the Falls region began more than a century ago. Borden (1874) and Guernsey (1939, 1942) were the first to work in this region. Both undertook limited investigations of several shell middens, such as the Old Clarksville (12Cl1) and Clark's Point (12Cl3) sites. These sites were extensive, with the Old Clarksville site being described as extending for more than two kilometers down the northern bank of the river from just below the bottom of the Falls of the Ohio River.

In 1969, Donald Janzen began a study of Late Archaic sites in the Falls region (Janzen 2016). He returned to Old Clarksville, but also investigated Hornung (15Jf60), Reid (12Fl1), and Ferry Landing (12Hr3) (Janzen 1977a, 2014). The work of Janzen and others (Borden 1874; Guernsey 1939, 1942; see also Angst 1998 and White 2004) identified two distinct periods of site development, usually represented by middens composed primarily of shell or rock. Based upon stratigraphic superpositioning, the middens, composed primarily of shell, appeared to predate the rock midden deposits (see Chapter 4; Figure 4.5).

One of the observations that Janzen (1977a:129) made based upon his initial work was that radiocarbon dates from sites in the alluvial floodplain clustered from 4300–2800 BCE and that there were no dates from 2800–1250 BCE. He (Janzen 1977a:141) attributed the gap in the radiocarbon dates to a rapid decline in Late Archaic settlement of the Falls region. Subsequent excavation of sites within the Falls region has narrowed this gap significantly, but there remains an obvious drop off in dates from 2500 to 2000 BCE (Table 5.2).

Archaeological investigations undertaken in the 1970s in advance of the construction of the Southwest Jefferson County Floodwall (Chapman and

Granger 1971; Collins 1979b; Dobbs and Dragoo 1976; Mocas 1976) encountered sizable Late Archaic settlements along the Ohio River. The excavation
of the Arrowhead Farm (15Jf237) (Mocas 1976), Spadie (15Jf14) (Boisvert
et al. 1979), Villier (15Jf110) (Robinson and Smith 1979), Longworth-Gick
(15Jf243), and Rosenberger (15Jf18) (Dobbs and Dragoo 1976; Driskell 1979;
Wolf and Brooks 1979) sites generated additional Late Archaic data. Of
these, the most intensively investigated component was associated with the
Rosenberger site. The deposits associated with this site appear to be extremely similar to those documented at RiverPark.

Investigation of the Rosenberger site resulted in the documentation of almost 400 cultural features and 164 burial pits (Driskell 1979:698). The burial
features contained the remains of 230 individuals (Wolf and Brooks 1979).
Grave goods were more utilitarian than ornamental, and their distribution
suggests that status was more achieved than ascribed. The site also contained a dog burial. The lithic assemblage was dominated by McWhinney
projectile points, and most of the interments were attributed to the Late
Archaic component. Of the 164 burials, 14 were found to have McWhinney points, and an additional burial had a cache of 41 bifaces that likely
are preforms for McWhinney points (Driskell 1979). The association with
McWhinney points suggests that the burials are generally contemporaneous with the early and middle Late Archaic burials at RiverPark. Calibrated
radiocarbon dates obtained from the site (Claassen 2015) place the occupation from 2857–2498 to 2463–2209 BCE (Table 5.2), but it is probable, based
upon the diagnostics recovered, that the site occupation extends from at
least 3500–2000 BCE.

The position of Rosenberger along an elevated alluvial ridge or bar landform is typical of Late Archaic sites within the Falls region. The repeated
occupations of the site resulted in a mixed, dark, organic midden. The lack
of stratigraphic separation of deposits makes it difficult or impossible to
reliably separate these occupations over time. Excavations at other large
riverine sites, such as Old Clarksville, Arrowhead Farm, Townsend (Mocas
2008), Railway Museum (15Jf630) (Anslinger et al. 1994), Habich (15Jf550)
(Granger et al. 1992), and Site 12Cl158 (White 2002:23), as well as the extensive sites within the interior wet woods environment, such as KYANG
(Bader and Granger 1989), Lone Hill (15Jf10) (Burnett 1963), and Minor's
Lane (15Jf36) (Janzen 1977a) encountered similar problems due to com-
pressed or mixed stratigraphic sequencing. The majority of the interpretations compiled for the Late Archaic for the region are based on these sites,
or based on sites with similar issues, and, consequently, change across the
period is difficult to understand or interpret. This lack of clarity within the

Table 5.2. Late Archaic radiocarbon ages from the Falls of the Ohio region

Site	Date Range (rcypb)[a]		2 sigma cal BCE[b]	No.	Reference
	Earliest	Latest			
EARLY LATE ARCHAIC					
Reid (12Fl1)	5480±90	4555±70	4495–3025	3	Janzen 1977a
Muddy Fork (12Cl199)	5387±28	4581±28	4334–3121	4	French et al. 2015
Breeden (12Hr11)	5380±40	4850±110	4334–3370	3	Burdin 2009
Townsend (12Hr481)	5360±70	4990±70	4340–3656	4	Stafford & Mocas 2008
12Fl73	5350±130	4950±40	4456–3648	2	Burdin 2002
Buffalo Run (15Bu463)	5250±50	4690±40	4231–3368	3	Wetzel et al. 2017
Miller (12Hr5)	5220±200		4451–3640	1	Janzen 1977a
Miles Rockshelter (15Jf671)	5208±28		4451–3637	1	Bader et al. 2018
Ashworth Shelter (15Bu136)	5020±270		4441–3100	1	DiBlasi 1981
KYANG (15Jf267)	5188±32	5010±80	4044–3656	3	Bader & Granger 1989, Stallings et al. 2013
Hornung (15Jf60)	5100±75	5085±85	4041–3667	5	Janzen 2014
Knob Creek (12Hr484)	5070±70		3990–3702	1	Stafford & Mocas 2008
Overflow Pond (12Hr12)	4950±130	4710±90	4036–3126	3	Burdin 2009
Lone Hill (15Jf10)	4790±40		3652–3384	1	Bader 2007
Railway Museum (15Jf630)	4780±80	4720±70	3701–3370	2	Anslinger et al. 1994
McNeely (15Jf200)	4749±28		3636–3383	1	Bader et al. 2018
RiverPark (15Jf597)	4649±36	4554±41	3520–3100	4	Simpson & Mocas 2017
Total				42	

MIDDLE LATE ARCHAIC

Site	RCYBP[a]	RCYBP[a]	cal BP[b]	n	Reference
RiverPark (15Jf597/598)	4493±30	4196±26	3347–2679	6	Simpson & Mocas 2017
Habich (15Jf550)	4480±80		3364–2925	1	Granger et al. 1992
Shadow wood (15Jf674)	4470±40	4430±40	3344–2922	2	Kreinbrink 2008
Old Clarksville (12Cl1)	4460±180	4180±180	3635–2289	3	Janzen 1977a
Clarks Point (12Cl3)	4450±40	4230±40	3338–2678	2	White 2002
Muddy Fork (12Cl199)	4440±27		3313–2922	1	French et al. 2015
Miles Rockshelter (15Jf671)	4431±26	4037±29	3323–2474	3	Bader et al. 2018
Lone Hill (15Jf10)	4365±185		3520–2494	1	Janzen 1977a
Hornung (15Jf60)	4315±60	4240±95	3262–2500	2	Janzen 2014
Arrowhead Farm (15Jf237)	4250±70		3078–2622	1	Mocas 2008
Breeden (12Hr11)	4200±200		3362–2211	1	Bellis 1981
Miles 12Cl158	4150±40	4140±40	2879–2585	2	White 2002
Rosenberger (15Jf18)	4085±28		2857–2498	1	Claassen 2015
Total				26	

LATE LATE ARCHAIC

Site	RCYBP[a]	RCYBP[a]	cal BP[b]	n	Reference
Muddy Fork (12Cl199)	3968±25		2571–2355	1	French et al. 2015
Lone Hill (12Jf10)	3940±100		2856–2140	1	Janzen 1977a
Stucky (12Hr482)	3900±50		2550–2207	1	Stafford & Mocas 2008
Rosenberger (15Jf18)	3862±34		2463–2209	1	Claassen 2015
RiverPark (15Jf598)	3861±29	3795±31	2461–2137	3	Simpson & Mocas 2017
Ashworth Shelter (15Bu136)	3850±165		2864–1885	1	DiBlasi 1981
Total				8	

[a] Radiocarbon years before present (rcybp).

[b] Calibrations performed with Calib 7.10 program using intcal13 (Stuiver et al. 2017).

archaeological record has produced a wide assortment of interpretations, and there is extensive debate on how to interpret various aspects of the Late Archaic occupation of the Falls region, including diagnostic materials, settlement patterns, and population estimates.

RiverPark

The RiverPark Late Archaic deposits accumulated over a span of fourteen hundred years, dating from approximately 3500–2100 BCE (Table 5.1). These occupations stretched across a set of alluvial ridge or bar locations, typical of other large, contemporaneous Late Archaic floodplain sites. The bars were divided by a narrow channel that appears to have acted as a flood chute (Figure 5.1). A broad wetland associated with the poorly drained floodplain of Beargrass Creek would have separated these bars from the older terraces lying above the floodplain to the south. This would have placed the archaeological remains across a series of undulating alluvial ridges more like small islands within a wetland environment than the broad terrace that is seen today. The development of this landscape is consistent with the pattern of landform development within the Falls region (Gray 1984; Stafford 2004).

Riverside bar deposits within the region form as either small islands, mid-channel bars, or side-channel bars, which usually are attached to the bank by a slough or a low saddle. During periods of flooding, these bars become loci for additional sedimentation. Deposition adjacent to the channel laterally extends the bar on the downstream end, and overbank deposition continues along the bar, building it above the level of frequent flooding (Gray 1984). As a result, the upstream end of the bar grows higher in elevation through progressive deposition of sediments and then slopes downstream as well as toward the main channel. The higher a bar aggrades, the finer textured the sediments that cover it become; this process then produces an upward fining overbank sequence (Stafford 2004). A series of bar ridges can be established that differentially aggrade or prograde, with the ridges acting as crevasse channels that distribute water down the floodplain (Gray 1984). Bars such as these have the potential to become macroforms as they coalesce to form a larger alluvial ridge, sometimes over a kilometer in length.

The resulting implication for archaeological deposits along a prograding bar landform, like that at RiverPark, is that the upstream deposits of the same temporal association would be situated higher in elevation than their downstream counterparts. In addition, subsequent flood deposits will slowly fill the small channels or swales, linking the bar deposit with the side

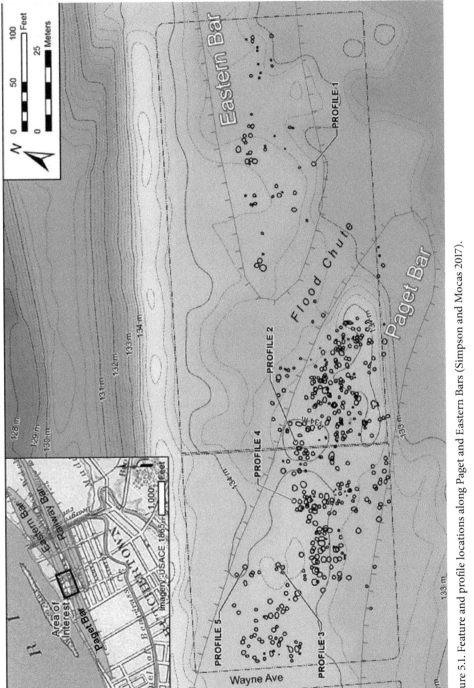

Figure 5.1. Feature and profile locations along Paget and Eastern Bars (Simpson and Mocas 2017).

of the channel, creating an undulating series of soil horizons that may or may not be of the same age. Excavation of these types of sites requires detailed stratigraphic work to understand the temporal and physical relationship between deposits lying both along the same landform and on adjacent landforms.

The investigation of RiverPark used detailed stratigraphic profiles along both bars (see Figure 5.1) to understand the depositional sequence. Radiocarbon dates and artifact analysis have provided a temporal understanding of the horizontal and vertical development of both landforms and relative and absolute means of temporally sequencing each of the strata. In addition, excavation data obtained from units and from trenching was used to remodel the surface elevations to represent the Late Archaic ground surface. Elevation data for each sampled feature or unit could then be used to place them into their correct vertical stratigraphic association.

This geomorphic analysis has indicated that the Late Archaic deposits at RiverPark extended over a series of rapidly accumulated soil packages that provided excellent stratification. The majority of the lower soil sequence consisted of rapidly deposited flood episodes that possessed little soil development and limited to no midden creation. Sediment accumulation rates slowed as the bar landform increased in elevation above the river, allowing for the formation of a series of dense, black midden horizons near the surface of the landform. These middens were composed primarily of organic material, with fire-cracked rock being found in minimal amounts. The soil sequence observed on each bar has been found to be fairly uniform, and by using the detailed wall profiles, a generalized stratigraphic sequence has been created for both bars that allows for all features, burials, and units to be placed in vertical order (Figure 5.2). The features were then subdivided according to the stratum from which they originated, separating them into smaller subsets (Figure 5.2). This subdivision produced isolated clusters of features across the bar landform. Clusters contained on average three to five features, which, when subdivided over the total number of features recovered, produced a conservative estimate of 40–70 occupations over the 1400-year span, or roughly one occupation every 10–20 years. This estimate is probably conservative, insofar as the interval between reoccupations may have been much shorter. The excavations have indicated repetitive placement of features and burials within individual strata that suggests a degree of prior knowledge of their specific locations by succeeding groups. Regardless of whether the estimates are too liberal or conservative, they are illustrative of the slow, incremental development of the site over an extended period.

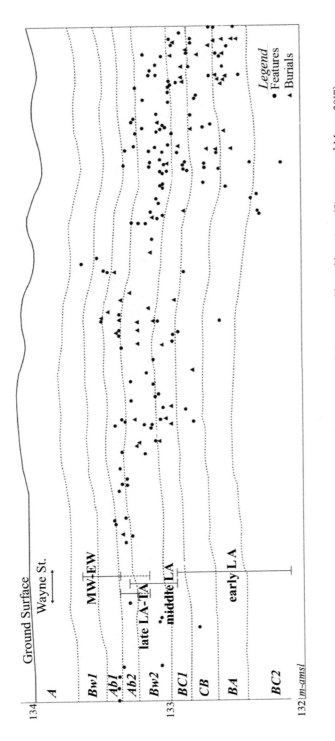

Figure 5.2. Generalized stratigraphic sequence along Paget Bar, depicting all features and burial locations (Simpson and Mocas 2017).

RiverPark Late Archaic

Temporal spans for the Late Archaic that have been derived for other areas, such as the early and late French Lick phases of the Patoka Lake area proposed by Munson and Cook (1980), are believed by some researchers to be applicable to the Falls region and were applied to the analysis of the Caesars Archaeological Project (CAP) sites (Stafford and Cantin 2009a). Division of the Late Archaic into early and late segments has been proposed for the Falls region (Granger 1988; Janzen 1977a; Munson and Cook 1980; Stafford and Cantin 2009a). Recent investigations within the Falls region indicate a finer separation of the Late Archaic Period is possible (Table 5.3). The 1400-year occupation of the RiverPark site spans the end of the early Late Archaic (3500 to 3200 BCE), the middle Late Archaic (3200 to 2500 BCE), and the initial portion of the late Late Archaic (2500 to 2100 BCE) subperiods.

In the following sections, four distinct aspects of RiverPark's archaeological record are examined: material culture, mortuary traditions, subsistence, and settlement patterns. These aspects of the archaeological record can provide an understanding of the changes that occurred in the Falls region from 3500–1900 BCE.

Material Culture

The overall analysis of the material remains recovered from RiverPark indicates a wide variety of tasks, including nut processing, hide preparation, general gathering and processing of resources, and the manufacture of beads and adornments, which were undertaken at the site. Projectile point production, including maintenance, was one of the primary tasks, with hafted bifaces being the most prolific artifact type recovered. The stratigraphic separation of the RiverPark deposits permits assignment of hafted bifaces to specific Late Archaic components. The radiocarbon dates associated with these projectile points confirm previous age estimates offered for the tools.

The cultural chronology of the region is closely tied to a shift from small, shallow side notched points, such as Matanzas and Brewerton Eared points, to the large, lanceolate Late Archaic Stemmed Cluster points (Justice 1987). These tools were used as criteria for the formulation of the French Lick phase of the Patoka Lake area to the northwest of the Falls region (Munson and Cook 1980). The succession of tool types in southern Indiana has been clarified and cogently outlined by Stafford and Cantin (2009a), and has been used to subdivide and to expand the range of the French Lick phase. The projectile point assemblage from RiverPark is well suited to offer

Table 5.3. Late Archaic to Terminal Late Archaic phases along the Ohio River

BCE	Lower Ohio River Valley*		Falls of the Ohio Region	
	Periods	Diagnostic Points	Diagnostic Points	Periods
950	Terminal Late Archaic	Buck Creek	Buck Creek	Terminal Late Archaic
1350				
2000		Riverton Merom, Trimble	Riverton Phase Merom	Late Late Archaic
2500	Late Late Archaic	Late French Lick Phase McWhinney	Lamoka, Ledbetter	
3200			McWhinney	Middle Late Archaic
4100	Early Late Archaic	Early French Lick Phase Brewerton Eared Matanzas	Brewerton Eared McWhinney Matanzas	Early Late Archaic
4300				Middle Archaic

perspective and to answer questions about the projectile point succession in the Falls region during the latter half of the Late Archaic.

Late Archaic Stemmed points, such as McWhinney and Oak Grove, account for 51.9 percent of the middle Late Archaic deposits at the RiverPark site (Figure 5.3). Observation of several other sites, such as Townsend (12Hr481), Knob Creek (12Hr484), and Railway Museum (15Jf630), has led to the conclusion that in addition to Late Archaic Stemmed points, a cluster of medium-sized, moderately broad bladed, parallel stemmed or expanding stemmed projectile points (Anslinger et al. 1994:Figures 7.1–3; Mocas 2008:Figure 8.9) forms a consistent minor constituent of the projectile point sequence around the time of the shift in popularity from Matanzas to Late Archaic Stemmed points. At RiverPark, these types of tools, which were classified as Saratoga Broad Bladed or Parallel Stemmed or Brewerton Side Notched (Figure 5.3), co-occur with Late Archaic Stemmed points, accounting for 22.8 percent of the recovered hafted bifaces. Like many of the projectile point types identified within the Falls region, these types gradually achieve prominence and subsequently decline concurrently with other types that have comparable but not identical periods of ascent and decline, creating a varied assemblage of points at any one site.

Figure 5.3. Projectile points, RiverPark: *top row*, McWhinney; *second row*, Oak Grove; *third row*, Brewerton Side Notched; *bottom row*, RiverPark (Simpson and Mocas 2017).

Figure 5.4. Pickwick point recovered from Burial 31 (Simpson and Mocas 2017).

Another group of tools does not fit readily into any of the established local point types, and rather than assign them to a known type with inapplicable characteristics, they were given the temporary label "RiverPark" points (Figure 5.3). They account for 15.2 percent of the middle Late Archaic projectile point collection. The points are characterized by thick, bi-convex, or asymmetrically bi-convex blades with steep, finely retouched lateral edges and narrow stems. They are almost exclusively made of high-quality Wyandotte or St. Louis cherts. The technology of the broad, thick blades of some RiverPark points resembles Table Rock Cluster points, but the stems and overall morphology are closer to Saratoga and Brewerton Side Notched points. In some studies, these tools have been classified as Benton points (e.g., Mocas 2008). Based on their horizontal and vertical distribution at the site, RiverPark points appear to reach their peak popularity slightly later than Saratoga and Brewerton Side Notched points.

Another small group of points appears to be linked to a widespread phenomenon of inclusion of inordinately large points with burials, as seen at KYANG, Millersburg (12W81), and Shafer in the Falls region and southern Indiana hill country. These bifaces have been classified as Pickwick points (Figure 5.4) to emphasize their incurvate/recurvate blades with fine, steep, lateral pressure flaking (Justice 1987:151–54). They share attributes, such as extreme length, narrow blades, and short stems, with Etley, Benton, and Elk River specimens (Justice 1987:111–14, 146–49). Like the RiverPark points, these tools resemble types that originated, or at least are best known, in the Midsouth and dispersed across much of the Midsouth and Midwest. All of the aforementioned stemmed and broad bladed types are consistent with the middle Late Archaic subperiod.

Groundstone tools and implements are common at Late Archaic sites within the Falls region. A wide assortment of groundstone implements, include nutting stones, pestles, hammerstones, axes, celts, and beads, have been recovered from RiverPark. The majority of these objects were associated with the site's use as a nut processing camp. Pestles, nutting stones, and hammerstones were the most common groundstone tool types and were associated with all of the Late Archaic occupations of the site. Pestles were the only groundstone tool recovered in sufficient quantities to reveal temporal shifts in form and spatial patterning. Bell-shaped pestles appear throughout the Late Archaic, but conical forms do not appear in the general record until the late Late Archaic. Examination of the spatial patterning of pestles within the RiverPark occupations also has provided data on site development that has implications for settlement patterns throughout the Falls region.

Over thirty pestles have been recovered from the site, the majority of which have been associated with midden contexts, whereas almost all of the axes and celts have been recovered from features. This consistent contextual difference is believed to indicate that the pestles were left on site following nut processing and represent "site furniture" rather than transported tools. On the other hand, the axes and celts were brought to the site for a specific purpose and then stored in pits for subsequent use. The storage of tools at selected sites would have allowed for the easy incorporation of a varied and ever-expanding array of plant resources without the need to significantly change the general mobile occupation pattern. The curation of nut processing tools suggests an intention to return to the locale repeatedly for specialized exploitation of resources, precludes the need for additional lithic manufacture, and lessens the need for sedentism, while allowing for an expansion of the overall diet within an ever-increasing population.

Subsistence

The excavations at RiverPark did not produce an extensive collection of faunal or botanical remains, but the little that was recovered documents the steady integration of a wider assortment of foods into the evolving Late Archaic diet. Because of the acidic soil and fluctuating water table, faunal preservation is poor at most Late Archaic sites along the Ohio River; consequently, there is no good data on the exploitation of fauna. One possible measure is the presence of relatively indestructible pharyngeal toothcaps of drumfish. Drum toothcaps are present in a moderate number of samples from the early Late Archaic component of RiverPark and are the only fish remains identified in the middle Late Archaic component (Simpson and Mocas 2017).

Native American plant food remains from RiverPark and other Late Archaic sites in the Falls region are dominated by wild plants, such as nuts and seeds from fleshy fruits and wetland sedges, but small amounts of native cultigens also are present at these sites. Late Archaic plant food remains are consistently dominated by nuts as a primary food source throughout the occupations at RiverPark. Hickory (*Carya* sp.) nut was by far the most ubiquitous botanical food consumed, with minor amounts of acorn (*Quercus* sp.), black walnut (*Juglans nigra*), butternut (*Juglans cinerea*), hazelnut (*Corylus* sp.), and pecan (*Carya illinoensis*) also present. The general nut consumption pattern identified at RiverPark is consistent with the broader regional record as seen at sites such as Townsend (12Hr481), Knob Creek (12Hr484), and Stucky (12Hr482) (Schroeder 2007), with species selection tied both to availability and to specific selective criteria.

Small collections of wild and cultivated plants have been recovered from RiverPark and other Late Archaic sites in the Falls region (Rossen 2017; Schroeder 2007). The shifting patterns of these resources seem to be tied to the dietary trends and changes across the period. Pondweed (*Potamogeton* sp.), spikerush (*Eleocharis* sp.), and ragweed (*Ambrosia trifida*) have all been recovered from the early and middle Late Archaic components at RiverPark, although these resources were apparently abandoned (Rossen 2017). This early adoption of wetland sedges and abandonment by the beginning of the late Late Archaic corresponds with increased reliance on starchy and oily-seeded plants, such as maygrass (*Phalaris caroliniana*) and chenopod (*Chenopodium berlandieri*) (Rossen 2000, 2017; see Chapter 9). This trend is consistent with broad patterns seen elsewhere along the Ohio River.

Sparse amounts of maygrass and chenopod have been found at River-Park, Townsend, Stucky, and Knob Creek by the onset of the early to middle Late Archaic, but use appears varied and enigmatic (Rossen 2017; Schroeder 2007). The recovery of 25 maygrass seeds from a single late Late Archaic (2310–2137 BCE) feature at RiverPark might be considered inordinately early, but may indicate that use of the cultigen was evolving by the end of the period. The data from the Falls region, as in Illinois, suggests that maygrass was an earlier and more common native cultigen (Smith 2011) relative to other plants that comprised the Eastern Agricultural Complex (EAC). Maygrass appears to be in place within the record of the Falls Region by at least the middle Late Archaic.

In addition to the native cultigens, fragments of gourd (*Lagenaria* sp.) and squash (*Cucurbita* sp.) are also present in Late Archaic plant assemblages from the region. However, like other native cultigens, their recovery in Late Archaic contexts is varied and enigmatic. While, overall, the subsistence record within the Falls of the Ohio region is limited for the Late Archaic due to a variety of factors, what has been recovered has shown that subsistence regimes were expanding commensurate with the broader settlement system. Limited use of native cultigens begins during this period, laying the groundwork for their eventual expansion into dietary mainstays during the succeeding Woodland period. The early integration of maygrass, a Midsouth cultigen, into the archaeological record of the Falls region reemphasizes the interaction at this time with groups to the south.

Mortuary Traditions

As Milner (2004:307) has noted, hunter-gatherers are usually viewed in terms of what they did to survive, with investigative emphasis on examining tools, the contents of features, and the exploitation of resources to provide evidence of their subsistence and settlement systems. While these issues are certainly relevant to understanding Archaic populations, other aspects of life, such as sociopolitical issues, conflict, and identification of ritual landscapes have been given less attention. Excavations at certain sites in which varied mortuary traditions have been identified, such as the large shell heaps along Kentucky's Green River (Crothers 1999, 2004; Marquardt and Watson 2005:637–39) and sites within the Falls region, like Rosenberger (Wolf and Brooks 1979) and KYANG (Bader and Granger 1989), appear to demonstrate more sociocultural complexity than is usually ascribed to Late Archaic groups. The mortuary traditions at RiverPark (Simpson and Ross-Stallings 2017) were highly varied and encompassed most forms documented at other sites within the Falls and Green River regions. Unlike most of these sites, RiverPark burials were stratified, which allows for examination of diachronic mortuary patterns during the Late Archaic.

A cemetery is one type of ritual landscape that people form to define, legitimize, and sustain the occupation of their traditional territories (Jefferies 2008:278). The development of these sacred spaces is not well-understood, insofar as they may be created for a wide variety of reasons, the majority of which are constrained by cultural practices that we as archaeologists struggle to understand and interpret. As Sassaman and Heckenberger (2004:215) note, it appears that once a cemetery was created a line was crossed, and there was no turning back: the cemetery or sacred space was encoded permanently in the earth and represented a persistent place on the landscape.

Certain landscapes have been noted that appear more valued as sacred spaces than others. For instance, Jefferies (2008:280) notes that in southern Indiana, sand dunes or ridges situated along the margins of wetlands appeared to be favored locations for interment.

A mix of primary interments, secondary burials, including bundles with skeletal elements from other individuals, cremations, and, in a few cases, disarticulated elements are common within the Late Archaic mortuary record of the Falls region. In some cases, the disarticulation has been associated with violence, but in most cases it appears more ritualistic in nature, speaking more to culture and group identity than to trauma. At a few Late Archaic sites in the Eastern Woodlands, elaborate and extensive postmortem processing has been documented for the skeletal material, as well as unique funerary layouts and inclusion of artifacts in the burial pits (Abel et al. 2001:294–96; Stothers et al. 2001:248–53; Webb and DeJarnette 1942:122–26, 239–47). These investigations document the variability that is common within the Late Archaic burial record. They also suggest that Archaic mortuary practices should be viewed as a continuum rather than as a specific set of cultural norms (Anderson 2004:270–71; Peacock et al. 2011:365). By looking at broad patterns of change within mortuary traditions rather than specific attributes of any one interment, it is possible to assess temporal trends in the treatment of the dead. The broad changes noted within the burial traditions at RiverPark form a continuum of change within and between individual Late Archaic subperiods.

At RiverPark, 57 interment pit features, which contained a minimum of 85 Late Archaic individuals, have been documented by Nancy Ross-Stallings (Simpson and Ross-Stallings 2017). Burials were distinguished by whether they were primary or secondary interments. Primary interments consisted of individuals who were interred in a semi-flexed to tightly flexed position on their sides (Figure 5.5a,b), flexed on their backs, fully extended, disarticulated, and fully extended with accompanying disarticulated elements. Secondary interments included bundles (Figure 5.5a), cremations, ossuaries, and single elements, such as skulls, legs, or mandibles. The general variability seen within the burial population is in some respects to be expected given that these individuals died and were buried over a period of 1400 years. While specific aspects of the burials were slightly different, they did conform to a few broad trends.

The early Late Archaic interments were represented by 33 individuals. Though burials tended to occur as clusters layered one on top of another, they do not appear to have been interred at the same time. Given the positioning of the burials, it is believed that they were related either within an

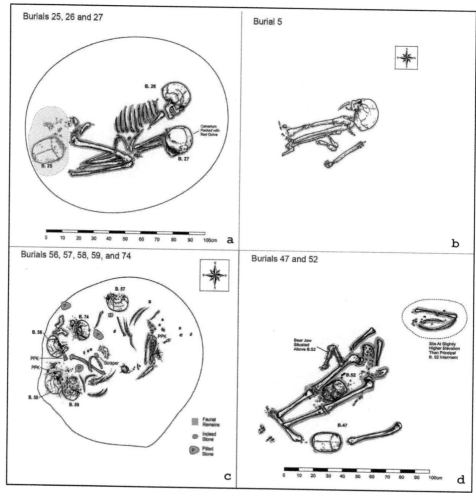

Figure 5.5. Burials: *a*, Late Archaic flexed on side; *b*, Late Archaic bundle; *c*, *d*, late Late Archaic burials (Simpson and Mocas 2017).

extended family unit or within a broad cultural group. During periodic revisits to the site, groups appear to have buried their dead along the edges of the bar, with habitation areas situated along the nearby crest. Similar use of sloped landforms for interment has been noted by other researchers (Bader 2011; Jefferies 2008). Burial pits appear to have been dug for the purpose of each interment, and relative to later interments, burial goods were associated with a higher percentage of the graves. Some limited blunt force trauma was noted on three of the interred, but this was a minor aspect of the overall burial population.

Red ochre was associated with almost fifty percent of the interments (Figure 5.5a). This practice may have originated in the Early and Middle Archaic subperiods (Mocas 1985; Schmidt et al. 2008). The tradition appears to have continued into the early and middle Late Archaic subperiods, insofar as it is present at several sites in the Falls region, including Geltmaker (12Fl73) (Burdin 2002), KYANG, Rosenberger (Driskell 1979), and Arrowhead Farm (15Jf237) (Mocas 1976). At RiverPark there is a significant reduction in the use of ochre by 3200 BCE—approximately the beginning of the middle Late Archaic.

At RiverPark, 10 of the 33 early Late Archaic burials had associated grave goods. Objects interred with the dead included 14 stone tools, five beads (bone or cannel coal), elk and deer antlers, and a human tooth. The most distinctive assemblage was associated with a young adult male who was surrounded by seven cache blades. In contrast to Rosenberger, where 98.0 percent of the grave goods were utilitarian in nature, a higher percentage of personal objects were interred with the dead at RiverPark. For instance, beads were found with 30.0 percent of the burials with grave goods.

At Rosenberger, few subadults had mortuary items and no one over the age of forty had grave goods. In comparison, grave goods were included with a wider range of individuals at RiverPark, with a cache blade being associated with one person at least thirty-five years old, a human tooth with a child, and a bead with an adolescent female.

The middle Late Archaic interments are represented by 41 individuals. While flexed interments and bundles still remained the primary modes of interment, the overall mortuary practice was far more varied, with cremations and large ossuary interments being exclusive to this component. Some limited blunt force trauma similar to that seen among the earlier interments has been noted, but this was a minor aspect of the overall burial population. Dog burials also were identified for the first time at the site.

Because of the use of refuse pits for interments and burial within the living area, it was difficult to confidently attribute artifacts to the middle Late Archaic burial features. Of the grave goods that could be verified, all were tools, with projectile points being associated with three graves (an adult male; an adult female; and a middle-aged female). While the burial artifacts that could be associated with the RiverPark burials from this period are far less extensive than those recovered from Rosenberger, the consistency of burial interment practices, presence of dog burials, and general material culture of the site suggest that the Rosenberger burial population dates primarily to the middle Late Archaic period.

Unlike the distinct cemeteries of the early Late Archaic, middle Late Archaic burials tend to be directly associated with habitation areas. Given the more scattered distribution of these interments, it is difficult to infer kinship between them or to calculate the length of time between interments. The intermixture of the graves with habitation features is similar to the patterns seen at nearby middle Late Archaic sites, such as Rosenberger (Wolf and Brooks 1979), Railway Museum (Anslinger et al. 1994), Arrowhead Farm (Mocas 1976), and Habich (Granger et al. 1993). The burial pits used for interment within the middle Late Archaic are similar in size and form (broad, deep basins) and contain fill similar to nearby contemporary subsistence activity pits. This raises the possibility that some habitation features may have been reused for burial purposes.

The late Late Archaic burial population is represented by only 11 individuals. All have been documented within the upper half of the dark Ab_2 midden deposit, which makes the burial pits difficult or impossible to define. The starkest difference between these interments and those of the two preceding subperiods was the level of trauma noted. In all, at least six, if not nine, of the deceased appear to have died by violent means (Figure 5.5c,d). Contained within this burial population is an ossuary of primarily crushed crania and a pair of trophy legs (Figure 5.5c). Another grave contains two disarticulated individuals with missing elements: the entire torso of one individual, and the left hand and lower forearm of another (Figure 5.5d).

While mortuary practices, such as ossuaries of disarticulated individuals or single crania, identified within this population were part of earlier burial rituals at the site, the distinctive aspects of this population are how the deceased were prepared for inclusion in a grave. Examples of the differing practices include disarticulation along the shafts of long bones rather than at joint locations and purposeful removal of some elements prior to interment. These practices often were evidenced by cut marks on long bones. In some instances, these cutting methods appeared to be for the removal of elements from the interred individual, but in others they appear to be a part of the overall burial preparation and not indicative of violence. Evidence of scalping also was noted within the late Late Archaic burial population at RiverPark.

Though individual elements were consistently noted with the earlier burials, they were not individually interred or crushed on purpose in the manner seen within the late Late Archaic burial population. The recovery of late Late Archaic trophy legs and the documentation of element removal from individuals within this population also represent distinctive departures from earlier mortuary traditions. In addition, while blunt force trauma has been noted on a few individuals from the earlier subperiods, no scalping has been identified.

The evidence of violence within the early and middle subperiod burial populations appears to be more enigmatic and could be consistent with interpersonal violence within or external to a group. The individuals from these early and middle subperiods were interred within the cemetery by their family or kin group. This sort of violence may be the result of conflicts within a group or it may be ritualistic in nature, perhaps serving a religious purpose for the group as a whole. Increased levels of mutilation and differing burial preparation methods indicate a significant shift in cultural norms that occurred during the late Late Archaic. These differing mortuary practices may be related to a cultural shift as a result of either increased violence between groups or a change in the ideology surrounding the mortuary behavior of the groups living in the Falls region or both. Increased intensity of violence between groups toward the end of the Late Archaic may have contributed to a significant drop in the occupational intensity of the Falls region after 2500 BCE.

Settlement Patterns

Late Archaic settlement patterns in the Falls region have been studied intermittently over the last fifty years. Several models for Late Archaic settlement have been offered for the region, none of which have been fully evaluated (Boisvert 1986; Granger 1988; Janzen 1977a; Winters 1969). A lack of vertical separation between site occupations has made it difficult to fully evaluate these models, especially at sites that may have been intermittently occupied over hundreds if not thousands of years. Another limiting factor has been the paucity of absolute dates from the Falls region.

The "base camp" model has been largely accepted by researchers in the mid-continent and in the Falls region as a central basis of Late Archaic settlement organization (Brown 1985; Brown and Vierra 1983; Emerson and McElrath 1983; Granger 1988; Jefferies 1988; Stafford and Cantin 2009a), insofar as it represents a very logical interpretation of how groups would incorporate increasingly diverse food resources into their subsistence strategies. An example of this logical interpretation for the Falls region would be Janzen's "hub and spoke" model. Janzen (1977:141) argued that the confluence of multiple environmental zones in the Falls region may have reduced the need for residential mobility on a seasonal basis. However, one could argue the opposite, concluding that given the great consistency and breadth of resources within the region, there would be no reason to stay in any one spot for longer than deemed necessary.

The "base camp" settlement system model has been evaluated by Boisvert (1986) as part of his dissertation research. Boisvert (1986:47) examined the concept of a "base camp" and the evidence that groups would separate and combine based upon seasonally scheduled events. Based on his research, he labeled this a "fission/fusion" concept of Late Archaic settlement and subsistence for the middle Ohio valley. He went on to suggest that perceived differences between short-term camp sites and "base camp" sites reflect frequency of reoccupation rather than the duration or intensity of the occupation (Boisvert 1986:112). In his model, a single group moves through a series of campsites but reoccupies some sites more than others, forming dense site assemblages at more frequented locales. The archaeological remnants of such sequential occupations could meet many of the expectations of a "base camp" site. Residential mobility has been consistently documented ethnographically for hunter-gatherer societies (Binford 2001), but the aspects of this mobility, such as frequency of movement, distance between sites, duration of occupation, and the group size, are all highly variable. If one accepts that variability was the norm for habitation duration or group size, then the evaluation of these broad models is extremely difficult, if not impossible, without horizontally or vertically stratified sites.

The horizontal and vertical separation of materials and features at RiverPark provides a good context within which to evaluate Boisvert's "base camp" model. The different loci at the site were found to consist of a series of short-term camps. The specific activities that took place during these visits consisted of hunting, gathering, fishing, wood chopping, nut acquisition and processing, and manufacturing of personal items. Adjacent to some of these activity areas were small cemeteries that consisted of a series of burials that accumulated over an extended period. Other burials were intermixed within habitation areas. The interval between groups reoccupying River-Park was highly variable, but may average as much as ten to twenty years between occupations based upon geomorphic analysis, as discussed previously. This sort of spacing between occupations would allow for a significant degree of variability.

The spatial separation of features and burials suggests that the same group or groups revisited the site during certain periods of RiverPark's history. If the same group reoccupied the site over hundreds of years, then they would more than likely have an entire system of potential preferred locations that would be visited based upon their economic needs. Any one of these localities could have been the point of origin from which a group revisited RiverPark, and the variability noted within the archaeological record could have been achieved without the need for significant logistical forays from the site. Based upon the patterning of deposits noted at a site, Boisvert's (1986) single group model appears consistent with the settlement and occupation of larger Late Archaic sites within the Falls region as compared with the more traditional "base camp" models.

DISCUSSION

RiverPark's development is consistent with the broad trends according to which the majority of sites dating to the Late Archaic in the Falls region formed and thus can be used to understand and interpret Late Archaic settlement patterns in this region. The overall occupation is dominated by large, broad, circular pits used for preparing nutmeat for storage, with a distinct subset of burial pits of varied sizes and shapes. These features lie along the crest of a series of linear bars separated by small wetland sloughs, a position typical of all larger Late Archaic riverine sites in the Falls region. It is this commonality of form, function, and assemblage that provides the greatest import in our interpretation and understanding of the Late Archaic subperiod. The stratified nature of the deposits documented at Riverpark provides an opportunity to evaluate how Late Archaic sites developed and how cultural changes are reflected in the archaeological record.

Several researchers (e.g., Jefferies 2008; Jefferies et al. 2005; Meadows and Bair 2000; Stafford and Cantin 2009a; Vickery 2008; Winters 1969) have suggested that relative to the Early and Middle Archaic subperiods, regional population levels peaked during the Late Archaic. They point to the significant increase in the size and number of Late Archaic sites relative to both the earlier Middle Archaic and the subsequent Early Woodland as evidence for this. Collins and Driskell (1979:1031–32) have offered an alternative explanation to the population increase/decrease model. They have observed that Archaic assemblages are highly varied, and sites are often not stratified and have numerous intrusive pits. This led them to question if the numerous Late Archaic sites actually represent an increase in population or if these sites had been used by the populations of the same size for shorter periods of time throughout the year. The archaeological record documented at RiverPark supports this reuse model, with indications that populations continued to steadily increase throughout the Archaic period rather than a population explosion.

This research has also confirmed Collins and Driskell's (1979) assertion that Late Archaic sites represent a palimpsest of smaller and varied occupations rather than large, multi-seasonal "base camp" sites. Based upon the development sequence documented at RiverPark, it would seem plausible that few, if any, actual Late Archaic base camps are present in the Falls region. Rather, large, complex Late Archaic sites represent "preferred camps" that grew in size incrementally for a specific array of economic reasons, such as nut processing or fishing, but were used differently over time. In the case of RiverPark, the recovery of cached tools, such as pestles, provides an indication of the cyclical reuse of these preferred localities within a broad settlement system rather than a concerted long-term occupation. The caching of tools for specific purposes would have allowed for the steady integration of larger amounts of plant resources into the burgeoning Late Archaic diet with little overall impact on sedentism, undercutting one of the major lines of evidence for the regional development of "base camp" type sites.

Analysis of materials recovered from the different RiverPark occupations is suggestive of continuity in the way inhabitants used the site throughout the Late Archaic. This overall continuity in occupation indicates that the groups who used this locality over time were in some manner affiliated, whether through broad kinship groups or as members of the established population who lived in the Falls region for millennia. The shifting changes observed within certain aspects of the site's occupation, such as mortuary traditions, indicate broad cultural changes that were occurring within the Falls region. Those cultural shifts, as seen in the mortuary traditions documented at RiverPark (see Chapter 6), indicate a better mechanism to separate the Late Archaic into smaller subperiods than any other aspect of the archaeological record.

The mortuary practices observed within the RiverPark burial population are highly varied when evaluated on an individual basis. This variability appears more a result of sporadic interment of individuals over time rather than a result of continually shifting cultural practices. While interment methods could be viewed as dynamic, certain mortuary traditions tend to be consistently associated with specific subperiods, and these associations can be used to identify diachronic changes in group cultural practices. Early Late Archaic mortuary traditions display a usage of ochre with interments placed in burial pits specifically created to inter an individual. Cemeteries were placed apart from habitation areas, appearing to lie on the edge of a landform rather than along the crest. Middle Late Archaic mortuary traditions saw the cessation or dissipation of ochre within the overall burial treatment, and individuals were placed in large mortuary features that appear to be intermixed with habitation areas. The larger interment pits are consistent in size and form with other domestic features and may indicate a reuse of pits for interment rather than the creation of burial-specific pits, as one can see in the preceding subperiod. The placement of limited amounts of grave goods, such as large points or beads, with the dead appears to be a consistent practice throughout the Late Archaic with no distinct variation noted in the archaeological record. Limited violence, in the way of blunt force trauma, has been noted on a small subset of individuals who died during early and middle Late Archaic times, with no distinct increase in the identified levels of violence from one subperiod to the other. This pattern appears to shift significantly within the late Late Archaic burial population.

The late Late Archaic mortuary traditions indicate a significant shift from the preceding periods. The recovery of trophy legs, the crania that were crushed on purpose, the removal of elements from individuals, and scalping have been noted within the burial population. None of these mortuary practices were part of the earlier cultural norms of the groups that lived within the Falls region. While the groups appear to remain the same as those that had lived within the region for generations, different mortuary practices appear to represent a significant change in the treatment of the dead. Regardless of whether these new mortuary programs represent increased violence between groups or changes in the norms surrounding the preparation of the dead, they represent a significant cultural shift in the region.

CONCLUSIONS

Late Archaic groups living in the Falls region moved continually throughout the year based upon seasonal resources. The duration of the stay at any one site was highly variable, and occupation may have happened multiple times in a single year or in multiple consecutive years depending on resource availability. This type of settlement pattern would lead to certain site locations being more preferred than others, possibly due to the variety of resources that might be obtained at one time or over repeated visits.

Mortuary practices associated with these localities appear to have changed through time. During the early Late Archaic, individuals were placed within cemeteries that contained pits that were dug for the purpose of their burial. Later, during the middle Late Archaic, they were interred within habitation areas in pits that were similar in size and shape to those dug for other purposes. This shift in burial location corresponds with decreased use of red ochre and is followed by increased interpersonal violence during late Late Archaic times. In the future, it may be possible to use changes in pit morphology, burial placement, and preparation methods to temporally order burials lacking stratigraphic or absolute temporal controls at other sites and to gain an understanding of their chronological position within the Late Archaic.

ACKNOWLEDGMENTS

The authors would like to thank all of the staff of Wood (formerly AMEC Earth & Environment) who assisted in the excavation and analysis of the RiverPark project. We especially would like to give credit to Dr. Hank McKelway, Dr. Nancy Ross-Stallings, and Richard Stallings for their editorial and technical assistance during the original research, as well as Daniel Conn and Chad Knopf for their artistry and skill in creating the graphics included in the current volume.

6

Increased Sedentism and Signaling during the Late Archaic

RICK BURDIN

By about 4000 BCE, nearly two thousand years of environmental change and human behaviors (see Chapters 3 and 4; Jefferies 2008) came to an end, resulting in a hunting and gathering lifeway that was very different compared to that of earlier populations. In that regard, this chapter is focused on the Late Archaic subperiod in the Falls region between 4000 and 2000 BCE. By about 3400 BCE in the Falls Region, the shell midden phenomenon declined, earth midden sites became dominant in the material record, and settlement locations were occupied more frequently and for longer periods. After around 2000 BCE settlement locations became sparse, many of the material cultural markers like bannerstones disappeared, mortuary and burial patterns changed, and increasing degrees of conflict between groups occurred (see Chapters 5 and 7).

Unlike other parts of the Ohio River valley, a great deal of data regarding the hunting and gathering way of life from 8000 to 1000 BCE in the Falls region has been collected over the last fifty years. Though much of this data set may be the result of archaeological investigations undertaken in advance of modern development, archaeologists must not lose sight of the unique natural setting of the Falls of the Ohio River. This landscape feature is the only natural barrier for river travel along the course of the river. It also was a major crossing, and the region surrounding the Falls of the Ohio River was an extremely rich resource area. As such, it has long been a preferred location for hunters and gatherers, providing a suite of resources and suitable places for settlement or prolonged use.

As evidenced by the preceding chapters, hunters and gatherers were attracted to the Falls region during the Archaic period. Throughout this period the environment increasingly became more suitable for prolonged human occupation. So much so that by the end of the Archaic, relatively modern conditions were present. While many social and cultural behaviors changed during this period, by ca. 4500 BCE hunters and gatherers had begun to intensify their use of aquatic species (Dye 1996), a variety of oily, starchy, seed-bearing plants (Gremillion 1997; Smith 1989, 1992), upland resources like nuts, and various species of terrestrial animals. These activities primarily appear to have been focused on resource-rich locations along the Ohio River, the surrounding uplands of the Falls region, and in some locations, inland areas along secondary streams (see Chapter 4; Stafford 1994).

During the course of the Archaic period, group mobility was reduced, being largely confined to smaller, more circumscribed territories (Anderson 1996; Brown 1985; Jefferies 2008). As territories became delineated, some sites were more intensely occupied more often and for longer periods. A sense of ancestral connection developed, and particular groups regularly returned to certain sites within these smaller home ranges (see Chapter 4). Some locations became venerated in that the deceased of succeeding generations were interred within their bounds (Buikstra and Charles 1999; see Chapter 4). What followed is likely a widespread view of group or familial ownership of these resource-rich but smaller home ranges. As a result, the relatively free movement across the landscape available to earlier populations was replaced, perhaps, by the requirements to coordinate such travel with neighbors and the limited/restricted use of the resources found there.

To facilitate communication between these groups, an overarching belief system that is best viewed by a similar approach to the treatment of the dead and ancestors seems to be in place by about 3500 BCE. In conjunction with the development of this geographically large-scale shared cosmology, a system of symbolic communication was developed to convey a variety of social messages (Burdin 2004; Jefferies 1997).

In the remainder of this chapter, a two-fold approach is taken in order to better understand the dynamic character of Late Archaic hunting and gathering lifeways in the Falls region. First, the reduction of mobility is viewed as a necessary precursor to significant organizational change within hunter-gatherer societies. While some Falls region Late Archaic sites were intensely occupied either seasonally or repeatedly for shorter periods (see Chapters 4 and 5), evidence of more permanence in settlement strategies has remained somewhat elusive. To date, the only documented Late Archaic house structures are subterranean house basins documented at the Overflow Pond (12Hr12) and Spadie 3 (12Jf54) sites (Figure 1.5). These structures are presented as important correlates of the adoption of a less mobile, more permanent settlement system (Brown and Vierra 1983; Ledbetter 1995;

Purtill 2015; Sassaman and Ledbetter 1996; cf., Jefferies 2008). After about 2000 BCE, structures apparently became more common within the Falls region (Mocas et al. 2009; see Chapter 8) and elsewhere (Harl et al. 2001; Purtill 2015).

Second, the reduction of mobility, a focus on smaller home ranges, and increased permanence of settlements at particular locations had an impact on the social aspects of hunting and gathering life. A major issue was the need to communicate with neighboring groups to continue past efforts to avoid conflict, share information, and exchange needed or desired goods. What seems to have intensified by the Late Archaic is the prevalence of efforts to convey group membership, communicate identity, and exhibit greater social differences. These types of communications are identified by examining symbolically charged objects (engraved bone pins and banner-stone stylistic variation) that demonstrate such interactions between groups living in the Falls region and their neighbors elsewhere in the lower Ohio River valley.

Late Archaic Architecture in the Falls Region

The remains of Late Archaic pit-house structures have been documented at two different Late Archaic sites in the Falls region. They represent the earliest known house floors/basins in this region. The first structure was documented at the Overflow Pond (12Hr12) site in Harrison County, Indiana. The site is located at the western edge of the Falls region near the confluence of Indian Creek and the Ohio River. It is situated on a Pleistocene terrace adjacent to an oxbow impoundment (the Overflow Pond) about 350–400 m inland from the Ohio River.

The Overflow Pond (12Hr12) site encompasses about 22,400 m^2 (Burdin 2008, 2009). The earth midden associated with this site is about 50 cm thick and has yielded calibrated median radiocarbon dates that range from 3753 to 2952 BCE (4950 to 4300 BP) (Burdin 2009:31). Among the features documented at this site is a large pit (Feature 15). Along the edge of this pit, 16 postholes have been documented (Figure 6.1). The pit extends downward to 110 cm below the surface and in profile is a bowl-shaped basin with steep walls.

The posts range in diameter from 8 to 17 cm (mean=10.4 cm) and in depth between 2 to 25 cm (mean=6.7 cm) (Burdin 2008, 2009). The two largest posts measure 17 cm in diameter and 25 cm deep, and 15 cm in diameter and 16 cm deep, respectively. Aside from their structural significance, the use of posts to demarcate the boundary of Feature 15 is significant in that

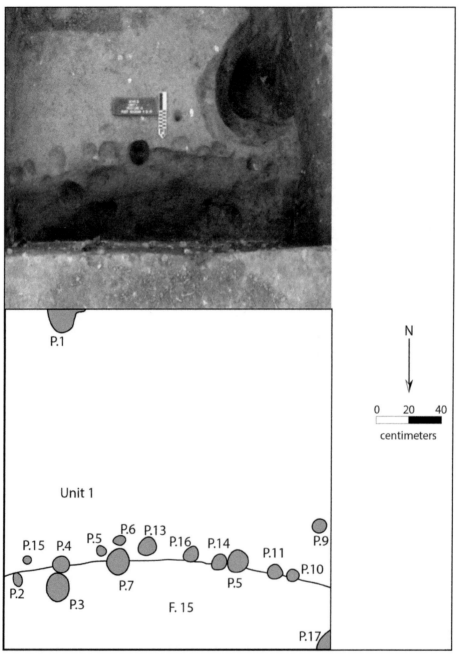

Figure 6.1. Floor plan showing posts along the edge of Feature 15 at the Overflow Pond site.

Figure 6.2. Projectile points: *left*, side notched (Overflow Pond); *right*, broad blade side notched (Spadie 3).

particular spaces within the site may have begun to be set aside, with some limitations regarding who could enter and use them.

Based on the portion of the feature excavated, Feature 15 is suggested to be the remains of a Late Archaic pit-house structure that had an estimated diameter of 8 to 10 m (floor area 50.27 to 78.54 m^2). Multiple lines of data suggest that this structure dates to the Late Archaic. The presence of a side notched projectile point (Figure 6.2:left), the recovery of chenopodium and seeds of the sunflower family, and calibrated median radiocarbon dates of 3743 BCE (4940±100 BP; ISGS Sample #6230) and 3753 BCE (4950±130 BP; ISGS Sample #6232) obtained from Post 13 and Stratum 1, respectively, all support a Late Archaic association (Burdin 2009).

Even though Feature 15 is the largest anomaly detected, results of the geophysical survey indicate there are several similar-sized anomalies in proximity to this structure (Burdin 2009:19) (Figure 6.3). These structures may be contemporary with Feature 15 or may represent similar structures that were occupied at different times. The presence of two other distinct, circular clusters of anomalies is suggestive of individual households or, at a minimum, discrete activity areas. In any case, the presence of house structures provides strong evidence that the people who lived at the Overflow Pond site were staying longer and investing more effort in the development of the settlement.

Feature 17, a large storage pit, provides additional evidence that people were occupying the Overflow Pond site for more extended periods of time. This feature was located about 30 m south of the Feature 15 structure along the edge of the steep bank of, and 4 m above, the Overflow Pond. Feature 17 appears to have been circular in shape, about 1 m in diameter, and, even though upper levels had been disturbed, at least 80 cm deep with a rounded basin. The location of this pit is perhaps the only setting within the site that would have been suited for underground storage. Most of the site is underlaid by hard-packed clay that does not drain well. However, near the edge of the Overflow Pond bank where Feature 17 is situated, the landform drops four meters over a relatively short distance (13 m) to the water level affording the necessary slope for drainage.

The presence of a dense midden and a remarkably large artifact assemblage, the documentation of a subterranean pit structure, a large storage pit, and what appears to have been discrete activity areas within the site is significant. These lines of evidence not only indicate that there was an intense use of the Overflow Pond site during the Late Archaic, but also that there was a degree of internal site organization and settlement permanence. It has been suggested that people lived at the Overflow Pond site for longer periods or more frequently than did earlier hunters and gatherers in the Falls region.

A second structure has been documented at the Spadie 3 (15JF54) site in the southwestern portion of Jefferson County, Kentucky. The site is situated on the first floodplain terrace 370 m inland from the Ohio River (Burdin 2010). During the investigation of this site, five pit features were documented. Feature 1 is the largest and represents the remains of a subterranean house structure.

The structure was documented at the base of the plowzone. It consists of an oval-shaped basin with sloping sides and a relatively flat bottom. The house basin has a diameter of 7.75 m (floor area of 47.15 m^2) and extends to a depth of 75 cm below the surface (Figure 6.4). The size of the house is consistent with the structure documented at the Overflow Pond site (8–10 m in diameter; minimum floor space of 50.27 m^2). A burnt pit feature is situated along the structure's northern edge, two posts have been documented along its southern boundary, and four posts have been associated with its

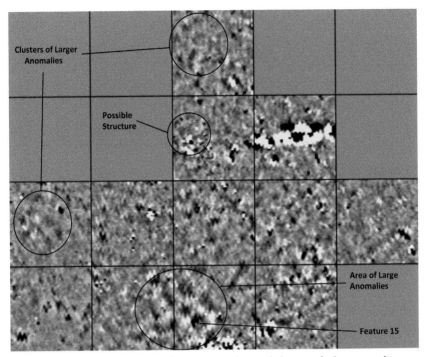

Figure 6.3. Magnetometer survey showing Feature 15 and clusters of other anomalies.

western boundary (Burdin 2010). It is dated to about 2000 BCE based on the presence of a Late Archaic broad blade projectile point (Figure 6.2:right).

Other artifacts recovered from the vicinity of this structure and associated features include chert debitage (n=538), a biface fragment, cores (n=2), edge-modified flakes (n=7), battered stones (n=2), a chopper, and a hammerstone. A moderate-to-dense concentration of fire-cracked rock was recovered from the house basin. The presence of these materials indicates that multiple day-to-day activities were conducted at the location of the structure and they are consistent with tasks that would be expected to take place in and around a house.

To summarize, these two Late Archaic subterranean houses are, to date, the only such structures documented in the Falls region between 5000 and 3000 BCE. Similar subterranean pit-house features appear in multiple locations throughout eastern North America during this period, (e.g., Ledbetter 1995; Otinger et al. 1982; Peterson 1973). Even so, there are no subterranean structures previously documented in the middle or lower portions of the Ohio River valley until after 2000 BCE (e.g., Mocas et al. 2009; Purtill 2015).

In this regard, the presence of structures at Late Archaic sites in the Falls

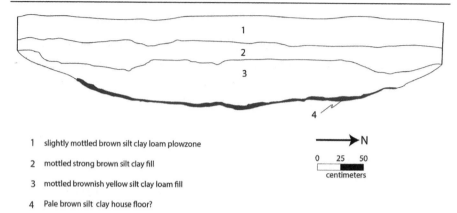

Level Line

1 slightly mottled brown silt clay loam plowzone

2 mottled strong brown silt clay fill

3 mottled brownish yellow silt clay loam fill

4 Pale brown silt clay house floor?

N

0   25   50
centimeters

Figure 6.4. West wall profile of Spadie 3 house basin.

region is currently unique in the majority of the Ohio River drainage. These structures suggest that a settlement strategy had been initiated that was focused on particular locations along interior river valleys and their tributaries. The construction of domestic structures also suggests that mobility had been reduced to relatively well-defined and smaller territories. Within a more restricted system of mobility and settlement, new mechanisms were needed to communicate and interact with neighbors living in surrounding regions.

The significance of these structures extends beyond their physical presence and has implications for how archaeologists think about hunter-gatherer settlement systems during the latter stages of the Archaic period. As Nabokov and Easton (1989:11; cf., Redmond 2015:1–2) note, when people begin to construct architecture, it involves more than design and decoration of buildings or making order and meaning of random space, but also includes the often unseen social and religious meanings in buildings and spatial domains. Redmond (2015:1–2) rightfully notes that the careful reconstructions of structures alone are insufficient. Rather, we should adopt a broader description of architecture in context of the entire built environment, including social and religious meanings.

As the groups living in the Falls region became more tethered to resource-rich locations within smaller home ranges, the construction of more permanent structures was accompanied by adjustments to social and religious practices. The increasing use of selected locations to bury the dead is a strong indicator of an intensifying religious belief system (see Chapter

4). Socially, the use of symbolic devices suggests that an increasing need to communicate a variety of socio-political messages had become an important aspect of a hunting and gathering life.

In this chapter the connections between the construction of more permanent structures and the social environment during the Late Archaic are addressed by examining the use of engraved bone pins and bannerstones, their stylistic attributes, and their spatial distributions in the Falls region and the lower Ohio River valley in general.

SYMBOLICALLY CHARGED OBJECTS

After about 4000 BCE, interactions within the large-scale exchange system that began during the late Middle Archaic intensified. In addition to the continuation of the economic exchange of goods, information, and mates, the communication of identity, conveying group membership and perhaps a degree of group status, also had become important (Burdin 2004; Jefferies 1997, 2008; Jefferies and Burdin 2007; cf., Winters 1968). In order to facilitate the transmission of particular social messages, such as identity, membership, and status, hunter-gatherers adopted a system of communication using a variety of symbolically charged objects by which such information was signaled (Bird and Smith 2005; Bird et al. 2001; cf., Conolly 2017; Jefferies and Burdin 2007).

Symbolic objects were highly visible for all to see (Whallon 2006) and thus are effective signaling devices (Bird and Smith 2005). These items are hyperstylized, and particular attributes are related to geographically distinct groups and their home territories (Burdin 2004; Jefferies 1997; cf., Wobst 1977). Within the Falls region and throughout the lower Ohio River, the presence and extent of interactions between distinct groups of hunters and gatherers are reflected in part by the spatial distribution of engraved bone pins (Jefferies 1997) and bannerstones (Burdin 2004).

Bone Pins

Jefferies (1996a, 1996b, 1997; cf., Goad 1980; Winters 1969) has demonstrated that by the late Middle Archaic, hunters and gatherers living in large portions of eastern North America were participating in long-distance exchange networks. As hunters and gatherers continued to become less mobile, activities within these large-scale networks intensified. As part of his research, Jefferies examined the kinds of inter-group interactions that occurred and suggested reasons why they were important, such as risk avoidance or conveying identity. As such, his research has moved the concept of exchange beyond simple down-the-line economics and has considered the social aspects of these interactions.

While Winters (1969) has suggested that degrees of social stratification may have arisen due to the exchange and use of exotic goods, as seen in mortuary contexts, there has been little recognition regarding the symbolic messaging value of these goods. Jefferies' (1997) study of engraved bone pins has provided the first documentation that material goods were used by late Middle Archaic hunters and gatherers living in the Falls region and throughout the lower Ohio River valley to symbolically convey a variety of social messages. As part of his study, Jefferies has identified seven morphological bone pin types and several distinct decorative engraving styles. In general, these pin types and decorative elements occur at sites located in the Falls region, and at locations downriver and up the Mississippi to its confluence area with the Missouri River.

Bone pin types found north of the Ohio River were generally widely distributed across the landscape. In contrast, those documented to the south in the middle Green River region were substantially different (Marquardt and Watson 1983). Jefferies (1997) has suggested that this reflects a lower level of interaction between groups living south of the Ohio River and those to the north. He has further suggested that interactions between hunter-gatherer groups resulted in stronger social ties, a broadening of social identities, and the emergence of a large regional group comprised of interdependent local groups (Jefferies and Burdin 2007; cf., Jefferies 2004:76).

In the Falls region, Bader (1992) has documented 31 bone pins and fragments collected from the KYANG (15Jf267) site (Bader and Granger 1989), which contains distinct late Middle Archaic and Late Archaic components (Bader 1992; Jefferies 1997). Jefferies (1997:478) has noted that nearly forty-two percent (n=13) of these bone pins were engraved with the concentric step motif, a pattern closely related to locations north of the Ohio River. The presence of these bone pins at a site south of the Ohio River suggests that within the Falls region, interactions between groups living to the north and south were not impeded. This contrasts with the pattern of interaction between groups living in the Green River and those living north of the Ohio River. Given the extremely rich resource base of the Falls region and the advantage that at periods of low water the Falls of the Ohio River was a natural crossing (cf., Jefferies 1997:483), such interactions should not be surprising.

Prior to the investigations at the Overflow Pond site (Burdin 2008), the most westerly site in the Falls region that had yielded engraved bone pins was the Crib Mound (12Sp1&2) site. Of the 14 bone pins and fragments recovered from the Overflow Pond site, the two examples of engraved bone pins were recovered from well-dated Late Archaic deposits. As identified by Jefferies (1997:478), these fragments exhibit a concentric square design and what appears to be a complex concentric engraved pattern. A complete pin with the concentric step decorative pattern has been collected from the site by an avocational artifact collector. The discovery of the pin and fragments in the unglaciated portion of the lower Ohio River valley begins to fill the spatial gap in our understanding of the use and meaning of these objects. Their distribution across the landscape suggests that interactions that began during the preceding late Middle Archaic subperiod continued into the Late Archaic.

Jefferies (2004) has noted that the spatial distribution of bone pin types and their decorative, stylistic attributes suggests that inter-group interactions were occurring within the region. The mechanism(s) by which bone pins were distributed across the landscape, such as economic exchange, the movement of people between groups, or the sharing of ideas about how they were made, is unclear. Even so, Jefferies (2004:76) has concluded that "long-term interaction among these late Middle Holocene hunter-gatherers resulted in the strengthening of social ties and the broadening of cultural identity, leading to the emergence of a larger regional group comprised of interdependent local groups." Based on the bone pin data, this network extended from the Falls of the Ohio River, near Louisville, Kentucky west to eastern Missouri, a distance of approximately 500 km (Jefferies and Burdin 2007).

Jefferies (1997:480) has further noted that "their frequent occurrence at some sites, along with their non-ceremonial disposal, suggests that bone pins were not considered to be particularly special or valuable in themselves." He also has suggested that their value might "have been the stylistic information that their various shapes and decorations conveyed concerning the wearer's social identity or affiliation." In contrast, other items occur primarily in burial contexts and were used by hunters and gatherers during the latter stages of the Archaic period to convey different messages, such as individual or group status.

At the time of the use of decorated bone pins, other items also were being used to symbolically convey social messages. Unlike the bone pins, these items are primarily found in burial contexts, including marine shell for personal adornment, engraved conch shell gorgets, and bannerstones. The distribution of bannerstone types and stylistic elements appears to coincide temporally and spatially with that noted for the bone pins. As such, they provide another way to view interactions between hunters and gatherers living in the Falls region.

BANNERSTONES

As with Jefferies' study of bone pins, the author's (Burdin 2004) examination of the spatial and temporal distribution of bannerstone forms and stylistic attributes in lower Ohio River drainage has identified similar interregional differences. Like bone pins, stylistic differences tended to distinguish those groups living to the north of the Ohio River from those living to the south of the Ohio River. Further, by the Late Archaic, stylistic characteristics can be associated with specific locations in the lower Ohio River valley and secondary drainages like the Green River in Kentucky.

Bannerstones were likely first used during the latter stages of the early Middle Archaic, with 49 specimens being documented in the lower Ohio River valley. By the late Middle Archaic/early Late Archaic, 119 specimens of multiple morphological forms (n=10) were widely distributed across the landscape. During this period, soft raw material was the preferred medium for production and banded slate was the dominant type of stone used. Like those of the early Middle Archaic, most late Middle Archaic/early Late Archaic bannerstone types were widely distributed throughout the region. At this time there are a few indicators that specific types were becoming associated with distinct geographical groups. For example, the Notched Butterfly type, primarily made of banded slate, occurs only north of the Ohio River at six specific locations, including the Overflow Pond site (n=2). South of the Ohio River, the composite shell, humped variety (n=10), is primarily restricted to sites located in the middle Green River drainage of Kentucky.

The number of lower Ohio River valley bannerstones associated with Late Archaic contexts more than doubles (n=262) from the late Middle/ early Late Archaic. However, a significant shift occurs after 4000 BCE in that there are only four primary forms being used: Bottle (n=12), Quartz Butterfly (n=22), Diamond (n=58), and Triangular (n=78) types (Burdin 2004:110). The Diamond variety is primarily distributed north of the Ohio River, and the Triangular form is most often found south of the Ohio River. This distribution is similar to that documented by Jefferies (1997) for bone pin types.

Lutz (2000:488–502) has suggested that there is a distinct bannerstone variety that is geographically associated with the Falls region, which he has defined as the Clarksville type. There appears to be a significant amount of variation of form and stylistic attributes within his definition of the Clarksville typology. Based on preliminary examinations by the author of available information and several specimens from the Falls region, a distinct Falls region bannerstone type exists, albeit based on only a few attributes like a

Figure 6.5. Bannerstones recovered from the Falls region (Photo courtesy of Anne Bader).

concave end and a smaller drilled hole. Even though more analysis needs to be completed, these attributes appear to be restricted to the Falls region and indicate that there are bannerstone forms and attributes that are directly associated with groups living in the Falls region (e.g., Figure 6.5).

The Bottle (n=12) and Quartz Butterfly (n=22) types are visually impressive and represent hyperstylized exotic forms that also are geographically restricted (Burdin 2004). While the majority of the Bottle form occurs downriver from the Falls region (n=10), one example is documented upriver just outside the Falls region, and one was recovered from the Overflow Pond site.

A cache of three bannerstones, documented by Lutz (2000:92), has been collected by an avocational artifact collector from an oval-shaped pit approximately sixty centimeters below the surface at the Overflow Pond site (Figure 6.6). The cache includes a quartz Bottle form, a mottled quartz Clarksville variety, and a green quartzite Horn type (a Diamond type with horn stylistic attributes). Lutz (2000:75–86) has suggested that this group represents a Three Atlatl Cache ceremonial trait. While the Diamond type primarily occurs to the north of the Ohio River, the horn attribute is completely restricted to that portion of the region. The numerically and geographically restricted Bottle form is only the second one documented in or near the Falls region and its presence points to limited, ceremonial interactions between groups living in the Falls region and those living farther downriver.

It is also significant that more dense raw materials like quartzite, ferruginous quartzite, quartz, and jasper were selected from which to manufacture bannerstones. These materials are significantly more difficult to shape compared to slate, siltstone, and limestone. The amount of labor invested to form these harder materials into a final shape, drill the central hole, add

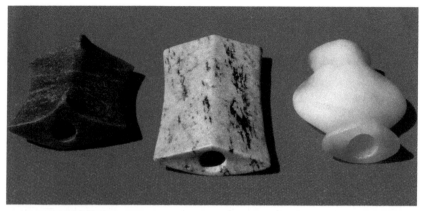

Figure 6.6. Butterfly bannerstones recovered from the Falls region (12Hr12) (Photo used with permission of Mr. Dave Lutz).

various stylistic elements, and then highly polish them was considerably more than the work dedicated to earlier bannerstones.

The elaboration of the saddle and hourglass elements and the addition of horn and hook attributes are remarkable (Burdin 2004:Figures 5.7 and 5.8). These stylistic attributes have no impact on the mechanical function of the bannerstone as an element of the spearthrower. Instead, the addition of these decorative, stylistic elements was about visual, symbolic messaging rather than mechanical function, and Late Archaic people living through-out the lower Ohio River valley considered it important enough to invest a considerable amount of skilled labor in it.

The spatial distribution of bone pins and bannerstones in the lower Ohio River valley indicates that during the Late Archaic these symbolically charged artifacts tended to be associated with specific group affiliated areas. By then, localities, such as the Falls region, had become important/persis-tent places on the landscape for hunting and gathering groups, where the conveyance of both individual and group identity was important.

Discussion

The documentation of two Late Archaic houses in the Falls region reflects an intensification of use of this area by the beginning of this subperiod. The Late Archaic occupation of the Overflow Pond site began around 3800 BCE and increased in intensity until about 3000 BCE. This increasing intensity of occupation is evidenced by the accumulation of a dense earthen midden that contains a large amount of lithic materials and faunal remains.

It is also evidenced by the hundreds of anomalies detected during the

Table 6.1. Other Late Archaic structures

Site	Dates	Source
Brinkley Midden, Ms	3500–2000 BCE[a]	Otinger et al. 1982
Overflow Pond, In	3753–3743 BCE	Burdin 2008
Unnamed Mill Branch, Ga	2350–2200 BCE	Ledbetter 1995
Ohio Region (several)	2300–700 BCE	Purtill 2015
Spadie 3, Ky	≤ 2000 BCE[a]	Burdin 2010

[a] Relative dates based on projectile point associations.

geophysical survey of the Overflow Pond site, and the identification of two-to-three clusters of anomalies within the midden area, the presence of which is suggestive of some degree of internal community organization (Figure 6.3). The association of a large pit-house structure and storage pit with one cluster and the possibility that other structures are located nearby reflect an intensification of use of this locality. Likewise, the presence of a Late Archaic house at the Spadie 3 site also reflects intensification of use of the Falls region. Other Late Archaic sites located near Spadie 3 include the Hornung (15Jf60), Villier (15Jf110), Rosenberger (15Jf18), and the Spadie site (15Jf14) (Boisvert 1979; Driskell 1979; Janzen 1977a; Robinson and Smith 1979).

These subterranean structures are, to date, the earliest known in the Falls Region and the only ones that date to the period between 4000 and 2000 BCE. This is somewhat surprising given the number of Late Archaic sites investigated in the Falls region. On the other hand, only a few such structures have been documented throughout eastern North America (e.g., Ledbetter 1995; Otinger et al. 1982; Peterson 1973).

The presence of Late Archaic structures in the Falls region is consistent with patterns documented elsewhere in the southeast and mid-continent regions of eastern North America (Table 6.1). The mere presence of these structures is remarkable, but their significance needs to be considered within the contexts of the natural and social environments in which they occur. It is no coincidence that they appear in the archaeological record near the beginning of the Late Holocene around 3000 BCE, when riverine settings became more suitable for longer periods of habitation. By this time, forests of oak and hickory covered much of the Falls region. Wetlands were present in low lying areas and near stream confluences. The Ohio River had relatively stabilized and was contained approximately within what is its modern channel.

As particular locations began to be occupied more intensively and for longer periods of time, they came to be identified with particular groups, perhaps due to familial or ancestral connections. In addition to these places as major areas of habitation, over time they became regionally important locations for social, economic, and political events (Burdin 2004). Archaeologically, the importance of these places is reflected in the spatial distributions of highly stylized and symbolically charged artifacts. Engraved bone pins and bannerstones (Jefferies 1997 and Burdin 2004, respectively) from the lower Ohio River valley indicate that certain areas within the region had become important focal points of hunter-gatherer life. Based on the spatial distributions of these artifacts, the Falls region was one such locality.

CONCLUSION

By the beginning of the Late Archaic period, hunting and gathering groups had become centered within smaller territories. People were staying longer, and they were occupying some sites more frequently. The construction of houses required a major reorganization of labor and time. Such an investment indicates that a change in settlement practices had occurred, or was occurring.

The presence of Late Archaic pit-house structures at the Overflow Pond and Spadie 3 sites indicates that people living within the Falls region were expending considerable effort to establish more permanent settlements. In both instances, the presence of substantial structures suggests that the sites were used for longer periods or more frequently compared to previous patterns of site use. As particular locations began to be occupied in these ways, they may have come to be identified with particular groups, perhaps due to familial or ancestral connections. In addition to these places being major areas of habitation, over time some became regionally important places for social, economic, and political events.

There is little doubt that the Falls region was an important place for Late Archaic groups. People residing in this region had a very broad base of rich and predictable resources, which could support a relatively large population. As the local hunter-gatherer groups became more sedentary, there was an increasing need to exchange goods and communicate with local and distant neighbors.

In the Falls region, individual identity, (possibly) status, and group membership may have been signaled through the shapes and motifs engraved on bone pins. At another level, the inclusion of bannerstones in burials, sometimes as caches, and the restricted distributions of particular bannerstone forms and added stylistic attributes indicate that they communicated group identity, status, and perhaps one's political-economic position within the Falls region. With over twenty bannerstones documented at locations in the proximity of the Falls of the Ohio River and fifty documented at and around the Overflow Pond area near the western limit of the Falls region, bannerstones and bone pins may have been used to signal one's identity not only within the Falls region but to outsiders as well.

The Falls region had, by the Late Archaic, become a major location of hunting and gathering life. Perhaps initially this happened because of the Falls of the Ohio River's unique setting on the landscape and the extremely rich resource base of the Falls region. By 4000 BCE, groups living in the Falls region were fulfilling a significant role in the socio-economic and political aspects of the broader lower Ohio River valley.

ACKNOWLEDGMENTS

The author wishes to acknowledge the many who participated in the investigations of the Overflow Pond area and the excavations of the Spadie 3 site. The author would like to thank Mr. David Lutz for allowing him to use the photograph of the Overflow Pond bannerstones (Figure 6.6). Mr. Richard Burnett took the photograph of the Figure 6.5 bannerstones. Dr. Richard Jefferies' work with Archaic bone pins was instrumental, but even more important were his insights and comments. The advice, suggestions, and discussions with Anne Bader and David Pollack were of great benefit. Finally, the comments and suggestions provided by the outside reviewers greatly enhanced this work.

7

Middle and Late Archaic Trophy-Taking in the Falls Region

CHRISTOPHER W. SCHMIDT

Trophy-taking in archaeological contexts is defined as the intentional removal of body parts from a recently killed person (see Chacon and Dye 2007). Over the last several decades, researchers have offered numerous explanations for this phenomenon, but for the most part, motivations for interpersonal conflict, in general, and trophy-taking, in particular, are difficult to discern, especially for Native American populations that lived thousands of years ago. Explanations tend to range from cosmology, to mourning, to military prowess, although it is possible that multiple factors simultaneously motivated the taking and burial of trophies (e.g., Hargrave et al. 2015; Jacobi 2007; Keeley 1996; Kelly 2000; Lambert 1997, 2002, 2008; Mensforth 2001, 2007; Milner 2007; Walker 2001; Willey 1990). Hypotheses, however, can be constructed using the ethnographic record. For example, Harner (1972) describes trophy-taking among the Jivaro of Amazonia. Here people were motivated to take heads because of the magical powers they held, which were particularly valuable in warfare. The trophies, called tsantsas, were smoked and dried heads with the cranium and mandible removed (i.e., "shrunken heads"). They were worn during conflicts in the belief that they protected the wearer from harm. But they also served as emblems of military prowess because they indicated that the wearer was capable of acquiring a human head.

Additionally, it is important to include a historical ecology perspective, which considers the feedback loop that connects humans and their environments: as people affect the natural world, it, in turn, affects them (see Szabó 2015). For example, the fact that trophy-taking was common in areas having sizable mussel beds that were, nonetheless, finite in time and space, and within forests that were favorites for silviculture may be more than coincidental. The economic potential of the Falls region, coupled with an increasing use of symbols and stylizations that indicate a heightened interest in group membership/identity and an increasing use of cemeteries indicating more territoriality (e.g., Charles and Buikstra 1983; Jefferies 1997; see also Chapters 4 and 5), may have formed a nexus whereby trophy-taking became a legitimized sociocultural phenomenon.

During the Middle and Late Archaic subperiods in the Eastern Woodlands of the United States, trophy-taking was common (e.g., Ross-Stallings 2007; Schmidt et al. 2010; Smith 1993, 1995, 1997; Snow 1948). Trophy items tended to be hard and soft tissue components of heads and limbs, although at times only soft tissues were taken, such as scalps and the tongue (e.g., Schmidt et al. 2010; Smith 1995). In Middle and Late Archaic contexts, trophies are typically found in cemeteries buried alongside a primary interment (e.g., Snow 1948; Webb 1946, 1950). Whether or not the trophy-takers were motivated in ways similar to those of the Jivaro, or similar to those of groups like the Jivaro, is unknown. But the contexts regarding how the trophies were taken, how they were treated by the trophy-takers, how long the tradition of trophy-taking lasted, and how trophies were disposed of provide insights into how they were viewed at the time of their taking and placement in a grave. Thus, while it is unlikely that we will ever fully understand the motivations for Archaic-era trophy-taking, it is possible to use the osteological and cultural data from each trophy-taking event to construct parsimonious explanations that include both site-specific nuances and region-wide similarities.

TROPHY-TAKING

In southern Indiana, there are six Middle and Late Archaic sites along the Ohio River where trophy-taking has been documented (Schmidt et al. 2010; see also Chapter 5) (Figure 7.1; Table 7.1). These sites include large and small cemeteries, as well as isolated cemeteries and those that are adjacent to habitation areas. At these sites, trophy elements tend to be heads and forelimbs (Table 7.1), with head removal present in four individuals at three of the six sites. Scalping was present at the Kramer site and perhaps at Site 12Hr6. Forelimb removal is present among nine people from four sites (Table 7.1). A single individual from the Bluegrass site had its head and all four limbs removed; this is the only person from Indiana to have had the lower limbs removed. But this person's burial context is unclear; it is difficult to discern if this person represents someone from the cemetery population, or if he is actually a trophy thorax brought in to accompany a grave in the cemetery.

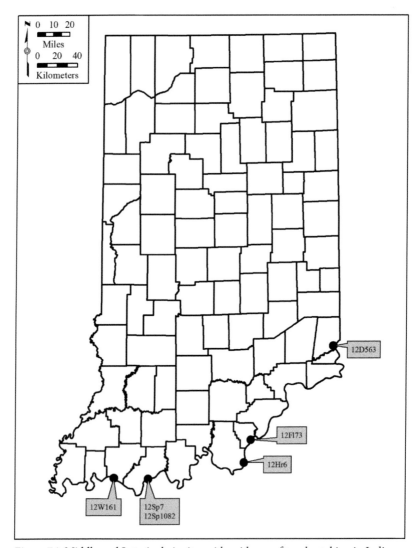

Figure 7.1. Middle and Late Archaic sites with evidence of trophy-taking in Indiana.

The thorax was found in a location that is somewhat isolated from the in situ graves, and so does not clearly represent an element buried with another person. In contrast, at Site 12Fl73, which is located within the greater Falls region, a cache of trophy forearms that came from victims not interred at the site has been documented. While Site 12Fl73 is the only trophy site in Indiana so far reported from within the Falls region, others are located on the Kentucky side of the Ohio River. For example, at the Late Archaic RiverPark site evidence of hand and lower limb removal and a cache of skulls have been documented (see Chapter 5).

Table 7.1. Evidence of Middle to Late Archaic trophy-taking in Indiana

Site	Victim(s)	Description
Firehouse—12D563[a]	1 male	Decapitation, removal of right forearm
12Fl73[a,f]	5 males	Removal of left and right forearms
12Hr6 (possibly an Early Woodland site)[a]	1 adult	Scalping, forearm removal
Kramer—12Sp7[b,d]	1 adult	Scalping
Meyer—12Sp1082[a,e]	1 subadult	Decapitation, tongue removal
Bluegrass—12W162[a,c]	2 adults	Female decapitated, left forearm removed; adult with head and all limbs removed

Note: Firehouse and site 12Hr6 do not have a published report.
[a] Schmidt et al. (2010).
[b] Schmidt (2013).
[c] Stafford et al. (2000).
[d] Bergman et al. (2013).
[e] Bader (2011).
[f] Burdin (2002).

In Indiana, trophy victims were men, women, and children. Most were young adult males, although a female victim was found at the Bluegrass site and a 12-to-15-year-old subadult, likely a male, was found at the Meyer site. The latter was found with his severed head placed in his right hand. Cut marks on his mandible make it very clear that his tongue had been removed. This case is of particular interest because it is the only subadult victim known in Indiana, and it is the most unique of all the Indiana trophy victims, because the head remains with the body (although outside of Indiana, but within the Falls region, a head remains with a body at the Hornung site in Kentucky [Anne Bader, personal communication 2017]). The perimortem removal of the Meyer site victim's head is unambiguous. Chop marks on the cervical vertebrae indicate that the head was taken around the time of death (Schmidt et al. 2010).

Experimental studies conducted by the author and by the University of Indianapolis graduate students indicate that in Indiana, trophy-takers used large bifacial stone tools to remove body parts. The cut marks on the bones were not created by incisive movements of the cutting tool. Instead, they were made by percussive strokes with what was probably a hafted tool. The cut marks are large, often nearly a millimeter wide, and almost half a millimeter deep; cuts of this size require a forceful blow to create. Slicing with a sharp flake, either unifacial or bifacial, does not create the kinds of cut marks seen on ancient bone. Likewise, steel tools like knives and trowels could not replicate the ancient cut marks. But groundstone celts and axes were capable of making them (Schnellenberger 2013). The cut marks were only found in areas where heads or limbs were missing, and none of the vic-tims exhibit evidence of bone cleaning, either perimortem or postmortem (Lockhart and Schmidt 2007, 2008; Lockhart et al. 2009).

The trophy-taking phenomenon lasted for over three thousand years, from the late Middle Archaic to the end of the Late Archaic subperiod. In-terestingly, the placement of the cut marks did not change over that span of time. For example, distal humeral cut marks only appear on the anterior, medial, and lateral aspects. They never appear on the posterior aspect of the humerus. This may indicate that the trophy-taking process had a par-ticular procedure that its practitioners followed; for example, Andrushko et al. (2005) has found evidence that Native Americans in California dis-membered people in the same fashion that they butchered animals. Another possibility is that the trophy-taking process was dictated by supernatural concerns. Perhaps it was important to carry out limb or head removal in a particular way in order to avoid supernatural repercussions.

SITE 12FL73

Although well-known to collectors for many years, Site 12Fl73 in Floyd County, Indiana (Figure 7.1) has, for the most part, eluded extensive study by qualified professional archaeologists. In 1998, the Indiana Department of Natural Resources Division of Historic Preservation and Archaeology (IDNR/DHPA) visited the site and collected human remains from along the Ohio River, which formed the site's eastern border. Controlled archaeo-logical work was initiated by Rick Burdin of the University of Kentucky, who surveyed the site in the early 2000s (Burdin 2002). In 2001, he found that the river bank was eroding. Examination of the profile documented an earthen midden situated above an approximately 5 cm thick shell midden, both extended intact for hundreds of meters. He also found exposed hu-man remains within the earthen midden and about two meters below the current road level. The only other features documented in the profile in the vicinity of the human remains were a couple of pits, including one that had fire-reddened sides, suggesting that it was a cooking pit or hearth. No ad-ditional excavations have been conducted at the site. A calibrated median date of 3728 BCE (4950±40 BP) has been obtained from the earthen midden and a calibrated median date of 4176 BCE (5350±130 BP) has been obtained from the shell midden (Burdin 2002).

Human Remains

Investigation of Site 12Fl73 by University of Indianapolis personnel in 2004 documented 10 human bone features; Burials 1, 2A, and 3 were partly in situ, but they were not complete skeletons (Figure 7.2). The rest of the features consist of ex situ clusters of remains (groups of bones from previous in situ interments). These remains had eroded from the river bank, and were recovered as clusters on the surface. Despite being partly in situ, much of Burial 1 was found ex situ, and so is grouped with the other ex situ remains in the discussion below.

The minimum number of individuals (MNI) recovered from the site is 11; there are five adults in the forearm cache, four additional adults, and two subadults (Table 7.2). The adults are from Burials 1, 2, 2A, 3, and 4. The subadults include a single infant cranial fragment found near Burial 2 and teeth and limb fragments of a 12-to-15-year-old from Burial 4. The highly disturbed condition of the remains makes age and sex determination difficult. Features 1, 2A, and 3 appear to be middle-aged adult males, and Feature 4 includes long bones from an adult female.

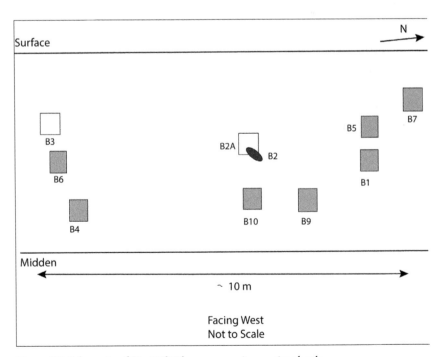

Figure 7.2. Schematic of Site 12Fl73 human remains on river bank.

Table 7.2. Burial inventory for Site 12Fl73

Burial	Summary	*In situ/Ex situ*
Burial 1	Age: Middle Adult, Sex ?; MNI=1	*Ex situ*
Burial 2	cache of human forearms; MNI = 5 (5 left ulnae, 5 right ulnae, 5 left radii, 5 right radii)	*In situ*
Burial 2A	Age: Adult, Sex = M; head to S/SW, flexed, right side? MNI =2; ex situ infant frag	*In situ* (partially, much of skeleton eroded away)
Burial 3	Age: adult; Sex=F, head to S, flexed, right side; MNI=1	*In situ* (partially, much of skeleton eroded away)
Burial 4	Fragments, adult female and subadult (age 15), MNI=2	*Ex situ*
Burial 5	Fragments	*Ex situ*
Burial 6	Fragments	*Ex situ*
Burial 7	Fragments	*Ex situ*
Burial 8	Fragments	*Ex situ*
Burial 9	Fragments	*Ex situ*
Burial 10	Fragments	*Ex situ*

Note: Includes bones recovered by Indiana DNR/DHPA in 1998 and the University of Indianapolis.

The northern and southern-most burials (Burials 7 and 3, respectively) are separated by approximately ten meters. Because only exposed burials have been excavated, it is impossible to estimate inter-burial space within the cemetery. Burials 1, 2A, and 3 have enough of their bones present that burial positions could be discerned. The burials were single, primary interments, flexed on the side, with the head to the south, or to the southwest. In addition to the human remains, ex situ burned animal remains have been recovered from the site.

Burial 2A

This 35-to-50-year-old male was found immediately adjacent to Burial 2, the forearm cache. The in situ part of his skeleton includes fragments from his skull, thorax, pelvis, lower limbs, and some forelimb bones. The presence of his radii and ulnae establishes that none of the remains in the cache come from him. The context of the cache suggests that it was intentionally placed next to this individual. Unfortunately, the eastern edge of Burial 2A's burial pit boundary was too disturbed to determine if Burials 2 and 2A were initially interred within the same pit.

Burial 2

Burial 2 is an oblong feature that measures approximately 50 × 20 cm in size. The long axis of this pit has the same orientation as Burial 2A and it is approximately 10 cm thick. Its fill is dark brown and just above it are pieces of fire-cracked rock. Together, these materials suggest that a hearth feature had been placed above the cache (see Chapter 3), although how long after is unknown. One of the first elements to erode out was a bone pin similar in morphology to the T-top pins from the Black Earth site in southern Illinois (Richard Jefferies, personal communication 2017; see also Jefferies 1997). It has no engraving and was found broken in two pieces that include the proximal end and part of the shaft. The distal end was not found. A bone pin is the only artifact found in direct association with any human remains at the site.

Upon excavation, five left and right ulnae, and five left and right radii, for a total of 20 forelimb long bones, was exposed. Several carpals and metacarpals also have been found in association with the arm bones (see Table 7.3 for a complete inventory). Most of the bones were not in a proper anatomical position, indicating that they had been curated and allowed to decompose before their placement in the ground. The exception was a radius-ulna pair that had a lunate immediately next to the distal radius. That forearm must have retained its soft tissues at the time of burial. The presence of other hand bones demonstrates that hands were intentionally included in the cache, even if they were from a heavily decayed limb.

The bones are fragmented, but overall the preservation is good. Based on size, color, and morphology, it appears that the forearm bones represent left and right forelimbs from five individuals. The fragmentation and disarticulation of the bones have required detailed study to find the pairs, but similarities in size and robustness have yielded left and right radius/ulna pairs. The numbers of metacarpals, carpals, and phalanges present have not changed the MNI of five.

Age and Sex Estimation

All of the limbs appear to be from adult males. All have their epiphyses completely fused and all are robust. It is difficult to determine their precise age, but none appear to be subadult, and none are so old that their articular surfaces are significantly arthritic. Two right ulnae have arthritis, and one has a sizable entheseal hypertrophy. A radius also has a deep entheseal depression on the radial tuberosity. These attributes, which are associated with

Table 7.3. Burial 2, forearm cache, inventory

Bone	MNI
Left Radius	5
Right Radius	5
Left Ulna	5
Right Ulna	5
Right Hamate	3
Right Lunate	3
Right Scaphoid	3
Right Trapezium	3
Left Triquetral	3
Left Capitate	2
Left Hamate	2
Left Lunate	2
Right Pisiform	2
Left Trapezium	2
Right Triquetral	2
Left MC 1	2
Right MC 4	2
Left MC 5	2
Right Pisiform	2
Left Trapezium	2
Right Triquetral	2
Left MC 1	2
Right MC 4	2
Left MC 5	2
Right MC 2	1
Right MC 3	1
Left MC 4	1
Right MC 5	1
Right Capitate	1
Left Pisiform	1
Right MC 1	1
Right MC 2	1
Right MC 3	1
Left MC 4	1
Right MC 5	1

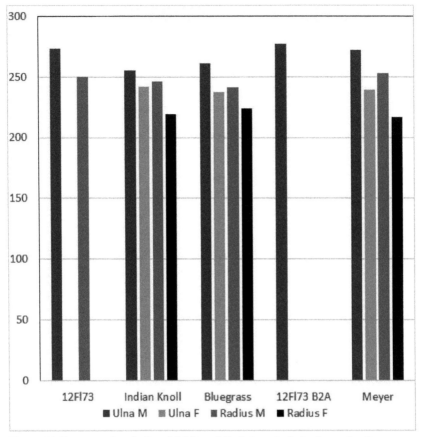

Figure 7.3. Summary data for Late Middle and Early Late Archaic ulna and radius maximum lengths compared to the Site 12Fl73 forearms. The Indian Knoll data are from Snow 1948.

repeated limb use, suggest that at least some of the males could have been closer to midlife rather than young adult.

Sex estimation comes from the maximum lengths of the ulnae and radii. The mean ulnae and radii lengths are 273 and 250 cm, respectively (Figure 7.3). When compared to other contemporary sites, the Burial 2 ulnae and radii lengths are more similar to male means than female means. For example, the mean male and female ulnae lengths at the Bluegrass site were 261 mm and 237 mm, respectively. At Meyer (12Sp1082), male ulnae averaged 272 mm and females averaged 239 mm. The adult male associated with Burial 2A had a measurable ulna of 277 mm. The trend is identical for the radii; the Burial 2 radii are very similar in maximum length to the other males and dissimilar to the females (Figure 7.3). It is possible to estimate stature from ulna and radius lengths, but appropriate reference samples do not exist for Archaic people of the Eastern Woodlands. If some leeway is allowed and a modern reference population is used as a proxy for an ancient reference sample, then the males in the cache stood approximately 168 to 177 cm (5' 6" to 5' 10") using a regression formula from Trotter and Gleser (1958) for Asians and Mexicans. (The goal of including the stature estimates is to underscore the overall robustness of the cache long bones. The estimates should not be used to characterize the entire burial population.)

Pathology and Taphonomy

There are no traumata or cut marks present on the arm and hand bones. The only pathological condition present is minor osteoarthritis. The taphonomy indicates no post-depositional disturbances and it appears that all of the remains were buried at one time. Having said this, it is clear the individuals who lost their forearms did not die at the same time. The disarticulated forearms came from people who died well before they were buried, but the articulated bones likely came from a person who died shortly before the individual was placed in the ground. There is no evidence that the limbs were exposed on the surface prior to interment since they lack solar bleaching and animal gnawing. The bones are not perforated and have no polishing or smoothing of their cortical surface. Thus, even though the remains must have been curated, they were not suspended from cordage as is seen in South America (e.g., Williams et al. 2001) or handled repeatedly.

Limb Removal Process

The forelimb removal process at Site 12Fl73 appears to be similar to that documented at contemporary Archaic sites in Indiana. The person removing the limbs would have rotated the arm medially and severed the biceps muscle using a hafted biface or a celt in a chopping motion. However, since the humerus is rotated, the cutmarks made there are linear and look like incisions; but they are not. They are the result of percussive strokes, just like the wedge-shaped chop marks on the medial and lateral distal humeral borders. The posterior aspect of the elbow joint was cut free perhaps by bending the elbow and cutting between the humerus and the ulna. Since there are no cut marks on the posterior humerus, it is unclear if this aspect of the removal process uses the same tool that was used to make the anterior cuts. Once the joint capsule was opened, the forearm could be detached. In the end, the limb could be removed expediently by an experienced person. None of the cache forelimb bones have cut marks. But, since cuts were not made on the posterior aspects of the arms, it is not a surprise for the cache ulnae and radii to lack them. Thus, it appears that the Site 12Fl73 forelimbs were taken in the same way as other forelimbs were taken at other sites, such as the Bluegrass and Firehouse sites in southern Indiana. An alternative explanation is that the Site 12Fl73 forelimbs lack cutmarks because they were not taken as trophies, but as elements pulled from long-dead ancestors. Although compelling, the veneration idea is not supported osteologically. Arguments that the cache represents trophies (rather than instances of veneration) are provided below.

Are the Site 12Fl73 Remains the Result of Violence?

There is overwhelming evidence that most Middle and Late Archaic trophies were taken from people who were killed just prior to the trophy-taking event (e.g., Mensforth 2007). These killings may or may not have been motivated by the taking of the trophy, but nonetheless resulted in the removal of a body part or parts. The direct evidence for killing is that trophy victims often bear unambiguous instances of perimortem trauma. Moreover, they have cut and chop marks located in areas where trophies were taken, for example, at the ends of humeri or on the cervical vertebrae. Thus, when trophy victims are found, it is fairly straightforward, from an osteological perspective, to interpret what happened to them.

When one finds a cache of bones, however, it is more difficult to understand the circumstances surrounding their placement in a grave when the taphonomy does not clearly indicate violence. This is the case for the remains from Site 12Fl73. Because they lack cutmarks, it is not immediately obvious that they are in fact skeletal trophies. But there is contextual evidence that indicates that the bones in the cache came from victims of violence. To begin with, the lack of cutmarks on the Site 12Fl73 bones does not preclude a violent origin. As noted earlier, their absence is not a surprise. As it turns out, there is no reason for someone to cut either the radius or the ulna when removing a forelimb.

Additional evidence for violence is that all of the bones are forelimbs, which were a preferred trophy element during the Middle and Late Archaic. Forelimbs are the most common Archaic trophy found at sites in Indiana and are common trophy elements at contemporary sites in Kentucky, including at RiverPark (see Chapter 5). In fact, forearms are one of the most commonly documented trophy elements in all of precontact North America (e.g., Chacon and Dye 2007). Moreover, at least one arm retained soft tissues at the time of burial. This means that it was taken from a fully fleshed person at or near their time of death. By contrast, ancestor veneration tends to use bones from people who have been allowed to decay (see Rakita et al. 2005 for examples).

The remains only represent adult males and include both forearms from each of the five victims. While trophies can come from females and children, they primarily come from adult males. Lastly, they were placed in the grave of another adult male, which is consistent with the manner in which trophies were interred in the Green River region of Kentucky (e.g., Snow 1948). The overall context, therefore, indicates that the Site 12Fl73 cache represents limbs taken from victims of violence.

Discussion

While trophy-taking occurs with some regularity in and around the Falls region (e.g., Ross-Stallings 2007; Schmidt et al. 2010), caches of human remains are uncommon. The Late Archaic component of RiverPark, however, includes a cluster of human heads that may represent a cache, as well as trophy legs, a torso, and at least one arm (see Chapter 7). RiverPark differs from Site 12Fl73 in a number of important ways, particularly in terms of overall size and time. The RiverPark cemetery contained 85 individuals from the Middle Archaic to the end of Late Archaic. That RiverPark includes a cache of human remains indicates a spatial/temporal distribution of caching in the greater Falls region; but being found at just two localities suggests it was not a widespread phenomenon.

In the Green River region of Kentucky, Mensforth (2001) reports a small collection (cache?) of drilled human teeth from the Ward site. Though numerous examples of trophy victims and buried trophies have been documented at Archaic sites in the Green River region, similar forelimb caches have yet to be found. On the other hand, artifact and shell caches have been documented at several Middle and Late Archaic sites in this region and elsewhere (e.g., Snow 1948). For example, at the Firehouse site, which is mostly a habitation locale, archaeologists recovered a cache of grooved axes (Jeff Plunkett, personal communication 2004).

Large collections of human body parts have been documented at Early and Middle Woodland sites in the Midwest. Windsor Mound, for example, in east central Indiana, contained over fifty crania (McCord and Cochran 1996). Accompanying some of the crania were the first and second cervical vertebrae, which indicates that soft tissues were present at the time of head removal and interment. Other collections of human crania and "cut" human jaws are reported from the Mount Vernon mound in Indiana; Turner, Seip, Harness, Hopewell, Marriot, Mound City, and Ater mound sites in Ohio; and Montezuma, Snyders Mound C, Dickison, and Pete Klunk mounds in Illinois (e.g., Johnston 2015; Moorehead 1922; Schmidt and Helmkamp 1997;

Seeman 1988, 2007; Shetrone 1926; see Hargrave et al. 2015 for detailed discussion of Woodland, Mississippian, and late precontact trophy-taking and
bone modification).

Until such time that archaeologists are able to find more human bone
caches, the collection of arm bones documented at Site 12Fl73 represents a
rare expression of Middle and Late Archaic trophy-taking and trophy burial
in the Ohio River valley, in general, and in the Falls region, in particular.
The same could be said for RiverPark (Chapter 5); it too represents a unique
form of trophy-taking and trophy burial. These two sites bear similarities
that indicate some level of functional/cosmological constancy that guided
the trophy removal, curation, and burial processes that apparently allowed
for substantial differences in the final disposition of trophy remains.

The emphasis on forelimb removal is not surprising given that forearm
removal has been documented at other Middle and Late Archaic sites (e.g.,
Mensforth 2007). A possible cosmological explanation for the forearm
cache is that the limbs offered protection in the afterlife to the adult male
who was interred in the adjacent grave. Alternatively, the forelimbs were
taken to render the victim helpless in the afterlife (e.g., Keeley 1996); an
armless person would have difficulty hunting or fighting. Of course, these
two speculations are not mutually exclusive, and perhaps several cosmological explanations are required to understand the cache's presence in the
cemetery. The point is that the trophy is part of a belief system that gives it
an existence or a "life" after it is taken from the victim (see Smith 2015).

Another possibility is that the forearms indicate fighting prowess; perhaps the male interred in the adjacent grave was able to take the lives of five
men. Archaic warfare tended to be small scale, but persistent (e.g., Jacobi
2007). Thus, it is plausible that the limbs acknowledge success in warfare. If
we reconsider the Jivaro example provided earlier, it seems likely that cosmology and prowess are linked, and that both contribute to the motivations
behind the creation of the cache.

To explore this point further, it is possible to contextualize the Site 12Fl73
cemetery by comparing it to the practices of groups known to recognize
fighting valor. In her study of Middle and Late Archaic, in addition to late
precontact violence, Lockhart (2008) has found that violence during the
former period generally led to only one or two people killed per cemetery,
very few multiple-person graves containing victims of violence, and trophies that focused on entire body elements like forelimbs and skulls. In
contrast, late precontact violence led to many victims per cemetery, graves
containing multiple victims of violence, and expedient trophies like scalps
and other soft tissue elements, including noses and ears (Lockhart and

Schmidt 2007, 2008; Lockhart et al. 2009; also see Milner et al. 1991; Willey 1990). Lockhart's insights on late precontact violence, coupled with proto-contact ethnographic accounts (see Chacon and Dye 2007), indicate that fighting prowess was highly prized. But, given the osteological and mortuary differences between the two periods, it seems unlikely that their respective patterns of violence had the same motivations. It is suggested here that Middle and Late Archaic motivations for trophy-taking were dominated by a cosmology that required the collection and burial of certain human body parts. An ethnographic example would be the belief system of the Asmat of New Guinea, who saw head removal as vital for maintaining cosmological balance (Zegwaard 1959).

Although caching human remains may be rare, placing human trophies in graves is not. During the Middle and Late Archaic, particularly in the Green River region of Kentucky, people were buried with sizable trophy elements. Excellent examples come from Indian Knoll and Ward. There, entire limbs, including forelimbs, were buried with or even draped over individuals in graves (Mensforth 2001; Snow 1948). And, like Site 12Fl73, only a small number of people out of hundreds in the cemetery were buried with trophy bones. Taken together, it may be that certain people during the Archaic were afforded a mortuary status that reflected a particular (shamanistic?) status in life. Thus, while the Site 12Fl73 cache is uncommon, the occurrence of one (or just a few) people buried with at least one trophy element is not.

Conclusion

The Site 12Fl73 cache is unique in that it contains several forearms, yet it is part of a regional Middle and Late Archaic trophy-taking phenomenon (Osterholt 2013). It is evident that the cache contains the remains from people who likely died violently, whether or not the forelimbs themselves were meant to symbolize or acknowledge violence. For archaeologists interested in understanding trophy remains, it is important to recognize, even if it is difficult to determine, the likely cosmological significance the cache had for the people who created it. Also, it is important to make sure that interpretations are driven by the osteological and contextual evidence. In sum, the Falls region includes sites like Site 12Fl73 that play important roles in our understanding of Middle and Late Archaic lifeways; Site 12Fl73 has a one-of-a-kind bone cache, one that represents the intricacies and complexities of people living in and around the Falls region. But it also indicates that life in the Falls region was linked to other regions that practiced similar, albeit not identical, trophy-taking behaviors.

8

The Riverton and Buck Creek Phases of the Falls Region

STEPHEN T. MOCAS AND DUANE B. SIMPSON

The period from 1600 to 700 BCE in the Falls region was marked by an increased focus on the Ohio River floodplain and its main tributaries for habitation and resource extraction. The material culture associated with these sites reflects participation in broad Midwestern trends. These trends are best expressed by changes in projectile point styles, with late Late Archaic Merom projectile points being associated with the Riverton phase and Terminal Archaic Buck Creek Barbed projectile points with the Buck Creek phase. These two phases also are characterized by a shift in preference from the use of river gravels and other local sources to manufacture projectile points to a preference for high-quality Wyandotte and St. Louis cherts. The Terminal Archaic also is associated with the production of Turkey-tail cache blades manufactured from Wyandotte chert for export over much of the Eastern Woodlands. The widespread distribution of Turkey-tail points and their association with mortuary practices are suggestive of participation of those living in the Falls region in broader rituals that may presage Adena and Hopewell rituals.

The marked differences among the lithic assemblages of earlier Late Archaic, and later Riverton, and Buck Creek could be indicative of the movement of ideas or populations into the region. However, the archaeological record of the Falls region has not been shown to reflect population replacement. Throughout the late Late Archaic and Terminal Archaic, the Falls region does not appear to be a border or frontier region. The adoption of Merom points, however, is suggestive of greater interaction with the lower Ohio valley, and Buck Creek Barbed points show a marked affinity to the Wade and Delhi types of the Midsouth and Mississippi valley. Turkey-tail points manufactured from Wyandotte chert are found in similar ritual contexts throughout much of the Eastern Woodlands, reflecting the spread of the symbolism and rituals associated with these artifacts.

Within the Falls region, during the Riverton phase some sites were visited repeatedly by small to medium-sized groups as has been documented for the Late Archaic in general (see Chapter 5), although some Riverton occupations may have lasted longer, and other sites show less intensive use. These trends continued into the Buck Creek phase, though the presence of sturdier seasonal structures at some sites suggests that groups were beginning to stay at some localities for longer periods of time. Subsistence practices reflect intensification of nut exploitation and diversification in the use of native cultigens. Intra-group factionalism and attempts to control access to resources in the late Late Archaic to the Terminal Archaic could be linked to increased intra- or inter-group violence documented in the archaeological record of the Falls region.

In this chapter, the Riverton and Buck Creek phases, as represented in the Falls region, are highlighted and contrasted. Emphasis is placed on characterizing and identifying trends in Riverton and Buck Creek material culture, settlement patterns, subsistence practices, and mortuary patterns. In particular, attention is given to the increased importance of Wyandotte chert in tool production and its role in the manufacture of items for participation in widespread ritual practices.

Riverton (Late Late Archaic)

The Riverton culture was initially defined by Winters (1969), based on his work in the lower Wabash River valley. Subsequent work has expanded the range of the Riverton culture to include much of the lower Ohio valley and all of southern Illinois, and it has essentially become a horizon style for the late Late Archaic throughout this region (Butler 2009:623). The recovery of Merom points from sites, such as Knob Creek (12Hr484)(Stafford and Cantin 2009a; Stafford and Mocas 2008; Stafford et al. 2008), Villier (15Jf110) (Collins 1979), Hornung (15Jf60) (Janzen 2014), and RiverPark (15Jf596, 15Jf597, and 15Jf598) (Simpson and Mocas 2017), in addition to smaller floodplain sites and sites in upland settings throughout the Falls region, has led to the identification of a Riverton phase in the Falls region (Anslinger et al. 1994; Mocas 1974; O'Malley et al. 1980; Driskell 1979; Seeman 1975; Sieber and Ottesen 1986). Among the sites with Riverton components, Knob Creek is one of the largest and most intensively investigated, not only in the Falls region but also throughout much of the lower Ohio River valley (Stafford and Cantin 2009a; Stafford and Mocas 2008; Stafford et al. 2008).

Figure 8.1. Terminal Archaic projectile points: *a–e*, Turkey-tails (cache from Zorn Avenue Village site); *f–h*, Buck Creek Barbed (12Cl199); *i–m*, Merom (Hornung site).

The five radiocarbon samples from the Knob Creek Riverton component have yielded calibrated medians that range from 1933 to 1704 BCE (Table 8.1). These dates place the occupation among the earliest documented thus far in the lower Ohio valley, and correlate well with the dates obtained from Riverton sites located in the lower Wabash valley (Winters 1969).

At the Knob Creek site, Riverton deposits extend for a kilometer along a levee in the Ohio River floodplain. In addition to 325 Merom points (Figure 8.1), researchers recovered six distinctive Riverton chipped stone axes (Winters 1969:65, Plate 31d-f), and a small number of microtools. Variable quality, readily available, bedrock and water-rolled cherts, such as those used to manufacture earlier Late Archaic Stemmed points, continued to be utilized during the Riverton phase in the Falls region. Analysis of the chipped stone materials recovered from this site has demonstrated that the diminutive size of the tools was not a product of limited raw material size (contra Winters 1969). Despite the availability of large pieces of raw material, the projectile points and other tools within the assemblage are markedly smaller than those associated with earlier and later assemblages. Additionally, point size trends smaller over the phase, perhaps indicating a higher degree of resharpening and tool curation as compared with the earlier examples.

Table 8.1. Late Late Archaic and Terminal Archaic radiocarbon dates

Temporal Period/Site	(rcybp)	2 Sigma Cal BCE	Median Cal BCE	Reference
LATE LATE ARCHAIC—RIVERTON				
Stucky (12Hr482) ISGS-116445	3900±50	2550–2207	2382	Stafford & Mocas 2008
Knob Creek (12Hr484)				
ISGS-4956	3580±70	2135–1746	1933	Stafford & Mocas 2008
ISGS-4957	3570±70	2133–1699	1919	
Beta-192410	3550±40	2015–1761	1894	
ISGS-4961	3430±70	1920–1535	1743	
ISGS-4985	3400±70	1884–1530	1704	
Habich (15Jf550)				Granger et al. 1992
Beta-42898	3480±100	2114–1531	1806	
TERMINAL ARCHAIC—BUCK CREEK BARBED				
Knob Creek (12Hr484)				
Beta-115655	3140+70	1605–1220	1405	Stafford & Mocas 2008
Beta-206922	3090+40	1436–1233	1346	
ISGS-4983	2980+70	1401–1013	1202	
Stucky (12Hr482)				
Beta-116443	3080+60	1495–1132	1335	Stafford & Mocas 2008
Spadie (15Jf14)				
TX-3013	3090±150	1682–932	1326	Boisvert 1979
Shippingport (15JF702)				
Beta-250737	3030+40	1407–1131	1282	Mocas et al. 2009
Beta-250738	3120+40	1495–1278	1387	
Beta-250735	2900+40	1215–949	1087	
Newcomb (12CL2)	2922+34	1217–1014	1119	Simpson et al. 2014
Muddy Fork (12CL199)				
D-AMS 005835	2911+29	1207–1014	1100	French et al. 2015

Note: Calibrations performed with Calib 7.10 program using intcal13.14c.

The main habitation area at the Knob Creek site contains clusters of small-to-moderate sized shallow pits (n=103) and basin-shaped hearths (n=25). Many of the pits appear to be associated with the processing of nuts (cf. Stafford 1991). Chert knapping loci and plant and animal processing areas also have been documented at this site. The distribution of features and middens suggests that this was a locale that was revisited numerous times during a series of substantial residential occupations and smaller, specialized short-term encampments (Stafford and Cantin 2009a; Stafford et al. 2008).

The Riverton settlement type represented at Knob Creek differs from those documented in the Wabash valley (Anslinger 1986; Winters 1969). For instance, at Robeson Hills and Riverton, the pits are larger and deeper than at Knob Creek, and there are baked clay floors and arcs of postholes indicative of possible houses, in addition to burials that are present. Despite intensive excavation, the Riverton component at Knob Creek has produced no posthole patterns. Nor are there any burials. Thus, many of the Falls region sites may have been used for shorter durations than those documented elsewhere in the lower Ohio valley.

Little is known about Riverton faunal exploitation patterns in the Falls region, but during the Riverton phase, there was an increase in nut and seed consumption (Schroeder 2007). The number of nut specimens per 10-liter flotation sample (n=230.5 liters) reflects a more intensive exploitation of mast resources relative to earlier and later components. Black walnut (45.9 percent) and hickory (49.6 percent) account for nearly equal percentages of the nut sample. The spatial distribution of Riverton ethnobotanical remains at the Knob Creek site suggests that it was a hub for seasonal gathering, and nut species may have been exploited both on a preferential and on an opportunistic basis during seasonal rounds (cf. Simon 2009; Stafford 1991).

As a means of mitigating the unpredictability of masts at specific times and places, the groups may have revisited the Knob Creek site repeatedly, because it provided a dependable level of nut productivity and abundant resources within a short distance. It is noteworthy that even during the subsequent Early Woodland and Middle Woodland subperiods, both hickory and black walnut were exploited extensively at this locale (see Chapter 9). It is evident that the environmental setting was instrumental in the choice of site location. In addition, the presence of hazelnut in the ethnobotanical record may reflect the alteration of the environment by site occupants from a closed forest to more open timber, or even the formation of an ecotone bordering a habitation clearing (either intentionally or by overuse) (Schroeder 2007:230).

There was a moderate seed density (2.6 seeds/10 liters) associated with the Riverton component at Knob Creek, indicating that starchy seeds and fleshy fruits (mostly grape) figured prominently in the diet (Schroeder 2007). Chenopodium was the most ubiquitous seed. Simon (2009:100) reports that chenopod was by far the most widely distributed of the EAC seeds during the Late Archaic, especially along major rivers, but they are usually found in only small numbers, and this is the case at Knob Creek.

The Riverton mortuary traditions in the Falls region appear to reflect a significant shift from preceding Late Archaic occupations (see Chapter 5). Though burials have not been documented at Knob Creek, the presence of trophy legs, scalping, intentionally crushed crania, and the removal of elements from individuals have been noted at RiverPark (Simpson and Mocas 2017). Many of the interments exhibited cuts along the shafts of long bones, which was not documented within earlier Archaic cemeteries at RiverPark (Simpson and Mocas 2017). In some instances, these cutting methods appear to be for the removal of elements from the interred individual, but in others it appears to be a part of the overall burial preparation and not indicative of violence. None of these practices were part of the earlier mortuary programs in the Falls region. Whether these new mortuary practices represent increased violence between groups or changes in the cultural norms, they indicate a significant cultural shift in the treatment of the dead.

BUCK CREEK (TERMINAL ARCHAIC)

Interest in the Terminal Archaic in the Midwest was advanced by Seeman's (1975) description of Buck Creek Barbed points that have been recovered from sites in the Falls region (Figure 8.1) and his recognition of their similarity to hafted bifaces recovered from sites in the American Bottom (Phillips and Brown 1983) and in the lower Illinois River valley (Farnsworth and Asch 1986). During the Terminal Archaic in these areas, nut exploitation reaches a peak, settlements gravitate toward major river valleys, and gardening of weedy and oily plants increases (Butler 2009; McElrath et al. 2009; Wiant et al. 2009).

As with the Riverton phase, the largest Buck Creek component in the Falls region has been documented at the Knob Creek site as indicated by the recovery of 86 Buck Creek Barbed points (Figure 8.1), though only four features could be confidently attributed to this component. Features directly associated with Buck Creek points have yielded calibrated medians of 1346 and 1202 BCE (Table 6.1). Within the Falls region, the Buck Creek phase is also well-represented at the Shippingport site (Mocas et al. 2009). The

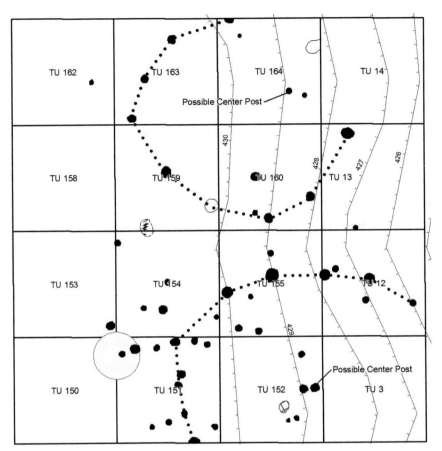

Figure 8.2. Structure A and Structure B, Terminal Archaic Zone 8, 15JF702. (adapted from Mocas et al. 2009).

three radiocarbon samples associated with the Buck Creek component at this site have yielded calibrated medians that range from 1282 to 1087 BCE. These dates correlate well with the Terminal Archaic dates from Newcomb (French et al. 2015; Simpson et al. 2013) and Site 12CL199, both of which have Buck Creek components (Table 6.1). The Hornung site also contains a substantial Buck Creek component (Janzen 2014), as do the Villier (Robinson and Smith 1979) and Rosenberger (Driskell 1979) sites.

At Shippingport, numerous postholes and two C-shaped structures with center posts (2.5 × 4.0 m and 2.5 × 5.0 m in size) have been documented (Figure 8.2). Based on their open sides, both are considered to be warm weather facilities. Perhaps by 1400 BCE, groups living in the Falls region were beginning to spend longer durations at certain localities, which may have necessitated the building of more durable structures (see Chapter 7).

Small numbers of Buck Creek points have been recovered from other flood-plain sites and upland settings throughout the Falls region, and they have a spatial distribution similar to earlier Merom points (Anslinger et al. 1994; Mocas 1974; O'Malley et al. 1980; Seeman 1975; Sieber and Ottesen 1986). At Knob Creek and Hornung, the presence of both Riverton and Buck Creek components reflects sequential use of the same landform.

The Terminal Archaic faunal remains from Shippingport (Ross-Stallings 2009) were dominated by freshwater drumfish, catfish, and unidentifiable fish remains, which as a group accounts for more than fifty percent of the faunal remains. Fish remains are so plentiful on the Buck Creek living floor that this area has been interpreted as representing a specialized resource procurement locale—a fishing camp where the fish were harvested, processed by removing the inedible portions, then smoked, and subsequently transported to a habitation site (Ross-Stallings 2009). In comparison, at Knob Creek, while fish remains (freshwater drum, catfish) are present, the faunal assemblage is dominated by white-tailed deer, with raccoon, river otter, and softshell turtle also present (Styles and Brand 2008). The faunal remains from Knob Creek, thus, reflect a broader animal exploitation pattern than those documented at Shippingport.

Plant remains recovered from Terminal Archaic sites in the Falls region reflect a continued reliance on nuts, supplemented by starchy and oily seeds (Rossen 2009; Schroeder 2007). The frequency of nutshell (1.8/liter) in Terminal Archaic flotation samples, however, at Shippingport (Rossen 2009) is much lower than what has been documented for the Riverton and Buck Creek components at Knob Creek (23/liter) (Schroeder 2007), which supports a different function for the site.

During the Buck Creek phase there is a marked contrast in the exploitation of lithic raw materials relative to the earlier Riverton phase. In particular, there is a much greater use of high-quality Wyandotte and St. Louis cherts for the manufacture of hafted bifaces. For instance, at Shippingport, Wyandotte chert was used to make 62.0 percent of the Terminal Archaic Barbed Cluster points, and relatively high-quality St. Louis chert was used for 31.0 percent. A similar preference for high-quality chert has been documented at the Knob Creek (Stafford et al. 2008:Table 13.15), Villier (Robinson and Smith 1979), and Rosenberger (Driskell 1979) sites. This shift in raw material preferences indicates that the technological cost/benefit factor and personal preference made acquisition of these materials during logistical forays a worthwhile endeavor. This preference for high-quality chert continued and intensified during the subsequent Woodland period (see Chapter 9).

During the Terminal Archaic, there also was a focus on the use of Wyandotte chert for the manufacture and export of Turkey-tail cache blades. In the late 1980s, Justice and Smith (1988) surveyed the western and central portions of Harrison County to locate and characterize important special purpose Wyandotte chert quarries and workshops. At that time they noted the presence of sizable numbers of distinctive bifacial retouch flakes from the manufacture of Turkey-tails. Terminal Archaic components have been found at five sites, and possible components have been found at three other sites.

It has been noted (Wiant et al. 2009:275) that in the lower Illinois valley some red ocher burials display episodes of "conspicuous consumption," in which as many as two hundred cache blades, including Turkey-tails made from Wyandotte chert, are arrayed in graves. The diversity of the implements in some caches, including items imported to a site specifically to be placed in burials, suggests that they may originate in several regions—and that the Falls of the Ohio area is one likely source. Although it is increasingly recognized that not all ceremonial bifaces made of blue-gray chert are made of Wyandotte chert (Morrow et al. 1992; Schenian 1987; Tankersley 1985), a significant portion appears to originate in the Falls region (Didier 1967; Justice 1987; Ritzenthaler and Quimby 1962). The value of Turkey-tails as ceremonial or ritual objects is substantiated by the frequent burning or breaking of the cache blades (Mocas 1977; Wiant et al. 2009:275)—perhaps as a means to emphasize the finality of the ritual; as a method of transition to use in the afterlife; as a means of magnifying the value by limiting the supply; or as a method of maintaining the need for additional ritual objects within a cycle. The acquisition and distribution of Turkey-tails appear to have originated in the Falls region and constitute an excellent example of the spread of ritual participation throughout much of the eastern United States. Unfortunately, little is known about Buck Creek phase mortuary patterns in the Falls region.

Conclusions

The Riverton and Buck Creek settlement systems in the Falls region focused on the floodplains and terraces of the Ohio River and its main tributaries, with upland, wetland, rockshelter, and sinkhole contexts also utilized. Observation of the sequential occupation of the landform of the Knob Creek site suggests that the location and the reuse of preferred sites were strongly influenced by combinations of environmental factors and that groups may have altered the environment to maintain or improve these features. The

Riverton subsistence system reflected an intensification of the exploitation of nut resources, with both preferential and opportunistic gathering in the floodplain and uplands. There also was an increased reliance on starchy seed plants of the Eastern Agricultural Complex (EAC). From the Buck Creek phase, there is evidence of temporary structures and specialized exploitation of fish. Plant use reflects a continuation of trends initiated during the Riverton phase.

The late Late Archaic of the Falls region displays attributes that securely link it to Riverton sites elsewhere, and the components show temporal and technological separation from other cultures sufficient to suggest that the local manifestation of Riverton is a distinct entity. There is a prominent shift in the mortuary behavior during the late Late Archaic, and whether it represents increased violence between groups or changes in the cultural norms surrounding the preparation of the dead, a significant cultural shift in the treatment of the dead is evident.

The Riverton phase in the Falls region is marked by the manufacture of Merom points, which are markedly smaller than earlier Late Archaic Stemmed varieties and later Buck Creek tools. There were abrupt and perceptible shifts in the technology and raw material preferences for the production of chipped stone tools at the beginning of and after the Riverton phase. Though Riverton groups living in the Falls region had access to a wide variety of chert raw materials, like their Late Archaic predecessors, they tended to focus on river gravels and nearby outcrops for raw materials. During the Buck Creek phase, high-quality Wyandotte and St. Louis became the preferred raw material for tool production, and in particular for the manufacturing of Turkey-tail points and preforms. The marked differences among the lithic assemblages of earlier Late Archaic, Riverton, and Buck Creek could be indicative of movement of ideas or populations into the region, though the latter is not supported by the archaeological record.

A prominent example of ritual participation and its spread is reflected in the manufacture and export of Turkey-tail cache blades. The rarity of tools and other objects manufactured from nonlocal materials in the Falls region supports the likelihood that Turkey-tail cache blades were exported more as ceremonial contributions than as reciprocal trade items (although perishable goods may have been what was received). It is possible that Turkey-tail points may have been used to demarcate "sacred areas" (Schenian 1987). The Turkey-tails manufactured in the Falls region could represent shared symbols for the establishment of communal ties, for maintenance of social continuity, or for reduction of social tensions and hostilities.

During the late Late Archaic and Terminal Archaic in the Falls region there is general continuity with the Ohio valley and with much of the Midwest. The adoption of Merom points is suggestive of interaction beyond the lower Ohio valley, and Buck Creek Barbed hafted bifaces show a marked affinity to the Wade and Delhi types of the Midsouth and Mississippi valley. The late Late Archaic and Terminal Archaic sites do not presage the cultural and technological boundaries seen at the beginning of the Early Woodland. It is apparent that the Riverton and Buck Creek phases had dynamic characteristics, rather than being linear extensions of earlier Late Archaic groups who lived in the Falls region.

9

The Woodland Period of the Falls Region

STEPHEN T. MOCAS

What is known about the Woodland period (1000 BCE–1000 CE) in the Falls region is primarily derived from several large-scale excavation projects (e.g., Caesars Archaeological Project (CAP); Clark Maritime Centre Archaeological Project (CMCAP); and RiverPark Place Archaeological Project) undertaken in the Ohio River floodplain not far from the Falls of the Ohio River. These investigations documented multi-component sites or clusters of several smaller sites that were positioned on the same or on comparable nearby landforms. While vertically stratified sites are relatively rare in the Falls region, exposure of large horizontal areas has generated data concerning the spatial distribution of domestic activities and the temporally distinct repeated use of particular locales. The data derived from Woodland period research permits inferences to be drawn concerning diachronic adaptations to the environment of the Falls region, changes in the exploitation of natural resources, and the characterization of local settlement patterns, subsistence practices, and mortuary patterns.

Throughout much of the Woodland period the Falls region was a border area, with ceramics in particular reflecting greater interaction with groups living in the middle Ohio valley. The degree to which the border was closed or permeable varied through time, but as a result of interactions with their neighbors, the Falls region had a local social identity that incorporated and often reinterpreted trends of other regions. Early and Middle Woodland settlement and subsistence patterns in the Falls region reflect a focus on floodplain localities, with an increase in house structure size and the presence of large storage pits. Subsistence practices reflect a steady increase in the reliance on starchy and oily seeds, and a decline in the consumption of nuts. At multi-seasonal camps, groups often focused on the processing of a particular plant during each visit. The repeated visits to these localities resulted in the opening and maintenance of garden plots. By the early Late

Woodland, smaller settlements were associated with floodplain and interior upland ridgetops, but by the end of the Woodland period, there was a renewed emphasis on floodplain localities, and by the end of the Terminal Late Woodland there was intensive exploitation of maize. Early and Middle Woodland faunal remains are poorly represented, but Late Woodland faunal remains reflect the consumption of a variety of animals and the appearance of specialized fishing camps.

The scarcity of data concerning mortuary patterns, burial mounds, and earthwork construction restricts comparison of ritual endeavors. However, the mining and export of high-quality Wyandotte chert resources during the Early and Middle Woodland subperiods represent extra-regional interaction and perhaps participation in broader regional rituals.

This chapter examines how Woodland hunter-gatherer-gardener settlement and subsistence systems interacted with and impacted the environment and the natural resources of the Falls region from the introduction of pottery to the establishment of village-based farming societies in the Falls region.

EARLY WOODLAND (1000–200 BCE)

Defining the beginning of the Early Woodland in the Falls region and elsewhere is difficult (Brown 1986). Gibbon (1986:89; see also Applegate 2008) wrote that the Early Woodland can be interpreted in a variety of ways: as the incidental addition of ceramics and a few lithic tools to an essentially stable Archaic lifeway; as a manifestation of Archaic florescence; as a technological stage marked by the ability to make pottery; or as the emergence of a new lifeway based on marked shifts in settlement/subsistence practices and monumental architecture.

For the purpose of this chapter, the beginning of the Early Woodland is placed at 1000 BCE (Applegate 2008). In the Falls region, the Archaic to Woodland transition (1600–700 BCE) does not appear to have been associated with a dramatic change in settlement and subsistence patterns and material culture. Zorn Avenue Village (15Jf250) (Mocas 1988); 12Cl109 (Sieber and Ottesen 1986; Mocas 1988); Knob Creek (12Hr484) (Mocas 2006), Townsend (12Hr481) (Mocas 2008), Shippingport (15Jf702) (Mocas et al. 2009); RiverPark Place sites 15Jf597 and 15Jf598 (Simpson and Mocas 2017); Hornung (15Jf60), and Riverwood Rockshelter (15Bu265) (Hill et al. 2017) (Figure 1.6) are some of the most informative Early Woodland sites in the Falls region. Radiocarbon dates obtained from ceramic-bearing pit features at these sites have calibrated medians that range from 660 to 252 BCE (Table

Table 9.1. Woodland radiocarbon dates (int13.14c; ib 7.0.4)

Temporal Period/ Site	rcybp	2 Sigma Cal BCE/CE	Median Cal BCE/CE	Reference
EARLY WOODLAND				
KNOB CREEK (12HR484)				
ISGS-4900	2550±70	822–430 BCE	660 BCE	Stafford & Mocas 2008
ISGS-4905	2400±70	766–383 BCE	525 BCE	
Beta-113984	2320±80	751–192 BCE	399 BCE	
ISGS-4984	2280±70	540–120 BCE	317 BCE	
ISGS-4971	2190±70	393–57 BCE	252 BCE	
SHIPPINGPORT (15JF702)				
Beta-205667	2470±60	771–413 BCE	609 BCE	Mocas et al. 2009
Beta-215903	2440±60	746–410 BCE	572 BCE	
RIVERWOOD (15BU265)				
M-2463	2450±140	887–203 BCE	576 BCE	Hill et al. 2017
TOWNSEND (12HR482)				
ISGS- 5189	2270±70	515–117 BCE	304 BCE	Mocas 2008
CLARK MARITIME 12CL109				
DIC-2616	2230±60	402–120 BCE	282 BCE	Sieber and Ottesen 1986
DIC-2619	2220±60	400–115 BCE	278 BCE	
EARLY MIDDLE WOODLAND				
RIVERPARK 15JF598				
D-AMS 001646	2190±31	361–177 BCE	287 BCE	Simpson and Mocas 2017
D-AMS 002084	2037±26	157 BCE-46 CE	40 BCE	
D-AMS 001648	2009±26	90 BCE-60 CE	9 BCE	
KNOB CREEK (12HR484)				
ISGS-4972	2100±70	358 BCE-49 CE	131 BCE	Stafford & Mocas 2008
ISGS-4903	2080±70	355 BCE-66 CE	107 BCE	
ISGS-4901	2070±70	354 BCE-73 CE	95 BCE	
ISGS-4904	2000±70	199 BCE-137 CE	10 BCE	

Temporal Period/ Site	rcybp	2 Sigma Cal BCE/CE	Median Cal BCE/CE	Reference
LATE MIDDLE WOODLAND				
CUSTER (15JF732)				
D-AMS 022103	1667±42	252–532 CE	376 CE	Mocas 2014a
Beta-240940	1510±40	428–636 CE	553 CE	
EARLY LATE WOODLAND				
<tbh>Shelby Lake (15SH17)				
<tb>(Beta-73163)	1480±60	428–655 CE	573 CE	Hocken-smith et al. 1998
(Beta-73162)	1430±60	431–757 CE	612 CE	
<tbh>Old Bear (15SH18)				
<tb>UGa-3706	1440±100	389–775 CE	594 CE	Brooks 1985
<tbh>SARA (15JF187)				
<tb>Beta-12720	1400±70	434–771 CE	632 CE	Mocas 1995
TERMINAL LATE WOODLAND				
<tbh>Shippingport (15JF702)				
<tb>Beta-250741	1180±40	721–969 CE	840 CE	Mocas et al. 2009
<tbh>M. Kraft (12CL935)				
<tb>D-AMS 001469	907±22	1039–1186 CE	1098 CE	Simpson et al. 2013
D-AMS 001466	913±22	1034–1181 CE	1095 CE	

Note: Calibrations performed with Calib 7.10 program using intcal13.14c.

9.1) (Hill et al. 2017; Mocas 2006; Mocas et al. 2009; Sieber and Ottesen 1986; Simpson and Mocas 2017).

Material Culture

Grit-tempered, cordmarked ceramics are present in the Falls region by at least 800 BCE, and are often associated with Kramer, Adena Stemmed, and hybrid forms of Adena/Turkey-tail points. The earliest pottery to be found west and north of the Falls region has been classified as Marion Thick (Clay 2002; Morgan 1992; Munson and Munson 2004). Comparable ceramics with a similar range of thickness, tempering materials of similar size and

Figure 9.1. Adena/Turkey-tail projectile point (*left*) and early Early Woodland ceramic vessel rim (Knob Creek site) (*right*).

density, and exterior and interior cordmarking have been recovered from sites in Falls region (Mocas 2006; Mocas et al. 2009).

Although some of the earliest ceramics in the Falls region resemble Marion Thick, some vessels differ from this trend. These vessels are neither thick nor as coarsely tempered as most Marion Thick sherds. Some of the ceramics from Knob Creek and Shippingport are well-made vessels with around ten-millimeter-thick walls with slightly constricted necks/rims, with closely spaced, vertical cordmarking on the exterior and horizontally oriented cordmarking on the interior of the rim (Figure 9.1). These sherds, which are primarily tempered with quartz-sand or chert, have cordmarking similar to Marion Thick vessels and slight shoulders like those of Marion vessels, although the shoulder is higher on the vessel (Mocas 2006; Mocas et al. 2009). Comparable thick and thinner ceramics have been recovered from Early Woodland sites in other regions (Conrad et al. 1986:195; Harn 1986; Morgan 1992; Morgan et al. 1986; Munson and Munson 2004). Thus, the earliest ceramics in the Falls region may be part of a widespread trend associated with the introduction of pottery to the Midwest.

By about 400 BCE, vessels tend to get thinner. These vessels generally have cordmarked exterior surfaces and are tempered with grit or chert and have flat bases, semi-globular bodies, and vertical or slightly constricted rims (Mocas 2006; Mocas et al. 2009; Sieber and Ottesen 1986; Simpson and Mocas 2017). In general, the cordmarking techniques and vessel forms bear closer resemblances to assemblages from middle Ohio valley sites, such as Peter Village (Clay 2002; Cramer 1989; Duerksen et al. 1992; Webb and Snow 1945), than to pottery recovered from sites in the lower Ohio valley, where Baumer/Crab Orchard ceramics dominate site assemblages (Applegate 2008). This suggests greater interaction with groups living in central and northern Kentucky. These vessels are associated primarily with Adena Stemmed projectile points.

In the latter portion of the Early Woodland, residents of the Falls region appear to have developed their own distinct ceramic type—Zorn Punctate (Figure 9.2), which incorporates decorative elements similar to those of Alexander Pinched pottery from the Tennessee and Mississippi River valleys (Mocas 1988) and Florence phase pottery of the American Bottom (Emerson 1983).

Attributes of atlatl weights and gorgets (expanded center, reel, quadraconcave, and keeled) (Dragoo 1963: 182–83, 215, Figure 10; Seeman 1975:55; Webb and Elliott 1942:437, Figure 29F; Webb and Snow 1974:84–85;) are comparable to those at sites in eastern Kentucky and West Virginia, and, as with the thicker ceramics, are suggestive of greater interaction with groups living upriver.

Analysis of the lithic assemblage from the Knob Creek site provides some insights into economic developments. The presence of numerous chert and groundstone adzes and celts indicates an increase in woodworking. Microwear analysis (Pope 2005) of the adzes suggests use for cleaving burned wood, possibly to make dugout canoes for navigation along the Ohio River. The paucity of pitted stones, metates, and pestles correlates with a decreased emphasis on nuts.

Throughout the Early Woodland there is a pronounced preference for high-quality Wyandotte and St. Louis cherts for local and nonlocal use. Local use is reflected by two concentrations of 10,000–30,000 Wyandotte and St. Louis chert flakes and the Hathaway Cache (Mocas 2006, 2014b). The flake concentrations reflect the production of tools, while the 20 preforms that compose the cache represent a logistical foray to the source of these cherts.

Extra-regional exchange of these high-quality cherts is manifested in the recovery of functional and ceremonial items manufactured from Wyandotte and St. Louis cherts at sites throughout the Eastern Woodlands. The widespread use of these chert types is reflected in the recovery of extremely large caches of bifaces/blanks (Justice and Smith 1988).

Settlement Patterns

While the Falls region has not yielded definitive evidence of large Early Woodland base camps, in the sense of a particular locale that was inhabited for all or most of the year, some locales appear to have been occupied on a multi-seasonal basis and to have been repeatedly visited over many years. For instance, at the Knob Creek site, Early Woodland deposits extend over four hundred meters along an Ohio River floodplain ridge (Mocas 2006). The main habitation area contained domestic structures, communal hearths, intensive cooking areas, flint knapping locations, and botanical and faunal processing areas.

The presence of these features is suggestive of intensive use of floodplain locales for short periods of time. The Terminal Archaic C-shaped structures present at Shippingport (Mocas et al. 2009) and the Early Woodland windbreak at Townsend (Mocas 2008) are likely warm-weather structures. On the other hand, the arrangement of postholes at the Knob Creek site (Mocas 2006) is suggestive of fully enclosed circular enclosures. Structures may also be present at Clark Maritime sites where Sieber and Ottesen (1986) have documented 100 postholes, but have not reported whether they formed a particular structure.

Although most of the seasonally occupied sites are associated with floodplain or terrace localities, some are located in the interior wetlands (e.g., Wallis Farm site [15Jf921]). Use of rockshelters along the periphery of the interior wetlands and in the uplands above tributary streams also has been documented. Some of the interior sites likely represent hunting camps, while others may be related to nut acquisition and processing. Upland sites located near Wyandotte chert outcrops (Justice and Smith 1988) reflect specialized Early Woodland lithic resource acquisition and manufacture of large quantities of bifacial implements for local use and exchange.

Subsistence

As was the case for Archaic groups, the environment of the Falls region provided abundant plant and animal resources for Woodland hunter-gatherers—plentiful game, massive quantities of nuts, a wide variety of botanical resources, and ready access to water and riparian resources. Relative to Archaic groups, the Early Woodland plant diet was more diverse. This is reflected by a greater emphasis on a mixture of spring and fall ripening seed species and a reduced reliance on fruits and nuts. For instance, at the Knob Creek site, the frequency of nut decreases from 230.5 to 34.2 per 10 liters of soil, while fleshy fruits decline tenfold (Schroeder 2007:216).

As elsewhere in the Ohio valley, the Early Woodland is marked by an increase in the consumption of starchy seeds, with maygrass, chenopodium, and erect knotweed being the primary plants consumed. Though more than three times as many maygrass (55.0 percent) seeds have been recovered relative to chenopodium (18.0 percent) seeds at the Knob Creek site, the latter have been recovered from more than half of the features (Schroeder 2007:239). In comparison, maygrass has been recovered from 43.0 percent of the features. The greater quantity of maygrass relative to other plants is somewhat deceptive, insofar as most were recovered from just two features.

In comparison to Knob Creek, where marshelder accounts for only two percent of the seed sample, at Site 12Cl109, it accounts for 88.0 percent of the seeds. The marshelder seeds from both sites may have been gathered from nearby mudflats and floodplains, since they do not appear to be of the domesticated variety (Schroeder 2007).

The presence of concentrations of maygrass at Knob Creek and marshelder at 12Cl109 may represent a focused or seasonal exploitation of a particular plant during one or more Early Woodland encampments. In addition, individual features with large quantities of nut remains reflect intensive seasonal mast exploitation.

The high ubiquity of elm/hackberry and black walnut/butternut wood among the features at Knob Creek points to the selection of fuel primarily from bottomland forest rather than from the valley slope. In addition, while hickory nuts were likely gathered from the slope, black walnut was a bottomland or ravine resource, and hazelnut came from open forests, forest margins, or grassland resource zones (Schroeder 2007:238, 242).

Due to extremely poor preservation, it is not possible to characterize Early Woodland faunal exploitation patterns in the Falls region.

Mortuary Patterns

Little is known about Early Woodland burial patterns in the Falls region because only one burial has been well documented. The Early Woodland burial encountered at RiverPark Place (15Jf598) suggests that there may have been a continuation of the interpersonal violence documented in mortuary patterns at the end of the Late Archaic (Simpson and Mocas 2017; see Chapter 7). This adult male was interred at the periphery of a short-term habitation area. He was buried in a seated position and showed perimortem trauma on his skull, and a projectile point fragment was found in or near the thoracic region. Large mammal bones, including a portion of a cougar mandible, were found in the grave and may have served as mortuary items.

Discussion

During the Early Woodland the inhabitants of the Falls region continued to maintain a hunter-gatherer economy with an increasing emphasis on horticulture. While occupation of sites did not entail year-round habitation or aggregation, the presence of structures suggests that people were staying

Figure 9.2. Zorn Punctate ceramics (Zorn Avenue Village site).

at some localities for longer periods of time relative to the Late Archaic. These changes in settlement patterns most likely were associated with an increased reliance on native cultigens. Still, horticulture remained a minor aspect of the economy, and the types of plants grown and consumed varied according to seasonal availability. Longer and more intensive occupations, coupled with a greater reliance on native cultigens, would have resulted in the creation and maintenance of more open areas and forest edges.

At this time the Falls region continued to be a border area, but relative to earlier Archaic groups, there were stronger affinities with groups living upstream and to the north than with those living downstream and to the south. These affinities are best expressed by ceramics, with vessels from the middle to late portion of the Early Woodland having forms and surface treatments similar to those from east-central and northern Kentucky, in addition to a virtual absence of Crab Orchard-like pottery in the Falls region. On the other hand, the distinctive decorative treatments exhibited by Zorn Punctate reflect brief interaction with groups living in the Midsouth and Mississippi valley. Interaction with groups outside of the Falls region is not only reflected in participation in general regional trends in ceramic production, but also in the quarrying of Wyandotte chert for export.

MIDDLE WOODLAND (200 BCE TO 400 CE)

In central and northern Kentucky the beginning of the Middle Woodland is marked by the construction of Adena earthen enclosures and the interment of the dead in mounds. To the north of the Ohio River, about two hundred years later, it is marked by subsequent Hopewell mound ceremonialism, and the construction of large geometric earthen enclosures (Applegate 2008). Though the residents of the Falls region appear to have participated in mound and earthwork construction to only a limited extent, they do appear to have participated in general trends in material culture and settlement and subsistence patterns. For the purposes of this section, the Middle Woodland is subdivided into the early Middle Woodland (200 BCE to 100 CE) and the late Middle Woodland (100 to 400 CE).

Early Middle Woodland (200 BCE to 100 CE)

The best data on the early Middle Woodland occupation of the Falls region is derived from the extensive excavations undertaken at the Knob Creek site (Mocas 2006); large scale investigations at Site 12Cl103 (Sieber and Ottesen 1986); examination of small components at Sites 15Jf596–98 at RiverPark Place (Simpson and Mocas 2017); surface collections and limited excavation at Zorn Avenue Village (Mocas 1988) and Hunting Creek (Mocas 1992); and a survey of quarry and workshop sites in Harrison County, Indiana (Justice and Smith 1988; Seeman 1975). Radiocarbon dates obtained from ceramic-bearing pit features at these sites have calibrated medians that range from 287 BCE to 107 CE (Table 9.1).

Material Culture

Early Middle Woodland pottery is typified by Falls Plain (Figure 9.3), a regional variant of Adena Plain (Mocas 2006; O'Malley 1983). As with Adena Plain, limestone is the dominant temper, and vessels are in the nearly cylindrical to semi-globular range and have partially flattened bases. Jar rims are straight to concave in form, of various heights, and everted to various degrees. Other distinctive attributes shared with Adena Plain include thinned necks, thickened and folded rims, and slightly convex bases. This close similarity suggests increased interaction/affinities with their neighbors living to the east.

Despite the seemingly abrupt shift from cordmarked to plain surfaced pottery in the Falls region, the ceramic assemblages from RiverPark and Knob Creek demonstrate that there were gradual changes in vessel morphology and tempering from the Early to Middle Woodland, and certain

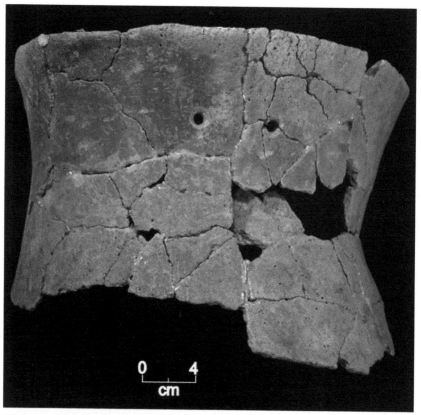

Figure 9.3. Falls Plain vessel (Knob Creek site).

vessels display transitional combinations of attributes that support the like-lihood of local population continuity. Once Falls Plain becomes the pre-ferred ceramic type in the region, it stays relatively unchanged for several hundred years. As was the case during the Early Woodland, Crab Orchard ceramics of the lower Ohio valley are virtually absent from the Falls region, again reinforcing the concept that the Falls region may have functioned as a border locale for societies upriver and downriver (Mocas 1988, 2006; Mocas et al. 2009).

The recovery of a large number of Zorn Punctate ceramics at the Zorn Avenue Village site, some with bands or columns of triangular and crescent shaped punctations, raises the possibility that important region-wide inte-grating rituals took place at this locale, and some of the ceramic motifs may have had symbolic local significance.

At about the same time Falls Plain pottery begins to appear, Affinis Sny-ders points become common in the archaeological record of the Falls region.

Although there is evidence of the presence of Adena Stemmed points at the earliest documented appearance of Falls Plain, eventually the type appears to have been supplanted by Snyders points (Mocas 2006). The adoption of a new projectile point style, however, does not appear to have greatly impacted the Knob Creek lithic industry, which reflects continuity from the Early Woodland in the numbers and types of tools, the amount of retouch and reworking, the lack of bladelets, the occurrence of comparable special purpose tools (Mocas 2006:175), and an overwhelming preference for Wyandotte and St. Louis cherts.

Blade cores and bladelets have not been recovered from Knob Creek, but bladelets are illustrated in the CMCAP report (Sieber and Ottesen 1986: Figure 6.3.4). Groundstone manos and metates are slightly more common in the Knob Creek lithic industry than during the Early Woodland, but neither component has showed evidence of intensive processing of nuts and seeds.

Participation in regional trends is indicated by the presence of personal items with morphologies comparable to those found at Adena sites in central and eastern Kentucky and portions of Indiana, Ohio, and West Virginia. These objects, however, were manufactured locally. For example, a conical tubular pipe (Figure 9.4a) found within Structure X at the Knob Creek site and a proximal pipe fragment from the Hunting Creek site have forms similar to those of tubular pipes recovered from the Fisher Mound (Webb and Haag 1947:62–65; 90–91); an elbow pipe (Figure 9.4b) from within the same structure at the Knob Creek site resembles a pipe associated with the larger of the Wright Mounds (Webb 1940:58–59; Figure 34S). Other examples include several locally manufactured gorgets (Mocas 2006:Figure 7.55; James Matthews Collection; Simpson and Mocas 2017) that are similar to those recovered from Adena mounds (Dragoo 1963; Funkhouser and Webb 1935; McCord and Cochran 2000; Swartz 1970; Webb and Elliott 1942:437; Webb 1940, 1941) (Figure 9.5). Unlike at most Adena sites, where these objects have been recovered from mortuary contexts, within the Falls region they tend to be associated with domestic contexts, but it is possible that they enter the archeological record as part of important community-based rituals.

Together, the ceramics and personal items recovered from early Middle Woodland habitation sites in the Falls region provide abundant evidence of the directions of influence and interaction with groups from other areas. As with the Early Woodland, stronger ties with societies to the east are evidenced by vessel forms and surface treatments that bear closer resemblances to assemblages from the middle Ohio River valley than to the lower Ohio River valley. On the other hand, aspects of the chipped stone industry, such as the presence of Affinis Snyders points, which are predominant in the

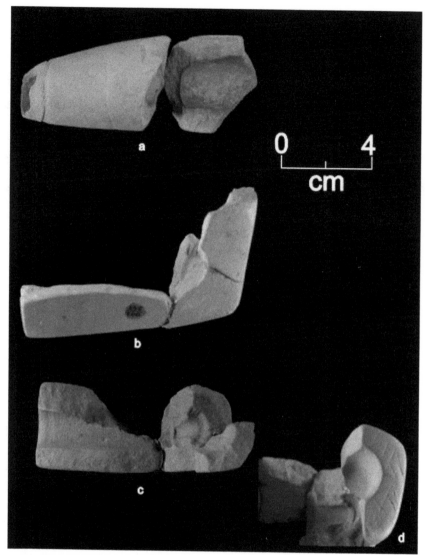

Figure 9.4. Pipes from Knob Creek site.

Havana area of the lower Ohio valley, and bladelets from CMCAP manufactured with the Fulton blade technique, reflect interaction over a broader
area, including downriver, indicating some degree of border permeability.

As was the case for the Early Woodland, during the Middle Woodland,
Wyandotte chert was quarried for use in the Falls region and for functional
and ceremonial use at Hopewell sites in other regions. Extra-regional exchange of local high-quality Wyandotte chert peaked with the production

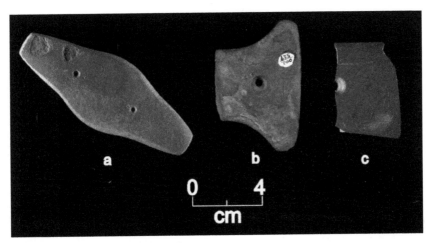

Figure 9.5. Gorgets from Knob Creek site.

of extremely large caches of Middle Woodland preforms that have been found along the Ohio River, as exemplified by Site 12Hr449, from which approximately one thousand two hundred cache blades have been taken by a collector (Justice and Smith 1988). It is also worth noting that 80.0 percent of the chert raw material at the Hopewellian Mann site, situated 200 km downstream from the Falls of the Ohio River, has been classified as Wyandotte (Kellar 1979:105).

The presence of nonlocal items, such as mica, lamellar blades, and Snyders points manufactured from Ohio Flint Ridge chert (Cantin and Stafford 2012), reflects interaction with more easterly groups. On the other hand, objects manufactured from Burlington chert from Illinois (Cantin and Stafford 2012) and the presence of a Havana/Hopewell zoned stamped sherd at the Newcomb site (Simpson et al. 2013) reflect limited interaction with groups living in the lower Ohio valley and perhaps in the Illinois valley (Cantin and Stafford 2012; Simpson et al. 2013). There appears to be a wider geographical area associated with the Hopewellian materials than with the materials related to domestic sites.

Settlement Patterns

The large Middle Woodland components at Site 12Cl103 and Knob Creek, in addition to smaller components at RiverPark, all made use of Ohio River floodplain bars. This reuse of previously occupied localities reflects continuity in settlement locations for seasonal and multi-seasonal habitation camps. At least one large settlement, the Zorn Avenue Village site, is associated with the bluffs overlooking the Ohio River.

Smaller early Middle Woodland camps are found in the floodplains of and on the ridges above the tributaries of the Ohio River; adjacent to minor streams in the uplands and lowlands; and occasionally adjacent to sinkholes or in rockshelters. Sizable quarry sites also have been documented in the region (Justice and Smith 1988).

At the Knob Creek site, a concentrated occupation area has more than one hundred pit features, some of which are extremely large storage pits (Figure 9.6 top). Located near these features are several circular tension-pole structures (Figure 9.6 bottom). These structures range in diameter from 6.4 to 7.3 m. The presence of these features, the recovery of abundant lithic and ceramic materials, and the manufacture of personal items reflect an amplification of sedentism that began in the Early Woodland.

Subsistence

Relative to the Early Woodland, the Middle Woodland is marked by an increased reliance on starchy and oily seeds (Crites 1986; Schroeder 2007; Simpson and Mocas 2017; see Chapter 10). For instance, at the Knob Creek site, Middle Woodland features yielded nearly twice the number of seeds per 10 liters of soil as those of the Early Woodland. Maygrass, chenopod, and erect knotweed have continued to be the most abundant and most ubiquitous seeds recovered. Despite the modest yield of carbonized seeds (20.3 per 10 liters of flotation soil), it is feasible that seed crops played a significant role in the economy, as suggested by the presence of a number of large bell-shaped storage pits (Schroeder 2007:243). Schroeder (2007:259) has noted that despite the lack of morphological evidence for grain domestication during the Early and Middle Woodland at Knob Creek, the greater frequencies suggest that the seed crops were being gardened to increase harvests. The botanical remains suggest that this site was occupied more extensively in the fall than in the spring (Schroeder 2007:253).

The presence of fleshy fruit seeds at Knob Creek shows that the harvesting of wild fruit continued to be a minor subsistence activity, while the amount of nuts consumed decreased slightly in comparison with the Early Woodland component at Knob Creek. The dominant nut species vary across the site, with a preponderance of hickory and acorn in the area of most intensive Middle Woodland occupation. Other locales show extensive exploitation of black walnut, possibly the result of the presence of one or more large trees within the site.

Relative to the Early Woodland component, a greater variety of wood species was associated with the Middle Woodland component. As with the Early Woodland, a high ubiquity of elm/hackberry, oak, and black walnut/

Figure 9.6. Knob Creek Middle Woodland component: *top*, large storage pit; *bottom*, structure X.

butternut wood among the features at Knob Creek points to the selection of fuel primarily from bottomland forest rather than from the valley slope. Minor wood types, such as cigartree and tulip tree, prefer low or rich woods, and American chestnut prefers drier, rocky habitat (Schroeder 2007: 245–46).

On different occasions, sites, such as Knob Creek, would have fulfilled a variety of roles within the local settlement and subsistence system, from a multi-seasonal camp, to a specialized resource extraction camp for the exploitation of various species of nuts and grains, to a processing locale for nuts and seeds, to a storage locus for grains. Within the Falls region, local Middle Woodland groups, while fundamentally remaining hunter-gatherers, maintained a focus on the exploitation of naturally occurring foodstuffs, while increasing their reliance on starchy and oily seeds. The distribution and volume of seeds and nuts vary sufficiently within and between sites to suggest that food items were processed and consumed in different quantities and proportions depending on the season.

Mortuary Patterns

The extent to which the Falls Middle Woodland population participated in mound ceremonialism and rituals is not known. Although the presence of burial mounds has been reported in the Falls region (O'Malley et al. 1980; Webb and Funkhouser 1932), few have been positively determined to date to the Woodland period. For instance, at least one conical mound and several smaller associated mounds have been identified on a bluff above the Ohio River floodplain in Harrison County, Indiana, and other examples have been reported by professional archaeologists in Clark County. To date, none have been investigated, and there is no information on early Middle Woodland mortuary patterns from domestic habitation sites.

Late Middle Woodland (100–400 CE)

The latter portion of the Middle Woodland is poorly documented in the Falls region and is known predominantly from the Custer site, a small habitation site located adjacent to the Falls of the Ohio (Mocas 2014a). Calibrated median dates of 376 CE and 553 CE suggest that the occupation of the site began in the late Middle Woodland and may have continued into the early Late Woodland. Though few late Middle Woodland sites have been excavated in the region, there is nothing in the archaeological record to suggest a hiatus in occupation of the Falls region at this time.

Late Middle Woodland ceramics in the Falls region are characterized by clay tempered, ellipsoidal jars with vertical or slightly inverted rims. Surface treatment consists of cordmarking and smoothed-over cordmarking. These attributes display a marked dissimilarity to earlier Falls Plain ceramics but presage limestone-tempered early Late Woodland ceramics. In general, the assemblage reflects participation in regional late Middle Woodland ceramic trends in vessel form, surface treatment, and the near absence of decoration seen throughout the middle Ohio valley. The recovery of a check-stamped sherd and the presence of mica at Custer reflect general middle Ohio River valley trends and some level of interaction with groups living in the Midsouth.

The chipped stone tool assemblage is dominated by Lowe Cluster and Copena Cluster bifaces, and Wyandotte chert continued to be the preferred raw material for tool production. Of note is the presence of bladelets that are similar to Ohio bladelets (Bader, personal communication 2007) but are manufactured from local cherts. Little is known about late Middle Woodland settlement, subsistence, and mortuary patterns in the Falls region.

Discussion

As was the case for the Early Woodland, throughout the Middle Woodland, the Falls region continued to be a border area, such that those living in the Falls region had stronger affinities with upriver groups than with those of the lower Ohio valley. Material culture links with groups to the east are reflected in the close similarity of Falls Plain and Adena Plain ceramics and by gorget and pipe forms. It is noteworthy that the predominant early Middle Woodland hafted biface is the Affinis Snyders point, which has strong ties to downriver societies and has a distribution that extends east of the Falls region, and that Fulton-style blades have been reported from Clark Maritime—an indication of a wider geographical range to some artifact types. The continued preference for high-quality Wyandotte and St. Louis cherts reflects continuity with the Early Woodland occupation of the region.

Archaeobotanical studies attest to the increased importance of starchy and oily seed plants to the local diet and the continued decline in the consumption of nuts. The environmental diversity of floodplain settings within the Falls region is well-suited to extended Woodland settlements, and the proximity of sites to relatively open floodplain areas and mudflats undoubtedly facilitated the development and expansion of horticulture. The presence of domestic structures that are more substantial than their earlier counterparts and are associated with large storage pits reflects intensive and sustained occupation of floodplain localities. Together, an increased reliance on starchy seeds and more intensively occupied settlements would have resulted in more floodplain areas being cleared and maintained.

The continued production of high-quality Wyandotte and St. Louis chert blanks for export and the recovery of mica and check-stamped pottery reflect participation in broader regional interactions. On the other hand, the limited evidence that local groups participated in mound or earthwork construction suggests that Middle Woodland groups in the Falls region may have chosen not to participate in Adena and Hopewell ceremonialism, or, if they did, they traveled to other regions to take part in these rituals, perhaps taking with them finished tools, preforms, and raw materials of Wyandotte, and possibly St. Louis, chert.

LATE WOODLAND (400–1000/1100 CE)

Combinations of material culture and subsistence-settlement lifeways of Late Woodland groups throughout the Ohio River valley exemplify the subperiod in a number of distinctive ways, and there is increasing recognition of developments in the form of population aggregation and intensified food production (Applegate 2008; Pollack and Henderson 2000). Although long distance trade may have declined, the movement of ideas, and perhaps populations, continued over a sizable geographic area, and groups adjusted to maintain stability and to facilitate their lifestyles. Pollack and Henderson (2000) note that the Late Woodland downriver from the Falls differs markedly from that upriver, and Redmond and McCullough (2000) substantiate further diversity within southern and central Indiana.

In the Falls region, the gradual transition from the Middle Woodland to the early Late Woodland (400–800 CE) is marked by a shift from clay-tempered to limestone-tempered, cordmarked pottery; the continued use of Copena and Lowe Flared Base points; and an increased reliance on native cultigens. The Terminal Late Woodland (800–1000/1100 CE) is marked by the introduction of the bow and arrow, a shift in ceramic attributes, and an intensification of the consumption of maize.

Early Late Woodland (400–800 CE)

Pollack and Henderson (2000) note that the transition from the late Middle Woodland to the early Late Woodland in Kentucky is in some instances barely perceptible, and this is the case in the Falls region. The early Late Woodland is primarily known from the SARA site (15Jf187) (Mocas 1995), Riverwood Rockshelter (Hill et al. 2017), Old Bear site (15Sh18) (Brooks 1985), and Shelby Lake site (15Sh17) (Hockensmith et al. 1998). Radiocarbon dates obtained from ceramic-bearing pit features at these sites have a two-sigma-calibrated range of 389–775 CE (Table 9.1).

Material Culture

In contrast to the predominantly clay-tempered pottery recovered from the Custer site, limestone was the most common raw material used to temper early Late Woodland jars. Water-rolled quartz-sand, finely crushed quartzitic rock, various kinds of grit, siltstone, and sandstone also were used. These vessels also exhibit a greater variety of rim forms and surface treatments, though the standard jar form is very similar. Most vessels are cordmarked, but plain and moderately burnished vessels also are present.

The most distinctive early Late Woodland ceramic attributes are castellated rims and angular shoulders that show a strong affinity with Newtown ceramics to the east (Hockensmith et al. 1998; Reidhead and Limp 1974). In addition to vessel forms seen during the late Middle Woodland, jars with short or tall, everted rims are present. Globular, thin-walled vessels that resemble Newtown vessels from the Haag site (Reidhead and Limp 1974:Figure 7) in southeastern Indiana may be indicative of changing cooking technology associated with an increased reliance on native cultigens (see Braun 1983). With the exception of occasional notched or cordmarked lips, decoration is extremely rare.

As with earlier Woodland groups, early Late Woodland knappers appear to have primarily utilized Wyandotte chert for the production of tools. A preference for high-quality raw material is seen even at interior sites situated at the eastern periphery of the Falls region some forty to fifty kilometers from Wyandotte chert outcrops. Lowe Cluster projectile points continue to be the predominant projectile point type. Bladelets found at these sites tend to be smaller than those recovered from Middle Woodland sites.

Settlement Patterns

Early Late Woodland settlements are associated with a variety of environmental settings, including floodplains, rockshelters, and interior ridgetops a considerable distance inland from the Ohio River. All appear to be short-term habitation sites, as exemplified by the presence of pit features and postholes at the SARA site.

Old Bear and Shelby Lake are good examples of upland fall-winter camps. The exclusive use of Wyandotte chert at these interior sites is suggestive of a settlement system that involved significant movement during a seasonal round that included acquisition of materials that outcrop forty to fifty kilometers to the west of the site.

Subsistence

Plant remains recovered from early Late Woodland sites are suggestive of exploitation of a variety of environmental zones. The recovery of black walnut, hickory, and acorn shells along with sunflower, sumac, and purslane at the SARA site is suggestive of late summer and fall (Mocas 1995). The seeds represent cultigens, domesticates, and wild plants.

Shelby Lake has been considered to be a late winter to early spring encampment or hunting camp, and there are very large amounts of hickory and small amounts of black walnut and three other nut species (Hockensmith et al. 1998). A small quantity of squash, one gourd fragment, and maygrass seeds are the only cultigens identified. A few possible chenopod seeds also have been recovered. It is evident that despite the practice of horticulture and the consistent use of seed crops, nuts were still exploited seasonally. The Old Bear site is considered to be a short-term encampment occupied between early fall and early spring by a small group, and four species of nutshell are present in the site's plant assemblage (Brooks 1985).

Unlike most Woodland sites in the Falls region, the Old Bear and Shelby Lake sites had good faunal preservation. At Old Bear and Shelby Lake, deer and bear were most common, with small amounts of turtle, raccoon, turkey, and other animals present (Hockensmith et al. 1998). Much of the bone was highly fragmented, and this has been attributed to intensive marrow extraction, which Brooks (1985) interprets as a possible sign of nutritional stress. The Old Bear faunal assemblage is suggestive of a fall-winter camp, while the Shelby Lake site appears to have been occupied from the late winter to early spring.

Plant and animal remains recovered from Late Woodland sites in the Falls region are suggestive of settlement/subsistence patterns that involved warm weather exploitation of floodplain locales and a shift to the interior during the cooler months.

Mortuary Practices

There is little available information on early Late Woodland mortuary practices in the Falls region. The partial remains of one human has been found in the two features at Old Bear (Brooks 1985).

Terminal Late Woodland (800–1000/1100 CE)

The Terminal Late Woodland subperiod is known from Site 12Hr15 (Mocas and Calton 2020), Newcomb (12Cl2) (Simpson et al. 2013), M. Kraft

(12Cl935) (Simpson et al. 2013), Shippingport (Mocas et al. 2009), and Muddy Fork/Hubbards Lane #3 (15Jf262) (Janzen 2008). The projectile points and ceramics from 12Hr15 and a calibrated median radiocarbon date from Shippingport of 840 CE suggest that both were occupied toward the beginning of the Terminal Late Woodland subperiod. The two radiocarbon dates obtained from the M. Kraft site (calibrated date range of 1034–1186 CE) place the occupation of this site as well as the Newcomb and the Muddy Fork site toward the end of the Terminal Late Woodland (Table 9.1) (Simpson et al. 2013), insofar as all three sites have comparable ceramic and lithic assemblages.

Material Culture

The lithic and ceramic assemblages from Site 12Hr15 (Mocas and Calton 2020) reflect the appearance of cultural materials that bear considerable similarities to those recovered from Intrusive Mound/Jack's Reef Horizon sites in southern Ohio and central/eastern Kentucky (Pollack and Henderson 2000; Redmond 2013; Seeman 1992; Seeman and Dancey 2000). In the Falls region, this pottery is tempered with crushed quartzitic rock and has imprecisely applied cord-wrapped paddle impressions on the exterior surface. Thickened rims bear the horizontal lines of cord-wrapped paddle edge impressions on the exterior and diagonally oriented paddle edge impressions on the lip crest. These materials probably predate the ceramics recovered from Newcomb and M. Kraft.

The Terminal Late Woodland assemblages from M. Kraft, Newcomb, and Muddy Fork have surface decorations that consist of pinching, incising, and punctation. The most common motif is one or more thin horizontal incised lines, in some instances intersected by converging lines that form a triangular design. Small, circular punctations in rows or columns occasionally are present, and fingernail impressions in intersecting rows and columns have been documented. Lip crests are decorated with cordmarks, cord-wrapped dowel impressions, notches, slashes, or fingernail impressions (Simpson et al. 2013). The most distinctive and most common temper variant is characterized by large numbers of ferric concretions in the paste (Janzen 2008; Simpson et al. 2013). Exterior surfaces exhibit cordmarking or smoothed cordmarking. Almost all two-ply cords are Z-twist.

These ceramics have some traits in common with the early Fort Ancient Beals Run series of central Kentucky (Henderson 1999; Pollack and Henderson 2000). The bar stamps, appliques, and grog temper that characterize Yankeetown ceramics of the lower Ohio valley are not found in the Falls region, although the presence of Wyandotte debitage and tools at Yankeetown sites (Redmond 1990; Smith and Mocas 1993:92) reflects some interaction with downriver groups.

Jack's Reef Cluster and Unnotched Pentagonal Cluster varieties (Justice 1987:215–20) typify the component at Site 12Hr15. Projectile points associated with other Terminal Late Woodland components are triangular in shape. The Terminal Late Woodland is marked by a change in chert preferences and procurement strategies. While throughout most of the Woodland period, Wyandotte and St. Louis cherts composed more than eighty percent of the chipped stone raw material, during the Terminal Late Woodland there was a sharp decline in the use of Wyandotte chert. It appears that it was no longer considered necessary to travel twenty to thirty kilometers to the Wyandotte deposits. St. Louis chert was of nearly the same quality and was available at a lesser distance, and although its use also declined, it was still exploited in moderation. Conversely, there was a significant increase in the use of Jeffersonville chert, available in river gravels, and Muldraugh chert from the nearby uplands.

Settlement Patterns

As with early Late Woodland settlements, Terminal Late Woodland sites tend to be small habitation sites. At this time there appears to be a lesser emphasis on upland areas, with an association of the best-known sites with floodplain contexts that were well-suited for horticulture and later for agriculture. Since only limited excavations have been conducted at these settlements, little is known about their internal organization.

Subsistence

Plant food remains from Terminal Late Woodland sites reflect a continuation of the earlier Late Woodland diet but with the addition of maize. The ethnobotanical sample from M. Kraft provides the earliest documented evidence of intensive consumption of maize in the Falls region and demonstrates that this occurred toward the end of the Terminal Late Woodland. The maize consists of small, low, crescent-shaped kernels consistent with a forerunner of the Midwestern Twelve variety that became dominant during Mississippian times (see Chapter 10). The maize consists almost exclusively of edible kernels, which are more closely associated with storage, food consumption, and discard, while the two waste product cupules represent earlier food processing (Rossen 2013). An increased reliance on maize toward the end of the Late Woodland is consistent with what has been documented elsewhere in the Ohio valley (Pollack and Henderson 2000:624–25, 632–33; Simon 2000:44–45; see Chapter 10).

The Shippingport site faunal collection consists primarily of deer and fish remains, with the latter accounting for more than fifty percent of the micro-fauna. The association of these remains with a large surface hearth suggests that areas in close proximity to the Falls of the Ohio River may have been used as warm weather, short-term fishing camps during the Terminal Late Woodland (Ross-Stallings 2009:311).

Discussion

As was the case for the Middle Woodland, early Late Woodland groups living in the Falls region maintained stronger ties with groups to the east than with those to the west, with the Falls region continuing to be a border area. Affinities with upstream Newtown groups are reflected in the material culture, in particular, ceramic attributes such as angular shoulders and castellation. The recovered plant remains have confirmed the ubiquity of native cultigens and the continued exploitation of nuts and wild plants on a seasonal basis. The faunal remains from the upland sites suggest that local groups may have experienced some nutritional stress during the winter months (Brooks 1985).

Early Late Woodland sites in the Falls region tend to be small, seasonally occupied sites associated with a variety of environments. Settlement and subsistence patterns involve warm weather exploitation of floodplain locales, perhaps to tend gardens, and a shift to the interior during the cooler months to hunt game. The presence of roasting pits, posts, and other features at these sites points to extended occupation, but none appear to have been occupied year-round. Terminal Late Woodland components also tend to be relatively small and are primarily associated with floodplain localities. With the addition of maize to local gardens, the seasonal movement of groups may have become more restricted as more time was needed to tend the crops.

The influx of Intrusive Mound/Jack's Reef Horizon ceramics and lithics may be of considerable significance. These materials are associated with the introduction of the bow and arrow, which may have precipitated a rapid economic shift, if not an actual movement of people into the area. While Terminal Late Woodland ceramics are suggestive of affinities with early Fort Ancient ceramics, the maize recovered from these sites suggests increased interaction with groups to the west. The maize recovered from sites in the Falls region is consistent with a forerunner of the Midwestern Twelve variety used by Mississippian groups and not the Eastern Eight variety preferred by Fort Ancient groups (see Chapter 10). Toward the end of the Late Woodland, affinities thus appear to have shifted toward the west (see Chapter 11).

Conclusions

Throughout the Woodland period the Falls region was a border area, but compared to the preceding Archaic period had greater affinities with groups living in the middle Ohio valley. These affinities are primarily reflected in ceramics with similarities to Fayette Thick, Adena Plain, Newtown Cordmarked, Intrusive Mound, and Beals Run ceramics being evident in the archaeological record. The sudden appearance of Zorn Punctate pottery, with its distinctive punctation, toward the end of the Early Woodland and continuing into the Middle Woodland, deviates from this pattern, insofar as the decorative treatments associated with this type are similar to Alexander Pinched ceramics from the Tennessee and Mississippi River valleys and Florence Phase pottery of the American Bottom. When the distinctive motifs associated with Zorn Punctate are considered with the Zorn Avenue site's association with a bluff overlooking the Ohio River, it is possible that this site may have fulfilled a region-wide integrative function within the Falls region during the early Middle Woodland.

The Early and Middle Woodland production of high-quality Wyandotte and St. Louis chert blanks for export and the recovery of small amounts of mica and check-stamped pottery from Woodland sites in the Falls region reflect participation in broader regional interactions. On the other hand, the limited evidence that local groups participated in mound or earthwork construction suggests that Middle Woodland groups in the Falls region may have chosen not to participate in those aspects of Adena and Hopewell ceremonialism, or, if they did, they traveled to other regions to take part in these rituals, perhaps taking with them finished tools, preforms, and raw materials of Wyandotte chert.

Archaeobotanical studies attest to the increased importance of starchy and oily seed plants, and to the decline in the consumption of nuts through most of the Woodland period. The environmental diversity of floodplain settings within the Falls region was well-suited to support extended Woodland settlements, and the proximity of many of these sites to relatively open floodplains and mudflats undoubtedly facilitated the development and expansion of horticulture in the Falls region. The presence of domestic structures and large storage pits reflects intensive and sustained occupation of these floodplain localities by the Middle Woodland subperiod. An increased reliance on starchy seeds and more intensive settlements would have resulted in more floodplain areas being cleared and maintained, resulting in groups staying at sites for longer periods of time, with some sites exhibiting multi-seasonal occupations.

While Terminal Late Woodland ceramics are suggestive of affinities with Intrusive Mound and early Fort Ancient Beals Run ceramics, the presence of the forerunner of the Midwestern Twelve variety of maize is suggestive of increased interaction with groups to the west. Toward the end of the Late Woodland it appears that affinities had begun to shift back toward the west (see Chapters 10 and 11).

10

Plant Use at the Falls of the Ohio

Ten Thousand Years of Regional Systems, a Sociocultural Boundary, and Interaction

JACK ROSSEN AND JOCELYN C. TURNER

Native people used the Falls region as both a central meeting place and a sociocultural boundary during its long history. This chapter summarizes and discusses more than thirty years of archaeobotanical research in the Falls region, and documents changes in local plant use systems through time. People living in and around the Falls region participated in broader regional patterns of plant use during the Archaic (when our archaeobotanical database begins, ca. 8000–1000 BCE) and Woodland (1000 BCE–1000 CE) periods. Dramatic shifts in plant use occurred ca. 1000 CE, when the developments of the more egalitarian Fort Ancient groups to the east and the more centralized Mississippian polities of the Falls region resulted in the formation of a sociocultural boundary situation (see Chapter 11). In terms of different corn-based agricultural systems, this frontier can now be discussed in terms of both boundary maintenance and permeability. By 1300 CE, with the abandonment of the Prather administrative center, this boundary situation became more fluid, and people and their plants and material culture intermingled.

There are two broad themes that unite this discussion, which focuses on a relatively small region but covers almost ten thousand years of time. The first is that the systematic water flotation collection of plant remains during archaeological investigations has allowed scholars to conduct fine-grained compilations of ancient plant use systems and to determine how they relate to cultural identity and change (Rossen 2008). Seemingly repetitive and intensive archaeobotanical studies throughout Kentucky and Indiana have brought depth and nuance, based on plant identifications, detailed plant morphologies, and densities per liter of floated soil of familiar plants like corn and nuts. Second, plant use systems may be used as markers of cultural identity on par with more traditional material culture, such as ceramics, as well as architecture and settlement patterns. For example, the distinctive plant use system of the Fort Ancient people from 1000 through 1700 CE should end notions that the Fort Ancient were merely an "archaeological construct" (Wagner 1987), an "Upper Mississippian," or a less-developed echo of neighboring polities (Henderson 1998, 2008). Instead, from a plant use perspective, they may be viewed as a cultural alternative to their Mississippian neighbors.

ARCHAIC PERIOD (CA. 8000–1000 BCE)

During Archaic times, people living in the Falls region participated as mobile hunter-gatherers in a broad regional plant use system as they gradually became more focused or "anchored" in resource territories. Nuts, particularly hickory (*Carya* sp.), but also black walnut (*Juglans nigra*), butternut (*Juglans cinerea*), hazelnut (*Corylus* sp.), acorn (*Quercus* sp.), American chestnut (*Castanea dentata*), pecan (*Carya illinoensis*), and beechnut (*Fagus grandifolia*), were the focal plant resource (see Chapters 2–7). Hickory was usually the principal nut exploited. The James Farnsley (12Hr520) site in Harrison County, Indiana, is unusual in presenting black walnut as more economically important than hickory during the Early Archaic (Schroeder 2007:369). Fleshy fruits, such as grape (*Vitis* sp.), persimmon (*Diospyros virginiana*), and sumac (*Rhus* sp.) also are staple Early Archaic plant foods (Schroeder 2007; Stafford and Cantin 2009b).

During the Middle and Late Archaic, hunter-gatherers continued their focus on nuts and added resources from the shrinking wetlands during the peak of the Hypsithermal Drying Trend (ca. 5500–3000 BCE), particularly edible pondweeds (*Potamogeton* sp.), hornedpondweeds (*Zannichellia* sp.), sedges (*Carex* sp., *Cyperus* sp.), bulrushes (*Scirpus* sp.), and spikerushes (*Eleocharis* sp.) (Collins and Driskell 1979; Janzen 1977a; Jefferies 1982, 1996b; Nance 1988; Neusius 1986; Rossen 2000, 2006) (Figure 10.1). Although these occur in low frequency in site assemblages, they were significant beyond their low archaeological visibility (Brown and Vierra 1983). Weedy dryland annuals, such as knotweeds and smartweeds (*Polygonum* sp.), marshelder (*Iva annua*), maygrass (*Phalaris caroliniana*), sunflower (*Helianthus* sp.), amaranth (*Amaranthus* sp.), and chenopod (*Chenopodium* sp.), appearing first as wild predecessors and later as cultivated versions of the Eastern

Figure 10.1. Edible wetland plants: *from left to right,* hornpondweeds, sedge, and spik-erush (mm scale).

Agricultural Complex (EAC) plants, are present in Middle and Late Archaic collections (Rossen 2000; Schroeder 2007; Stafford and Mocas 2009:490).

Two plants cultivated in the hunting-gathering lifeway by the Middle Archaic are gourd (*Lagenaria* sp.) and squash (*Cucurbita* sp.), used for containers, fish floats, and edible seeds (Hart et al. 2004; Hudson 2004). DNA evidence suggests that gourds, which have no wild American plant relatives, were introduced throughout North America from Africa by transoceanic drift, and that both squash and gourds were domesticated several times at different places in North America (Kistler et al. 2014). The unusually early cultivation of both squash and gourd may have been stimulated as early as 6000 BCE by food scarcity caused by the disappearance of the great megafauna (including mastodons and mammoths) who maintained disturbed habitat and distributed seeds (Kistler et al. 2015). In the Falls region, one squash rind fragment has been identified in an early Middle Archaic charcoal dump feature at Ireland Cave (15Jf839), with an associated calibrated median date of 5420 cal BCE (see Table 3.1; Rossen 2019).

Between 3000 and 2000 BCE, the first evidence of EAC plants being purposefully grown is evident in the archaeological record of the Falls region. Maygrass was present at the RiverPark (15Jf596, 15Jf597, and 15Jf598) site at this time (see Chapter 5), and this appears to be a broad regional trend (Smith 2009, 2011), although some early maygrass seeds have been attributed to intrusion from later Woodland components (Stafford and Mocas 2009:492). Because of its ecology and native range near the Gulf Coast of Florida, Alabama, Mississippi, and Louisiana, any maygrass in Kentucky and Indiana must have been cultivated, although it never shows morphological changes associated with selection (Cowan 1978) (Figure 10.2).

The use of native cultigens in Middle and Late Archaic times does not signify a major lifestyle change in terms of plant use. The low frequencies of these seeds, combined with nuts and wetlands plants, suggests low-risk experimentation with cultivation within a continuing hunter-gatherer lifeway, which Jack Harlan (1992) termed an "extension of collecting." One

Figure 10.2. Maygrass.

lingering question is why dryland annuals eventually became cultivated, while wetlands plants were abandoned. Was it simply the expediency of dryland weedy annuals over the potential greater maintenance and energy inputs of wetlands plants?

WOODLAND PERIOD (CA. 1000 BCE–1000 CE)

During Woodland times, people living throughout the Falls region participated in broad regional plant use changes. Nuts remained a focal plant resource, but frequencies and densities gradually decreased through time. It is possible that changing plant economies and a reduced emphasis on nutshell as fuel were factors in this trend. The six EAC plants (chenopod, marshelder, maygrass, squash, sumpweed, and sunflower) became more important, indicating the establishment of garden horticulture and a mixed wild/cultivated plant economy. Woodland sites on all sides of the Falls region yielded similar large nutshell and native cultigen collections (Davis et al. 1997; Hockensmith et al. 1998; Pollack and Henderson 2000; Redmond and McCullough 2000; Rossen 1999, 2007; Simon 2000; see Chapter 8).

Gardens were the culmination of at least two thousand years of experimentation with weedy annual plants for their starchy and oily seeds. By 1000 BCE, gardening was in place over a wide geographical area, ranging from

Illinois in the west to Arkansas in the south, West Virginia in the east, and Pennsylvania in the northeast (Smith 2011). Different EAC plants dominated in sectors of this large area (Cowan 1985; Cowan et al. 1981; Gremillion 1998; Johannessen 1984; Simon 2000). In western Kentucky and the Falls region, maygrass appears to have been the first and dominant EAC plant (Pollack and Railey 1987). At Shippingport (15Jf702), other than a single chenopod specimen, all native cultigen seeds are maygrass in Terminal Archaic, Early Woodland, and Late Woodland contexts (Rossen 2010). RiverPark also exemplifies this pattern, with only maygrass appearing in middle Late Archaic contexts, while chenopod, erect knotweed, and sunflower appear with maygrass in Early and Middle Woodland contexts (Simpson and Mocas 2017:16). At M. Kraft (12Cl935), maygrass appears in both Middle and Late Woodland samples as the sole native cultigen (Rossen 2013).

Middle Woodland Appearance of Corn

Corn (*Zea mays*) macroremains appeared in the Eastern Woodlands during the Middle Woodland (ca. 100–400 CE). Claims for pollen and phytolith evidence are much earlier (Hart 2008), but we will concentrate on the evidence provided by macroremains. The supposedly early corn specimens vary in terms of their morphological credibility (that is, whether they exhibit the small crescent-shaped kernels, closed cupules, and heavy glumes of Midwestern Twelve or the long low crescent-shaped and open cupules of Eastern Eight), and direct dates have not always verified context-related dates. For example, reexamination of corn from the Holding site in Illinois, once thought to be the oldest directly dated Middle Woodland corn in the Eastern Woodlands, has determined the corn identification to be in error (Simon 2017). However, Middle Woodland AMS dates on corn at the Edwin Harness site in Ohio and Icehouse Bottom in Tennessee appear to support the low frequency presence of Middle Woodland corn (Crawford et al. 1997; Fritz 1993). Possibly the largest multi-site collection of Middle Woodland corn is from Owl Hollow Phase sites in central Tennessee. Small, crescent-shaped kernels have been recovered from several sites of this phase, including the Hurricane Branch site, the Owl Hollow (type) site, and sites of the Normandy Reservoir Project (Chapman and Crites 1987; Crites 1978, 1994; Rossen 1984; Shea 1977, 1978). It is notable that corn is absent from some large and well-preserved Middle Woodland archaeobotanical assemblages (Rossen 1999), particularly west of the Falls region (Butler and Wagner 2000). The gap between the Middle Woodland introduction of corn in the Owl Hollow region and its later appearance in the Mississippi Valley represents a diffusion process that would have presumably crossed the Falls region (Nassaney 2000:717).

Small amounts of corn are associated with many Late Woodland sites across the Midwest (Pollack and Henderson 2000; Railey 1996). Near the Falls, at the M. Kraft site, corn is not present in the two Middle Woodland features, but appears in all three analyzed Terminal Late Woodland features, including a cache of more than one thousand small, low, crescent-shaped kernels that are consistent with a forerunner of Mississippian Midwestern Twelve (Rossen 2013; see Chapter 9).

Another secure, large, Terminal Late Woodland assemblage comes from 120 kilometers northeast of the Falls region. The Ronald Watson Gravel site collection exhibits the typical pattern: small amounts of corn dispersed throughout the site in several contexts within a typical Woodland nuts and native cultigens collection without later overlying deposits (Huebchen 2006; Rossen and Hawkins 1995).

At Shippingport, small amounts of corn are present in Late Archaic, Early Woodland, and Late Woodland contexts. However, given the vast amounts of corn associated with the site's Mississippian component, these materials may be intrusive (Rossen 2010; see also Chapter 9).

The introduction of corn into the Falls region and throughout the Ohio Valley is a key unresolved archaeobotanical issue. One scenario is that corn arrived by Middle Woodland times and was in low-level use in selected places for centuries. A combination of environmental and cultural factors would have been involved in preventing its greater immediate use. Tropical corn had to be adapted to the temperate climates and shorter growing seasons of the Eastern Woodlands. Additionally, people may have delayed heavy use of corn until its ritual and supernatural cultural contexts could develop (see Staller et al. 2009). In this scenario, corn simmered as a low-level use plant for centuries (or if the pollen data are correct, millennia) before exploding into roles as a dominant dietary and ritual plant.

The alternative scenario that is sometimes presented is that Middle Woodland corn specimens will be clarified by correct identification, carbon isotope assessment, and direct dating, showing that the introduction and development of corn as a dominant staple food was more immediate and less protracted (Simon 2017). In this scenario, corn did not have to undergo as much environmental or ritual adaptation to the Eastern Woodlands as previously believed, and it easily supplanted EAC starchy and oily seed plants in a rapid transition from house garden horticulture to multi-family agriculture. This model views corn as an earlier version of the relatively

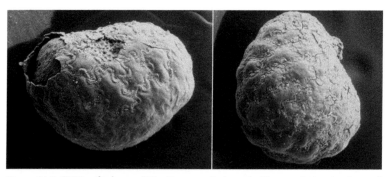

Figure 10.3. SEMs of tobacco (*Nicotiana rustica*) seeds. Note variation in the surface reticulation. This is suggestive of the use of multiple varieties by Late Mississippian times.

sudden introduction and diffusion of *Phaseolus* beans, which were introduced between 1000 and 1400 CE (Hart 2008; see discussion below). The authors currently support the model of an earlier introduction and long-term, low-level development of corn.

Worthy of mention is tobacco (*Nicotiana rustica*). Although notoriously difficult to recover even by water flotation, tobacco seeds appear as early as 100 BCE and are sporadically present in low frequencies throughout the Eastern Woodlands after 300 CE. There are tobacco species native to the Eastern Woodlands, yet most scholars view tobacco as a plant diffused from Mexico and South America. Tobacco seeds have been recovered predominantly from domestic contexts, which does not necessarily preclude ritualistic use of the plant (Wagner 2000). Tobacco recovered from Slack Farm (15Un28) suggests that multiple species were utilized by Caborn-Welborn times (Rossen 1996; Figure 10.3).

MISSISSIPPIAN (CA. 1000–1300 CE)

The Kentucky East-West Model, first published more than three decades ago, describes the Falls region as a key boundary point between distinctive regional plant use systems (Rossen and Edging 1987). The model states that from 1000–1300 CE, Fort Ancient and Mississippian groups, both long recognized as corn agriculturalists, had greatly different plant subsistence systems. Specifically, beneath the umbrella of corn, Fort Ancient groups adopted and heavily used *Phaseolus* beans, while their Mississippian neighbors did not. On the other hand, Mississippians continued and even intensified the use of native starchy and oily seeded cultigens like maygrass and marshelder, which disappeared entirely from most Fort Ancient sites. The only EAC native cultigen to continue in use in Fort Ancient territory

Figure 10.4. Corn varieties: *top*, Eastern Eight row corn with thick open cupules; *bottom*, Midwestern Twelve corn with closed cupules and heavy glumes.

is chenopod. Likewise, nut use as measured by density indices was an important component of Mississippian diets, even to the point of suggesting hickory silviculture (Munson 1973, 1984, 1986), while nut densities are uniformly much lower at Fort Ancient sites, suggesting a strong deemphasis of that time-honored resource. Even corn used by each group appears to be distinctive, with the Fort Ancient favoring an open cupule, eight-row variety known as Eastern Eight and Mississippians tending to grow a closed cupule, twelve-row variety known to archaeologists as Midwestern twelve (Figure 10.4).

By ca. 1000 CE, Falls Mississippian settlements were situated along the northeastern boundary of two different plant use systems. The contrasting plant use systems developed among contemporary groups: the Mississippian polities of the lower Ohio Valley, and the egalitarian Fort Ancient groups, including Oliver (thought by some scholars be a Fort Ancient variant), who lived on the eastern and northern peripheries of those polities (Bush 2004; Henderson 1992b, 1998, 2008; Madsen et al. 2016; McCullough 2000, 2010; Pollack et al. 2010; Swihart and Nolan 2014). It is difficult to think of the plant use differences of the East-West Model as being environmentally or climatically based. Instead, differing cultural choices to adopt or reject new plants and to discard or intensify use of time-honored plants offer insights into each group's social identity. This boundary was maintained for at least three hundred years, but around 1300 CE, it became more permeable.

Introduction of the Common Bean (*Phaseolus vulgaris*)

One key distinction in the plant use systems of the East-West Model was the use of the common bean (*Phaseolus vulgaris*), a tropical introduction that was separate from and much later than corn (Hart 2008). The Falls region lies along the western boundary of the eastern *Phaseolus* bean zone, which stretches from the Florida panhandle through Georgia to New York and New England (Ashley and White 2012; Blakely 1988; Chacon et al. 2005; Hally 1994; Keene 2004; Scarry and Scarry 2008). While an introduction from the lower Great Lakes has been proposed (Crites and Baumann 2017), the archaeological distribution suggests a largely untested entry path through the Caribbean, a region that has been modeled as a "superhighway" for cultural influences (Lathrap and Oliver 1986; Riley et al. 1990; Siegel 1991).

The general consensus is that beans entered the eastern U.S. as a rapid introduction and broad geographic diffusion around 1200 CE (Hart and Scarry 1999), a date supported by glottochronological evidence (Brown 2008). In contrast, scholars working in Tennessee are using an earlier date of 1050 CE as a baseline date for the southeastern introduction of *Phaseolus* beans, based on research involving the use of gas chromatography that is interfaced with mass spectrometry on heirloom beans (Baumann et al. 2015; Baumann and Crites 2016; Crites and Baumann 2017).

We are still exploring odd case studies like the beans from Muir, an early eleventh-century Fort Ancient site in central Kentucky (Turnbow and Sharp 1988). The Muir specimens are too large and wide to be wildbeans (*Phaseolus polystachus* or *Strophostyles* sp.). David Asch has examined a complete cotyledon specimen and has concluded, "the combination of cross-sectional shape and thickness of the specimen differs substantially from what is expected of a carbonized *Phaseolus* cotyledon. Size and shape are otherwise consistent with it being *P. vulgaris*" (Asch 2008). Bill Best, renowned expert

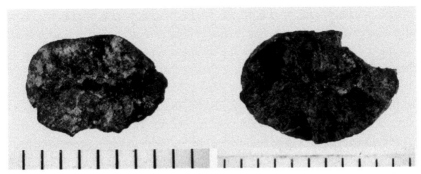

Figure 10.5. The eleventh-century specimens of *Phaseolus* beans from the Muir site (mm scale).

on heirloom Kentucky beans, has examined the Muir specimens and thinks that they could be a *Phaseolus vulgaris* variety commonly known as "cut short bean" for having one rounded edge and one flat edge (Best 2017; Henderson 2017; Figure 10.5).

INTERMINGLED PLANT USE AT THE BOUNDARY

The Fort Ancient-Mississippian plant use dichotomy with its boundary in the Falls region was thought to have had well-defined margins. However, four plant assemblages from the Falls region have altered and nuanced our view of this boundary zone: Prather, Newcomb, Eva Bandman, and Shippingport. All four sites show the intermingling of Fort Ancient and Mississippian plant use traits, and not necessarily the same type of comingling present in other artifact assemblages, such as ceramics.

The Prather and Newcomb sites were occupied during Early Mississippian times (1000–1300 CE) (Munson et al. 2006; Turner 2006, 2011; see Chapter 11). With respect to material culture, and in particular the ceramics, there is little evidence of Mississippian/Fort Ancient interaction. Several corn kernels and cupules have been recovered from Prather, but no row numbers have been determined. However, at Newcomb, Midwestern Twelve corn (along with nutshell and fleshy fruits) is ubiquitous in Mississippian samples (Rossen 2013). An earlier analysis of other samples from the same site has revealed that about a third of the recovered corn is eight row (Turner 2006). A single early Mississippian house at Shippingport has revealed twelve row corn and the native cultigens maygrass, marshelder, and chenopod, all usually associated with Mississippian plant use. The presence of two beans in this house may be evidence of Fort Ancient influence in the early Mississippian, or it may be merely an intrusion from the plentiful plant materials associated with the later Mississippian component of the site. These data reflect an intermingling of plant use traditions, plus a level of interaction across the Falls region that is not necessarily suggested by early Mississippian material culture.

Later in Mississippian times (1300–1450 CE), the material culture, and in particular the ceramics, recovered from Eva Bandman and Shippingport suggest the presence of Fort Ancient households or potters within Mississippian communities (Madsen et al. 2016; Pollack et al. 2010; see also Chapter 12). The botanical remains recovered from both sites point to an intermingling of Mississippian and Fort Ancient plant use patterns, with the Eva Bandman collection exhibiting more Fort Ancient influence and Shippingport showing more Mississippian influence. As such, both the material culture and the plant remains recovered from these two sites are indicators of a more permeable boundary after 1300 CE (see Chapter 12).

At Eva Bandman, varieties of corn associated with both Mississippian (Midwestern Twelve) and Fort Ancient (Eastern Eight) groups are present within several different contexts. The *Phaseolus* beans in this collection are exclusively associated with Fort Ancient populations to the east, and the presence of cultivated chenopod also matches the Fort Ancient pattern. The absence of other native cultigens, like maygrass (*Phalaris caroliniana*) and marshelder (*Iva annua*), which were heavily used and hybridized by Mississippian groups, is significant. Plants like sumac, blackberry, grape, and paw-paw are all generally associated with the Fort Ancient, who more strongly maintained a wild plant collecting component that emphasized fleshy fruits. Low nutshell densities are more like Fort Ancient than Mississippian patterns, though overall poor preservation may depress the site statistics. In addition to the presence of Midwestern Twelve corn, other markers of Mississippian plant use that are absent from most Fort Ancient collections, such as pecan and wildbean (*Strophostyles* sp.), are present at Eva Bandman. Overall, the Eva Bandman collection displays the mixed plant use indicators of a permeable boundary, but with a stronger influence from the Fort Ancient lifeway in terms of plant use (Madsen et al. 2016).

The Shippingport site is an unusually large and significant collection, including materials from 145 flotation samples representing 1,240 liters of soil. The result is a massive collection of more than 145,000 specimens from houses with early (1000–1300 CE) and late (1300–1450 CE) Mississippian architecture (Rossen 2010). Except for the one early Mississippian house discussed above, most of the artifacts and plant remains have been recovered from the late Mississippian deposits. As with the contemporary

Eva Bandman site, the ceramic collection is primarily Mississippian with a substantial Fort Ancient presence (Pollack et al. 2010; see also Chapter 12), and varieties of corn associated with both Fort Ancient (Eastern Eight) and Mississippian (Midwestern Twelve) peoples are present. Also, like Eva Bandman, the *Phaseolus* beans of Shippingport are associated with Fort Ancient populations. In contrast to Eva Bandman, however, the presence of native cultigens, particularly maygrass and marshelder, is significant as a clear-cut Mississippian plant use trait. Similarly, the high nutshell densities of Shippingport are much more like Mississippian than Fort Ancient patterns. Overall, the Shippingport collection displays the mixed indicators of a permeable boundary, but with a stronger influence from the Mississippian lifeway in terms of plant use.

Together, the Eva Bandman and Shippingport sites help to refine our understanding of boundaries and relationships among Mississippian and Fort Ancient groups in the Falls region. During early Mississippian times there is little evidence of Mississippian and Fort Ancient interaction (see Chapter 11), but after 1300 CE, plant assemblages clearly show the complexities of both separation and interaction at a sociocultural border. In some respects, the boundary looks well-defined in terms of plant use, with clear-cut traits that typify a Fort Ancient or a Mississippian plant use system. But examples of intermingled plant use, coupled with the presence of Fort Ancient ceramics within Mississippian settlements, are suggestive of increased relationships between Fort Ancient and Mississippian peoples (see Chapter 12).

Discussion

Plant use over ten thousand years in the Falls of the Ohio area can be divided into four eras: 1) Archaic broad-spectrum hunting-gathering that gradually came to focus on nuts and wetland plants; 2) the development of starchy-oily seed plant house gardening from a long-term "extension of collecting" by at least 1000 BCE; 3) the staggered introduction of tropical cultigens (the exact chronology of which is still unclear) leading to mixed economies and differing emphases with the native cultigens, complex plant use decision-making, and the development of a sociocultural boundary at the Falls around 1000 CE; and 4) the abandonment of the Prather mound center around 1300 CE and the subsequent development of movements of people from the east into the Falls region, which resulted in a more permeable plant use boundary.

Modeling Plant Use Systems in the Falls Region

Archaic hunter-gatherers have been viewed as oriented to river valleys with a gradual pull toward oak-hickory and mixed forest zones (Jefferies 1982:1483; Munson and Cook 1980:735–37; Smith 2011), even to the point of reduced mobility and semi-sedentism (Janzen 1977a:141; Jefferies 1982:1484–85; Munson and Cook 1980:674). Behavioral models emphasized long-term changes from broad-spectrum to more specialized collecting of fewer nut species through time (Stafford 1991, 1994). The role and significance of wetlands plants remain unknown, with some scholars, including the present authors, viewing them as essential and archaeologically underrepresented (Brown and Vierra 1983; Rossen 2000, 2006), while others have depicted them as merely an additional minor patch to be exploited outside of basic logistical strategies (Stafford 1991, 1994). More recent models of the Falls region tend to emphasize the pull toward wetlands resources, while also recognizing the continued use of upland plant resources, particularly the use of drought-tolerant mast forests during the Middle Archaic. The shift to the wetlands was thus conducted within a "short-distance movement pattern" that was intermediate between earlier fully mobile hunting-gathering and subsequent Late Archaic semi-sedentary and sedentary house gardening (see Chapters 3 and 4).

The Eastern Agricultural Complex began during the Archaic period within a reduced mobility hunter-gatherer framework and evolved during Woodland times into a more sedentary dispersed settlement pattern and house gardening system. The EAC thus represented an era of long-distance plant diffusion, along with complex and varied decisions of plant adoption and rejection. The EAC, in part, represented a movement away from wetland plants in favor of better drained upland environments and dryland weedy annuals. Within the large EAC region, there was diversity in the regional emphasis on particular plants and the relative importance of house gardening in general (Asch and Asch 1978, 1985a; Johannessen 1984).

Models involving behavioral ecology consider factors of changing environments and resource availabilities (Bird and O'Connell 2006; Gremillion 1996; Piperno 2006). These models move away from environmental determinism by placing a premium on social learning and patterns of human decision-making, in combination with traits of particular plants, such as phenotypic plasticity (Gremillion and Piperno 2009). As these models have become refined, two somewhat competing ideas for modeling the development of starchy-oily seed cultigens have been presented. The first is niche construction theory and models, developed from evolutionary biology

(Laland and O'Brien 2010; Odling-Smee et al. 2003). These models emphasize human manipulation of environmental niches leading to resource enhancement. The importance of human agency in developing new food resources at low risk is central (Rossen 2011:190–92; Smith 2011).

A second contrasting model involves optimality, a sophisticated descendant of early optimal foraging theory. According to these models, gradual population rise, reduced mobility, even circumscription, and resource depression led to exploitation and then cultivation of seed plants. Scholars presenting optimality models contend that the high yield return of nut trees would never necessitate lower yield seed plant collection without being spurred by resource shortfalls caused by population growth (Zeanah 2017).

In both types of models, the goal is to understand how relatively low-yield seed plants were added to the plant economy and eventually cultivated to the point of transforming settlement patterns and contributing to increased sedentism. The fundamental debate is whether human plant use change related to the EAC was induced by pressure forces of population and environment (optimality) or was the product of human creativity in manipulating and enhancing the environment in the absence of pressures (niche construction). There are also compromise models that attempt to combine aspects of both niche construction and optimality (Stiner and Kuhn 2016). Given the later role of EAC plants in the East-West Model, when both the retention and deemphasis of EAC starchy-oily seed plants seem to have been connected to group identity and boundary maintenance, we tend to favor models that acknowledge human creativity and niche construction. This is particularly true insofar as it relates plant use to emerging group identities.

The transformation around 1000 CE of the Falls region from the center of broad plant use traditions to a boundary zone between different systems is of particular interest. In some Mississippian regions, this is essentially a shift from house gardening to multi-family and corporate agriculture, including the development of hoe blade manufacturing, distribution, and use technologies, which is often viewed as a mechanism of specialization and social stratification (Cobb 2000; Hammerstedt and Hughes 2015; Sussenbach 1993). However, there are not many chert hoes in the Falls region, and the local nature of this change in plant use is less clear.

In the 1980s, the Fort Ancient people were routinely referred to as an "Upper Mississippian" people and as an "archaeological construct" (Wagner 1987). These terms imply that there was not enough evidence to consider the Fort Ancient archaeological record as truly representative of a distinctive people, and that they were a distant reflection or echo of their more centralized neighbors. Systematic archaeobotanical work has been vital not only in defining a true Fort Ancient cultural identity, but also in showing that their plant use decisions were complex and independent. Fort Ancient groups living east of the Falls, along with the Oliver variant of Indiana, abandoned or deemphasized time-honored food resources, such as nuts and most native cultigens. They simultaneously and rapidly accepted newly introduced *Phaseolus* beans as a staple. By comparison, their Mississippian neighbors living at (and west of) the Falls region seem conservative, not adopting the bounty of beans, which they surely knew about, and continuing or even intensifying their efforts on traditional plant foods like nuts and native cultigens. We wonder what sociocultural controls conditioned those plant use decisions and maintained the distinctiveness of each system, since as stated above these appear to be cases of agency as well as internal acceptance and rejection of available plants, rather than environmentally conditioned decisions.

Because of the energy advantage provided by beans, especially in producing complete proteins when eaten with corn, there is a certain irony in the acceptance of *Phaseolus* beans by the Fort Ancient farmers east of the Falls but not by Mississippian groups west of the Falls. It would seem logical that the protein energy increase of beans would be associated with the greater centralization and mound building of Mississippian groups near the Falls of the Ohio, but this is not the case. It is tempting to speculate that the decision not to adopt beans as a crop was a factor in the decline of the Middle Mississippian settlements, particularly when considered in light of the thriving later Mississippian Caborn-Welborn population that did grow beans.

In the Falls region, the cultural plant use distinctions began to cross the Falls boundary at some point after 1300 CE. Simultaneously, aspects of the Fort Ancient material culture appear at Shippingport and Eva Bandman (see Chapter 12). As with ceramics, the archaeobotanical record of the Falls region reflects a diffusion and intermingling of two cultures in a locally reorganizing world after 1300 CE.

The East-West Model holds no implications for the relative importance of native versus introduced tropical cultigens to regional cultural centralization or egalitarianism. The model does, however, call attention to the diversified agricultural economy of the Mississippians, who selectively added new tropical plants (except in most cases beans) to the existing economy of native cultigens (Edging 1995). It does not, however, explain the decisions of the Mississippians to reject beans, or of Fort Ancient people to deemphasize or to drop time-honored food sources like nuts and most native cultigens. The Falls region was the fulcrum of the development, gradual dissolution, and end of the plant use systems and sociocultural boundary associated with the East-West Model. To the east, Fort Ancient plant use remained unchanged for several hundred more years at most sites, with key exceptions like Fox Farm. Further, Caborn-Welborn groups living downstream from the Falls region adopted Fort Ancient beans within a system that overall still resembled a Mississippian plant use system. In the Falls region itself, the two plant use systems were intermingled in different ways at particular sites.

After 1300 CE, plant use in and around the Falls region shows how different plant use systems migrated and meshed during times of culture change and reorganization. We also think that the shifting plant systems in the post–1300 CE Falls region help to illustrate how plant adoption-rejection decisions were made based on intercultural relations that were not governed by environmental capabilities and constraints. As in the present world, in times of cultural change and uncertainty, people migrate looking for a better life, bringing their plants with them and influencing the people and cultures around them.

11

The Early Mississippian Occupation in the Falls Region

A View from the Prather Mound Center

CHERYL ANN MUNSON AND ROBERT G. MCCULLOUGH

The post–1050 CE occupation of the Falls region represents the northeastern Mississippian frontier. The nearest broadly contemporary populations were Fort Ancient communities upstream to the east (Henderson 2008) and to the north (Oliver) (McCullough 2005), in addition to the Mississippian communities of the Angel phase downriver to the southwest (Green and Munson 1978). A Mississippian presence, defined by shell-tempered ceramics, a variety of pottery vessel forms, and reported stone box graves, has been recognized in the Falls region since the nineteenth century. The adoption of Mississippian symbols and beliefs by residents of the Falls region was recognized by E. Y. Guernsey, who was the first to investigate Mississippian sites on the Indiana side of the Falls region. Guernsey sent sketches of discoidals (Bader and Etenohan 2017:78–80) and reports of ceramic human head effigies to Eli Lilly during his early investigations (E. Guernsey to E. Lilly, letter, August 22, 1933, Erminie Wheeler-Voegelin Archives [EWVA], Glenn Black Laboratory of Archaeology, Indiana University). Griffin (1978:551) summarized Guernsey's findings at Prather and other sites. Since then, Jon Muller, in his overview of Ohio valley archaeology, suggested that the Falls region was "a somewhat backwoods kind of Mississippian from the traditional point of view" (Muller 1986:250). Subsequent archaeological investigations in the Falls region, however, have challenged his characterization, documenting a Mississippian settlement hierarchy and a range of artifacts, as well as evidence of trade relations and an occupation lasting around 1050–1450 CE.

To understand Mississippian development and change in this region, and to compare it with other regions of the Midwest and South, we must also reference the nature and extent of Terminal Late Woodland (ca. 800–1100 CE) components in the Falls region (see Chapter 9). Archaeological evidence for large-scale population replacement between the Late Woodland and Mississippian occupations of the Falls region is lacking. Instead, researchers are finding increasing evidence of a transition from "Late Woodland-ness" to "Mississippian-ness" in the form of transitional ceramics from household and mound fill contexts that combine a mixed temper of shell and grit, or shell and other materials, as opposed to distinct shell-tempered Mississippian and grit-tempered Woodland pottery in the excavated features or strata.

Our goals in this chapter are: 1) to identify Mississippian components in the Falls region; 2) to review the radiocarbon dates; 3) to distinguish early and late Mississippian components; and 4) to provide an overview of the early Mississippian occupation of the Falls region, 1050–1300 CE (see Chapter 12 for the late Mississippian occupation).

MISSISSIPPIAN SITES AND SETTINGS

The Falls region contains 21 identified Mississippian sites, based on the presence of shell-tempered pottery, state site records, and reports (Table 11.1). In Indiana, the surveys and excavations of Guernsey, funded by business leader and avocational archaeologist Eli Lilly (1937), are a primary but very limited source of Mississippian site information, since Guernsey (1939, 1942) wrote only brief summary reports. The earlier archaeological reports of pioneering geologists (Borden 1874; Cox 1874, 1875) guided Guernsey's work. These early reports refer to a series of sites along the Ohio River floodplain and terraces, in close proximity to the Falls of the Ohio River, that have Mississippian components. Subsequent professional investigations have confirmed the presence of Mississippian components at several of these sites: Aydelotte-Reid (12Fl1), the upper portions of which are nearly destroyed (Angst 1998; Duerksen and Bergman 1995); Elrod-Kelly-Old Clarksville (12Cl1) at the mouth of Silver Creek; Newcomb (12Cl2) (Bader 2004; Munson 2011; Simpson et al. 2013); Clark's Point-Collins (12Cl3); Hale-Spond (12Cl890) (Munson 2011); and site 12Fl57 (Cantin and Stafford 2012) (Figure 1.7). The investigations of Newcomb (Munson 2011; Simpson et al. 2013) suggest that the Mississippian component at Elrod-Kelly-Old Clarksville may simply be an extension of the Newcomb occupation. In

Table 11.1. Mississippian sites in the Falls region

Setting	Sites	Attributes	References
INDIANA			
Alluvial Valley	Aydelotte-Reid (12Fl1)	OH, B	Lilly 1937; Guernsey 1939, 1942
	12Fl57	OH	Cantin and Stafford 2012
	Elrod-Kelly-Old Clarksville (12Cl1)	OH, SBG, B	Guernsey 1939, 1942
	Newcomb (12Cl2)	OH, SBG, B	Guernsey 1939, 1942
	Clark's Point-Collins (12Cl3)	OH, SBG	Guernsey 1939, 1942
	Hale-Spond, Upper (12Cl890)—terrace	OH	Munson 2011
Uplands	Prather (12Cl4)	OH, FB, EB, 4 mounds	Guernsey 1939, 1942; Janzen 1975; Munson and McCullough 2004; Munson et al. 2006
	Willey (12Cl16)	OH, SBG	Guernsey 1939, 1942
	Spangler-Koons	OH, SBG	Guernsey 1939, 1942; Adams et al. 2004; Bupp et al. 2005
	Ellingsworth (12Cl127)	OH, B	Arnold and Graham 2011b
	Smith-Sutton (12Cl130)	OH, B	Wells et al. 2008; Arnold & Graham 2011a
	Devil's Backbone (12Cl14)	Fortified, SBG	Borden 1874; Cox 1874, 1875; Putnam 1875; Janzen 1972; Arnold and Graham 2013
KENTUCKY			
Alluvial Valley	Shippingport (15Jf702)	OH, FB	French 2010
	Eva Bandman (15Jf638)—terrace	OH, FB	Pollack 2008
	Petey Day (15Sp3/202/250)	OH, *	Janzen 1978; Anne Bader, personal communication; Fisher 2013
	Edwards(15Sp5/204/252)	OH, FB, *	Janzen 1978; Anne Bader, personal communication
Uplands	15Jf561	OH	Bader 2003
	15Jf650	OH	Bader 2003
	15Jf651	OH	Bader 2003
	Armstrong	OH, SBG	Bader 2003
	Miles (15Jf671)	Rockshelter	Bader 2003

Key: OH = open habitation; B = burials; FB = flexed burials; EB =extended burials; SBG = stone box graves

* = reported mounds not confirmed

addition, Newcomb's accretional alluvial floodplain setting contrasts with the outwash terrace setting of the Hale-Spond site, where Mississippian and Woodland ceramics occur in shallow soils at similar depths with no stratigraphic separation.

In the Indiana uplands, Mississippian components have been identified at Prather (12Cl4) (Janzen 1975, 2016; Munson and McCullough 2004; Munson et al. 2006); Willey (12Cl16) and Spangler-Koons (Adams et al. 2003:111–13; Bupp et al. 2005:5-39-40, 5-43-45); Ellingsworth (12Cl127) (Arnold and Graham 2011b); and Smith-Sutton (12Cl130) (Arnold and Graham 2011a; Wells et al. 2008). The Devil's Backbone (12Cl14), a naturally fortified upland bluff overlooking the river, was reported to contain stone walls, stone mounds, stone box graves, and shell-tempered pottery (Borden 1874; Cox 1874, 1875; Janzen 1977b; Putnam 1875), although a survey by Arnold and Graham (2013) did not confirm the presence of the ceramics.

Mississippian sites located in Kentucky are similarly situated in both the Ohio River floodplain and its uplands. The Shippingport site (15Jf702), on what is now an island below the Falls of the Ohio River, is the most extensively excavated Mississippian site in the Falls region (French 2010). Eva Bandman (15Jf638), on a terrace along the river, had more limited investigations (Pollack 2008:680–82). Farther south in the Salt River valley are Mississippian components at the Edwards site (15Sp5/204/252) (Fiegel 1985; Janzen 1978; Anne Bader, personal communication 2017) and at the Petey Day site (15Sp3/202/250) (Fisher 2013; Janzen 1978; Anne Bader, personal communication 2017), both of which have been minimally investigated.

The uplands along the South Fork of Beargrass Creek include three Mississippian open habitation sites (15Jf561, 15Jf650, and 15Jf651) and a little-known stone box cemetery (Bader 2003), none of which have been systematically investigated. Another stone box grave site was noted by Bader (2003:16) in what is now downtown Louisville on the basis of reports made in 1894. Early historical descriptions and accounts noted by Joseph Granger (Bader 2003:16) suggest that a possible Mississippian settlement, with mounds, was located in the vicinity of downtown Louisville. The extent of the Louisville mounds and their association with either the early or the late Mississippian subperiods, however, cannot be determined at this time. In the uplands south of Louisville is the Miles Rockshelter (15Jf671), where avocational excavations and professional investigations have yielded shell tempered pottery as well as triangular points (Bader 2003:32–33).

CHRONOLOGY

Guernsey (1939) was the first to suggest there was an earlier and later Mississippian occupation of the Falls region, based on an apparent shift in burial patterns. Radiocarbon dates obtained from Mississippian components in the region (Table 11.2; Figure 11.1) not only support his observation but are evidence of a continuing Mississippian presence in the Falls region for approximately 450 years.

Of the 21 recorded Mississippian sites, nine have two or more radiocarbon dates. The Mississippian period in the Falls region extends around 1000–1450 CE, with early and late Mississippian being divided somewhat arbitrarily at about 1300 CE (Lewis 1996; Pollack 2008). The beginning of the early Mississippian subperiod overlaps with dates for the Terminal Late Woodland subperiod in the range of 1000–1200 CE (e.g., dates from Prather and Shippingport's House 4 and from M. Kraft [see Chapter 9]). More precise dating of assemblages may temporally separate Terminal Late Woodland and early Mississippian components or may confirm that there is indeed a temporal overlap with contemporary Terminal Late Woodland and Mississippian lifeways within the region and perhaps even at some sites. Terminal Late Woodland assemblages are well dated only at M. Kraft but are also present at the adjacent Newcomb site and may be present at Prather. Early Mississippian components are recognized based on dates at Prather, Newcomb, and Shippingport. Ellingsworth has multiple dates for Mississippian contexts that postdate Prather but straddle the 1300 CE dividing line; the limited information from this site will be discussed with the other late Mississippian sites (see Chapter 12). Petey Day and Edwards also have dates that straddle the dividing line, but their small collections are minimally analyzed and are not considered further.

EARLY MISSISSIPPIAN SETTLEMENT PATTERNS AND SITE CHARACTERISTICS

Early Mississippian settlements in the Falls region consist of Prather, a four-mound center, and several smaller habitation sites. The mound center's anomalous upland location, nearly five kilometers from the Ohio River, stands in sharp contrast to the alluvial or near-riverine setting of other early Mississippian habitation sites in the Falls region. While it is the only documented Mississippian site with mounds in the region, it is not geographically situated at the center of known early Mississippian sites or of Mississippian sites regardless of age. The two other identified early Mississippian

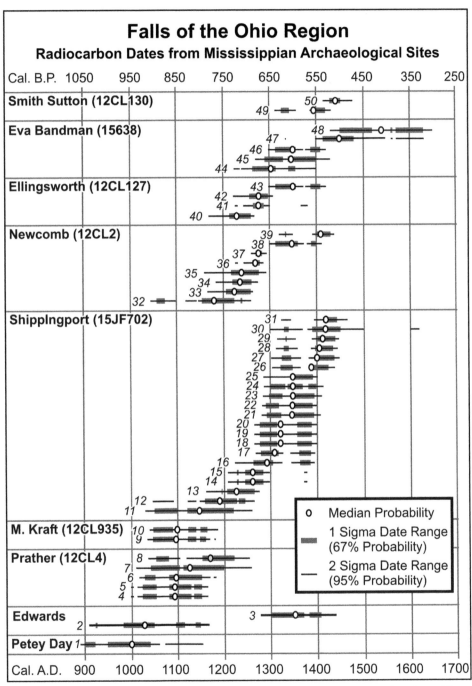

Figure 11.1. Calibrated radiocarbon dates for Mississippian sites in the Falls region, keyed to Table 11.2.

Table 11.2. Calibrated radiocarbon dates for Mississippian sites in the Falls region, keyed to Figure 11.1

Site/Sample No., [Figure 11.1 reference]	rcybp	2 Sigma Cal CE Range	Cal CE Median Probability (context)	References
EDWARDS (15SP5/204/252)				
UGa-838[s] [3]	600±75	1276–1437	1351 (bp)	Fiegel 1985;
UGa-839[s] [2]	1020±60	893–1157	1015 (?)	Janzen 1978
UGa-837[s] [*]	1215±55	673–961	807* (?)	
ELLINGSWORTH (12CL127)				
Beta-277798[a] [43]	580±40	1298–1421	1350 (wt)	Arnold and
Beta-277797[a] [42]	720±40	1222–1386	1277 (wt)	Graham 2011a;
D-AMS 029660[a] [41]	722±31	1226–1382	1276 (wt)	Simpson et al.
D-AMS 029661[a] [40]	812±29	1169–1268	1230 (wt)	2019
EVA BANDMAN (15F638)				
Beta-185612[s] [*]	200±70	1521–1950	1762*(mi)	Madsen et al.
Beta-185614[s] [48]	370±70	1430–1650	1539 (mi)	2016: Table 8.1
Beta-184844[s] [47]	490±50	1334–1631	1449 (mi)	
Beta-145638[s] [46]	580±40	1298–1421	1350 (mi)	
Beta-184845[s] [45]	620±70	1273–1427	1347 (mi)	
Beta-184847[s] [44]	690±60	1224–1400	1304 (mi)	
Beta-145639[s] [*]	760±40	1191–1294	1255*(po)	
M. KRAFT (12CL935)				
DAMS-001469[a] [10]	907±22	1039–1186	1098 (co)	Simpson et al.
DAMS-001466[a] [9]	913±22	1034–1181	1095 (he)	2014: Table 6.6
NEWCOMB (12CL2)				
DAMS-001473[a] [39]	533±29	1320–1438	1409 (wt)	Bader and
DAMS-001472[a] [38]	596±29	1298–1410	1346 (wt)	French, pers.
DAMS-001474[a] [37]	723±23	1260–1294	1276 (he)	comm. 2006;
DAMS-001471[a] [36]	744±23	1226–1287	1269 (pi)	Munson et al.
Beta-212869[s] [35]	780±50	1159–1293	1239 (sb)	2006: Table
DAMS-001470[a] [34]	800±30	1184–1275	1236 (pi)	7.5; Simpson et
DAMS-001475[a] [33]	819±30	1166–1264	1224 (po)	al. 2013: Table
Beta-221497[s] [32]	860±40	1044–1260	1180 (sb)	7.15
PETEY DAY (15SP3/202/250)				
UGa-808[s] [1]	1035±55	887–1154	999 (pi)	Fisher 2013;
UGa-807[s] [*]	1450±60	430–672	597*(mi)	Janzen 1978

Site/Sample No., [Figure 11.1 reference]	rcybp	2 Sigma Cal CE Range	Cal CE Median Probability (context)	References
PRATHER (12CL4)				
Beta-215869[a] [8]	870±40	1043–1104	1169 (bp)	Munson and
UGa-308[s] [7]	905±70	1020–1258	1124 (wt)	McCullough
Beta-215870[a] [6]	950±40	1016–1182	1095 (po)	2004:16; Mun-
Beta-215871[a] [5]	960±40	998–1164	1092 (sb)	son et al. 2006:
Beta-215872[a] [4]	960±40	998–1164	1092 (md)	Table 7.5
SHIPPINGPORT (15JF702)				
Beta-258131[a] [*]	420±40	1420–1630	1468*(bt)	French 2010:
Beta-258127[a] [31]	490±40	1324–1465	1426 (ss)	Table 16.1
Beta-190224[s] [30]	500±60	1300–1620	1418 (ss)	
Beta-258135[s] [29]	520±40	1315–1447	1412 (sw)	
Beta-258133[a] [28]	530±40	1312–1444	1405 (ss)	
Beta-248840[s] [27]	530±50	1302–1448	1400 (pi)	
Beta-248836[a] [26]	550±40	1304–1438	1388 (pi)	
Beta-258125[a] [25]	630±40	1285–1401	1348 (pi)	
Beta-258130[s] [24]	610±50	1286–1413	1348 (ss)	
Beta-258132[s] [23]	620±50	1284–1410	1348t(ss)	
Beta-258134[a] [22]	640±40	1282–1399	1347 (ss)	
Beta-258126[s] [21]	630±50	1281–1407	1346 (pi)	
Beta-258129[s] [20]	670±50	1265–1399	1321 (sw)	
Beta-250382[s] [19]	670±50	1265–1399	1321 (ss)	
Beta-250381[s] [18]	670±50	1265–1399	1321 (ss)	
Beta-248839[a] [17]	670±40	1268–1395	1317 (ss)	
Beta-215968[s] [16]	700±50	1223–1394	1292 (wt)	
Beta-258128[s] [15]	750±40	1208–1378	1261 (ss)	
Beta-250384[s] [14]	750±40	1208–1378	1261 (ss)	
Beta-250740[s] [13]	810±40	1161–1276	1226 (ss)	
Beta-250383[s] [12]	850±40	1046–1265	1190 (ss)	
Beta-210231[s] [11]	880±70	1030–1260	1146 (ss)	
SMITH-SUTTON (12CL130)				
Beta-294673[s] [50]	450±30	1415–1478	1441 (mi)	Arnold and
Beta-294674[s] [49]	550±30	1312–1432	1395 (wl)	Graham 2011b

[1] INTCAL 13 (Reimer et al. 2013); [a] AMS radiocarbon method;
[s] Standard radiocarbon method; * Date not reliable, excluded from Figure 11.1
(Dated Contexts): bp = burial pit; bt = burned timber; co = concentration of maize; he = hearth; mi = midden; md = mound soil core; pi = pit; po = post feature; sb = structure basin; ss = single-set post structure; wl = wall; wt = wall trench structure

habitation sites, Shippingport and Newcomb, are situated in alluvial, near-riverine settings 13 km away from the contemporary occupation at Prather. Several undated smaller habitation sites, such as Spangler-Koons, Willey, and the Miles Rockshelter, as well as the later Mississippian Ellingsworth and Smith-Sutton sites, also are situated in upland settings. The little-known Petey Day and Edwards sites are situated about fifty kilometers to the southeast of Prather in the Salt River valley.

THE PRATHER MOUND CENTER

Situated between Fort Ancient societies to the north and east, and other Mississippian societies to the west and south, Prather is the northeasternmost Mississippian mound center in the Eastern Woodlands (Honerkamp 1975; Janzen 1971; Munson et al. 1977). During early Mississippian times the Prather site, with its four platform mounds, was truly a center, serving for a time as the religious and political focal point for the Falls region. Its remote setting, compared to the early Mississippian components at Shippingport and Newcomb, suggests that the upland siting of Prather was intentional; a cluster of permanent springs at the edge of the site, associated with a dolomite outcrop and a series of bedrock mortars, would have afforded a perpetual water source. In addition, the construction of the platform mounds, the cutting of trees for houses and firewood, and the clearing of agricultural fields represent an investment in a particular locality and a modification of the surrounding environment.

Prather encompasses more than eleven hectares, with the Mississippian component covering about seven hectares (Munson and McCullough 2004; Munson et al. 2006) (Figures 11.2a, 11.2b, and 11.3). This is remarkably small for a mound center that includes four mounds, possibly oriented to the cardinal directions, and a residential core area around the mounds. Importantly, the plaza and the distribution of ceramics, lithics, and faunal remains mirror those of the site's earlier Woodland settlement, suggesting perhaps an in situ development—or Mississippianization—of a local population concurrent with the rise of Cahokia.

Prather is the only Mississippian site in the Falls region where spatial distribution data are available. Investigations in 2003 and 2005 employed a tractor-mounted posthole auger to systematically map and sample the entire site. Soils from these augers were screened, which provided the basis for comparing various classes of material for spatial analysis, in particular Woodland (Figure 11.2a) and Mississippian (Figure 11.2b) ceramics. The survey successfully identified the layout of the village: a central

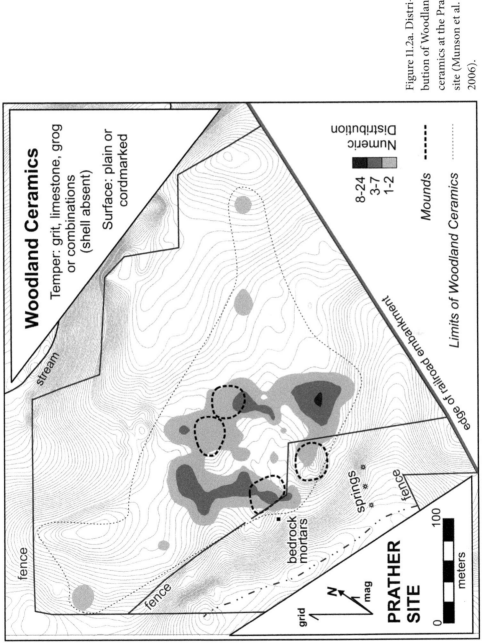

Figure 11.2a. Distribution of Woodland ceramics at the Prather site (Munson et al. 2006).

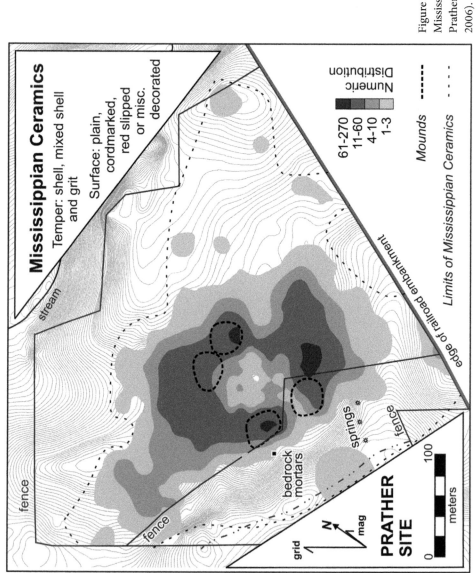

Figure 11.2b. Distribution of Mississippian ceramics at the Prather site (Munson et al. 2006).

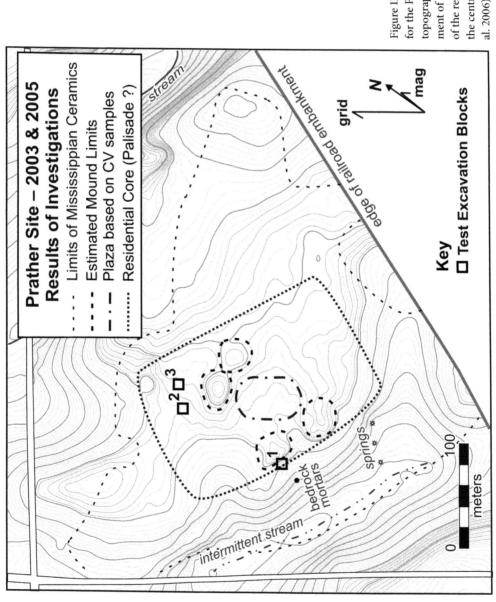

Figure 11.3. Survey results for the Prather site, showing topography, the arrangement of mounds, the extent of the residential core, and the central plaza (Munson et al. 2006).

plaza, a surrounding residential core that encompasses the four mounds, and a periphery of Mississippian occupation that includes the long western slope of the site near the springs and the bedrock mortars (Munson et al. 2006:146–48) (Figure 11.2b). The plaza's extent was subsequently confirmed by the excavation of fifty-×-fifty-centimeter sample units placed on a ten-×-ten-meter grid over the plaza area and into the residential core (Figure 11.3). The sharp fall-off in Mississippian ceramics at the outer margins of the residential core suggests a palisade enclosure with a rectangular configuration. Woodland ceramics also ring the plaza, co-occurring with Mississippian ceramics in the residential core around the mounds (Figures 11.2a and 11.2b). There are also several scattered areas where Woodland ceramics or Mississippian ceramics do not co-occur; perhaps these are outlying households.

Investigations in the 1930s by Guernsey, in the early 1970s by Janzen (1975, 2016:70–71), and in 2003 and 2005 by Munson and McCullough (2004; Munson et al. 2006) documented a structure, hearths, pits, and burials. A radiocarbon date obtained from a rectangular wall-trench structure floor in what is probably the Northwest Mound showed Prather's occupation to be early (Janzen 2016:71, 77), with a calibrated median date of 1124 CE (Table 11.2). A geoarchaeological study of soil cores (Stafford 2006) and the profile of an excavated unit placed in the severely eroded edge of the Southwest Mound suggest that it was built with redeposited midden over soils that were dug down to the Bt horizon, providing a clean base for the monument (Munson et al. 2006). Subsequent radiocarbon dates point to an occupation range for the site of about 1092 to 1160 CE (Table 11.2), with the earliest dates coming from the Southwest Mound (1092 and 1095 CE).

In one of two 2005 test blocks placed in the residential area around the mounds, a portion of a probable house basin was documented. Postholes were present near the margins of the basin, similar to the early Mississippian single-set post house at Shippingport, and no wall trenches were recognized in or near the basin (Munson et al. 2006). (Other data on domestic architecture is equally limited, but classic Mississippian rectangular wall-trench architecture was found by Janzen in early Mississippian contexts on Prather's largest mound [Munson and McCullough 2004:16].)

Flexed and extended burials were identified at the site. Flexed burials were found beneath floors of rectangular wall-trench structures on mounds and beneath floors of residential area "houses," as well as in pit features (Guernsey 1939:28; Janzen 1975; Munson et al. 2006). In one of the smaller mounds, Guernsey uncovered an extended burial with accompanying prestige goods that point to elite status: a copper-covered wooden "eagle" effigy at the head (Munson and McCullough 2004: Figure 7; Munson et al. 2006); a bone pin over the falconid's tail; a pottery jar and a long-necked bottle at the feet; and a circular, ring-shaped conch shell gorget near the shoulder. A nearby flexed burial had a small (6 cm diameter), perforated, bi-concave stone discoidal and pottery vessels (Bader and Etenohan 2017:96–97; E. Guernsey to E. Lilly, letter, September 10, 1934, EWVA). Guernsey also reported in a brief later visit the discovery of a hammered copper nugget on the surface of the largest mound (E. Guernsey to E. Lilly, letter, July 16, 1935, EWVA; Guernsey's notes and maps of his excavations do not survive, but at least portions of his collections are curated at the Glenn Black Laboratory of Archaeology, Indiana University, and at the Museum of Anthropology, University of Michigan).

Non-Mound Settlements

The two early Mississippian non-mound settlements are Shippingport and Newcomb, located adjacent to the Ohio River. Both sites have been impacted by erosion and soil borrow, which makes their size difficult to assess. Additionally, both have Late Mississippian components, as evident in ceramic collections and radiocarbon dates.

At Shippingport, a good example of an early Mississippian single-set post structure was excavated (French and Schatz 2010:88–91). Exposed in its entirety, House 4 (Figure 11.4) is rectangular in shape and oriented approximately with the cardinal directions. Its area of 8.2 m^2 and a length/width ratio of 1.4 are consistent with early Mississippian houses in other regions (Milner et al. 1984; Pauketat 1998). This structure apparently burned and does not show evidence of later rebuilding. A conventional radiocarbon date from a combination of wood charcoal and burnt thatch, both from basin fill, returned a calibrated median date of 1146 CE for House 4. In addition to this house, portions of 12 other Mississippian single-set post houses also were documented at the site, and eight have been dated. Median calibrated radiocarbon dates for single-set post house construction span the period 1146–1426 CE (Table 11.2; Figure 11.1) (French 2010) and extend into the late Mississippian subperiod. Three other houses built with wall trenches also had single-set post walls, but three radiocarbon samples from one of these structures has placed it in the late Mississippian subperiod. Seven Mississippian burials have been identified at the site, but their dating is unknown (Ross-Stallings 2010a).

Across the river at Newcomb, Guernsey's excavations in the 1930s yielded a curated artifact collection without associated notes and maps. Subsequent

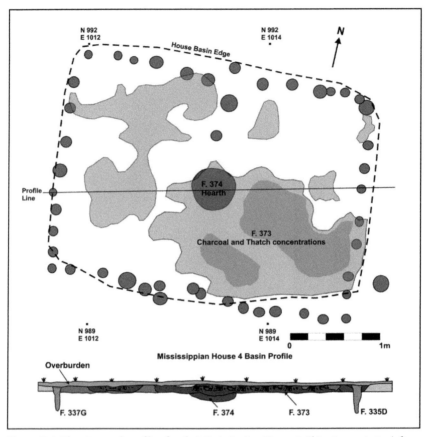

Figure 11.4. Planview and profile of early Mississippian House 4, Shippingport site (after French and Schatz 2010: Figure 17.14).

excavations (Bader 2004) in response to riverbank erosion have identified a burial and three burned house basins, two of which returned calibrated median radiocarbon dates of 1180 CE and 1239 CE (Table 11.2; Figure 11.1). One house basin yielded a loop-handled rim sherd similar to those of early Mississippian vessels from the Angel site (Hilgeman 2000). During a subsequent survey, shovel probe excavations extended the limits of the greatly impacted Newcomb site and identified a Mississippian wall-trench house with associated burned maize cupules and cob fragments (Munson 2011). More extensive excavations (Simpson et al. 2013) found two wall-trench structures that postdate 1300 CE at two sigma, a possible early Mississippian house basin located near a smudge pit that dates to 1236 CE (Table 11.2; Figure 11.1), and two unexcavated burials. The known size of Newcomb coupled with its "overwhelmingly utilitarian" ceramic collection probably indicates that it was a relatively small settlement occupied over a length of time (Simpson et al. 2013:405).

Intensity of occupation can at times be indicated by depth of midden. Midden deposits may be compared in upland and terrace settings, where floodplain silts do not contribute to the depth of the cultural soil profile. At Prather, in areas away from the slope wash from mounds, observed midden depths are variable (Munson and McCullough 2004:63–69, Figures 47–51, Appendix II); in some places, midden soils extend below an average 25 cm thick plowzone to depths of 40–55 cm below surface, but in most parts of the site, midden deposits have been fully incorporated into the plowzone. Soil borrow for mound construction undoubtedly altered the depth and distribution of middens. At smaller settlements, such as Ellingsworth (Arnold and Graham 2011a:Figures 4.40 and 4.47) and Shippingport (French 2010), midden depths reach 5 and 40 cm, respectively, below surface in some areas. At the Hale-Spond Upper terrace location, Mississippian midden deposits are similarly variable, but extend below an average 25 cm thick plowzone in places to 30–40 cm below surface (Munson 2011:Figures 4.30–4.34, Table 4.7). At Eva Bandman, also on a terrace, midden deposits were 30 cm thick (Pollack 2008:680). These data suggest that there is little difference in the intensity of site occupation between the early and late Mississippian occupations of the Falls region.

MATERIAL CULTURE

Assessment of the characteristics of early Mississippian material culture is hindered by the paucity of excavated feature contexts that can be unquestionably assigned to this subperiod. At Prather the bulk of the collections derive from auger samples and controlled-volume, hand-excavated samples of plowzone and shallow midden contexts; dated features in the eroded face of the Southwest Mound; and a probable house basin feature in Block 2 of the residential area. The materials recovered from these contexts represent a minor portion of the entire Prather site collection. All four of the radiocarbon dates from these contexts are early Mississippian in age (Table 11.2), and the bulk of the collections are probably associated with this subperiod. Sherds classified as Woodland on the basis of the absence of shell temper represent less than three percent of the ceramic collection; some may be contemporary with the early Mississippian occupation, or were redeposited in the fill of early Mississippian features and mound fill. Additionally, Janzen's radiocarbon date obtained from the Northwest Mound is somewhat later but still within the early Mississippian subperiod (Table 11.2). However, the collections from his excavations have not been catalogued or analyzed. In contrast to Prather, Shippingport and Newcomb have ceramics from both early and late Mississippian radiocarbon dated contexts, with Shippingport having a much higher proportion of late contexts.

Lithic Implements

At early Mississippian sites, the abundance of lithic implements is greatly limited compared to ceramics, particularly at Shippingport. The lithic tool kit consists of artifacts generally common throughout the Midwest at this time and made primarily from local cherts. At Prather, these include chipped-stone triangular projectile points (straight to slightly incurvate sides) and sidescrapers in roughly equal numbers; spokeshaves, drills, and perforators in lesser quantities; and a few groundstone tools, including a celt (Munson and McCullough 2004; Munson et al. 2006:111, 113). The chipped stone raw materials were overwhelmingly derived from local sources, predominantly New Chapel and Jeffersonville cherts, with Wyandotte and Allens Creek cherts combining for twelve percent and nonlocal materials present in only minor amounts (Cantin 2006:188–91). Notably absent in the assemblage is evidence of hoes, adzes, or gouges: no whole specimens, fragments, or re-sharpening flakes were identified. These implements and refurbishing debitage are present at many Angel phase sites in the lower Ohio valley (Munson 1994). At most Mississippian sites, these tools were commonly made from imported cherts and were received in the form of finished products or tool preforms. Given the absence of these tools, it is not surprising that the types of chert that were widely traded in Mississippian times—Mill Creek, Dover, and Kaolin (Cobb 2000)—also are absent in the Prather collections (Munson et al. 2006:111). Groundstone tools recovered from Prather during the 2003 and 2005 investigations include hammerstones, grinding slabs, pitted "nutting stones," and celts. In addition to these materials, Guernsey's collection includes multiple nutting stones, granite celts, and a polished, perforated stone discoidal (Munson and McCullough 2004:15).

Lithic tools associated with Shippingport's House 4 are limited to eight utilized flakes and two biface fragments; the small size of the stone tool assemblage makes it difficult to compare with those from other sites or from later contexts. The chert debris recovered from this house, however, showed a different knapping trajectory and procurement pattern relative to later houses (Stallings et al. 2010:294).

Lithic implements recovered from Newcomb include drills, triangular knives, and six varieties of triangular arrow points that depart from defined types to some degree (Simpson et al. 2013:262). The Newcomb collection includes points from Late Woodland, Mississippian, and mixed contexts, but the variation is comparable to that at Prather. These varieties also overlap with the 26 varieties of triangular points identified at Shippingport that were assigned primarily to the late Mississippian subperiod (Stallings et al. 2010:247–52). Guernsey's collection from Newcomb additionally includes nutting stones, celts, and a small fragmentary discoidal similar to the one found at Prather.

Ceramics

Early Mississippian pottery in the Falls region is characterized by the use of crushed shell alone or by a mixture of shell and grit, limestone, or grog as temper, and (rarely) shell with a sandy paste. Vessel forms are dominated by jars, with little morphological variation, such that plain surfaces predominate. Most of the early Mississippian ceramics have been recovered from the Prather site, with much smaller collections being recovered from Shippingport and Newcomb.

At Prather, the 4,908 analyzed Mississippian sherds (Munson and Mc-Cullough 2004; Munson et al. 2006) were tempered with shell alone (63.2 percent) or with shell mixed with other aplastics (36.8 percent). Jars (91.7 percent)—typically having short-to-medium-long rims with flaring or outcurving profiles and rounded bodies—are far more common than bowls (5.0 percent) (Figure 11.5). Jar bodies are generally globular with rounded bases. Single examples of wide-mouth and narrow-neck bottles (3.3 percent) are represented by rim and neck sherds. Soup bowl–like plates and shallow pans are so far unknown. Other vessel forms, represented by body fragments, include several examples of sharply angled jar shoulders rather than the usual rounded forms. Vessel attachments are not common, but consist of wide to intermediate strap and loop handle varieties (Hilgeman 2000), in addition to a few examples of horizontal, rounded lugs.

As with other early Mississippian sites in the Falls region, Mississippi Plain and Bell Plain surfaces predominate over cordmarked. Some cordmarked jars have smoothed necks and rims. Absent are identifiable examples of Kimmswick Fabric Impressed, but this type is present in Guernsey's and Janzen's collections from the Northwest Mound. As befits a mound center, the Prather collection also contains a variety of decorated ceramic types, such as Old Town Red, Pouncey Pinched, Mound Place Incised, Wolf Creek Check Stamped, and a Fort Ancient–like incised sherd. A few sherds were classified as Ramey Incised–like and Powell Plain–like. The lack of burnishing and other morphological attributes of the Ramey-like sherds suggests that these were locally made copies of the iconic Cahokia vessels (Emerson

Figure 11.5. Pottery vessels from the Prather site (jars are Mississippi Plain): *left to right*, jar, donated by Dr. W. W. Work to E. Y. Guernsey (Glenn A. Black Laboratory of Archaeology [GBL], Indiana University); jar donated by Ace Soliday, local artifact collector, to the Falls of the Ohio State Park; Bell Plain bowl found in a spring, donated to the Clark County Museum; jar excavated by Guernsey, 1934 (GBL); reconstructed jar recovered in auger sampling (Munson and McCullough 2004: Figure 21, curated at GBL).

1989, 1991, 1997; Pauketat and Emerson 1991) (Figure 11.6). In addition to these ceramic types, Janzen's collection at the University of Louisville includes an unclassifiable black-on-buff, negative-painted bottle sherd, and Janzen (1975) notes the presence of a scalloped rim and a human head effigy that perhaps was part of a bottle.

The early Mississippian ceramics recovered from Shippingport and Newcomb are similar to those of Prather: shell tempering mixed with other aplastics predominates, as do jars and plain surfaces. At both sites, jars are primarily tall, with short, flared, or slightly flared rims. Few handles and refined wares are present, and there is an effective absence of decoration and nonlocal forms (Pollack et al. 2010; Simpson et al. 2013:405). The Shippingport early Mississippian ceramic collection (Pollack et al. 2010:164) includes all sherds regardless of temper categories from House 4 (n=66) plus the sherds from other contexts having a mixed temper of shell and other aplastics (n=176). This assignment may have overrepresented Mississippian sherds with mixed shell and non-shell temper and possibly increased the proportion of cordmarking over plain, since cordmarked sherds have somewhat less shell in the various temper combinations. Overall, Shippingport's early Mississippian collection is dominated by Mississippi Plain (57.0 percent), Bell Plain (7.9 percent), and cordmarked (33.5 percent). Fabric Impressed, Wolf Creek Check Stamped, and unclassified trailed account for less than one percent (Pollack et al. 2010). Like Prather, jars (88.4 percent) dominate the Shippingport assemblage, with bowls (11.6 percent) being the

Figure 11.6. Ramey Incised-like jar rim fragments from the Prather site (after Munson and McCullough 2004:Figure 36a-b; Munson et al. 2006: Figure 6.5a).

only other identified vessel form. Two incurved/recurved jars have trailed lines reminiscent of the Ramey Incised–like sherds found at Prather.

The Newcomb assemblage consists of sherds tempered with shell alone or with shell and other aplastics (Simpson et al. 2013). Of the 476 analyzed sherds, 448 have been classified as Mississippi Plain, with only eight classified as Bell Plain. As at Shippingport, Newcomb's early Mississippian ceramic assemblage is marked by a limited range of forms. In addition to jars and bowls, only four pan sherds and two strap handle fragments have been identified, leading Simpson et al. (2013:212) to label the assemblage "overwhelmingly utilitarian." However, there are some significant differences in other aspects of the ceramic assemblage. Shell tempering alone accounts for almost all of the Mississippian pottery (96.6 percent). In addition, the jar to bowl ratio (1.1:1) at Newcomb is significantly lower compared to both Shippingport (9:1) and Prather (18:1). Some of the discrepancy in temper (and surface treatment) can be accounted for by different classification schemes, but other factors will need to be evaluated in future investigations.

While the analyzed assemblage from Newcomb is drawn from domestic contexts, earlier minimally reported surveys and excavations by Guernsey included a diverse array of Mississippian pottery, such as Pouncey Pinched jars, fabric-impressed pans, human effigies, a hooded water bottle, soup bowl–style plates, wide strap handles, and sherds with Fort Ancient–like trailed/incised designs (Munson et al. 2006:90). Guernsey also reported red-slipped pottery (Bader and Etenohan 2017:56) and effigies, including "a little pottery head a funny human grotesque, quite Mexican in concept" (E. Guernsey to E. Lilly, letter, August 22, 1933, EWVA). The bottle, plates, and handle style point to the possibility of a later Mississippian component, perhaps in a part of the site now lost to riverbank erosion or soil borrow, but the other ceramic characteristics provided by Guernsey's work are evidence of continuity with Prather. The prospect of a later Mississippian occupation at Newcomb is supported by two post–1300 CE radiocarbon dates from wall-trench houses (Table 11.2).

In brief, early Mississippian ceramics are very similar at Prather and Newcomb, with over ninety percent being Mississippi Plain or Bell Plain. Shippingport stands out in having the greatest incidence of early Mississippian cordmarking, a surface treatment that does not continue into late Mississippian at the site. The occurrence of mixed shell-tempered ceramics at all three sites suggests a temper recipe that is transitional between the Woodland grit (or grit and other temper types) and Mississippian unmixed shell temper. These variable temper combinations may have been in use at the same time or may have shifted in popularity over time.

SUBSISTENCE

Analysis of the small suites of plant and animal remains recovered from Prather showed that maize and nuts were the common plant foods (Turner 2006), while animal remains include terrestrial and aquatic fauna (Garniewicz 2006). Specialized facilities for processing plant foods are the bedrock metates and mortars along the site's western slope. In samples of charcoal from hand-excavated contexts, hickory and black walnut shells, corn kernels, cupules, cob fragments, and a single large pawpaw seed were identified. In six flotation samples, corn kernels are ubiquitous and occur in much greater density than cupules. Nutshell and a low number of wild seeds also are present in the flotation samples, but an interregional comparison of sites suggests that "use of corn may have been more intense at Prather than at other Late Prehistoric communities," including Angel (Munson et al. 2006:115–18; Turner 2006). Faunal analysis of two hand-excavation units at Prather identified 13 mammal, three bird, five reptile, two amphibian, and six fish species, as well as five mollusk species, with deer, turkey, and raccoon dominating the assemblage (Garniewicz 2006). The limited exploitation of fish seen at Prather contrasts with that found in early Mississippian household contexts located along the Ohio River at Shippingport, where the ratio of mammal to fish elements is about 1.8:1, but is similar to that documented at the contemporary upstream Fort Ancient sites and to that documented at the later Eva Bandman site (Breitburg 1992; Madsen et al. 2016; Ross-Stallings 2010a:Tables 23.6 and 23.7; see Chapter 12). The upland setting did not deter the Prather inhabitants from consuming fish and practicing other classic Mississippian foodways, but it may have shaped their emphases. Economic costs of the upland setting at Prather would have included less fertile soils compared to the alluvial valley, as well as travel time to transport fish and mussels, or production costs for goods to exchange with riverside villagers for aquatic foods.

Early Mississippian sites elsewhere in the Falls region also reflect the intensity of maize agriculture (Rossen 2010, 2014). At Shippingport, corn kernels and cupules dominated the plant remains from the Early Mississippian component; gourd rind, three native cultigens, nutshell, and wild plant seeds also were recovered (Rossen 2010:355–56), as were beans, but their association with these deposits may be a result of mixing, since some archaeologists argue beans postdate 1300 CE (Rossen 2010:360).

Although no corncobs were identified at Prather or Shippingport, at Newcomb, cob segments and fragments of both eight-row and twelve-row varieties were recovered, suggesting interactions between early Mississippian and Fort Ancient groups that are not reflected in the early Mississippian material culture (Rossen 2013; Turner 2011; see Chapter 10). The macrobotanical analysis at Newcomb also found "evidence of broad spectrum wild plant collecting, including fleshy fruits and medicine. . . . The nutshell density is within known values for other Mississippian sites, far greater than in the contemporary Fort Ancient areas" (Rossen 2013:308).

Mississippian Identity and Exchange Relations

The limited amount of early Mississippian excavated contexts in the Falls region makes it difficult to determine the extent and frequency of trade in extra-regional goods. The recovery of a conch shell gorget, a copper nugget, and the copper eagle or falcon representation indicates that the Prather elites were participating, at least minimally, in wider Mississippian extra-regional trade networks. Thus far, only sumptuary goods found in special high-status contexts have been recorded, while the exotic cherts and stone hoes traded throughout the Mississippian world (Cobb 2000) are not evident in Falls region early Mississippian contexts.

What is clear is that the most tangible sign of exchange relationships is the participation in a network of Mississippian ideas and symbols. The people occupying the Falls region incorporated what it was to be Mississippian into most aspects of their lives, ranging from construction of flat-top mounds and plaza spaces, and development of a religious/political center, to architectural forms, iconography, foodways, and material culture. In one of the more visible mediums, local populations emulated Mississippian pottery manufacturing techniques, such as shell tempering, jar morphology, a wider diversity of vessel forms, and non-textured surfaces. The temporal lag in a shift to shell tempering and plain surfaces that is seen with the early Mississippian pottery strengthens the case for an in situ Mississippianization of the local population, with the earliest shell-tempered ceramics in both domestic and mound contexts at Prather radiocarbon dated between 1012 and 1164 CE (Table 11.2; Figure 11.1). This local adoption of style is also evident with the Ramey Incised–like vessels from Prather, in which the motifs are stylized representations of the Ramey design. Ramey vessels manufactured at Cahokia have a distinctive seam where the neck was attached to the shoulder of the vessel. This is a result of the standardization of production within the Cahokian region and a hallmark of the vessels made there. Thus far, this distinctive attribute has not been observed in early Mississippian contexts in the Falls region.

The wide geographic distribution of Ramey Incised imitations is better known north and northwest of Cahokia (Emerson 1991; Finney and Stoltman 1991) but is seldom noted to Cahokia's east. The Ramey Incised–like sherds at Prather, and possibly Shippingport, are similar to Ramey Incised copies elsewhere in the greater Ohio valley: at Angel (Hilgeman 2000), at the Annis Mound in western Kentucky (Hammerstedt 2005), and at the Fort Ancient sites of Turpin and State Line (Riggs 1986; Vickery et al. 2000). While geographic distance might suggest Angel as the point of inspiration for Ramey symbolism at Prather and elsewhere east of Angel, it is remarkable that the far more common decorated vessels at Angel—the negative painted plates—are unknown at Prather and elsewhere in the Falls region until the late Mississippian subperiod (Pollack et al. 2010; see Chapter 12). Further, the dates for Angel's largest mound (Mound A) are about a half century later than those for Prather's Southwest Mound (Monaghan and Peebles 2010). Thus, it seems more plausible that during the early Mississippian subperiod, both Prather and Angel received Ramey symbols from Cahokia, rather than one from the other.

It is also clear that this exchange of Mississippian ideas continues through time. The wider temporal trends evident in the Mississippian world are reflected in the Falls region. For example, changes in jar rim morphology across much of the Mississippian world occur in rims found at the sites in the Falls region. Compared to early Mississippian ceramics, later contexts in the Falls region show a proliferation of other pottery vessel forms and a greater occurrence of nonlocal ceramic styles (Pollack et al. 2010; see Chapter 12), demonstrating an increase in the exchange of ideas among Mississippian groups over a broad area. In domestic architecture, structures from limited excavated contexts in the Falls region (French 2010; Simpson et al. 2013) follow the general Mississippian shift from single-set posts to an increased frequency of wall-trench construction through time (Hammerstedt 2005; Lacquemont 2007; Pauketat 1998). Roof shape and house appearance followed this construction shift, with bent-pole, rounded roofs shifting to hip roofs or gabled, peaked roofs (e.g., Alt and Pauketat 2011). Radiocarbon dates suggest that wall-trench architecture was established at the Prather mound center earlier than at other sites, perhaps with the initial emplacement of Mississippian ideology (Table 11.2).

Recognizing exchange relationships outside the Mississippian sphere of influence is more difficult. From an examination of the material culture recovered thus far, there does not appear to be any significant exchange between those living in the Falls region and the Fort Ancient groups upriver during the early Mississippian subperiod. In fact, the presence of significant quantities of Fort Ancient pottery is a major hallmark of the later Mississippian occupations of the Falls region (Madsen et al. 2016; Pollack et al. 2010). Yet there is evidence of exchange with groups north of Indianapolis at the Castor site (McCullough 2015). Castor is a later Late Woodland group with a Great Lakes affiliation that eventually combined with middle Fort Ancient people to form the Oliver phase. In the fill of a large communal structure basin, a small, shell-tempered vessel with a stylized Ramey–like design (McCullough 2005:152) was recovered. This example is similar to the Ramey–like pottery recovered from the Prather site. Several other early Mississippi Plain rim sherds recovered from the same basin fill also were similar those recovered from Prather. Three radiocarbon dates place the filling of this structure contemporary with Prather at a two sigma maximum range of 1020–1285 CE (McCullough 2015:Table 1).

Conclusions

The early Mississippian mound center at Prather, in addition to the occupation of smaller settlements throughout the Falls region, is a mystery in many ways. Prather was the earliest Mississippian site in the Falls region and dates only slightly later than the initial Mississippian centers in the Mississippi River valley. Comparable to the Aztalan site in southern Wisconsin (Birmingham and Goldstein 2006; Goldstein and Richards 1991), Prather may have been founded by a small group of immigrants from the west—perhaps from the Cahokia center (Fowler 1997; Pauketat 2009)—who introduced Mississippian mound ceremonialism and lifeways to the Late Woodland people who had lived for centuries in the Falls region. Missionaries from Cahokia are thought to have brought Mississippian beliefs and lifeways to Trempealeau in Wisconsin (Pauketat et al. 2015), Collins in eastern Illinois (Butler 2016; Douglas 1976), and other distant regions (e.g., Emerson 1991; Finney and Stoltman 1991), where Late Woodland cultures appear to have been Mississippianized. Alternatively, Falls region Terminal Late Woodland people may have brought with them new knowledge and beliefs upon their return home from visits to Cahokia, a process suggested for the Yankeetown culture of southwestern Indiana (Alt 2006, 2010). The returnees may have been related to those who made the grit-tempered, primarily cordmarked pottery at the M. Kraft site or the grit-tempered, primarily plain pottery at Prather.

Between the Mississippian sites in the Falls region and those of the Angel phase centered at the mouth of the Green River (Green and Munson 1978; Hammerstedt 2005), there is a well-documented eighty-five-kilometers-long "no-Mississippians-land" (Munson et al. 1977). To the east and upstream from Prather were contemporary Fort Ancient villages. These groups did not construct platform mounds and had a more egalitarian lifestyle (Pollack and Henderson 1992). Extra-regional interaction between early Mississippians living in the Falls region and early Fort Ancient groups is not evident in the archaeological record, though surely these groups were aware of each other. The nearest known Fort Ancient village that may be contemporaneous with Prather is the Casey site (15Sh6), located in Shelby County, Kentucky, about fifty kilometers southeast of Prather (Sharp 1990:476). Upriver from the Falls of the Ohio, there is a paucity of Fort Ancient villages along the Ohio River until Boone County, Kentucky, and Ohio County, Indiana, around the mouth of Laughrey Creek, making another thinly occupied area stretching over ninety-five kilometers to the northeast.

The early Mississippian occupation, then, was buffered on each side by stretches of thinly occupied land where there would have been little competition for resources. From a regional perspective, however, Prather's location between the Mississippian Angel polity to the southwest and Fort Ancient groups to the east suggests that an understanding of its development as a frontier Mississippian outpost is more appropriate than its classification as a "dilute" form of Mississippian. Prather participated in interregional exchange—copper and marine shell—and employed other classic Mississippian artifacts and symbols, including discoidals, diverse ceramic vessel forms, negative painted bottles, Ramey Incised–like pottery vessels, and depictions of falconids. But only about two centuries after Prather became a borderland Mississippian outpost and religious center, with little evidence of Fort Ancient interaction, the mound center was abandoned and multicultural communities of Mississippians and Fort Ancient peoples were established closer to the Ohio River in the Falls region (see Chapter 12). The Fort Ancient presence at later Mississippian sites, such as Shippingport and Eva Bandman, stands in sharp contrast to the virtually unmixed Mississippian character of the early Mississippian occupation.

ACKNOWLEDGMENTS

First and foremost, we give our most sincere thanks to Dr. T. Harold Martin, who has owned and cared for the Prather site for more than forty-five years, ceasing the deep plowing of the site and employing no-till farming that halted the erosion of its mounds. Dr. Martin, along with his family and Donna Kinser, welcomed our research project and provided gracious hospitality. Our colleagues and coauthors in research at Prather, Russell Stafford and Michael Strezewski, were crucial in that work. Additional contributors were Leslie Bush, Mark Cantin, Rex Garniewicz, Laura Kozuch, Susan Spencer, Jocelyn Turner, and Andrew White. Perry Harrell assisted in both field seasons. Ms. Jeanne Burke, Ms. Jane Sarles, and Ms. Bett Etenohan, all local historians, were generous with their time and local knowledge, as were archaeologists Phil DiBlasi, Duane Simpson, Steve Mocas, Michael French, Anne Bader, and David Pollack, who shared their archaeological knowledge of the Falls area. Thank you also to members of the Falls of the Ohio Archaeological Society and students at the University of Louisville who assisted with fieldwork at the Prather site, as well as to Patrick Munson who helped in field and lab work and in preparation of this chapter. We also wish to acknowledge the assistance of the Glenn A. Black Laboratory of Archaeology, Indiana University, and the Department of Anthropology, University of Louisville, for making collections available for our examination. Finally, we are especially grateful to Anne, David, Justin, and Dot McCullough for their skill and patience in editing numerous iterations of this chapter.

12

Mississippian/Fort Ancient Interaction and Identity in the Falls Region

MICHAEL W. FRENCH AND DAVID POLLACK

Archaeological research in the Falls region has documented a 450-year sequence of Mississippian use of this area: a sequence that parallels the development of Mississippian polities elsewhere in the lower Ohio valley. Though on the northeastern periphery of the distribution of Mississippian polities, as noted by Munson and McCullough, there is nothing in the archaeological record to suggest that the residents of the Falls region were not fully integrated into the Mississippian world (see Chapter 11). Based on research conducted at early and late Mississippian sites in the Falls region, we view Falls Mississippian as a regional expression distinguished from its Mississippian neighbors to the west and Fort Ancient neighbors to the east by a shared collective social identity (Comaroff and Comaroff 1992; Emberling 1997; Jones 2002; McBrinn and Webster 2008; Neitzel 2000). This shared identity can be expressed in a variety of ways (e.g., material culture, subsistence practices, and architectural styles).

Early in the Mississippian history of the Falls region, a broader social identity is reflected in ceramic forms and decoration (e.g., adoption of bowls and pans, in addition to the use of Ramey-like motifs to decorate jars), the presence of a mound center, and the construction of wall-trench houses. The establishment of a mound center, the clearing of land for agricultural fields, and the use of local resources for the construction of houses and for firewood would have altered the local environment and would have created challenges for the residents of Prather and associated settlements through soil degradation and depletion of other natural resources.

From 1000–1300 CE, shared experiences with Mississippian groups to the west also may have led to the adoption of religious practices tied to an agricultural way of life, and the rise of leaders (elites) who had some control over who had access to new information (see Chapter 11). These changes in social and political organization led to the adoption of a local Mississippian identity that resulted in the establishment of Prather (12Cl4) as a mound center and the development of a more hierarchical society (see Chapter 11), at least relative to earlier Woodland groups and contemporary village farming neighbors to the north and east.

By 1300 CE, there appears to have been changes in the Mississippian social order within the Falls region and elsewhere. The Prather mound center was abandoned, or at least was not being intensively occupied. With its decline, households seem to have relocated to smaller villages or hamlets, such as Shippingport (15Jf702) (French 2010), Smith-Sutton (12Cl130), Ellingsworth (12Cl27) (Arnold and Graham 2011a, 2011b; Wells et al. 2008), and Eva Bandman (15Jf668) (Madsen et al. 2016) (Figure 1.7; Tables 11.1 and 11.2). Following this reorganization of people on the local landscape and a decentralization of power, the residents of the Falls region continued to maintain relationships with the downstream Angel polity. At the same time, they increased their interactions/entanglements with neighboring Fort Ancient groups to the east. These interactions may have led some Fort Ancient households to relocate to the Falls region.

In the remainder of this chapter, we examine late Mississippian ceramics, subsistence practices, and settlement patterns in the Falls region for what they can tell us about social identity and Mississippian/Fort Ancient interaction.

CERAMICS

Throughout the Ohio valley and elsewhere, social identity and social networks are often reflected in ceramics (Hegmon et al. 2008; Henderson 1992b; Nelson et al. 2011; Peeples 2011; Pollack 2004; Pollack and Henderson 2000), and the Falls region is no exception. Within small scale societies, pottery production is a learned behavior and most ceramic vessels are produced locally and used in a variety of domestic activities or during certain rituals (Arnold 1985, 1989; Peeples 2011:360; Pollack 2004). Characteristics (e.g., surface treatment, vessel form, temper type and size, and decoration) of the pottery recovered from Shippingport (Pollack et al. 2010) and Eva Bandman (Madsen et al. 2016) were used to distinguish ceramics manufactured by Mississippian potters from their Fort Ancient counterparts. These characteristics also were used to identify the presence of ceramics, such as fragments of negative painted vessels, that may have been manufactured

Figure 12.1. Ceramic jar handles: *top row*, Mississippi Plain; *bottom row*, Fort Ancient.

elsewhere and transported to the Falls region by those who had visited the downstream Angel site.

Falls region late Mississippian ceramic assemblages are characterized by Mississippi and Bell Plain jars, bowls, plates and bottles, and Kimmswick Fabric Impressed or Kimmswick Plain pans. Appendages consist primarily of handles (Figure 12.1), lugs, nodes, and effigy rimriders. There are only a few Mississippian ceramic traits that serve to distinguish Falls region ceramics from their Mississippian neighbors. The most prominent is the annular ring associated with some bowl bases. Though most prevalent at Eva Bandman, bowls with these rings have also been found at Shippingport and Smith-Sutton (Arnold et al. 2012; Madsen et al. 2016; Pollack et al. 2010).

In general, surface treatment, vessel form, decoration, and appendage forms are most similar to those of the Angel 3 component (1325–1450 CE) at the Angel site (Hilgeman 2000; Munson 1994; Pollack et al. 2010). Among the most obvious similarities is a preference for the use of a red slip (Old Town Red) rather than incised or trailed motifs to decorate jars and bowls (Hilgeman 2000; Madsen et al. 2016; Pollack et al. 2010). The overall similarity of the ceramic assemblages recovered from the Falls and Angel regions reflects interregional interaction (Hilgeman 2000; Munson 1994; Pollack et

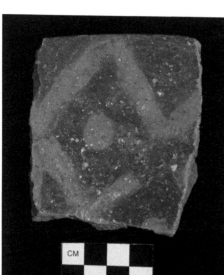

Figure 12.2. Angel Negative Painted plate.

al. 2010). The presence of types, such as Tolu Fabric Impressed, reflects interaction with groups located downstream from Angel, and in the case of Parkin Punctate, those who lived in the central Mississippi valley.

It is quite likely that the Angel/Kincaid Negative Painted ceramics recovered from Shippingport were manufactured at the Angel site (Figure 12.2) and were transported to the site by those who had visited this important regional center. As has been argued for Ramey Incised, negative painted vessels may have had symbolic significance within Mississippian society, and possession of even a fragment of a vessel may have increased one's prestige (cf., Pauketat and Emerson 1991). This symbolism may be reflected in a negative painted sherd recovered from the floor of House 3 at the Shippingport site (Figure 12.2). The rectangular shape of the sherd, with the dot-in-diamond motif centered on the interior surface, suggests that this motif had symbolic significance within the Shippingport community.

The presence of substantial amounts of Fort Ancient ceramics serves to distinguish the late Falls Mississippian collections from Eva Bandman and Shippingport (Figure 11.1), not only from their neighbors living at Smith-Sutton and Ellingsworth, but also from Mississippian groups living downstream in the lower Ohio River as well (Madsen et al. 2016; Pollack et al. 2010). At Eva Bandman and Shippingport, Fort Ancient ceramic types account for about twenty to twenty-five percent, respectively, of each site's ceramic assemblage. In contrast to the high percentage of Fort Ancient

Figure 12.3. Oliver Cordmarked jars.

pottery at these two sites, only a few Fort Ancient sherds have been recovered from Smith-Sutton and none have been recovered from Ellingsworth (Arnold and Graham 2011b; Wells et al. 2008).

Most of the Fort Ancient ceramics from the Falls region resemble late middle Fort Ancient (1300–1400 CE) Anderson Ceramic Series, particularly Anderson Shell-Tempered, *variety Anderson,* found primarily in southeastern Indiana/southwestern Ohio/northern Kentucky, and early late Fort Ancient (1400–1500 CE) Madisonville Cordmarked found throughout the entire Fort Ancient region (Essenpreis 1982; Griffin 1943; Henderson 1993; Turnbow and Henderson 1992). This resemblance is attributed to similarities in temper (predominance of shell temper), vessel form (jars with rimfold/rimstrip/rimstrip-like thickened rims, and rounded or rounded-pointed lips), decoration (high percentage of guilloche designs), thin fine cordmarking, and a predominance of thin triangular strap handles (Griffin 1943; Henderson 1993) (Figure 12.1).

In addition to Anderson/Madisonville-like pottery, the presence of a small number of Oliver ceramics reflects interaction with more northerly Fort Ancient groups who resided in central Indiana along the White River (Madsen et al. 2016; McCullough 2000, 2005; Redmond and McCullough 2000; Pollack et al. 2010) (Figure 12.3). Though not as prevalent as the Anderson Series ceramics, some of the Fort Ancient ceramics resemble Oliver Cordmarked and Oliver Plain from south-central Indiana (McCullough 2000; Redmond and McCullough 2000). Attributes shared in common by these ceramics with Oliver ceramics include a predominance of grit or grit-sand as a temper agent, decorated rimfolds/rimstrips, and guilloche designs.

About one quarter of the Fort Ancient ceramics at Shippingport and Eva Bandman are decorated, which is similar to the amount of decoration documented at the early Madisonville horizon Capitol View (15Fr101) (Henderson 1992a) and New Field (15Bb45) (Henderson and Pollack 1996:214; Lacy 1996:179) sites. In general, within the Fort Ancient region, the end of the middle Fort Ancient subperiod and the beginning of the late Fort Ancient subperiod is marked by an increase in jar neck decoration (Turnbow and Henderson 1992). This trend is reflected in the Shippingport and Eva Bandman Fort Ancient ceramic materials.

The Mississippian and Fort Ancient ceramic vessels found at Eva Bandman and Shippingport were recovered from the same contexts and exhibit similar spatial distributions within their respective sites. At both sites, these vessels were produced from local alluvial clays and lack manganese or hematite concretions that are common in the clays used by interior Fort Ancient groups to manufacture ceramic vessels (Madsen et al. 2016; Pollack et al. 2010). The archaeological evidence thus suggests that the ceramic assemblages from both sites were produced locally by Mississippian and Fort Ancient potters. That Fort Ancient ceramics account for about one quarter of the sherds recovered from Eva Bandman and Shippingport raises the possibility that Fort Ancient families were residing within each village.

Surprisingly, in the Falls region there was a lack of hybridization or blending of Mississippian and Fort Ancient ceramic traits, as for instance occurred when Caborn-Welborn potters incorporated Oneota designs within their ceramic motifs/decorative tradition (Pollack 2004). Rather, in the Falls region, Mississippian ceramics look like Mississippi Plain jars, Bell Plain bowls, and Kimmswick Plain and Fabric Impressed pans. Likewise, Anderson-like and Oliver cordmarked and plain jars look like their Fort Ancient counterparts. In addition, there are no obvious signs that Mississippian potters attempted to emulate Fort Ancient ceramic jars or vice versa. The jars are well-made, and the vessel forms and execution of the decorative motifs are consistent with late middle/early late Fort Ancient ceramics recovered from sites to the east and north of the Falls region (Henderson 1992b, 1993). We interpret the large percentage of Fort Ancient pottery present at Shippingport and Eva Bandman to be indicative of Fort Ancient people residing within these Mississippian settlements, as opposed to the pottery merely being acquired through trade. The lack of hybridization may illustrate how these people held on to their social identity even while living in the same village and perhaps even intermarrying.

SUBSISTENCE PRACTICES

Plant remains recovered from Eva Bandman and Shippingport reflect aspects of Mississippian and Fort Ancient social identity based on the foods they consumed or those that were not eaten (see Chapter 10). As with material culture, elements of both Fort Ancient and Mississippian plant use systems have been identified in the botanical remains recovered from Eva Bandman and Shippingport (Madsen et al. 2016; Rossen 2010). Varieties of corn associated with both cultures (Fort Ancient "Eastern Eight" and Mississippian "Midwestern Twelve") are present. In the Ohio valley, prior to 1300 CE, *Phaseolus* beans are almost exclusively associated with Fort Ancient populations. This suggests that beans were brought to the Falls region by Fort Ancient households. The presence of native cultigens, particularly maygrass (*Phalaris caroliniana*) and marshelder (*Iva annua*), which were heavily used and hybridized by western Kentucky Mississippians, is a clear-cut Mississippian plant use trait. In contrast, plants like sumac, blackberry, grape, and pawpaw are generally associated with Fort Ancient groups, who more strongly maintained a wild plant collecting component that emphasized fleshy fruits. The high nutshell densities are much more like Mississippian than like Fort Ancient patterns (see Chapter 10).

Overall, the botanical collections from Shippingport and Eva Bandman display plant use indicators of a permeable boundary. The former exhibits a continued preference for a Mississippian plant use strategy. On the other hand, the near absence of native cultigens, low nutshell densities, and the presence of beans at Eva Bandman is more consistent with Fort Ancient subsistence strategies. The plants consumed at both villages reflect the social choices of the residents of each village (Rossen 2010). While both Shippingport and Eva Bandman showed permeability along the cultural boundary, the residents of Shippingport appear to have been more culturally conservative in that they retained a more Mississippian plant use strategy (see Chapter 10).

Also significant is the environmental reconstruction based on an enormous wood charcoal collection. Shippingport clearly exhibits the diverse oak-hickory hardwood forest that has been documented throughout much of northeastern and western Kentucky (Rossen 2010). This contrasts with the oak-chestnut-elm forest cul-de-sac that has been indicated by the Eva Bandman wood collection. As noted by Rossen (2010), these cul-de-sac areas have been documented ethnohistorically. While variation in forest composition may have led to the establishment of a settlement at a particular locality, it probably did not influence community subsistence practices.

Rather, plant use near the Mississippian-Fort Ancient boundary after 1300 CE reflects choices made by those living in the Falls region. These decisions led them to incorporate aspects of both Mississippian and Fort Ancient domesticated tropical plants, native starchy-oily seeded cultigens, and a wide variety of native plants from various ecosystems within their subsistence strategies (Rossen 2010).

Social identity also may be reflected in Falls Mississippian faunal exploitation, though the patterns are not entirely clear. Based on her analysis of the faunal remains from Eva Bandman, Peres (Madsen et al. 2016) suggests that animal exploitation practices were primarily based on environment and geographical location, with cultural practices and traditions exhibiting less influence over animal subsistence practices. She goes on to note that the paucity of fish remains at Eva Bandman, coupled with a reliance on bear and elk, is more consistent with Fort Ancient than with Mississippian animal consumption. On the other hand, the Shippingport faunal assemblage, with its relatively high percentage of fish remains, is more typical of Mississippian faunal exploitation patterns (Ross-Stallings 2010b). These differences in animal exploitation parallel plant use choices made by the residents of these communities.

SETTLEMENT PATTERNS

In general, village size, house size, and construction methods (wall-trench construction) in the Falls region are consistent with those of a small Mississippian village (Shippingport [2.5 ha], Smith-Sutton [1.2 ha], and Ellingsworth [1.1 ha]) (Green and Munson 1978; Pollack 2004). A geophysical survey of Smith-Sutton identified 33 anomalies that have been interpreted as the remains of Mississippian structures surrounding a central plaza (Arnold and Graham 2011b; Arnold et al. 2012:17, 20). Examination of the distribution of these anomalies suggested that they were aligned in rows or clusters (Arnold et al. 2012:17). As with Smith-Sutton, the houses at Shippingport appear to have been organized around a central plaza, though the interpretation of this pattern may be influenced by the placement of the borrow pit in the middle of the site. A possible palisade was delineated along the southeastern edge of the Smith-Sutton site (Wells et al. 2008). It is not known if palisades were associated with other late Mississippian sites in the Falls region.

Limited excavations at Smith-Sutton and Ellingsworth have documented the association of wall-trenches with some of the structures (Arnold and Graham 2011a; Arnold et al. 2012). Late Mississippian wall-trench structures

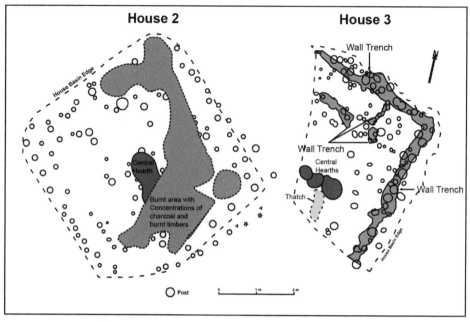

Figure 12.4. Mississippian houses (after French and Schatz 2010: Figure 17.10 and 17.14).

also have been documented at Shippingport (French 2010), though most of the structures are of single pole construction (Figures 12.4 and 12.5). Structures were probably present at Eva Bandman, but none have been documented in the limited area investigated.

Based on the size of various anomalies documented at Smith-Sutton, it has been suggested that houses at this village measured approximately 6-×-8-m (Arnold et al. 2012). This is somewhat larger than the structures at Shippingport, which ranged in size from 4-×-4-m to 5.0-×-5.5-m (French 2010). These differences in house size may be related to the geophysical anomalies at Smith-Sutton, which are larger than the living surface enclosed by the wall-trenches. Since the geophysical data measures the size of the house basin, the large anomalies may incorporate areas that extend beyond the structure's walls, making them look larger than the structures at Shippingport.

At Shippingport, houses tended to be oriented between 58 and 66 degrees west of north (Figure 12.5). When structures were rebuilt, they continued to be oriented in a similar manner. Structures often had a prepared central hearth, with evidence of hearth cleaning, reuse, and reconstruction being documented at the site (Figure 12.4). Small storage or discard pits, and possible benches or interior racks, were found in association with several structures.

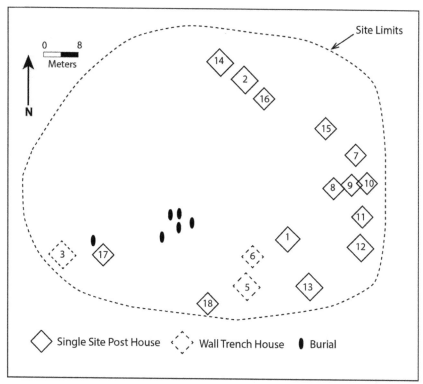

Figure 12.5. Distribution of houses and burials at Shippingport site (after French and Schatz 2010:Figure 17.8).

In comparison to Shippingport, Smith-Sutton, and Ellingsworth, Eva Bandman may have been a smaller settlement, though this may be a deceptive impression, since over the years the site has been severely impacted by development. Though this multi-component site encompasses 8 ha, the spatial distribution of Mississippian materials is not known insofar as the investigated area encompasses only 450 m². What Eva Bandman does share with the other late Mississippian sites is an intensive trash disposal area consisting of pits and midden. The presence of a small cemetery has been documented at this site and at Shippingport, and the presence of burials has been noted at Smith-Sutton. At Shippingport, the cemetery would have been situated between the edge of what may have been a plaza, and the domestic structures. At Eva Bandman and Smith-Sutton, the possible relationship of the burials to domestic structures could not be determined.

In general, late Mississippian house construction in the Falls region is consistent with that found elsewhere in the lower Ohio River valley. Houses tend to be square and can be constructed within single set posts or wall-trenches. Most have formal hearths, and rebuilding in place is common. Unfortunately, the manner in which space was used in late Mississippian villages in this region is poorly known. Overall, late Mississippian settlement patterns in the Falls region reflect a continuation of Mississippian traditions.

MISSISSIPPIAN-FORT ANCIENT ENTANGLEMENTS

The presence of a large number of Fort Ancient ceramics within Mississippian settlements does raise a critical question. Why would the inhabitants of the Falls region, who previously had limited interaction with their eastern neighbors (see Chapters 10 and 11), at least as reflected in their material culture and plant subsistence strategies, welcome Fort Ancient households into their communities? What spurred these increased/new entanglements among groups that seemingly avoided one another for countless prior generations, and why is there more evidence of this interaction at some villages but not at others?

The answer likely is in part explained by changes that were underway throughout much of the Mississippian and Fort Ancient worlds toward the end of the fourteenth century. The period from 1300 to 1450 CE in the Southeast and Midwest, including the lower and middle Ohio River valleys, was a time of change. People were reorganizing themselves on the landscape, with many Mississippian regional mound centers and associated communities being abandoned (Cobb and Butler 2002; Pollack 2004). Downstream from the Falls of the Ohio River, following the collapse of the Angel polity, during the subsequent Caborn-Welborn phase, the bulk of the population relocated to villages centered at the mouth of the Wabash River. Upstream from the Falls region, this trend coincided with population aggregation within reconfigured Fort Ancient villages. These changes in settlement patterns correspond with changes in social and political organization (Henderson 1992b, 2008; Pollack and Henderson 2000). Throughout the lower and middle Ohio valley, this time period also is marked by a reorientation and expansion of long-distance exchange relationships with Mississippian groups to the south and Oneota groups to the north. After 1400 CE, Fort Ancient site assemblages, as well as those associated with downstream Caborn-Welborn Mississippian sites, are marked by an increased presence of marine shell objects, some engraved with Mississippian iconography, catlinite pipes, and later copper and brass objects (Henderson 2008; Pollack 2004, 2008).

While the Mississippian settlements in the Falls region appear to have maintained strong relations with the downstream Angel polity throughout the fourteenth century, their access to other Mississippian polities may have been curtailed. This situation may have led the residents of late Mississippian villages in the Falls region to establish new external relationships. In so doing, they may have looked to the east and the north, and they may have increased their interaction and entanglements with their Fort Ancient neighbors. It also is possible that as Fort Ancient groups reorganized themselves on the landscape and became more outward looking, they became interested in forging new relationships with Mississippian communities. As a result, some Fort Ancient households may have relocated to established Mississippian communities to solidify newly negotiated relationships between Fort Ancient groups and Falls region Mississippian villages.

Contextualized in this manner, late Falls Mississippian settlements represent communities that were negotiating new social entanglements along the Mississippian periphery in order to maintain and reaffirm their sense of community and identity. These social negotiations occurred both externally with their Fort Ancient neighbors as well as internally among village residents. New relations between otherwise different and separate cultural traditions may have made sense at this time, as leaders sought to maintain their positions within Falls Mississippian society. Fort Ancient households may have moved into or may have moved closer to Mississippian communities as a way of formalizing these new external social relations.

Conclusions

The intensification of social and economic ties between Falls region late Mississippian groups and their Fort Ancient neighbors coincides with extensive social changes that were occurring throughout the lower Ohio and Green River valleys. By the late fourteenth century, many Mississippian polities situated to the east and south of the Falls Region had collapsed or were in decline. The social networks that had helped to sustain the Falls region's Mississippian identity for more than three hundred years had become unreliable. Cut off from some past alliances, though still maintaining a strong relationship with the downstream Angel polity, the residents of the Falls region appear to have looked elsewhere for groups with whom to forge new mutually beneficial relationships. These new entanglements may have led Fort Ancient households to relocate to Shippingport and Eva Bandman. Within both communities the social identity of these newcomers was reflected in the ceramics they or their household produced and in their subsistence practices. The lack of hybridization of Mississippian and Fort Ancient ceramics suggests that the social identities of those who manufactured these vessels were maintained throughout the life of both communities.

Though the late Mississippian residents of the Falls region were able to establish new external relationships with their Fort Ancient neighbors following the abandonment of the Prather site, they do not appear to have been able to sustain them. Unlike their Caborn-Welborn neighbors to the west and their Fort Ancient neighbors to the east, who were able to do so until the established networks were disrupted following European contact, those living in the Falls region were not as successful. As a result, by 1450 CE there were no remaining substantial Mississippian settlements in the Falls region.

ACKNOWLEDGMENTS

The authors would like to thank the staff of Wood (formerly AMEC Earth & Environment), who assisted in the excavation of the Shippingport site, analysis, and report preparation. We also would like to thank Hayward Wilkirson for taking the artifact photographs.

13

The Falls

A Changing Cultural Landscape

DAVID POLLACK, ANNE TOBBE BADER,
JUSTIN N. CARLSON, AND RICHARD W. JEFFERIES

As the only major natural impediment along the one-thousand-five-hun-
dred-kilometers course of the Ohio River, the Falls of the Ohio River was a
constant and recognizable landmark for millennia. Because it was a difficult
landscape feature to pass without a portage, mobile hunter-gatherer groups
often stopped and camped there. At the Falls, the river was rocky and shallow. The river bed consisted of Devonian period fossil beds, which allowed
for easy pedestrian crossing of the river during periods of low water. The
river also was a major corridor leading from the northeast to the far south
(and *vice versa*) via its juncture with the Mississippi River. The Falls of the
Ohio River thus became a crossroads where travelers and traders converged.
It is, therefore, not surprising that interaction between and influences from
other groups that once inhabited adjacent parts of the Midwest and Southeast are evident in the archaeological record of the Falls region.

A FALLS REGION HISTORICITY

Archaeological data from the Falls region, when considered from a historical ecological perspective, provides an opportunity to examine the interplay of societal and environmental changes on a defined landscape over
several millennia (Balée 2006; Crumley 1994). Notions such as historicity,
in which cultural developments occur in a time of specific interweaving of
social, political, and environmental conditions, are integral to this approach
(Balée 2006; Crumley 1994; Håkansson and Widgren 2014; Sassaman 2010).
One of the greatest strengths of this volume's chapters is that they highlight

numerous environmental and cultural variables that played a role in the everyday lives of groups that lived in the Falls region.

Over several millennia, Native Americans anchored themselves to the Falls region, making significant cultural investments. This region's rich resource base may have initially attracted them, but it soon became the locus of their daily lives. This process of settling in was neither smooth nor simple, and though the landform was an anchor, the region's history was marked by dynamic social, economic, and environmental shifts and perturbations. Efforts to maintain stasis, as well as renegotiations with the land and with other groups, are seen through communication, such as signaling affiliations by the objects that they manufactured.

Holistic examination of available interdisciplinary archaeological and environmental data has allowed for in-depth and meaningful discussions concerning the lifeways of groups during specific chronological eras and the transitions between them. By the Early Archaic, the Falls region had become a part of the social memory of indigenous groups (Chapter 2). Perhaps the strongest indications of this social memory lie in the eventual anchoring of familial ties to the landscape through mortuary practices, the construction of houses, and the maintenance of settlements during the Middle and Late Archaic.

Whether they are the locations of long-term settlement or slowly deposited accumulations of midden, some sites, such as shell and rock middens with spatially segregated domestic and mortuary components, are suggestive of the sustained reuse of some localities (Chapter 4). These places were special, revisited, added to, and remembered. Perhaps they became localities that held a special significance for ancestral veneration and social memory. Intraregional conflict may be attributable to efforts to establish and maintain territorial boundaries, and to protect or restrict access to mussel beds and forest stands with potential for silviculture (Chapters 4, 5, and 7). Modification of the environment and selective harvesting of plants occurred (Chapter 8). The establishment of long-term settlements through construction of houses and platform mounds further demonstrates an intention to invest in this region and to call it home (Chapters 6, 8, 9, 11, and 12). As Burdin notes in Chapter 6, by the Late Archaic, a sense of ancestral connection had developed, with particular groups regularly returning to certain loci within smaller home ranges. Over time, the Falls of the Ohio River may have taken on new or different cultural or ideological meanings.

Human landscape use is patterned in the archaeological record of any given region. For instance, Stafford suggests that Early Archaic hunter-gatherers aggregated to procure chert and to manufacture flaked stone tools

(Chapter 2). On the other hand, Middle Archaic hunter-gatherers dispersed across the landscape, possibly as a response to patchy resource distributions associated with the Holocene Climatic Optimum (Chapter 3). Expansion of settlements into wetland areas toward the end of the Middle Archaic may be associated with the establishment of social boundaries brought about by population growth or by increased immigration of groups into the region (Chapter 4). This may have led to competition with established groups for existing resources, such as wetland plants and animals. By the early Late Archaic, competition for resources may have led to increased interpersonal violence (Chapters 4, 5, and 7). Throughout the Woodland period, local groups increased their reliance on the starchy-oily seeds of the Eastern Agricultural Complex (EAC) (Chapters 8, 9, and 10). As noted by Rossen and Turner (Chapter 10), an increased reliance on EAC plants represents a move away from the wetlands in favor of better drained upland environments and associated weedy annuals, in addition to the construction of niches favorable to plant cultivation. By ca. 1000 CE local groups increased their reliance on corn. With the environment of the Falls region being attractive to a Mississippian way of life, they established a mound complex at the Prather site (Chapter 11).

Native Americans impacted the landscape in specific and sometimes still identifiable ways (Kidder 2013; Thompson 2013). Doubtless, these activities indicate an investment in these landforms. Sustained activities in a single location may leave intensive scatters of cultural debris that have some impact on the soil characteristics at a site. A focus on nut mast during the Middle Archaic may have led to silviculture and the promotion of these species through selective forest clearance and burning. The traces of some environment-altering activities, such as the widespread burning of grasslands and forests, also are identifiable in the archaeological record of the Falls region (Rossen 2019). It also is plausible that high sedimentation rates documented at some Middle Archaic sites could have been partially caused by trampling or land clearance during the Middle Holocene (Carlson 2019a; Carlson and Pollack 2019; see Chapter 3).

Chert Resources

One of the most important natural resources for Archaic through Mississippian groups was chert, which was used in flaked stone tool production and often was exchanged with other groups for nonlocal goods. The Falls region is a chert-rich landscape, with high-quality Wyandotte, St. Louis, and Muldraugh cherts widely available. This important economic resource would have initially led groups to repeatedly visit the Falls region as part of their

seasonal rounds. Over time, these visits appear to have evolved into occupations that lasted for increasingly extended periods of time. During the
Early Archaic, Wyandotte chert was the preferred raw material for flaked
stone tool production, although if the high-quality variety of Muldraugh
was available, it was used as well. The importance of acquiring high-quality
tool stone for many of their implements appears to have influenced Early
Archaic group movement across the local landscape. As noted by Stafford
(Chapter 2), although Early Archaic hunter-gatherers in the Falls region
were highly mobile, their settlement patterns were at least partially structured by the availability of high-quality lithic material, which resulted in
some groups being tethered to specific locations on the landscape during
(at least) portions of their seasonal rounds.

During much of the Middle and Late Archaic, Muldraugh chert and other
immediately local but poorer quality fossiliferous materials and cherty river
cobbles were often used in preference to the high-quality Wyandotte chert
(Carlson and Pollack 2019). By the middle of the Late Archaic subperiod,
however, some projectile points, such as the RiverPark type, were almost
exclusively made of high-quality Wyandotte or St. Louis cherts (see Chapter 5). This trend continued into the Terminal Archaic (Chapter 8), when
there appears to have been a decided preference for Wyandotte chert for the
production of most formal flaked stone tools and, in particular, Turkey-tail
projectile points (see Figure 8.1). The distribution of this projectile point
style throughout the Eastern Woodlands and its association with Terminal
Archaic/Early Woodland ritual contexts suggest that by the beginning of
the Woodland period, Wyandotte chert had been ascribed symbolic significance. This led to its association with caches and burials some distance
from the Falls region. A preference for Wyandotte chert for formal tools
in the Falls region and its use in important rituals beyond the Falls region
continued into the Middle Woodland and is reflected in the production of
extremely large caches of Middle Woodland preforms (see Chapters 8 and
9). By the end of the Late Woodland subperiod and continuing into the
Mississippi period, a greater emphasis was once again placed on local lithic
resources, such as Muldraugh chert and river gravels (see Chapter 9).

Social Identity and Boundedness

For over twelve thousand years, the Falls region was variably a destination, a
central meeting place, a boundary, and a bridge. Though one should be careful in equating objects with social identity, individuals and groups often use
material culture to express who they are and to distinguish themselves from

their neighbors (Diaz-Andreu et al. 2005:1; Jefferies 1997; Peeples 2011:2; see Chapters 6 and 12). As noted in Chapter 1, during the course of a lifetime, individuals can have multiple identities constructed through interaction, informed by history, culturally mediated, and acquired through agency (Barth 1969; Calhoun 1995; Díaz-Andreu et al. 2005; Emberling 1997; Jenkins 2008; Jones 2002; Peeples 2011). Within the Falls region, identity was often expressed by projectile point styles, ceramic decoration, bannerstone styles, bone pin decoration, mortuary practices, and subsistence choices.

By at least the Early Archaic, the rich environment of the Falls region was attracting groups from north (associated with Thebes points) and south (Kirk points) of the Ohio River (Chapter 2). A local identity is reflected in the Pine Tree Kirk variety of the Falls region, and by the early Middle Archaic by Knob Creek Stemmed points (Chapter 3). During the early portion of the Middle Archaic, those living in the region appear to continue to have had greater affinities with those living to the south, with an emphasis on corner notched biface technologies, as reflected by the presence of Middle Archaic Corner Notched points. Toward the end of the Middle Archaic, however, there was greater interaction with groups downriver to the west-southwest, as reflected by the presence of shell middens, Matanzas projectile points, and decorated bone pins (Chapter 4). This more westerly interaction continued into the Late Archaic. During this subperiod, a distinctive Falls area identity appears to emerge, reflected by a distinctive bannerstone style and the local RiverPark projectile point style (Chapters 5 and 6).

A subsequent local identity is reflected by Early Woodland ceramics, such as Zorn Punctate, a ceramic type unique to the Falls region (Chapter 9). Toward the end of the Early Woodland, those groups living in the Falls region appear to have had greater affinities and interactions with groups living to the east. This is reflected by Falls Plain pottery, a variety of Adena Plain. This similarity in material culture did not extend to the construction of monumental architecture in the Falls region, such as the burial mounds and earthen enclosures found in central Kentucky. This suggests that Falls region Middle Woodland groups may have chosen not to participate in Adena and Hopewell rituals, or if they did, they traveled to other regions to take part in these ceremonies. When they did so, they may have taken Wyandotte raw material, preforms, and finished tools to be used in rituals undertaken at those earthen enclosures or mortuary events. The large number of Wyandotte preforms and tools recovered from sites throughout the Eastern Woodlands suggests that this resource was traded over relatively long distances.

More easterly interaction continued into the Late Woodland, with the presence of ceramics resembling the Newtown ceramic series of the middle Ohio River valley (Chapter 9). By around one thousand years ago, the affinity of those living in the Falls region again shifted, this time to the west as local residents embraced Mississippian religion, settlement patterns, and material culture. As noted by Munson and McCullough in Chapter 11, by ca. 1000 CE, the Falls region represented the northeastern frontier of a Mississippian way of life and religion. Surprisingly, Munson and McCullough point to relatively little interaction with neighboring Fort Ancient groups from 1000–1300 CE. Interaction with these groups seems to have provided little in the way of political, economic, or social benefits.

In a border situation, the establishment and maintenance of ethnic and social identities are especially critical. All societies recognize boundaries that separate or distinguish them from other groups (Feuer 2018:37). People often use new objects and practices for their own political agendas and assign new meanings to them according to their own cosmologies, political perspectives, and cultural perceptions (Dietler 1998:299). Through their daily decision-making, they are agents of change by constructing new forms of cultural identity along cultural boundaries.

Following the collapse of the Prather polity, the Mississippian/Fort Ancient border appears to have become more permeable. As noted by French and Pollack (Chapter 12), by 1300 CE, Fort Ancient potters/households were living in small villages located along the edge of the Ohio River. Throughout the occupation of these communities, the Mississippian residents appear to have continued to interact with their downstream Angel neighbors, as reflected by the presence of Angel Negative Painted ceramics and Falls potters, who continued to produce vessels that distinguished them from their Fort Ancient neighbors living in the same village. The comingling of Mississippian and Fort Ancient potters within these communities did not lead to a melding of ceramic traditions, as has been documented at villages after 1400 CE downstream and upstream from the Falls region (Henderson 1992b; Pollack 2004). French and Pollack (Chapter 12) argue that families living in late Mississippian villages within the Falls region continued to maintain and signal to others their distinctive social identities. As more work is undertaken in the Falls region, it may be possible to gain a better handle on the extent to which material culture and subsistence strategies reflect social identity.

A more permeable border ca. 1300 CE also is reflected in Mississippian plant use strategies. As noted by Rossen and Turner (Chapter 10), after 1300 CE, plant use in the Falls region reflects a melding of Mississippian and Fort Ancient subsistence strategies. For instance, both Midwestern Twelve (Mississippian) and Eastern Eight (Fort Ancient) corn varieties were consumed, as were beans, which prior to 1400 CE are rarely found at Mississippian sites in the lower Ohio River valley. Rossen and Turner go on to suggest that late Mississippian subsistence practices in the Falls region illustrate how plant adoption-rejection decisions were made based on intercultural relations that were only loosely governed by environmental capabilities and constraints.

The realignment and expansion of exchange networks that coincided with the widespread fifteenth-century collapse of Mississippian societies, in addition to competition with Mississippian groups downstream and Fort Ancient groups upstream from the Falls region for access to nonlocal goods, may have led to the abandonment of Mississippian villages by 1450 CE. Following village abandonment, Native American use of the Falls region did not leave a substantial archaeological presence. In early historic accounts, however, the Falls region continued to be an important landscape feature for indigenous Native American groups (Hanna 1911).

For more than twelve thousand years, groups living in the Falls region responded to changing social and environmental conditions. As a result, at times the Falls region was a crossroads, a social interaction zone, and a frontier/boundary. Depending on historical conditions, human relationships within the Falls region and between neighboring groups were likely renegotiated and reoriented. As people adapted to and altered the environment, they created a local social identity that was reflected in their material culture, settlement patterns, and subsistence strategies. Today the Falls of the Ohio River remains an important cultural and natural landmark.

References

Abel, Timothy J., David M. Stothers, and Jason M. Koralewski

2001   The Williams Mortuary Complex: A Transitional Archaic Regional Interaction Center in Northwestern Ohio. In *Archaic Transitions in Ohio and Kentucky Prehistory,* edited by Olaf H. Prufer, Sara E. Pedde, and Richard S. Meindl, pp. 290–327. Kent State University Press, Kent, Ohio.

Adams, Brian, Alice Berkson, Ilona Matkovski, and G. Walz

2003   *Phase Ia Archaeological Reconnaissance of 3,450 Acres at the Former Indiana Army Ammunition Plant in Clark County, Indiana.* Research Report 73. Public Service Archaeology Program, University of Illinois, Urbana-Champaign.

Ahler, Steven R.

1993   Stratigraphy and Radiocarbon Chronology of Modoc Rock Shelter, Illinois. *American Antiquity* 58(3):462–89.

1998   Early and Middle Archaic Settlement Systems in the Modoc Locality, Southwest Illinois. *Illinois Archaeology* 10(1/2):1–109.

Alt, Susan

2006   The Power of Diversity: The Roles of Migration and Hybridity in Culture Change. In *Leadership and Polity in Mississippian Society,* edited by Brian M. Butler and Paul D. Welch, pp. 289–308. Occasional Paper 33. Center for Archaeological Investigations, Southern Illinois University, Carbondale.

2010   *Investigation of Two Yankeetown Sites in Posey County.* Department of Anthropology, Indiana University, Bloomington.

Alt, Susan M., and Timothy R. Pauketat

2011   Why Wall Trenches? *Southeastern Archaeology* 30:108–22.

Anderson, David G.

1996   Approaches to Modeling Regional Settlement in the Archaic Period Southeast. In *Archaeology of the Mid-Holocene Southeast,* edited by Kenneth E. Sassaman and David G. Anderson, pp. 157–76. University Press of Florida, Gainesville.

2004   Archaic Mounds and the Archaeology of Southeastern Tribal Societies. In *Signs of Power: The Rise of Cultural Complexity in the Southeast,* edited by Jon L. Gibson and Philip J. Carr, pp. 270–99. University of Alabama Press, Tuscaloosa.

Anderson, David G., and Glen T. Hanson

1988   Early Archaic Settlement in the Southeastern United States: A Case Study from the Savannah River Valley. *American Antiquity* 53:262–86.

Andrefsky, William, Jr.
1998   *Lithics: Macroscopic Approaches to Analysis.* Cambridge University Press, Cambridge.

Andrushko, Valerie A., Kate Latham, Diane Grady, Allen Pastron, and Phillip Walker
2005   Bioarchaeological Evidence for Trophy-Taking in Prehistoric Central California. *American Journal of Physical Anthropology* 127:375–84.

Angst, Michael G.
1998   *Archaeological Salvage Excavation at the Reid Site (12FL11) Floyd County, Indiana.* Archaeological Resource Management Service, Ball State University, Muncie, Indiana.

Anslinger, C. Michael
1986   *The Riverton Culture: Lithic Systems and Settlement Parameters.* Unpublished Master's thesis, Department of Anthropology, Washington State University, Pullman.

Anslinger, C. Michael, Albert M. Pecora, Charles M. Niquette, and Jonathan P. Kerr
1994   *Salvage Excavations at the Railway Museum Site (15JF630) Jefferson County, Kentucky.* Contract Publication Series No. 94–15. Cultural Resource Analysts, Lexington, Kentucky.

Applegate, Darlene
2008   Woodland Period. In *The Archaeology of Kentucky: An Update. Volume 1,* edited by David Pollack, pp. 339–604. Kentucky Heritage Council, Frankfort.

Arnold, Craig R., and Colin Graham
2011a   *Intensive Investigations on the Smith-Sutton Farm and Phase Ia Survey of 12CL127 in Clark County, Indiana.* Reports of Investigations 1102. IPFW Archaeological Survey, Fort Wayne, Indiana.
2011b   Archaeological Investigations at the Ellingsworth Site (12Cl127), a Mississippian Hamlet of the Falls Mississippian Complex of Southeastern Indiana. *Indiana Archaeology* 6(1):24–48.
2013   *Phase Ia Archaeological Reconnaissance of 12CL171 (Rose Island Amusement Park) for the Placement of Interpretive Exhibits and Signage, and a Phase Ia Archaeological Reconnaissance of 12CL14 (Devil's Backbone) in Charlestown State Park, Clark County, Indiana.* Reports of Investigations 1116. IPFW Archaeological Survey, Fort Wayne, Indiana.

Arnold, Craig R., Robert G. McCullough, Colin D. Graham, and Leslie (Nocton) Arnold
2012   Recent Archaeological Investigations of the Falls Mississippian Complex 14 Ellingsworth and Smith-Sutton Sites. *Indiana Archaeology* 7(1):14–34.

Arnold, Dean E.
1985   *Ceramic Theory and Cultural Process.* New Studies in Archaeology. Cambridge University Press, Cambridge.
1989   Patterns of Learning, Residence, and Descent among Potters in Ticul, Yucatan, Mexico. In *Archaeological Approaches to Cultural Identity,* edited by Stephen J. Shennan, pp. 174–84. Unwin Hyman Ltd., London.

Asch, David L.
2008   Notes on a Carbonized "Bean" from 15JS86 (Muir Site, Kentucky). Manuscript submitted to New York State Museum, in author's possession.

Asch, David L., and Nancy B. Asch

1978   The Economic Potential of *Iva annua* and Its Prehistoric Importance in the Lower Illinois Valley. In *The Nature and Status of Ethnobotany,* edited by Richard I. Ford, pp. 300–41. Anthropological Paper No. 67. Museum of Anthropology, University of Michigan, Ann Arbor.

1985a   Prehistoric Plant Cultivation in West-Central Illinois. In *Prehistoric Food Production in North America,* edited by Richard I. Ford, pp. 149–203. Anthropological Papers No. 75. Museum of Anthropology, University of Michigan, Ann Arbor.

1985b   Archaeobotany of the Campbell Hollow Archaic Occupations. In *The Campbell Hollow Archaic Occupations: A Study of Intrasite Spatial Structure in the Lower Illinois Valley,* edited by C. Russell Stafford, pp. 82–107. Center for American Archeology Press, Kampsville, Illinois.

1986   Woodland Period Archeobotany of the Napoleon Hollow Site. In *Woodland Period Occupations of the Napoleon Hollow Site in the Lower Illinois River Valley,* edited by M. D. Wiant and C. R. McGimsey, pp. 427–512. Research Series 6. Center for American Archeology Press, Kampsville, Illinois.

Ashe, Thomas

1808   *Travels in America, Performed in 1806.* John Abraham, London.

Ashley, Keith and Nancy Marie White

2012   *Late Prehistoric Florida: Archaeology at the Edge of the Mississippian World.* University Press of Florida, Gainesville.

Bader, Anne Tobbe

1988   Another Look at Shellmiddens and Sedentism. Manuscript on file, Corn Island Archaeology, Louisville.

1992   *An Analysis of Bone and Antler Tool Use Pattern from the Kentucky Air National Guard Site.* Unpublished Master's thesis, Department of Anthropology, University of Kentucky, Lexington.

2003   Late Prehistoric Occupation at the Falls of the Ohio River: Somewhat More Than Speculation, Somewhat Less Than Conviction. *Currents of Change: Journal of the Falls of the Ohio Archaeological Society* 1(1):3–42.

2004   *Interim Report: A Management Summary of the Archaeological Investigations at the Newcomb Site (12CL2), Emery Crossing Road, Clark County, Indiana.* CRM Report 04-45. AMEC Earth and Environmental, Louisville.

2005a   Why Dig Yet Another Late Archaic Site in the Falls of the Ohio River Region? Insights into Corporate Identity through an Examination of Mortuary Behavior at the KYANG Site, Jefferson County, Kentucky and the Meyer Site, Spencer County, Indiana. Paper presented at the 2005 Annual Kentucky Heritage Council Meeting, Lexington.

2005b   *Data Recovery Plan for Archaeological Mitigation of Cultural Resources Located in the Proposed 30-Acre Riverpark Place Condominium Development in Louisville, Kentucky.* AMEC Earth and Environmental, Louisville.

2007   *Phase III Data Recovery and Construction Monitoring of the Lone Hill Site (15Jf562/15Jf10) Jefferson County, Kentucky.* Granger Consultants, Louisville.

2011   Evidence of Ritualized Mortuary Behavior at the Meyer Site: An Inadvertent Discovery in Spencer County, Indiana. *Indiana Archaeology* 5(2):10–49.

2017   *The Meyer Site.* Falls of the Ohio Archaeological Society, Clarksville, Indiana.

Bader, Anne Tobbe and Bett Etenohan (editors)

2017   E. Y. Guernsey at the Falls. *Currents of Change: Journal of the Falls of the Ohio Archaeological Society* 9:1–132.

Bader, Anne Tobbe and Joseph E. Granger

1989   *Recent Archaeological Investigations on the Kentucky Air National Guard Site (15Jf267), Jefferson County, Kentucky.* Granger Consultants, Louisville.

Bader, Anne Tobbe, Joseph E. Granger, Tammy Seiter, and Chris M. Rohe

1998   *A Phase I Archaeological Reconnaissance of the Cedar Creek Residential Relocation Project.* Granger Consultants, Louisville.

Bader, Anne Tobbe, Kathryn J. McGrath, Edgar E. Hardesty, and Joseph E. Granger

2018   *A Phase II Evaluation of the Miles Rockshelter Site (15Jf671), Jefferson County, Kentucky.* Corn Island Archaeology, Louisville.

Balée, William

2006   The Research Program of Historical Ecology. *Annual Review of Anthropology* 35:75–98.

Barrett, John C.

1999   Chronology of Landscape. In *The Archaeology and Anthropology of Landscape,* edited by Peter J. Ucko and Tobert Layton, pp. 21–30. Routledge, London and New York.

Barth, Frederick (editor)

1969   *Ethnic Groups and Boundaries.* Waveland Press, Prospect Heights, Illinois.

Baskin, Jerry M., Carol C. Baskin, and Edward R. Chester

1994   The Big Barrens Region of Kentucky and Tennessee: Further Observations and Considerations. *Castanaea* 59(3):226–54.

Bassett, John L., and Richard L. Powell

1984   Stratigraphic Distribution of Cherts in Limestones of the Blue River Group in Southern Indiana. In *Prehistoric Chert Exploitation: Studies from the Midcontinent,* edited by Brian M. Butler and Ernest E. May, pp. 239–52. Occasional Paper No. 2. Center for Archaeological Investigations, Southern Illinois University, Carbondale.

Baumann, Timothy E., and Gary D. Crites

2016   The Age and Distribution of the Common Bean (*Phaseolus vulgaris*) in Tennessee and the Southeastern U.S. Paper presented at the Eighty-First Annual Meeting of the Society for American Archaeology, Orlando, Florida.

Baumann, Timothy E., Gary D. Crites, and Lynne Sullivan

2015   The Emergence and Distribution of Common Bean (*Phaseolus vulgaris*) in the Southeastern U.S. Paper presented at Eightieth Annual Meeting of the Society for American Archaeology, San Francisco, California.

Bellis, James O.

1981   Test Excavation Conducted at the Breeden Site, 12Hr11, in Harrison County, Indiana. *Proceedings of the Indiana Academy of Science* 91:78–92.

Beneš, Jaromír and Marek Zvelebil

1991   A Historical Interactive Landscape in the Heart of Europe: The Case of Bohemia. In *The Archaeology and Anthropology of Landscape,* edited by Peter J. Ucko and Tobert Layton, pp. 73–90. Routledge, London and New York.

Bergman, Christopher, Tanya P. Lemons, and Christopher W. Schmidt

2013   Scientific Recovery Investigations at the Kramer Mound (12Sp7): Prehistoric Artifact Assemblages, Faunal and Floral Remains, and Human Osteology. Report submitted to the Department of Natural Resources, Division of Historic Preservation and Archaeology, Indianapolis, Indiana.

Best, Bill

2017   *Kentucky Heirloom Seeds: Growing, Eating, Saving.* University of Kentucky Press, Lexington.

Binford, Lewis R.

1979   Organization and Formation Processes: Looking at Curated Technologies. *Journal of Anthropological Research* 35:255–73.

1980   Willow Smoke and Dogs' Tails: Hunter-Gatherer Settlement Systems and Archaeological Site Formation. *American Antiquity* 45:4–20.

1982   The Archaeology of Place. *Journal of Anthropological Archaeology* 1:5–31.

2001   *Constructing Frames of Reference: An Analytical Method for Archaeological Theory Building Using Hunter-gatherer and Environmental Data Sets.* University of California Press, Berkeley.

Bird, Douglas W., and James F. O'Connell

2006   Behavioral Ecology and Archaeology. *Journal of Archaeological Research* 14(2):143–88.

Bird, Rebecca B., and Eric A. Smith

2005   Signaling Theory, Strategic Interaction and Symbolic Capital. *Current Anthropology* 46(2):221–48.

Bird, Rebecca B., Eric A. Smith, and Douglas W. Bird

2001   The Hunting Handicap: Costly Signaling in Human Foraging Strategies. *Behavioral Ecology and Sociobiology* 50:9–19.

Birmingham, Robert A., and Lynne G. Goldstein

2006   *Aztalan: Mysteries of an Ancient Indian Town.* Wisconsin Historical Society Press, Madison.

Blaauw, Maarten, and J. Andres Christen

2011   Flexible Paleoclimate Age-depth Models Using an Autoregressive Gamma Process. *Bayesian Analysis* 6(3):457–74.

Blakely, Robert L.

1988   *The King Site: Continuity and Contact in Sixteenth-Century Georgia.* University of Georgia Press, Athens.

Boisvert, Richard A.

1979   Excavations at the Spadie Site (15JF14). In *Excavations at Four Archaic Sites in the Lower Ohio River Valley, Jefferson County, Kentucky,* edited by Michael B. Collins, pp. 804–82. Occasional Papers in Anthropology No. 1. Department of Anthropology, University of Kentucky, Lexington.

1986   *Late Archaic Settlement Models in the Middle Ohio Valley: A Perspective from Big*

Bone Lick, Kentucky. Unpublished PhD dissertation, Department of Anthropology, University of Kentucky, Lexington.

Boisvert, Richard A., Boyce N. Driskell, Kenneth W. Robinson, Steven D. Smith, and Lathel F. Duffield

1979   Materials Recovered. In *Excavations at Four Archaic Sites in the Lower Ohio River Valley, Jefferson County, Kentucky,* edited by Michael B. Collins, pp. 60–470. Occasional Papers in Anthropology No. 1. Department of Anthropology, University of Kentucky, Lexington.

Borden, William W.

1874   *Report of a Geological Survey of Clark and Floyd Counties.* Indiana Geological Survey Annual Report 5. Indiana Geological Survey, Indianapolis.

Boulding, J. Russell

1995   Geomorphology and Geoarchaeology of the Swan's Landing Site (12Hr304) on the Ohio River, Harrison County, Indiana. In *Archaeological Subsurface Investigations at the Swan's Landing Site (12Hr304), Harrison County, Indiana,* edited by Stephen T. Mocas and Edward E. Smith, pp. 25–46. Reports of Investigations 95-34. Glenn A. Black Laboratory of Archaeology, Indiana University, Bloomington.

Bradley, Bruce A.

1997   Sloan Site Biface and Projectile Point Technology. In *Sloan: A Paleoindian Dalton Cemetery in Arkansas,* edited by Dan F. Morse, pp. 53–57. Smithsonian Institution Press, Washington, D.C.

Braun, David P.

1983   Pots as Tools. In *Archaeological Hammers and Theories,* edited by James Anthony Moore and Arthur S. Keene, pp. 107–34. Academic Press, New York.

Breitburg, Emanuel

1992   Vertebrate Faunal Remains. In *Fort Ancient Cultural Dynamics in the Middle Ohio Valley,* edited by A. Gwynn Henderson, pp. 209–41. Monographs in World Archaeology No. 8. Prehistory Press, Madison, Wisconsin.

Brooks, Robert L.

1985   The Old Bear Site (15Sh18): An Upland Camp in the Western Outer Bluegrass Region. In *Woodland Period Research in Kentucky,* edited by David Pollack, Thomas Sanders, and Charles Hockensmith, pp. 110–23. Kentucky Heritage Council, Frankfort.

Brown, Cecil H.

2008   Prehistoric Chronology of the Common Bean in the New World: The Linguistic Evidence. *American Anthropologist* 108(3):507–16.

Brown, James A.

1985   Long-Term Trends to Sedentism and the Emergence of Complexity in the American Midwest. In *Prehistoric Hunters-Gatherers: The Emergence of Cultural Complexity,* edited by T. Douglas Price and James A. Brown, pp. 201–31. Academic Press, New York.

1986   Early Ceramics and Culture: A Review of Interpretations. In *Early Woodland Archeology,* edited by Kenneth B. Farnsworth and Thomas E. Emerson, pp. 598–608. Center for American Archeology Press, Kampsville, Illinois.

Brown, James A., and Robert K. Vierra

1983   What Happened in the Middle Archaic? Introduction to an Ecological Approach to Koster Site Archaeology. In *Archaic Hunters and Gatherers in the American Midwest*, edited by John L. Phillips and James A. Brown, pp. 165–95. Academic Press, New York.

Buikstra, Jane E., and Douglas K. Charles

1999   Centering the Ancestors: Cemeteries, Mounds, and Sacred Landscapes of the Ancient North American Midcontinent. In *Archaeology of Landscape*, edited by Wendy Ashmore and A. Bernard Knapp, pp. 201–28. Blackwell Publishers, Malden, Massachusetts.

Bupp, Susan L., Christopher L. Bowen, Laurie Paonessa, and Ruth Trocolli

2005   *Phase II Investigations of Six Archaeological Sites, Indiana Army Ammunition Plant, Charlestown, Clark County, Indiana.* Parsons, Fairfax, Virginia.

Burdin, Sheldon R.

2002   *An Archaeological Assessment of Site 12FL73 in Floyd County, Indiana.* Department of Anthropology, University of Kentucky, Lexington.

2004   *Interaction, Exchange, and Politics among Hunter-Gatherers in the Midcontinent—Evidence from the Lower Ohio River Valley: Bannerstone Use from 6600 to 3000 B.P.* Unpublished Master's thesis, Department of Anthropology, University of Kentucky, Lexington.

2008   *Archaeological Investigations of the Overflow Pond Area in Harrison County, Indiana: The 2007 Survey and Excavations at the Breeden (12Hr11) and Overflow Pond (12Hr12) Sites.* Department of Anthropology, University of Kentucky. Lexington.

2009   Preliminary Results of the 2007 Investigations of Two Late Middle to Late Archaic (ca.6000–3000 B.P.) Sites in Harrison County, Indiana: The Breeden (12Hr11) and Overflow Pond (12Hr12) Sites. *Indiana Archaeology* 4(1):9–34.

2010   *An Archaeological Survey and Limited Excavations of the Spadie 3 Site in Jefferson County, Kentucky.* Report No. 190. Kentucky Archaeological Survey, Lexington.

Burnett, Richard

1963   Lone Hill. *Central States Archaeological Journal* 10(3):84–90.

Bush, Leslie L.

2004   *Boundary Conditions: Macrobotanical Remains and the Oliver Phase of Central Indiana, A.D. 1200–1450.* University of Alabama Press, Tuscaloosa.

Butler, Amanda J.

2016   A Mound with a Mission: New Excavations at the Collins Site in East-Central Illinois. Midwest Archaeological Conference, Program and Abstracts, 43, Iowa City, Iowa.

Butler, Brian M.

2009   Land between the Rivers: The Archaic Period of Southernmost Illinois. In *Archaic Societies: Diversity and Complexity Across the Midcontinent*, edited by Thomas D. Emerson, Dale L. McElrath and Andrew C. Fortier, pp. 607–34. State University of New York Press, Albany.

Butler, Brian M., and Mark J. Wagner

2000   Land between the Rivers: The Late Woodland Period of Southernmost Illinois. In *Late Woodland Societies: Tradition and Transformation across the Midcontinent,* edited by Thomas E. Emerson, Dale L. McElrath, and Andrew C. Fortier, pp. 685–712. University of Nebraska Press, Lincoln.

Butzer, Karl W.

1978   Changing Holocene Environments at the Koster Site: A Geo-Archaeological Perspective. *American Antiquity* 43(3):408–13.

Calhoun, Craig

1995   *Critical Social Theory: Culture, History, and the Challenge of Difference.* Blackwell Publishers, Oxford.

Campbell, Julian J. N.

1985   *The Land of Cane and Clover: Presettlement Vegetation in the So-called Bluegrass Region of Kentucky.* Manuscript on file, School of Biological Sciences, University of Kentucky, Lexington.

Cantin, Mark E.

2006   Chert Usage Analysis. In *Archaeological Investigations at the Prather Site, Clark County, Indiana: The 2005 Survey and Excavations,* edited by Cheryl Ann Munson, Michael Strezewski, and C. Russell Stafford, pp. 187–96. Reports of Investigations 802. IPFW Archaeological Survey, Fort Wayne, Indiana.

2009   Projectile Point Technology of a Kirk Cluster Assemblage from the James Farnsley Site (12Hr520). In *Early Archaic Occupations at the James Farnsley Site, Caesars Archaelogical Project, Harrison County, Indiana,* edited by C. Russell Stafford and Mark E. Cantin, pp. 142–89. Technical Report 39. Indiana State University Archaeology and Quaternary Research Laboratory, Terre Haute.

Cantin, Mark E., J. E. Conkin, and Stephen T. Mocas

2007   Lithic Resources in the CAP Locality. In *Caesars Archaeological Project Overview: Geomorphology, Archeobotany and Other Specialty Analyses,* edited by C. Russell Stafford, pp. 268–334. Technical Report 36. Indiana State University Archaeological and Quaternary Research Laboratory, Terre Haute.

Cantin, Mark E., and C. Russell Stafford

2012   *Archaeological Phase Ic Subsurface Investigations of the Duke Energy Gallagher Pipeline, Floyd and Harrison Counties, Indiana.* Indiana State University Archaeology and Quaternary Research Laboratory, Terre Haute.

Carlson, Justin N.

2019a   *Middle to Late Holocene (7200–2900 cal. BP) Archaeological Site Formation Processes at Crumps Sink and the Origins of Anthropogenic Environments in Central Kentucky, USA.* Unpublished PhD dissertation. Department of Anthropology, University of Kentucky, Lexington.

2019b   Appendix A: McNeely Lake Projectile Points. In *Native American Utilization of Caves and Rockshelters in the Floyds Fork Drainage of Jefferson and Bullitt Counties,* edited by Justin N. Carlson and David Pollack. Research Report No. 14. Kentucky Archaeological Survey, Lexington.

Carlson, Justin N., and David Pollack

2019   *Native American Utilization of Caves and Rockshelters in the Floyds Fork Drainage of Jefferson and Bullitt Counties.* Research Report No. 14. Kentucky Archaeological Survey, Lexington.

Carlson, Justin N., and Claiborne Daniel Sea

2019   Chipped and Ground Stone. In *Native American Utilization of Caves and Rockshelters in the Floyds Fork Drainage of Jefferson and Bullitt Counties,* edited by Justin N. Carlson and David Pollack. Research Report No. 14. Kentucky Archaeological Survey, Lexington.

Carmody, Stephen B.

2009   *Hunter/Gatherer Foraging Adaptations during the Middle Archaic Period at Dust Cave, Alabama.* Unpublished Master's thesis, Department of Anthropology, University of Tennessee, Knoxville.

Carr, Lucien and Nathaniel S. Shaler

1876   *On the Prehistoric Remains of Kentucky.* Volume 1. Part 4. Memoirs of the Geological Society of Kentucky, Frankfort.

Casseday, Ben

1852   *The History of Louisville from Its Earliest Settlement to the Year 1852.* Hull and Brother, Louisville, Kentucky.

Chacon, Maria I., Barbara Pickersgill, and Daniel G. Debouck

2005   Domestication Patterns in Common Bean (*Phaseolus vulgaris* L.) and the origin of Mesoamerican and Andean Cultivated Varieties. *Theoretical and Applied Genetics* 110(3):432–44.

Chacon, Richard J., and David H. Dye

2007   *The Taking and Displaying of Human Body Parts as Trophies by Amerindians.* Springer Science, Business Media, New York.

Chapman, Jefferson

1976   The Archaic Period in the Lower Little Tennessee River Valley: The Radiocarbon Dates. *Tennessee Anthropologist* 1:1–12.

Chapman, Jefferson and Gary D. Crites

1987   Evidence for Early Maize (*Zea mays*) from the Icehouse Bottom Site, Tennessee. *American Antiquity* 52(2):352–54.

Chapman, Lloyd and Joseph E. Granger

1971   *A Report of an Archaeological Survey of the Southwestern Jefferson County Local Flood Protection Project.* Report 5. University of Louisville Archaeological Survey, Louisville, Kentucky.

Charles, Douglas K., and Jane E. Buikstra

1983   Archaic Mortuary Sites in the Central Mississippi Drainage: Distribution, Structure, and Behavioral Implications. In *Archaic Hunters and Gatherers in the American Midwest,* edited by James L. Phillips and James A. Brown, pp. 117–45. Academic Press, New York.

Chilton, Elizabeth S.

2009   The Origin and Spread of Maize (*Zea mays*) in New England. In *Histories of Maize: Multidisciplinary Approaches to the Prehistory, Linguistics, Biogeography,*

Domestication, and Evolution of Maize, edited by John Staller, Robert Tykot, and Bruce Benz, pp. 539–48. Left Coast Press, Walnut Creek, California.

Claassen, Cheryl

1992   Shell Mounds as Burial Mounds: A Revision of the Shell Mound Archaic. In *Current Archaeological Research in Kentucky: Volume Two,* edited by David Pollack and A. Gwynn Henderson, pp. 1–12. Kentucky Heritage Council, Frankfort.

2015   *Beliefs and Rituals in Archaic Eastern North America: An Interpretive Guide.* University of Alabama Press, Tuscaloosa.

Clay, R. Berle

1991   Adena Ritual Development: An Organizational Type in a Temporal Perspective. In *The Human Landscape in Kentucky's Past: Site Structure and Settlement Patterns,* edited by Charles Stout and Christine K. Hensley, pp. 30–36. Kentucky Heritage Council, Frankfort.

2002   Deconstructing the Woodland Sequence from the Heartland: A Review of Recent Research Directions in the Upper Ohio Valley. In *The Woodland Southeast,* edited by David G. Anderson and Robert C. Mainfort Jr., pp. 162–84. University of Alabama Press, Tuscaloosa.

Cobb, Charles R.

2000   *From Quarry to Cornfield: The Political Economy of Mississippian Hoe Production.* University of Alabama Press, Tuscaloosa.

Cobb, Charles R., and Brian M. Butler

2002   The Vacant Quarter Revisited: Late Mississippian Abandonment of the Lower Ohio Valley. *American Antiquity* 67:625–44.

Collett, John

1878   *Geological Report of Harrison and Crawford Counties, Indiana. Eighth, Ninth, and Tenth Annual Reports of the Geological Survey of Indiana made during the years 1876, 1877, 1878,* pp. 419–21. Indianapolis, Indiana.

Collins, Michael B.

1979a   The Longworth-Gick Site (15Jf243). In *Excavations at Four Archaic Sites in the Lower Ohio River Valley, Jefferson County, Kentucky,* edited by Michael B. Collins, pp. 471–589. Occasional Papers in Anthropology No. 1. Department of Anthropology, University of Kentucky, Lexington.

Collins, Michael B. (editor)

1979b   *Excavations at Four Archaic Sites in the Lower Ohio Valley, Jefferson County, Kentucky. 2 Volumes.* Occasional Papers in Anthropology No. 1. Department of Anthropology, University of Kentucky, Lexington.

Collins, Michael B., and Boyce N. Driskell

1979   Summary and Conclusions. In *Excavations at Four Archaic Sites in the Lower Ohio Valley, Jefferson County, Kentucky, Volumes 1 and 2,* edited by Michael B. Collins, pp. 1023–42. Occasional Papers in Anthropology No. 1. Department of Anthropology, University of Kentucky, Lexington.

Comaroff, John L., and Jean Comaroff

1992   *Ethnography and the Historical Imagination.* Westview Press, Boulder, Colorado.

Conolly, James
2017   Costly Signaling in Archaeology: Origins, Relevance, Challenges, and Pros-
         pects. *World Archaeology* 49(4):435–45.

Conrad, Lawrence A., Susan L. Gardner, and J. Joe Alford
1986   A Note on the Late Archaic, Early Woodland, and Early Middle Woodland Oc-
         cupations of the Lima Lake Locality, Adams and Hancock Counties, Illinois.
         In *Early Woodland Archeology,* edited by Kenneth B. Farnsworth and Thomas
         E. Emerson, pp. 191–206. Center for American Archeology Press, Kampsville,
         Illinois.

Cook, Thomas Genn
1976   Koster: An Artifact Analysis of Two Archaic Phases in Westcentral Illinois.
         Prehistoric Records No. 1. Koster Research Reports No. 3. Northwestern Ar-
         cheological Program, Evanston, Illinois.

Cowan, C. Wesley
1978   The Prehistoric Use and Distribution of Maygrass in Eastern North America:
         Cultural and Phytogeographical Implications. In *The Nature and Status of Eth-
         nobotany,* edited by Richard I. Ford, pp. 263–88. Anthropological Papers No. 67.
         Museum of Anthropology, University of Michigan, Ann Arbor.
1985   Understanding the Evolution of Plant Husbandry in Eastern North America:
         Lessons from Botany, Ethnography and Archaeology. In *Prehistoric Food Pro-
         duction in North America,* edited by Richard I. Ford, pp. 205–43. Anthropo-
         logical Papers No. 75. Museum of Anthropology, University of Michigan, Ann
         Arbor.

Cowan, C. Wesley, H. Edwin Jackson, Katherine Moore, Andrew Nichelhoff, and Tris-
tine L. Smart
1981   The Cloudsplitter Shelter, Menifee County, Kentucky: A Preliminary Report.
         Southeastern Archaeological Conference Bulletin 24:60–76.

Cox, E. T.
1874   Mounds and Mound Builder's Implements. In *Fifth Annual Report of the Geo-
         logical Survey of Indiana, Made during the Year 1873,* pp. 126–27. Indianapolis,
         Indiana.
1875   Antiquities. In *Sixth Annual Report of the Geological Survey of Indiana, Made
         during the Year 1874,* pp. 124–25. Indianapolis, Indiana.

Cramer, Ann C.
1989   *The Dominion Land Company Site: An Early Adena Mortuary Manifestation in
         Franklin County, Ohio.* Unpublished Master's thesis, Kent State University, Kent,
         Ohio.

Crawford, Gary W., David G. Smith, and Vandy E. Bowyer
1997   Dating the Entry of Corn (*Zea mays*) into the Lower Great Lakes Region. *Amer-
         ican Antiquity* 62(1):112–19.

Crites, Gary D.
1978   Plant Food Utilization Patterns during the Middle Woodland Owl Hollow
         Phase in Tennessee: A Preliminary Report. *Tennessee Anthropologist* 3:79–92.
1986   Ecofacts. In *Phase III Mitigation of the Clark Maritime Archaeological District,*

Clark County, Indiana: Final Report, edited by Ellen Sieber and Ann T. Ottesen, pp. 327–85. Resource Analysts, Bloomington, Indiana.

1994   Plant Remains from the Southwind Site. In *Southwind: Archaeological Data Recovery at a Mississippian Village in Southwest Indiana,* edited by Cheryl Munson. Glenn A. Black Laboratory for Archaeology, Indiana University, Bloomington.

Crites, Gary D., and Timothy E. Baumann

2017   Timing the Arrival of Domesticated Beans in the Southeast. *Current Research.* McClung Museum of Natural History and Culture, University of Tennessee, Knoxville

Crothers, George M.

1999   *Prehistoric Hunters and Gatherers, and the Archaic Period Green River Shell Middens of Western Kentucky.* Unpublished PhD Dissertation, Department of Anthropology, Washington University, St. Louis, Missouri.

2004   The Green River in Comparison to the Lower Mississippi Valley during the Archaic: To Build Mounds or Not to Build Mounds. In *Signs of Power: The Rise of Cultural Complexity in the Southeast* edited by Jon L. Gibson and Philip J. Carr, 86–96. University of Alabama Press, Tuscaloosa.

Crumley, Carole L.

1994   Historical ecology: A Multidimensional Ecological Orientation: In *Historical ecology: cultural knowledge and changing landscapes,* edited by Carole L. Crumley, 1–16. School of American Research Advanced Seminar Series, Santa Fe, New Mexico.

Crumley, Carole L., Anna Westin, and Tommy Lennartsson

2018   Is There a Future for the Past? In *Issues and Concepts in Historical Ecology: The Past and Future of Landscapes and Regions,* edited by Carole L. Crumley, Tommy Lennartsson, and Anna Westin, 1–9. Cambridge University Press, Cambridge.

Darlington, William M.

1893   Christopher Gist's Journals with Historical, Geographical and Ethnological Notes and Biographies of His Contemporaries. J. R. Weldin, Pittsburgh, Pennsylvania.

Davis, Daniel B., Leon Lane, Nancy O'Malley, and Jack Rossen

1997   *Phase II Testing and Phase II Mitigation of Three Sites in the Bardstown Industrial Park, Nelson County, Kentucky.* Archaeological Report No. 386. Program for Cultural Resource Assessment, University of Kentucky, Lexington.

Delcourt, Hazel R.

1979   Late Quaternary Vegetation History of the Eastern Highland Rim and Adjacent Cumberland Plateau of Tennessee. *Ecological Monographs* 49(3): 255–80.

Delcourt, Paul A., Hazel R. Delcourt, Cecil R. Ison, William E. Sharp, and Kristen J. Gremillion

1998   Prehistoric Human Use of Fire, the Eastern Agricultural Complex, and Appalachian Oak-Chestnut Forests: Paleoecology of Cliff Palace Pond, Kentucky. *American Antiquity* 63(2): 263–78.

De Rego, Kathryn G.

2012   *Holocene Landscape Evolution of the Ohio River Valley from Knob Creek to Rose-wood Bottom.* Unpublished Master's thesis, Department of Earth and Environmental Systems, Indiana State University, Terre Haute, Indiana.

Diaz-Andreu, Margarita, Sam Lucy, Stasa Babic, and David N. Edwards

2005   *The Archaeology of Identity: Approaches to Gender, Age, Status, Ethnicity and Religion.* Routledge, London.

DiBlasi, Philip J.

1981   *A New Assessment of the Archaeological Significance of the Ashworth Site (15BU236): A Study of the Dynamics of Archaeological Investigation in Cultural Resource Management.* Unpublished Master's thesis, Department of Interdisciplinary Studies, University of Louisville, Louisville.

Didier, Mary E.

1967   A Distributional Study of the Turkey-tail Point. *Wisconsin Archeologist* 48(1): 3–73.

Dietler, Michael

1998   Consumption, Agency and Cultural Entanglement: Theoretical Implications of a Mediterranean Colonial Encounter. In *Studies in Culture Contact: Interaction, Culture Change and Archaeology,* edited by James G. Cusick, 288–315. Occasional Paper No. 25. Center for Archaeological Investigations, Southern Illinois University, Carbondale.

2010   *Archaeologies of Colonialism: Consumption, Entanglement, and Violence in Ancient Mediterranean France.* University of California Press, Berkeley.

Dobbs, Clark A., and Don W. Dragoo

1976   *Prehistoric Cultural Resources of Section Two, Southwestern Jefferson County Local Flood Protection Project: Test Excavations.* Environmental Consultants, Dallas, Texas.

Douglas, John G.

1976   *Collins: A Late Woodland Ceremonial Complex in the Woodfordian Northeast.* Unpublished PhD dissertation, University of Illinois, Urbana-Champaign.

Dragoo, Don W.

1963   Mounds for the Dead: An Analysis of the Adena Culture. *Annals of the Carnegie Museum* 37. Pittsburgh, Pennsylvania.

Driese, Steven G., Sally P. Horn, Joanne P. Ballard, Mathew S. Boehm, and Zhengua Li

2017   Micromorphology of late Pleistocene and Holocene sediments and a new interpretation of the Holocene chronology at Anderson Pond, Tennessee, USA. *Quaternary Research* 87(1): 82–95.

Driese, Steven G., Zheng-Hua Li, and Sally P. Horn

2005   Late Pleistocene and Holocene climate and geomorphic histories as interpreted from a 23,000 14C yr B.P. paleosol and floodplain soils, southeastern West Virginia, USA. *Quaternary Research* 63: 136–49.

Driese, Steven G., Zheng-Hua Li, and Larry D. McKay

2008   Evidence for multiple, episodic, mid-Holocene Hypsithermal recorded in two soil profiles along an alluvial floodplain catena, southeastern Tennessee, USA. *Quaternary Research* 69(2): 276–91.

Driskell, Boyce N.

1979   The Rosenberger Site (15JF18). In *Excavations at Four Archaic Sites in the Lower Ohio Valley, Jefferson County, Kentucky,* edited by Michael B. Collins, pp. 697–803. Occasional Papers in Anthropology No. 1. Department of Anthropology, University of Kentucky, Lexington.

Duerksen, Kenneth and Christopher A. Bergman

1995   *Phase 1 Archaeological Survey of a Proposed 50 Acre Sand and Gravel Quarry in Floyd County, Indiana.* Project C7505.01. Cultural Resources Program, 3D/Environmental, Cincinnati, Ohio.

Duerksen, Kenneth, John F. Doershuk, Christopher A. Bergman, Teresa W. Tune, and Donald A. Miller

1992   Fayette Thick Ceramic Chronology at the West Runway Site (15BE391), Boone County, Kentucky. In *Current Archaeological Research in Kentucky Volume Three,* edited by John F. Doershuk, Christopher A. Bergman and David Pollack, pp. 70–88. Kentucky Heritage Council, Frankfort.

Dye, David H.

1996   Riverine Adaptation in the Midsouth. In *Of Caves and Shell Mounds,* edited by Kenneth C. Carstens and Patty Jo Watson, pp. 140–58. University of Alabama Press, Tuscaloosa.

Edging, Richard B.

1995   *Living in a Cornfield: The Variation and Ecology of Late Prehistoric Agriculture in the Western Kentucky Confluence Region.* Unpublished PhD dissertation, Department of Anthropology, University of Illinois, Urbana-Champaign.

Emberling, Geoff

1997   Ethnicity in Complex Societies: Archaeological Perspectives. *Journal of Archaeological Research* 5:295–344.

Emerson, Thomas E.

1983   The Early Woodland Florence Phase Occupation. In *The Florence Street Site: American Bottom Archaeology,* edited by Thomas E. Emerson, George R. Milner, and Douglas K. Jackson, pp. 19–178. University of Illinois Press, Urbana.

1989   Water, Serpents, and the Underworld: An Exploration into Cahokian Symbolism. In *The Southern Ceremonial Complex: Artifacts and Analysis; The Cottonlandia Conference,* edited by Patricia Galloway, pp. 45–92. University of Nebraska Press, Lincoln.

1991   Some Perspectives on Cahokia and the Northern Mississippian Expansion. In *Cahokia and the Hinterlands: Middle Mississippian Cultures of the Midwest,* edited by Thomas E. Emerson and R. Barry Lewis, pp. 221–38. University of Illinois Press, Urbana.

1997   *Cahokia and the Archaeology of Power.* University of Alabama Press, Tuscaloosa.

Emerson, Thomas E., and Dale L. McElrath

1983   A Settlement-Subsistence Model of the Terminal Late Archaic Adaptation in the American Bottom, Illinois. In *Archaic Hunters and Gatherers in the American Midwest,* edited by James L. Phillips and James A. Brown, pp. 219–42. Academic Press, New York.

Essenpreis, Patricia S.

1982   *The Anderson Village Site: Redefining the Anderson Phase of the Fort Ancient Tradition of the Middle Ohio Valley.* Unpublished PhD dissertation, Department of Anthropology, Harvard University, Cambridge, Massachusetts.

Fairclough, Graham

1999   Protecting Time and Space: Understanding Historic Landscape for Conservation in England. In *The Archaeology and Anthropology of Landscape,* edited by Peter J. Ucko and Tobert Layton, pp. 119–33. Routledge, London and New York.

Farnsworth, Kenneth B., and David L. Asch

1986   Early Woodland Chronology, Artifact Styles, and Settlement Distribution in the Lower Illinois Valley Region. In *Early Woodland Archeology,* edited by Kenneth B. Farnsworth and Thomas E. Emerson, pp. 326–457. Center for American Archeology Press, Kampsville, Illinois.

Feathers, James

2007   Luminescence Dating of Ohio River Alluvial Sediments from Southern Indiana. In *Caesars Archaeological Project Overview: Geomorphology, Archeobotany and Other Specialty Analyses,* edited by C. Russell Stafford, pp. 162–76. Technical Report 36. Indiana State University Archaeology and Quaternary Research Laboratory. Terre Haute.

Federal Register

2013   *Notice of Inventory Completion: National Guard Bureau/A7AN, Air National Guard, Joint Base Andrews, MD.* Volume 78, Number 33, Tuesday, February 19, 2013, pp. 11676–77.

Feuer, Brian A.

2016   *Boundaries, Borders and Frontiers in Archaeology.* McFarland, Jefferson, North Carolina.

2018   Modeling Differential Cultural Interaction in Late Bronze Age Thessaly. In *Modeling Cross-Cultural Interaction in Ancient Borderlands,* edited by Ulrike Matthies Green and Kirk E. Costion, pp. 35–63. University Press of Florida, Gainesville.

Fiegel, Kurt H.

1985   An Assessment of Impacts on the Edwards Site, 15SP252. Report prepared for the Kentucky Transportation Cabinet, Frankfort.

Finney, Fred A., and James B. Stoltman

1991   The Fred Edwards Site: A Case of Stirling Phase Culture Contact in Southwestern Wisconsin. In *New Perspectives on Cahokia: Views from the Periphery,* edited by James B. Stoltman, pp. 229–52. Prehistory Press, Madison, Wisconsin.

Fisher, William Travis

2013   *Site 15SP202 and the Mississippian Presence at the Falls of the Ohio River.* Unpublished Master's thesis, Department of Anthropology, University of Louisville, Louisville, Kentucky.

Flagg, Edmund

1906   Part 1 of Flagg's Far West, 1836–1837. In *Early Western Travels, 1748–1846, Volume 26,* edited by Reuben Gold Thwaites, pp. 13–121. Arthur H. Clark, Cleveland, Ohio.

Fowler, Melvin

1997   *The Cahokia Atlas: A Historical Atlas of Cahokia Archaeology.* Studies in Archae-
        ology 2. Illinois Transportation Archaeological Research Program, University
        of Illinois, Urbana-Champaign.

French, Michael W.

1998   *Early Archaic Settlement Mobility, Lithic Resource Use, and Technological Orga-
        nization in the Lower Ohio River Valley: A Perspective from the Longworth-Gick
        Site (15Jf243).* Unpublished Master's thesis, Department of Anthropology, Uni-
        versity of Kentucky, Lexington.

French, Michael W. (editor)

2010   *Final Report: Intensive Archaeological Investigations at the McAlpine Lock and
        Dam, Louisville, Kentucky, Volume II: Mississippian Components at the Ship-
        pingport Site (15JF702).* CRM Report 2009–17. AMEC Earth and Environmen-
        tal, Louisville, Kentucky.

French, Michael W., Dawn M. Bradley, Richard J. Stallings, Stephen T. Mocas, Susan C.
Andrews, and Kimberly D. Simpson

2015   *Phase III Archaeological Data Recovery of Site 12CL199 in the Muddy Fork of
        Silver Creek Watershed in Clark County, Indiana.* AMEC Environment and In-
        frastructure, Louisville, Kentucky.

French, Michael W., and David W. Schatz

2010   Mississippian Feature Descriptions. In *Final Report: Intensive Archaeological
        Investigations at the McAlpine Lock and Dam, Louisville, Kentucky, Volume II:
        Mississippian Components at the Shippingport Site (15JF702)*, edited by Michael
        W. French, pp. 57–126. CRM Report 2009–17. AMEC Earth and Environmen-
        tal, Louisville, Kentucky.

Fritz, Gayle J.

1993   Early and Middle Woodland Period Paleoethnobotany. In *Foraging and Farm-
        ing in the Eastern Woodlands,* edited by C. Margaret Scarry, pp. 39–56. Univer-
        sity Press of Florida, Gainesville.

Funkhouser, William D., and William S. Webb

1935   The Ricketts Site in Montgomery County, Kentucky. *Department of Anthro-
        pology, Reports in Anthropology and Archaeology 3(3).* University of Kentucky
        Press, Lexington.

Gardner, Paul S.

1997   The Ecological Structure and Behavioral Implications of Mast Exploitation
        Strategies. In *Peoples, Plants, and Landscapes: Studies in Paleoethnobotany,* ed-
        ited by Kristen J. Gremillion, pp. 161–78. University of Alabama Press, Tusca-
        loosa.

Garniewicz, Rexford

2006   Preliminary Analysis of Vertebrate Faunal Remains. In *Archaeological Investiga-
        tions at the Prather Site, Clark County, Indiana: The 2005 Survey and Excava-
        tions,* edited by Cheryl Ann Munson, Michael Strezewski, and C. Russell Staf-
        ford, pp. 209–12. Reports of Investigations 802. IPFW Archaeological Survey,
        Fort Wayne, Indiana.

Gibbon, Guy
1986   Does Minnesota Have an Early Woodland. In *Early Woodland Archeology,* edited by K. B. Farnsworth and T. E. Emerson, pp. 84–91. Center for American Archeology Press, Kampsville, Illinois.

Goad, Sharon I.
1980   Patterns of Late Archaic Exchange. *Tennessee Anthropologist* 5:1–16.

Goldstein, Lynne G., and J. D. Richards
1991   Ancient Aztalan: The Cultural and Ecological Context of a Late Prehistoric Site in the Midwest. In *Cahokia and the Hinterlands: Middle Mississippian Cultures of the Midwest,* edited by Thomas E. Emerson and R. Barry Lewis, pp. 193–206. University of Illinois Press, Urbana.

Goodrich, Calvin
1929   The Pleurocerid Fauna of the Falls of the Ohio. *The Nautilus* 43(1):1–17.

Granger, Joseph E.
1985   *Archaeology at McNeely Lake: A Survey and Planning Study.* University of Louisville Archaeological Survey, Louisville, Kentucky.
1988   Late/Terminal Archaic Settlement in the Falls of the Ohio River Region of Kentucky: An Examination of Components, Phases, and Clusters. In *Paleoindian and Archaic Research in Kentucky,* edited by Charles D. Hockensmith, David Pollack, and Thomas N. Sanders, pp. 153–203. Kentucky Heritage Council, Frankfort.

Granger, Joseph E., Philip J. DiBlasi, and Jan Marie Hemberger
1981   *The Search for a Research and Management Design Process: Cultural Studies in the Falls Region of Kentucky, Volume 3.* University of Louisville Archaeological Survey, Louisville, Kentucky.

Granger, Joseph E., Edgar E. Hardesty, and Anne Tobbe Bader
1992   *Phase III Data Recovery Archaeology at Habich Site (15Jf550) and Associated Manifestations at Guthrie Beach, Jefferson County, Kentucky.* Archaeology Resources Consultant Services, Louisville, Kentucky.
1993   *Phase III Data Recovery Archaeology at the Habich Site (15JF550) and Associated Manifestations at Guthrie Beach, Jefferson County, Kentucky, Volume II: Special Analyses.* Report of Investigation 90–92. Archaeological Resource Consultant Services, Louisville, Kentucky.

Gray, Henry H.
1984   Archaeological Sedimentology of Overbank Silt Deposits on the Floodplain of the Ohio River near Louisville, Kentucky. *Journal of Archaeological Science* 11:421–32.

Green, Thomas J., and Cheryl A. Munson
1978   Mississippian Settlement Patterns in Southwestern Indiana. In *Mississippian Settlement Patterns,* edited by Bruce D. Smith, pp. 293–330. Academic Press, New York.

Green, Stanton W., and Stephen M. Perlman
1985   Frontiers, Boundaries, and Open Social Systems. In *The Archaeology of Frontiers and Boundaries,* edited by Stanton W. Green and Stephen M. Perlman, pp. 3–13. Academic Press, Orlando, Florida.

250 · References

Gremillion, Kristen J.
1996   Diffusion and Adaptation of Crops in Evolutionary Perspective. *Journal of Anthropological Archaeology* 15(2):183–204.
1997   New Perspectives on the Paleoethnobotany of the Newt Kash Shelter. In *People, Plants, and Landscapes Studies in Paleoethnobotany,* edited by Kristen J. Gremillion, pp. 23–41. University of Alabama Press, Tuscaloosa.
1998   3,000 Years of Human Activity at the Cold Oak Shelter. In *Current Archaeological Research in Kentucky: Volume Five,* edited by Charles Hockensmith, Kenneth Carstens, Charles Stout, and Sara Rivers, pp. 1–14. Kentucky Heritage Council, Frankfort.
Gremillion, Kristen J., and Dolores R. Piperno
2009   Human Behavioral Ecology, Phenotypic (Developmental) Plasticity, and Agricultural Origins: Insights from the Emerging Evolutionary Synthesis. In *Rethinking the Origins of Agriculture,* edited by Mark N. Cohen. *Current Anthropology* (Special Issue) 50:709–11.
Griffin, James B.
1943   *The Fort Ancient Aspect: Its Cultural and Chronological Position in Mississippi Valley Archaeology.* University of Michigan Press, Ann Arbor.
1978   Late Prehistory of the Ohio Valley. In *Handbook of North American Indians, The Northeast (Vol 15),* edited by Bruce Trigger, pp. 547–59. The Smithsonian Institution Press, Washington, D.C.
Guernsey, Elam Y.
1939   Relationships among Various Clark County Sites. *Proceedings of the Indiana Academy of Science* 48:27–32.
1942   The Culture Sequence of the Ohio Falls Sites. *Proceedings of the Indiana Academy of Science* 51:60–67.
Hajic, Edwin R.
1990   *Koster Site Archeology I: Stratigraphy and Landscape Evolution.* Center for American Archaeology Press, Kampsville, Illinois.
Håkansson, N. Thomas and Mats Widgren (editors)
2014   *Landesque Capital: The Historical Ecology of Enduring Landscape Modifications.* Left Coast Press, Walnut Creek, California.
Hally, David J.
1994   *Ocmulgee Archaeology, 1936–1986.* University of Georgia Press, Athens.
Hammerstedt, Scott W.
2005   Mississippian Status in Western Kentucky: Evidence from the Annis Mound. *Southeastern Archaeology* 24(1):11–27.
Hammerstedt, Scott W., and Erin R. Hughes
2015   Mill Creek Chert Hoes and Prairie Soils: Implications for Cahokia Production and Expansion. *Midcontinental Journal of Archaeology* 40(2):149–65.
Hammon, Neal O.
1978   Early Louisville and the Beargrass Stations. *The Filson Club History Quarterly* 52(2):147–65.

Hanna, Charles A.

1911   *The Wilderness Trail or the Ventures and Adventures of the Pennsylvania Traders on the Allegheny Path.* G. P. Putnam's Sons, New York.

Hargrave, Eva A., Shirley J. Schermer, Kristin M. Hedmen, and Robin M. Lillie

2015   *Transforming the Dead: Culturally Modified Bone in the Prehistoric Midwest.* University of Alabama Press, Tuscaloosa.

Harl, Joseph L., Mary Jo Cramer, Cynthia L. Balek, Marjorie B. Schroeder, and Elizabeth M. Scott

2001   *Data Recovery Investigations at the Callaway Farms Site (23CY227): A Terminal Late Archaic Village within Callaway County, Missouri.* Research Report No. 96. Archaeological Research Center of St. Louis, St. Louis, Missouri.

Harlan, Jack R.

1992   *Crops and Man.* 2nd edition. American Society of Agronomy and Crop Science Society of America, Madison, Wisconsin.

Harn, A. D.

1986   The Marion Phase Occupation of the Larson Site in the Central Illinois River Valley. In *Early Woodland Archeology,* edited by Kenneth B. Farnsworth and Thomas E. Emerson, pp. 244–79, Center for American Archeology Press, Kampsville, Illinois.

Harner, Michael J.

1972   *The Jivaro: People of the Sacred Waterfalls.* University of California Press, Berkeley.

Harrell, Glenn Perry

2005   A Survey of Paleoindian Points: Their Distribution in Clark County, Indiana. *Currents of Change: Journal of the Falls of the Ohio Archaeological Society* 4(1):95–102.

Hart, John P.

2008   Evolving the Three Sisters: The Changing Histories of Maize, Bean, and Squash in New York and the Greater Northeast. In *Current Northeast Paleoethnobotany II,* edited by John P. Hart, pp. 87–100. Bulletin Series No. 512. New York State Museum, Albany.

Hart, John P., Robert A. Daniels, and Charles J. Sheviak

2004   Do *Cucurbita pepo* Gourds Float Fishnets? *American Antiquity* 69(1):141–48.

Hart, John P., and C. Margaret Scarry

1999   The Age of Common Beans (*Phaseolus vulgaris*) in the Northeastern United States. *American Antiquity* 64(4):653–58.

Haskell, Bruce S., Robert Arm, John R. Stoop III, and John Shaunessy

1985   The Role of the Dentist in Archaeologic Investigation: An Unusual Facial Fracture with Healing Occurring 3,000 Years Ago. *Quintessence International* 16(1):95–101.

Hegmon, Michelle, Mathew A. Peeples, Ann P. Kinzig, Stephanie Kulow, Cathryn M. Meegan, and Margaret C. Nelson

2008   Social Transformation and Its Human Costs in the Prehispanic U.S. Southwest. *American Anthropologist* 110(3):313–24.

Henderson, A. Gwynn

1992a   Capitol View: An Early Madisonville Horizon Settlement in Franklin County, Kentucky. In *Current Archaeological Research in Kentucky, Volume Two,* edited by David Pollack and A. Gwynn Henderson, pp. 223–40. Kentucky Heritage Council, Frankfort.

1993   *Prehistoric Research at Petersburg, Boone County, Kentucky.* Archaeological Report No. 289. Program for Cultural Resource Assessment, University of Kentucky, Lexington.

1998   *Middle Fort Ancient Villages and Organizational Complexity in Central Kentucky.* Unpublished PhD dissertation, Department of Anthropology, University of Kentucky, Lexington.

1999   *Beals Run Series Ceramics: Implications for the Development of Fort Ancient Culture in Central Kentucky.* Paper presented at the Sixteenth Annual Kentucky Heritage Council Archaeological Conference, Lexington.

2008   Fort Ancient Period. In *The Archaeology of Kentucky: An Update. Volume 2,* edited by David Pollack, pp. 739–902. Kentucky Heritage Council, Frankfort.

2017   Foreword. In *Kentucky Heirloom Seeds: Growing, Eating, Saving,* by Bill Best, pp. ix-xxv. University of Kentucky Press, Lexington.

Henderson, A. Gwynn (editor)

1992b   *Fort Ancient Cultural Dynamics in the Middle Ohio Valley.* Monographs in World Archaeology No. 8. Prehistory Press, Madison, Wisconsin.

Henderson, A. Gwynn and David Pollack

1996   The New Field Site: An Early Madisonville Horizon Community in Bourbon County, Kentucky. In *Current Archaeological Research in Kentucky, Volume Four,* edited by Sara L. Sanders, Thomas N. Sanders, and Charles Stout, pp. 169–233. Kentucky Heritage Council, Frankfort.

Hensley, Christine K.

1991   The Middle Green River Shell Mounds: Challenging Traditional Interpretations Using Internal Site Structure Analysis. In *The Human Landscape in Kentucky's Past: Site Structure and Settlement Patterns,* edited by Charles Stout and Christine K. Hensley, pp. 78–93. Kentucky Heritage Council, Frankfort.

Hilgeman, Sherri L.

2000   *Pottery and Chronology at Angel.* University of Alabama Press, Tuscaloosa.

Hill, Fred

1974   Laboratory Analysis Notes. Notes on file, Corn Island Archaeology, Louisville, Kentucky.

Hill, William, Stephen Mocas, and Anne Bader

2017   *Riverwood Rockshelter (15BU265), Bullitt County, Kentucky.*

Hockensmith, Charles D., David Pollack, Valerie Haskins, and Jack Rossen

1998   The Shelby Lake Site: A Late Woodland Upland Camp in Shelby County, Kentucky. In *Current Archaeological Research in Kentucky: Volume Five,* edited by Charles D. Hockensmith, Kenneth Carstens, Charles Stout, and Sara Rivers, pp. 121–62. Kentucky Heritage Council, Frankfort.

Homsey-Messer, Lara
2015   Revisiting the Role of Caves and Rockshelters in the Hunter-Gatherer Task-
           scape of the Archaic Midsouth. *American Antiquity* 80(2):332–52.
Honerkamp, Marjorie W.
1975   *The Angel Phase: An Analysis of a Middle Mississippian Occupation in South-
           western Indiana.* Unpublished PhD dissertation, Department of Anthropology,
           Indiana University, Bloomington.
Howard, James H.
1981   *Shawnee! The Ceremonialism of a Native American Tribe and Its Cultural Back-
           ground.* Ohio University Press, Athens.
Hudson, Jean L.
2004   Additional Evidence for Gourd Floats on Fishing Nets. *American Antiquity*
           69(3):586–87.
Huebchen, Karl
2006   *The Ronald Watson Gravel Site (15Be249): An Examination of the Late Wood-
           land/Fort Ancient Transition in Boone County, Kentucky.* Unpublished Master's
           thesis, Department of Anthropology, University of Cincinnati, Cincinnati.
Jacobi, Keith P.
2007   Disabling the Dead: Human Trophy Taking in the Prehistoric Southeast. In *The
           Taking and Displaying of Human Body Parts as Trophies by Amerindians,* edited
           by Richard J. Chacon and David H. Dye, pp. 299–338. Springer Science Busi-
           ness Media, New York.
Janzen, Donald E.
1968   The Lone Hill Site, an Archaic Site in Jefferson County, Kentucky. Paper pre-
           sented at the Annual Meeting of the Eastern States Archaeological Federation,
           Ann Arbor, Michigan.
1971   Excavations at the Falls of the Ohio River. *The Filson Club History Quarterly*
           45(4):373–80.
1972   Archaeological Investigations in Louisville and Vicinity: A Historical Sketch.
           The Filson Club History Quarterly 46(4):305–21.
1975   Report of 1971 Excavations at the Prather Site: A Mississippian Site in Clark
           County, Indiana. Manuscript on file, Corn Island Archaeology, Louisville, Ken-
           tucky.
1977a   An Examination of Late Archaic Development in the Falls of the Ohio Area. In
           For the Director: Research Essays in Honor of James B. Griffin, edited by Charles
           E. Cleland, pp. 123–43. Museum of Anthropology, University of Michigan, Ann
           Arbor.
1977b   The Devil's Backbone of Clark County, Indiana, and the Evolution of a Legend.
           The Filson Club History Quarterly 51(4):303–14.
1978   Notes on Excavations at 15BU33, 15SP3, and 15SP5. Manuscript in possession of
           Anne T. Bader, Louisville, Kentucky.
2008   *Unearthing the Past: The Archaeology of the Falls of the Ohio River Region.* Butler
           Books, Louisville, Kentucky.
2014   The Temporal Relationship of Four Archaic Projectile Point Types at the Hor-

nung Site, Jefferson County, Kentucky. *Currents of Change: Journal of the Falls of the Ohio Archaeological Society* 7:65–78.

2016   An Archaeological Study of the Falls of the Ohio River Region. *Currents of Change: Journal of the Falls of the Ohio Archaeological Society* 8:1–94.

Jefferies, Richard W.

1982   Archaeological Overview of the Carrier Mills District. In *The Carrier Mills Archaeological Project: Human Adaptation in the Saline Valley, Illinois,* edited by Richard W. Jefferies and Brian M. Butler, pp. 1461–510. Research Paper No. 33. Center for Archaeological Investigations, Southern Illinois University, Carbondale.

1988   Archaic Period Research in Kentucky: Past Accomplishments and Future Directions. In *Paleoindian and Archaic Research in Kentucky,* edited by Charles D. Hockensmith, David Pollack, and Thomas N. Sanders, pp. 85–126. Kentucky Heritage Council, Frankfort.

1990   A Technological and Functional Analysis of Middle Archaic Hafted Endscrapers from the Black Earth Site, Saline County, Illinois. *Midcontinental Journal of Archaeology* 15(1):1–36.

1996a   The Emergence of Long-Distance Exchange Networks in the Southeastern United States. In *Archaeology of the Mid-Holocene Southeast,* edited by Kenneth E. Sassaman and David G. Anderson, pp. 222–34. University Press of Florida, Gainesville.

1996b   Hunters and Gatherers After the Ice Age. In *Kentucky Archaeology,* edited by R. Barry Lewis, pp. 39–77. University Press of Kentucky. Lexington.

1997   Middle Archaic Bone Pins: Evidence of Mid-Holocene Regional Scale Social Groups in the Southern Midwest. *American Antiquity* 62(3):464–87.

2004   Regional Scale Interaction Networks and the Emergence of Cultural Complexity along the Northern Margins of the Southeast. In *Signs of Power: The Rise of Cultural Complexity in the Southeast,* edited by Jon L. Gibson and Phillip J. Carr, pp. 71–85. University of Alabama Press, Tuscaloosa.

2008   *Holocene Hunter-Gatherers of the Lower Ohio River Valley.* University of Alabama Press, Tuscaloosa.

2009   Archaic Cultures of Western Kentucky. In *Archaic Societies: Diversity and Complexity across the Midcontinent,* edited by Thomas E. Emerson, Dale L. McElrath, and Andrew C. Fortier, pp. 635–66. State University of New York Press, Albany.

Jefferies, Richard and Sheldon R. Burdin

2007   Holocene Hunter-Gatherer Interaction in the North American Midcontinent. Paper presented at the Seventy-Second Annual Meeting of the Society for American Archaeology, Austin, Texas.

Jefferies, Richard W., and B. Mark Lynch

1983   Dimensions of Middle Archaic Cultural Adaptation at the Black Earth Site, Saline County, Illinois. In *Archaic Hunters and Gatherers in the American Midwest,* edited by James L. Phillips and James A. Brown, pp. 299–322. Academic Press, New York.

Jefferies, R. W., V. D. Thompson, and G. R. Milner
2005   Archaic Hunter-Gatherer Landscape Use in West-Central Kentucky. *Journal of Field Archaeology* 30:3–22.

Jenkins, Richard
2008   *Social Identity.* 3rd edition. Routledge, London.

Johannessen, Sissel
1984   Paleoethnobotany. In *American Bottom Archaeology,* edited by Charles J. Bareis and James W. Porter, pp. 197–224. University of Illinois Press, Urbana.

Johnston, Cheryl A.
2015   More Than Skulls and Mandibles: Culturally Modified Human Remains from Woodland Contexts in Ohio. In *Transforming the Dead: Culturally Modified Bone in the Prehistoric Midwest,* edited by Eva A. Hargrave, Shirley J. Schermer, Kristin M. Hedmen, and Robin M. Lillie, pp. 61–78. University of Alabama Press, Tuscaloosa.

Jones, Andrew
2007   *Memory and Material Culture.* Cambridge University Press, Cambridge.

Jones, Sian
2002   *The Archaeology of Ethnicity: Constructing Identities in the Past and Present.* Routledge, London.

Joutel, Henri
1906   *Joutel's Journal of La Salle's last voyage, 1684–7.* J. McDonough, Albany, New York.

Justice, Noel D.
1987   *Stone Age Spear and Arrow Points of the Midcontinental and Eastern United States.* Indiana University Press, Bloomington.

Justice, Noel D., and Edward E. Smith
1988   *An Archaeological Reconnaissance of Quarry and Workshop Sites in the Vicinity of Harrison County, Indiana.* Reports of Investigations 88–111. Glenn A. Black Laboratory of Archaeology, Indiana University, Bloomington.

Keeley, Lawrence H.
1996   *War before Civilization.* Oxford University Press, Oxford.

Keene, Deborah A.
2004   Reevaluating Late Prehistoric Coastal Subsistence and Settlement Strategies: New Data from Grove's Creek Site, Skidaway Island, Georgia. *American Antiquity* 69(4):671–88

Kellar, James H.
1979   The Mann Site and "Hopewell" in the Lower Wabash-Ohio Valley. In *Hopewell Archaeology: The Chillicothe Conference,* edited by David Brose and Naomi Greber, pp. 100–107. Kent State University Press, Kent, Ohio.

Kelly, Raymond C.
2000   *Warless Societies and the Origin of War.* University of Michigan Press, Ann Arbor.

Kepferle, R. C.
1972   *Geologic Map of Parts of the Brooks Quadrangle, Jefferson County, Kentucky.* U.S. Geological Survey, Geologic Quadrangle Map GQ-1202, scale 1:24,000.

1974   *Geologic Map of Parts of the Louisville West and Lanesville Quadrangle, Jefferson County, Kentucky.* U.S. Geological Survey, Geologic Quadrangle Map GQ-1202, scale 1:24,000.

Kidder, Tristram R.

2013   Observations about the Historical Ecology of Small-Scale Societeis. In *The Archaeology and Historical Ecology of Small Scale Economies*, edited by Victor D. Thompson and James C. Waggoner Jr., pp. 176–183. University Press of Florida, Gainesville.

King, James E., and William H. Allen

1977   A Holocene Vegetation Record from the Mississippi River Valley, Southeastern Missouri. *Quaternary Research* 8:307–23.

Kistler, Logan, Alvaro Montenegro, Bruce D. Smith, John A. Gifford, Richard E. Green, Lee A. Newsom, and Beth Shapiro

2014   Transoceanic Drift and the Domestication of the African Gourds in the Americas. *Proceedings of the National Academy of Sciences* 111(8):2937–41.

Kistler, Logan, Lee A. Newsom, Timothy M. Ryan, Andrew C. Clarke, Bruce D. Smith, and George H. Perry

2015   Gourds and Squashes (*Cucurbita* sp.) Adapted to Megafaunal Extinction and Ecological Anachronism through Domestication. *Proceedings of the National Academy of Sciences* 112(49):15107-12.

Klippel, Walter E.

1971   *Graham Cave Revisited: A Reevaluation of Its Cultural Position During the Archaic Period.* Memoir No. 9. Missouri Archaeological Society, Columbia.

Klippel, Walter E., and Paul W. Parmalee

1982   Diachronic Variation in Insectivores from Cheek Bend Cave and Environmental Change in the Midsouth. *Paleobiology* 8(4):447–58.

Kocis, James J.

2011   *Late Pleistocene and Holocene Hydroclimate Change in the Southeastern United States: Sedimentary, Pedogenic, and Stable Carbon Isotope Evidence in Tennessee River Floodplain Paleosols.* Unpublished Master's thesis, Department of Geology, University of Tennessee, Knoxville.

Kreinbrink, Jeannine

2008   *Site 15JF674 Phase II Testing Report, Jefferson County, Kentucky.* Natural and Ethical Environmental Solutions, Cincinnati, Ohio.

Lacquemont, Cameron H. (editor)

2007   *Architectural Variability in the Southeast.* University of Alabama Press, Tuscaloosa.

Lacy, Denise M.

1996   [New Field] Ceramics and Other Baked Clay Objects. In *Current Archaeological Research in Kentucky, Volume Four,* edited by Sara L. Sanders, Thomas N. Sanders, and Charles Stout, pp. 171–80. Kentucky Heritage Council, Frankfort.

Laland, Kevin N., and Michael J. O'Brien

2010   Niche Construction and Archaeology. *Journal of Archaeological Method and Theory* 17(4):303–22.

Lambert, Patricia M.

1997   Patterns of Violence in Prehistoric Hunter-Gatherer Societies of Coastal Southern California. In *Troubled Times: Violence and Warfare in the Past,* edited by Debra L. Martin and David W. Frayer, pp. 77–110. Gordon and Breach Publishers, Amsterdam.

2002   The Archeology of War: A North American Perspective. *Journal of Archaeological Research* 10(3):207–41.

2008   The Osteological Evidence for Indigenous Warfare in North America. In *North American Indigenous Warfare and Ritual Violence,* edited by Richard J. Chacon and Ruben G. Mendoza, pp. 202–21. University of Arizona Press, Tucson.

Lathrap, Donald W., and José R. Oliver

1986   The Pan-Caribbean Project: Quarry Sources and Redistribution of Exotic Lapidary Materials. Unpublished Manuscript in author's possession.

Ledbetter, R. Jerald

1995   Archaeological Investigations at Mill Branch Sites 9WR4 and 9WR11, Warren County, Georgia. Technical Report No. 3. Interagency Archaeological Services Division, National Park Service, Atlanta, Georgia.

Levi, Lily E.

1921   Traditions of Shippingport. Lecture presented at The Filson Historical Society, Louisville, Kentucky.

Lewis, R. Barry (editor)

1986   *Mississippian Towns of the Western Kentucky Border: The Adams, Wickliffe, and Sassafrass Ridge Sites.* Kentucky Heritage Council, Frankfort.

1996   *Kentucky Archaeology.* University of Kentucky Press, Lexington.

Lilly, Eli

1937   *Prehistoric Antiquities of Indiana.* Indiana Historical Bureau, Indianapolis.

Littleton, J., and H. Allen

2007   Hunter-gatherer Burials and the Creation of Persistent Places in Southeastern Australia. *Journal of Anthropological Archaeology* 26:283–98.

Lockhart, Rachel A., and Christopher W. Schmidt

2007   Evidence of Decapitation and "Trophy Taking" during the Late Archaic in Southern Indiana. Abstract in *American Journal of Physical Anthropologists, Supplement* 44:158.

2008   Patterns in Head and Forearm Removal Traumata during the Late Archaic in Southern Indiana. Abstract in *American Journal of Physical Anthropologists, Supplement* 46:141.

Lockhart, Rachel A., Christopher W. Schmidt, and Stephen A. Symes

2009   Understanding Middle and Late Archaic Forearm Removal. *American Journal of Physical Anthropologists, Supplement* 48:177.

Logansport Telegraph

1837   October 27. Lasselle and Dillon, 1837–49. Logansport, Indiana.

Lutz, David L.

2000   *The Archaic Bannerstone: Its Chronological History and Purpose from 6000 B.C. to 1000 B.C.* Hynek Printing, Richland Center, Wisconsin.

Madsen, Andrew, A. Gwynn Henderson, Rebecca Madsen, Tanya Peres, Jack Rossen, Christopher T. Begley, Jay Balil, Sheldon R. Burdin, Myrisa Byrd, Steve Culler, Alison Hadley, John A. Hunter, Donald W. Linebaugh, Patrick Wallace, and Steven Ahler

2016   *A Phase III Archaeological Data Recovery of Eva Bandman (Site 15JF668), Associated with the River Road Relocation Project, Jefferson County, Kentucky.* Technical Report 440. Program for Archaeological Research, University of Kentucky, Lexington.

Mallott, Clyde C.

1922   The Physiography of Indiana. In *Handbook of Indiana Geology,* edited by W. N. Logan, E. R. Cummings, C. A. Mallott, S. S. Visher, W. M. Tucker, and J. R. Reeves, pp. 66–255. Publication 21. Indiana Department of Conservation, Indianapolis.

Manzano, Bruce

2019   Faunal Remains. In *Native American Utilization of Caves and Rockshelters in the Floyds Fork Drainage of Jefferson and Bullitt Counties,* edited by Justin N. Carlson and David Pollack. Research Report No. 14. Kentucky Archaeological Survey, Lexington.

Marquardt, William and Patty Jo Watson

1983   Shell Mound Archaic of Western Kentucky. In *Archaic Hunters and Gatherers in the American Midwest,* edited by James L. Phillips and James A. Brown, pp. 323–39. Academic Press, New York.

2005   The Green River Shell Mound Archaic: Conclusions. In *Archaeology of the Middle Green River Region, Kentucky,* edited by William Marquardt and Patty Jo Watson, pp. 629–49. Institute of Archaeology and Paleoenvironmental Studies, Monograph 5. Florida Museum of Natural History, University of Florida, Gainesville.

Martindale, Andrew

2009   Entanglement and Tinkering: Structural History in the Archaeology of the Northern Tsimshian. *Journal of Social Archaeology* 9(1):59–91.

McBrinn, Maxine E., and Laurie D. Webster

2008   Creating an Archaeology without Borders. In *Archaeology without Borders: Contact, Commerce, and Change in the U.S. Southwest and Northwestern Mexico,* edited by Laurie D. Webster, Maxine E. McBrinn, and Eduardo Gamboa Carrera, pp. 1–24. University Press of Colorado, Boulder.

McCord, Beth K., and Donald A. Cochran

1996   *Windsor Mound: A Synthesis of an Adena Mound in Randolph County.* Report of Investigations 37. Ball State University, Muncie, Indiana.

2000   *A Survey of Collections: An Archaeological Evaluation of Eight Earthworks in Eastern Indiana.* Archaeological Resources Management Service, Ball State University, Reports of Investigations 58, Muncie, Indiana.

McCullough, Robert G.

2000   *The Oliver Phase of Central Indiana: A Study of Settlement Variability as a Response to Social Risk.* Unpublished PhD dissertation, Department of Anthropology, Indiana University, Bloomington.

2010   Oliver Phase: Fort Ancient's Westernmost Expression, A.D. 1200–1450. Paper

presented at the Sixty-Seventh Annual Meeting of the Southeastern Archaeological Conference, Lexington, Kentucky.

2015   Building Community on the White River in Central Indiana: Structures as Re-
flective of Societal Change at the Late Prehistoric Castor Farm Site. In *Building
the Past: Prehistoric Wooden Post Architecture in the Ohio Valley–Great Lakes,*
edited by Brian G. Redmond and Robert A. Genheimer, pp. 252–94. University
Press of Florida, Gainesville.

McCullough, Robert G. (editor)

2005   *Late Prehistoric Archaeology of a Frontier.* Reports of Investigations 502. IPFW
Archaeological Survey, Fort Wayne, Indiana.

McElrath, Dale and Madeleine Evans

2006   *Is the Leading Middle Archaic Point Type All Washed Up?—A Return to Matanzas Beach.* Paper presented at the Fiftieth Annual Meeting of the Midwest Archaeological Conference, Urbana, Illinois.

McElrath, Dale L., Andrew C. Fortier, Brad Koldehoff, and Thomas E. Emerson

2009   The American Bottom: An Archaic Cultural Crossroads. In *Archaic Societies:
Diversity and Complexity across the Midcontinent,* edited by Thomas D. Emer-
son, Dale L. McElrath, and Andrew C. Fortier, pp. 317–75. State University of
New York Press, Albany.

McGlade, James

1999   Archaeology and the Evolution of Cultural Landscapes: towards an Interdisciplinary Research Agenda. In *The Archaeology and Anthropology of Landscape,*
edited by Peter J. Ucko and Robert Lampton, pp. 458–80. Routledge Press, London and New York.

McGrain, Preston and James C. Currens

1978   *Topography of Kentucky.* Kentucky Geological Survey, Series X. Special Publication 25. University of Kentucky, Lexington.

McMillan, R. Bruce and Walter E. Klippel

1981   Post-glacial Environmental Change and Hunting-gathering Societies of the
Southern Prairie Peninsula. *Journal of Archaeological Science* 8:215–45.

Meadows, William C., and Charles E. Bair

2000   *An Archaeological Survey of High Probability Water Course Development Area in
the East Fork White River Watershed in South Central Indiana.* Reports of Investigations 00–07. Glen A. Black Laboratory of Archaeology, Indiana University,
Bloomington.

Mensforth, Robert P.

2001   Warfare and Trophy Taking in the Archaic Period. In *Archaic Transitions in
Ohio and Kentucky Prehistory,* edited by Olaf H. Prufer, Sara E. Pedde, and
Richard S. Meindl, pp. 110–40. Kent State University Press, Kent, Ohio.

2007   Human Trophy Taking in Eastern North America during the Archaic Period:
The Relationship to Warfare and Social Complexity. In *The Taking and Dis-
playing of Human Body Parts as Trophies by Amerindians,* edited by Richard J.
Chacon and David H. Dye, pp. 222–77. Springer Science Business Media, New
York.

Milner, George R.

2004   Old Mounds, Ancient Hunter-Gatherers and Archaeologists. In *Signs of Power: The Rise of Cultural Complexity in the Southeast,* edited by Jon L. Gibson and Philip J. Carr, pp. 300–15. University of Alabama Press, Tuscaloosa.

2007   Warfare, Population, and Food Production in Prehistoric Eastern North America. In *North American Indigenous Warfare and Ritual Violence,* edited by Richard J. Chacon and Ruben G. Mendoza, pp. 182–201. University of Arizona Press, Tucson.

Milner, George R., Eve Anderson, and Virginia G. Smith

1991   Warfare in Late Prehistoric West-Central Illinois. *American Antiquity* 56(4):581–603.

Milner, George R., Thomas E. Emerson, Mark W. Mehrer, Joyce A. Williams, and Duane Esarey

1984   Mississippian and Oneota Periods. In *American Bottom Archaeology: A Summary of the FAI-270 Project Contribution to the Culture History of the Mississippian River Valley,* edited by Charles J. Bareis and James W. Porter, pp. 158–86. University of Illinois Press, Urbana.

Milner, George R. and Richard W, Jefferies

1998   The Read Archaic Shell Midden I Kentucky. *Southeastern Archaeology* 17:119–132.

Mires, Ann Marie Wagner

1991   Sifting the Ashes: Reconstruction of a Complex Archaic Mortuary Program in Louisiana. In *What Mean These Bones? Studies in Southeastern Bioarchaeology,* edited by Mary Lucas Powell, Patricia S. Bridges, and Ann Marie Wagner Mires, pp. 114–30. University of Alabama Press, Tuscaloosa.

Mocas, Stephen T.

1974   Prehistoric Settlement at the Confluence of Two Streams, Jefferson County, Kentucky. Submitted to Kentucky Department of Transportation, Frankfort.

1976   *Excavations at Arrowhead Farm (15JF237).* Louisville Archaeological Survey, University of Louisville, Louisville, Kentucky.

1977   Excavations at the Lawrence Site, 15Tr33, Trigg County, Kentucky. Manuscript on file, Kentucky Department of Transportation, Frankfort.

1985   An Instance of Middle Archaic Mortuary Activity in Western Kentucky. *Tennessee Anthropologist* 10:76–91.

1988   Pinched and Punctated Pottery of the Falls of the Ohio River Region: A Reappraisal of the Zorn Punctate Ceramic Type. In *New Deal Era Archaeology and Current Research in Kentucky,* edited by David Pollack and Mary Lucas Powell, pp. 115–42. Kentucky Heritage Council, Frankfort.

1992   Falls Plain: A Middle Woodland Ceramic Type from the Falls of the Ohio River Region. In *Current Archaeological Research in Kentucky, Volume Two,* edited by David Pollack and A. Gwynn Henderson, pp. 55–78. Kentucky Heritage Council, Frankfort.

1995   The SARA Site: An Early Late Woodland Site in the Falls of the Ohio River Region. In *Current Archaeological Research in Kentucky, Volume Three,* edited by John F. Doershuk, Christopher A. Bergman, and David Pollack, pp. 113–36. Kentucky Heritage Council, Frankfort.

2006   *Early Woodland and Middle Woodland Occupations at the Knob Creek Site (12HR484), Caesars Archaeological Project, Harrison County, Indiana.* Caesars Archaeological Project Report Volume 2. Technical Report 36. Indiana State University Archaeology and Quaternary Research Laboratory, Terre Haute.

2008   Early Archaic and Late Archaic Occupations at the Townsend Site (12HR481), Caesars Archaeological Project, Harrison County, Indiana. In *The Middle, Late, and Terminal Archaic Occupations at the Caesars Archaeological Project, Harrison County, Indiana,* edited by C. Russell Stafford and Stephen T. Mocas, pp. 44–258. Technical Report 38. Indiana State University Archaeology and Quaternary Research Laboratory, Terre Haute.

2014a   Custer Site Ceramics: An Initial Look at Late Middle Woodland Pottery in the Falls of the Ohio River Region. *Currents of Change: Journal of the Falls of the Ohio Archaeological Society* 7:1–13.

2014b   The Hathaway Cache. *Currents of Change: Journal of the Falls of the Ohio Archaeological Society* 7:57–63.

Mocas, Stephen T., and Danny Calton

2020   Late Woodland Pottery from Western Harrison County, Indiana. *Currents of Change: Journal of the Falls of the Ohio Archaeological Society* 11:6–16.

Mocas, Stephen T., Michael W. French, and Duane B. Simpson (editors)

2009   *Intensive Archaeological Investigations at the McAlpine Locks and Dam, Louisville, Kentucky: Volume I Project Background and Investigations of the Late Archaic and Woodland Components at the Shippingport Site (15JF702).* CRM Report No. 2009-17. AMEC Earth and Environmental, Louisville, Kentucky.

Mocas, Stephen T., and Edward E. Smith

1995   *Archaeological Subsurface Investigations at the Swans Landing Site (12Hr304), Harrison County, Indiana.* Reports of Investigations 95-134. Glenn A. Black Laboratory of Archaeology, Indiana University, Bloomington.

Moeller, Roger W.

2007   1993–1994 Phase III Data Recovery Botanical Analysis. In *Phase III Data Recovery and Construction Monitoring of the Lone Hill Site (15JF562/15Jf10), Jefferson County, Kentucky,* edited by Anne Tobbe Bader, pp. 212–16. AMEC Earth and Environmental, Louisville, Kentucky.

Monaghan, G. William and Christopher S. Peebles

2010   The Construction, Use, and Abandonment of Angel Site Mound: A Tracing of the History of a Middle Mississippian Town through Its Earthworks. *American Antiquity* 75(4):935–53.

Moore, Christopher R., and Victoria G. Dekle

2010   Hickory Nuts, Bulk Processing and the Advent of Early Horticultural Economies in Eastern North America. *World Archaeology* 42(4):595–608.

Moore, Christopher R., and Victor D. Thompson

2012   Animism and Green River Persistent Places: A Dwelling Perspective of the Shell Mound Archaic. *Journal of Social Archeology* 12(2):264–84.

Moorehead, Warren K.
1922   *The Hopewell Mound Group of Ohio.* Publication No. 211. Field Museum of Natural History, Anthropological Series, Volume VI, No. 5.

Morgan, David T.
1992   Ceramics. In *Early Woodland Occupations at the Ambrose Flick Site in the Sny Bottom of West-Central Illinois,* edited by C. R. Stafford, pp. 127–49. Research Series 10. Center for American Archeology Press, Kampsville, Illinois.

Morgan, D. T., D. L. Asche, and C. R. Stafford
1986   Marion and Black Sand Occupations in the Sny Bottom of the Mississippi Valley. In *Early Woodland Archeology,* edited by K. B. Farnsworth and T. E. Emerson, pp. 208–30. Seminars in Archeology No. 2. Center for American Archeology Press, Kampsville, Illinois.

Morrow, Carol, J. Michael Elam, and Michael D. Glasscock
1992   The Use of Blue-Gray Chert in Midwestern Prehistory. *Midcontinental Journal of Archaeology* 17(2):166–97.

Morrow, Toby M.
1996   Lithic Refitting and Archaeological Site Formation Processes: A Case Study from the Twin Ditch Site, Greene County, Illinois. In *Stone Tools: Theoretical Insights into Human Prehistory,* edited by George H. Odell, pp. 345–73. Plenum Press, New York.

Muller, Jon
1986   *Archaeology of the Lower Ohio Valley.* Academic Press, New York.

Munson, Cheryl Ann (editor)
1994   Archaeological Investigations at the Southwind Site, a Mississippian Community in Posey County, Indiana. Report on file, Indiana Department of Natural Resources, Division of Historic Preservation and Archaeology, Indianapolis.
2011   *Phase 1 Archaeological Survey of the Lewis and Clark Trail, Town of Clarksville, Indiana (INDOT Des. No. 0200120).* Department of Anthropology, Indiana University, Bloomington.

Munson, Cheryl Ann and Thomas G. Cook
1980   The Late Archaic French Lick Phase: A Dimensional Description. In *Archaeological Salvage Excavations at Patoka Lake, Indiana: Prehistoric Occupations of the Upper Patoka River Valley,* edited by Cheryl A. Munson, pp. 721–40. Research Reports No. 6. Glenn A. Black Laboratory of Archaeology, Indiana University, Bloomington.

Munson, Cheryl Ann, William F. Limp, and David Barton
1977   *Cultural Resources of the Ohio River Valley in Indiana.* Glenn A. Black Laboratory of Archaeology, Indiana University, Bloomington.

Munson, Cheryl Ann and Robert G. McCullough
2004   *Archaeological Investigations at the Prather Site, Clark County, Indiana: The 2003 Baseline Archaeological Survey.* Department of Anthropology, Indiana University, Bloomington.

Munson, Cheryl Ann, Michael Strezewski, and C. Russell Stafford
2006   *Archaeological Investigations at the Prather Site, Clark County, Indiana: The 2005*

Survey and Excavations. Reports of Investigations 802. IPFW Archaeological Survey, Fort Wayne, Indiana.

Munson, Patrick J.

1973 The Origins and Antiquity of Maize-Beans-Squash Agriculture in Eastern North America: Some Linguistic Evidence. In *Variations in Anthropology,* edited by Donald W. Lathrap and Jody Douglas, pp. 107–35. Illinois Archaeological Survey, Urbana.

1984 *Experiments and Observations on Aboriginal Wild Food Utilization in Eastern North America.* Indiana Historical Society, Indianapolis.

1986 Hickory Silviculture: A Subsistence Revolution in the Prehistory of Eastern North America. In *Emergent Horticultural Economies of the Eastern Woodlands,* edited by W. F. Keegan, pp. 1–20. Southern Illinois University, Carbondale.

Munson, Patrick J., and Cheryl A. Munson

2004 Marion Culture (Early Woodland) Occupations in the Wabash and White River Valleys, Indiana and East Central Illinois. In *Aboriginal Ritual and Economy in the Eastern Woodlands: Essays in Honor of Howard D. Winters,* edited by A. M. Cantwell, L. Conrad, and J. E. Reyman, pp. 133–46. Illinois State Museum, Springfield.

Nabokov, Peter and Robert Easton

1989 *Native American Architecture.* Oxford University Press, New York and Oxford.

Nance, Jack D.

1988 The Archaic Period in the Lower Tennessee-Cumberland-Ohio Region. In *Paleoindian and Archaic Research in Kentucky,* edited by Charles D. Hockensmith, David Pollack, and Thomas N. Sanders, pp. 127–52. Kentucky Heritage Council, Frankfort.

Nassaney, Michael S.

2000 The Late Woodland Southeast. In *Late Woodland Societies: Tradition and Transformation across the Midcontinent,* edited by Thomas E. Emerson, Dale L. McElrath, and Andrew C. Fortier, pp. 713–30. University of Nebraska Press, Lincoln.

Neitzel, Jill E.

2000 What Is a Regional System? In *The Archaeology of Regional Interaction: Religion, Warfare, and Exchange across the American Southwest and Beyond,* edited by M. Hegmon, pp. 25–40. University of Colorado Press, Boulder.

Nelson, Margaret C., Michelle Hegmon, Stephanie R. Kulow, Matthew A. Peeples, Keith W. Kintigh, and Ann P. Kinzig

2011 Resisting Diversity: A Long-Term Archaeological Study. *Ecology and Society* 16(1):25. https://www.ecologyandsociety.org/vol16/iss1/art25.

Neusius, Sarah W.

1986 *Foraging, Collecting, and Harvesting: Archaic Period Subsistence and Settlement in the Eastern Woodlands.* Occasional Paper No. 6. Center for Archaeological Investigations, Southern Illinois University, Carbondale.

Odell, George H.

2000 *Lithic Analysis.* Springer, New York.

Odling-Smee, F. John, Kevin N. Laland, and Marcus W. Feldman
2003   *Niche Construction: The Neglected Process in Evolution.* Monograph in Population Biology No. 37. Princeton University Press, Princeton.

Olliges, Paul
2015   Eyewitnesses to the Rapids at the Falls of the Ohio. Manuscript on file, The Filson Historical Society, Louisville, Kentucky.

O'Malley, Nancy
1983   Adena Mound Ceramics in Retrospect. In *New Deal Era Archaeology and Current Research in Kentucky,* edited by David A. Pollack and Mary Lucas Powell, pp. 46–62. Kentucky Heritage Council, Frankfort.

O'Malley, Nancy, Boyce Driskell, Julie Riesenweber, and Richard Levy
1980   *Stage 1 Archaeological Investigations at Fort Knox, Kentucky.* Archaeological Report 16. Department of Anthropology, University of Kentucky, Lexington.

Osterholt, Amber
2013   *Defining a Region of Trophy Taking Concentration in the Eastern Woodlands.* Unpublished Master's thesis, University of Indianapolis, Indianapolis, Indiana.

Otinger, Jeffery L., Charles M. Hoffman, and Robert H. Lafferty III.
1982   *The F. L. Brinkley Midden (22Ts729) Archaeological Investigations in the Yellow Creek Watershed, Tishomingo County, Mississippi.* Report of investigations No. 36. Office of Archaeological Research, University of Alabama, Tuscaloosa.

Pauketat, Timothy R.
1998   *The Archaeology of Downtown Cahokia: The Tract 15A and Dunham Tract Excavations.* Studies in Archaeology 1. Illinois Transportation Archaeological Research Program, University of Illinois, Urbana-Champaign.
2009   *Cahokia: Ancient America's Great City on the Mississippi.* Viking-Penguin, New York.

Pauketat, Timothy R., Robert F. Boszhardt, and Danielle M. Benden
2015   Trempealeau Entanglements: An Ancient Colony's Causes and Effects. *American Antiquity* 80(2):260–89.

Pauketat, Timothy R., and Thomas E. Emerson
1991   The Ideology of Authority and Power of the Pot. *American Anthropologist* 93:919–41.

Peacock, Evan, Philip J. Carr, Sarah E. Price, John R. Underwood, William L. Kingery, and Michael Lilly
2011   Confirmation of an Archaic Mound in Southwest Mississippi. *Southeastern Archaeology* 29(2):355–68.

Peeples, Matthew A.
2011   *Identity and Social Transformation in the Prehispanic Cibola World: A.D. 1150–1325.* Unpublished PhD dissertation, Arizona State University, Tempe.

Peres, Tanya M., and Kelly L. Ledford
2016   Archaeological Correlates of Population Management of the Eastern Wild Turkey (*Meleagris gallopavo silvetris*) with a Case Study from the American South. *Journal of Archaeological Science,* Report No. 10:547–56.

Peterson, Drexel A., Jr.
1973   *The Spring Creek Site, Perry County, Tennessee: Report of the 1972-1973 Exca-*

vations. Occasional Papers No. 7. Anthropological Research Center, Memphis State University, Memphis, Tennessee.

Phillips, James A, and James L. Brown (editors)

1983　　*Archaic Hunters and Gatherers in the American West.* Academic Press, New York.

Piperno, Dolores R.

2006　　A Behavioral Ecological Approach to the Origins of Plant Cultivation and Domestication in the Seasonal Tropical Forests of the New World. In *Foraging Theory and the Transition to Agriculture,* edited by Douglas Kennett and Bruce Winterhalder, pp. 137–66. University of California Press, Berkeley.

Pirtle, Alfred

1910　　River Reminiscences. The Alfred Pirtle Papers (1837–1926). Papers on file, The Filson Historical Society, Louisville, Kentucky.

Pollack, David

2004　　*Caborn-Welborn: Constructing a New Society after the Angel Chiefdom Collapse.* University of Alabama Press, Tuscaloosa.

2008　　Mississippi Period. In *The Archaeology of Kentucky: An Update. Volume 2,* edited by David Pollack, pp. 605–738. Plan Report 3. Kentucky Heritage Council, Frankfort.

Pollack, David and A. Gwynn Henderson

1992　　Toward a Model of Fort Ancient Society. In *Fort Ancient Cultural Dynamics in the Middle Ohio Valley,* edited by A. Gwynn Henderson, pp. 281–94. Monographs in World Archaeology 8. Prehistory Press, Madison, Wisconsin.

2000　　Late Woodland Cultures in Kentucky. In *Late Woodland Societies: Tradition and Transformation across the Midcontinent,* edited by Thomas E. Emerson, Dale L. McElrath, and Andrew C. Fortier, pp. 613–41. University of Nebraska Press, Lincoln.

Pollack, David, A. Gwynn Henderson, and Melissa L. Ramsey

2010　　Late Prehistoric and Late Woodland Ceramic Artifacts. In *Final Report: Intensive Archaeological Investigations at the McAlpine Lock and Dam, Louisville, Kentucky, Volume II: Mississippian Components at the Shippingport Site (15JF702),* edited by Michael W. French, pp. 127–202. CRM Report 2009-17. AMEC Earth and Environmental, Louisville, Kentucky.

Pollack, David and Jimmy A. Railey

1987　　*Chambers (15Ml109): An Upland Mississippian Village in Western Kentucky.* Kentucky Heritage Council, Frankfort.

Pope, Melody

2005　　A Microwear Study on a Sample of Bifacial Tools from 12HR484. Submitted to Indiana State University Anthropology Laboratory, Terre Haute.

Purtill, Mathew P.

2015　　Dwelling on the Past: Late Archaic Structures of the Ohio Region. In *Building the Past: Prehistoric Wooden Post Architecture in the Ohio Valley-Great Lakes,* edited by Brian G. Redmond and Robert A. Genheimer, pp. 8–28. University Press of Florida, Gainesville.

Putnam, Frederic W.

1875   Archaeological Exploration in Kentucky and Indiana. *American Naturalist* 9:410.

Rafinesque, Constantine S.

1824   *Ancient History or Annals of Kentucky: Introduction to the History and Antiquities of the State of Kentucky.* Frankfort, Kentucky.

Railey, Jimmy A.

1996   Woodland Cultivators. In *Kentucky Archaeology,* edited by R. Barry Lewis, pp. 79–126. University Press of Kentucky, Lexington.

Rakita, Gordon F. M., Jane E. Buikstra, Lane A. Beck, and Sloan R. Williams

2005   *Interacting with the Dead: Perspectives on Mortuary Archeology for the New Millennium.* University of Florida Press, Gainesville.

Ray, Louis L.

1974   *Geomorphology and Quarternary Geology of the Glaciated Ohio Valley: A Reconnaissance Study.* Professional Paper 826. U.S. Geological Survey, Washington, D.C.

Redman, Kim

2007   1993–1994 Phase III Data Recovery Faunal Analysis. In *Phase III Data Recovery and Construction Monitoring of the Lone Hill Site (15JF562/15Jf10), Jefferson County, Kentucky,* edited by Anne Tobbe Bader, pp. 217–22. AMEC Earth and Environmental, Louisville, Kentucky.

Redmond, Brian G.

1990   *The Yankeetown Phase: Emergent Mississippian Cultural Adaptation in the Lower Ohio River Valley.* Unpublished PhD dissertation, Department of Anthropology, Indiana University, Bloomington.

2013   Intrusive Mound, Western Basin, and the Jack's Reef Horizon: Reconsidering the Late Woodland Archaeology of Ohio. *Archaeology of Eastern North America* 41:113–44.

2015   Building the Past, an Introduction. In *Building the Past: Prehistoric Wooden Post Architecture in the Ohio Valley-Great Lakes,* edited by Brian G. Redmond and Robert A. Genheimer, pp. 1–7. University of Florida Press, Gainesville.

Redmond, Brian G., and Robert McCullough

2000   The Late Woodland to Late Prehistoric Occupations of Central Indiana. In *Late Woodland Societies: Tradition and Transformation across the Midcontinent,* edited by Thomas E. Emerson, Dale L. McElrath, and Andrew C. Fortier, pp. 643–85. University of Nebraska Press, Lincoln.

Reidhead, Van A., and William F. Limp

1974   The Haag Site (12D19): A Preliminary Report. *Indiana Archaeological Bulletin* 1(1):4–19. Indiana Historical Society, Indianapolis.

Riggs, Rodney E.

1986   New Stratigraphic Sequences from the Lower Miami Valley. *West Virginia Archaeologist* 38(2):1–21.

Riley, Thomas J., Richard Edging, and Jack Rossen

1990   Prehistoric Cultigens in Eastern North America: Changing Paradigms. *Current Anthropology* 31(5):525–41.

Ritzenthaler, Robert E., and George I. Quimby
1962   The Red Ocher Culture of the Upper Great Lakes and Adjacent Areas. *Fieldiana* 36:243–75. Chicago Natural History Museum, Chicago.

Robinson, Brian S., Jennifer C. Ort, William A. Eldridge, Adrian L. Burke, and Bertrand G. Pelletier
2009   Paleoindian Aggregation and Social Context at Bull Brook. *American Antiquity* 74(3):423–47.

Robinson, Kenneth W., and Steven D. Smith
1979   The Villier Site (15JF110 Complex). In *Excavations at Four Archaic Sites in the Lower Ohio River Valley, Jefferson County, Kentucky*, edited by Michael B. Collins, pp. 590–696. Occasional Papers in Anthropology No. 1. Department of Anthropology, University of Kentucky, Lexington.

Rossen, Jack
1984   Botanical Remains. In *Prehistory of the Middle Cumberland River Valley: The Hurricane Branch Site, Jackson County, Tennessee*, edited by Tom D. Dillehay, Nancy O'Malley, and Thomas Gatus, pp. 234–52. Occasional Papers in Anthropology No. 4. Department of Anthropology, University of Kentucky, Lexington.
1996   The Archaeobotanical Record of the Late Mississippian Caborn-Welborn Culture: The Slack Farm, Caborn, and Hovey Lake Sites. Manuscript on file, Department of Anthropology, University of Kentucky, Lexington.
1999   Archaeobotanical Remains. In *Woodland Occupations along Clear Creek in Southeastern Kentucky*, edited by B. Jo Stokes and Carl R. Shields, pp. 73–86. Research Report No. 2. Kentucky Archaeological Survey, Lexington.
2000   Archaic Plant Utilization at the Hedden Site, McCracken County, Kentucky. In *Current Archaeological Research in Kentucky, Volume Six*, edited by David Pollack and Kristen J. Gremillion, pp. 1–24. Kentucky Heritage Council, Frankfort.
2006   Archaeobotanical Remains. In *The Highland Creek Site: Middle to Late Archaic Wetland Utilization in Western Kentucky*, edited by Greg Maggard and David Pollack, pp. 73–87. Research Report No. 5. Kentucky Archaeological Survey, Lexington.
2007   Description and Analysis of Paleobotanical Remains. In *Dreaming Creek: A Phase III Data Recovery of an Early Late Woodland Site in Madison County, Kentucky*, edited by James Fenton and David McBride, pp. 8.1–8.16. Archaeology Report No. 7. Wilbur Smith Associates, Lexington, Kentucky.
2008   Exploring New Dimensions in the Study of Archaeological Plants. In *Current Northeast Paleoethnobotany II*, edited by John P. Hart, pp. 191–98. Bulletin Series No. 512. New York State Museum, Albany.
2009   Late Archaic and Woodland Period Archaeobotanical Analysis. In *Intensive Archaeological Investigations at the McAlpine Locks and Dam, Louisville, Kentucky: Volume 1. Project Background and Investigations of the Late Archaic and Woodland Components at the Shippingport Site (15JF702)*, edited by Stephen T. Mocas, Michael W. French, and Duane B. Simpson, pp. 217–38. CRM Report No. 2009–17. AMEC Earth and Environmental, Louisville, Kentucky.
2010   Mississippian Period Archaeobotany. In *Final Report: Intensive Archaeological Investigations at the McAlpine Lock and Dam, Louisville, Kentucky, Volume II:*

Mississippian Components at the Shippingport Site (15JF702), edited by Michael W. French, pp. 351–67. CRM Report 2009–17. AMEC Earth and Environmental, Louisville, Kentucky.

2011 Preceramic Plant Gathering, Gardening, and Farming. In *From Foraging to Farming in the Andes: New Perspectives on Food Production and Social Organization,* edited by Tom D. Dillehay, pp. 177–92. Cambridge University Press, Cambridge.

2013 Macrobotanical Analysis. In *The Archaeological Evaluation of the Newcomb (12CL2) and M. Kraft (12CL935) Sites Located in the Proposed Lewis and Clark Trail Project (DES 0200120) Clarksville, Clark County, Indiana,* edited by Duane Simpson, Stephen T. Mocas, and Dawn Bradley, pp. 282–303. AMEC Environment and Infrastructure, Louisville, Kentucky.

2019 Botanical Remains. In *Native American Utilization of Caves and Rockshelters in the Floyds Fork Drainage of Jefferson and Bullitt Counties,* edited by Justin Carlson and David Pollack. Research Report No. 14. Kentucky Archaeological Survey, Lexington.

Rossen, Jack, and Richard Edging
1987 East Meets West: Patterns in Kentucky Late Prehistoric Subsistence. In *Current Archaeological Research in Kentucky, Volume One,* edited by David Pollack, pp. 225–34. Kentucky Heritage Council, Frankfort.

Rossen, Jack and Rebecca Hawkins
1995 The Plant Subsistence Transition of A.D. 1000: The View from Boone County, Kentucky. Paper presented at the Twelfth Annual Kentucky Heritage Council Archaeological Conference, Richmond, Kentucky.

Ross-Stallings, Nancy A.
2007 Trophy Taking in the Central and Lower Mississippi Valley. In *The Taking and Displaying of Human Body Parts as Trophies by Amerindians,* edited by Richard J. Chacon and David H. Dye, pp. 339–70. Springer Science Business Media, New York.

2009 Late Archaic and Woodland Period Faunal Analysis. In *Intensive Archaeological Investigations at the McAlpine Locks and Dam, Louisville, Kentucky: Volume 1. Project Background and Investigations of the Late Archaic and Woodland Components at the Shippingport Site (15JF702),* edited by Stephen T. Mocas, Michael W. French, and Duane B. Simpson, pp. 238–312. CRM Report No. 2009–17. AMEC Earth and Environmental, Louisville, Kentucky.

2010a Mississippian Period Burial Analysis. In *Final Report: Intensive Archaeological Investigations at the McAlpine Lock and Dam, Louisville, Kentucky, Volume II: Mississippian Components at the Shippingport Site (15JF702),* edited by Michael W. French, pp. 431–94. CRM Report, 2009–17. AMEC Earth and Environmental, Louisville, Kentucky.

2010b Mississippian Period Faunal Analysis. In *Final Report: Intensive Archaeological Investigations at the McAlpine Locks and Dam, Louisville, Kentucky: Volume II. Mississippian Components at the Shippingport Site (15JF702),* edited by Michael W. French, pp. 369–430. CRM Report 2009–17. AMEC Earth and Environmental, Louisville, Kentucky.

Rush, Dorothy
1994   Early Accounts of Travel to the Falls of the Ohio: A Bibliography with Selected Quotations, 1765–1833. *The Filson Club History Quarterly* 68(2):254.

Sassaman, Kenneth E.
2010   *The Eastern Archaic Historicized.* Alta Mira Press, Lanham, Maryland.

Sassaman, Kenneth E., and Michael J. Heckenberger
2004   Crossing the Symbolic Rubicon in the Southeast. In *Signs of Power: The Rise of Cultural Complexity in the Southeast,* edited by Jon L. Gibson and Philip J. Carr, pp. 214–33. University of Alabama Press, Tuscaloosa.

Sassaman, Kenneth E., and Gerald Ledbetter
1996   Middle and Late Archaic Architecture. In *Archaeology of the Mid-Holocene Southeast,* edited by Kenneth E. Sassaman and David G. Anderson, pp. 75–95. University of Florida Press, Gainesville.

Saunders, Lorraine P.
1986   KYANG Bioarchaeology Report. Report prepared for the University of Louisville Archeological Survey. Manuscript on file, Corn Island Archaeology, Louisville, Kentucky.

Scarry, C. Margaret and John F. Scarry
2008   Native American "Garden Agriculture" in Southeastern North America. *World Archaeology* 37(2):259–74.

Schenian, Pamela A.
1987   The Crick Cache (Site 15Cw96). In *Current Archaeological Research in Kentucky, Volume 1,* edited by David Pollack, pp. 1–12. Kentucky Heritage Council, Frankfort.

Schlanger, Sarah H.
1992   Recognizing Persistent Places in Anasazi. In *Space, Time, and Archaeological Landscapes,* edited by Jaqueline Rossignol and LuAnn Wandsnider, pp. 91–113. Plenum, New York.

Schmidt, Christopher W.
2013   Human Osteology. In *Scientific Recovery Investigations at the Kramer Mound (12Sp7): Prehistoric Artifact Assemblages, Faunal and Floral Remains, and Human Osteology.* Report Submitted to the Department of Natural Resources, Division of Historic Preservation and Archaeology, Indianapolis, Indiana.

Schmidt, Christopher W., and R. Criss Helmkamp
1997   Analysis of the Human Dental Remains. In *General Electric Company Hopewell in Mt. Vernon: A Study of the Mt. Vernon Site (12-Po-885),* edited by the General Electric Company, pp. 67–84. General Electric Company, Mount Vernon, Indiana.

Schmidt, Christopher W., Rachel A. Lockhart, Christopher Newman, Anna Serrano, Melissa Zolnierz, Anne T. Bader, and Jeffrey A. Plunkett
2010   Skeletal Evidence of Cultural Variation: Mutilation Related to Warfare and Mortuary Treatment. In *Human Variation in the Americas: The Integration of Archaeology and Biological Anthropology,* edited by Benjamin M. Auerbach, pp. 215–37. Occasional Paper No. 38. Center for Archaeological Investigations, Southern Illinois University, Carbondale.

Schmidt, Christopher W., Curtis Tomak, Rachel A. Lockhart, Tammy R. Greene, and Gregory A. Rinehardt

2008   Chapter 14. Early Archaic Cremations from Southern Indiana. In *The Analysis of Burned Human Remains*, edited by Christopher W. Schmidt and Steven A. Symes, pp. 227–237. Academic Press, imprint of Elsevier Press, Boston.

Schnellenberger, Jack

2013   Confocal Microscopy of Cut Marks on a Middle Archaic Cranial Fragment. Paper presented at the 128th Annual Meeting of the Indiana Academy of Science, Indianapolis.

Scholl, Nate C.

2008   *Geoarchaeological and Paleolandscape Reconstructions in the Lower Ohio River Valley: Late Wisconsin and Early Holocene Landforms in Knob Creek Bottom.* Unpublished Master's thesis, Department of Geography, Geology and Anthropology, Indiana State University, Terre Haute.

Schroeder, Marjorie

2007   Carbonized Plant Remains from the Caesars Archaeological Project, Harrison County, Indiana. In *Caesars Archaeological Project Overview: Geomorphology, Archeobotany and Other Specialty Analysis, Caesars Archaeological Project Report Volume 1*, edited by C. Russell Stafford, pp. 177–267. Technical Report 36. Indiana State University Archaeology and Quaternary Research Laboratory, Terre Haute.

Schultz, Christian

1810   *Travels on an Inland Voyage Through the States of NY, PA, VA, OH, KY and TN and Through the Territories of IN, LA, Miss., and New Orleans, performed in the Years 1807 and 1808.* Two Volumes. Filson Historical Society, Louisville, Kentucky.

Seeman, Mark F.

1975   The Prehistoric Chert Quarries and Workshops of Harrison County, Indiana. *Indiana Archaeological Bulletin* 1(3):47–67).

1988   Hopewell Trophy-Skull Artifacts as Evidence for Competition in Middle Woodland Societies circa 50 B.C.-A.D. 350. *American Antiquity* 53:565–77.

1992   The Bow and Arrow, the Intrusive Mound Complex, and a Late Woodland Jack's Reef Horizon in the Mid-Ohio Valley. In *Cultural Variability in Context: Woodland Settlements of the Mid-Ohio Valley*, edited by Mark F. Seeman, pp. 41–51, Special Paper 7. Midcontinental Journal of Archaeology, Kent State University Press, Kent, Ohio.

1994   Intercluster Lithic Patterning at Nobles Pond: A Case for "Disembedded" Procurement among Early Paleoindian Societies. *American Antiquity* 59:273–88.

2007   Predatory War and Hopewell Trophies. In *The Taking and Displaying of Human Body Parts as Trophies by Amerindians*, edited by Richard J. Chacon and David H. Dye, pp. 167–89. Springer Science Business Media, New York.

Seeman, Mark F., and William S. Dancey

2000   The Late Woodland Period in Southern Ohio: Basic Issues and Prospects. In *Late Woodland Societies, Tradition and Transformation Across the Midcontinent,* edited by Thomas E. Emerson, Dale L. McElrath, and Andrew C. Fortier, pp. 583–611. University of Nebraska Press, Lincoln.

Sharp, William T.

1990   Fort Ancient Period. In *The Archaeology of Kentucky: Past Accomplishments and Future Directions. Volume 2,* edited by David Pollack, pp. 467–557. Kentucky Heritage Council, Frankfort.

Shea, Andrea B.

1977   *Comparison of Middle Woodland and Early Mississippian Subsistence Patterns: Analysis of Plant Remains from an Archaeological Site in the Duck River Valley, Tennessee, Supplemented by the Potentially Exploitable Native Flora.* Master's thesis, Department of Botany, University of Tennessee, Knoxville.

1978   An Analysis of Plant Remains from the Middle Woodland and Mississippian Components on the Banks V Site and a Paleoethnobotanical Study of the Native Flora of the Upper Duck Valley. In *Fifth Report of the Normandy Archaeological Project,* edited by Charles H. Faulkner and Major C. R. McCollough, pp. 596–699. Report of Investigations No. 20. Department of Anthropology, University of Tennessee, Knoxville.

Sherwood, Sarah C., and Tristram R. Kidder

2011   The Davincis of Dirt: Geoarchaeological Perspectives on Native American Mound Building in the Mississippi River Basin. *Journal of Anthropological Archaeology* 30:69–87.

Shetrone, Henry C.

1926   Exploration of the Hopewell Group of Prehistoric Earthworks. *Ohio Archaeological and Historical Quarterly* 35:1–227.

Sieber, Ellen and Ann I. Ottesen

1986   *Final Report on the Phase III Mitigation of the Clark Maritime Archaeological District, Clark County, Indiana.* Resource Analysts, Bloomington.

Siegel, Peter E.

1991   On the Antilles as a Potential Corridor for Cultigens into Eastern North America. *Current Anthropology* 32(3):332–34.

Simon, Mary L.

2000   Regional Variation in Plant Use Strategies in the Midwest during the Late Woodland. In *Late Woodland Societies: Tradition and Transformation across the Midcontinent,* edited by Thomas E. Emerson, Dale L. McElrath, and Andrew C. Fortier, pp. 37–75. University of Nebraska Press, Lincoln.

2009   A Regional and Chronological Synthesis of Archaic Period Plant Use in the Midcontinent. In *Archaic Societies: Diversity and Complexity Across the Midcontinent,* edited by Thomas D. Emerson, Dale L. McElrath and Andrew C. Fortier, pp. 81–114. State University of New York Press, Albany.

2017   Reevaluating the Evidence for Middle Woodland Maize from the Holding Site. *American Antiquity* 82(1):140–50.

Simpson, Duane, Anne Bader, Tim Sullivan, William Hill, and Mickey Loughlin

2019   *A Phase II Evaluation of the Ellingsworth Site (12CL127), Clark County, Indiana.* Corn Island Archaeology, Louisville, Kentucky.

Simpson, Duane B., and Stephen Mocas

2017   *RiverPark Place: Documenting 5000 Years of Occupation along the Ohio River through Excavations at Sites 15JF594, 15JF596, 15JF597, 15JF598 and 15JF599, Louisville, Jefferson County, Kentucky. Volume 2: Prehistoric Archaeology.* Wood Group, Louisville, Kentucky.

Simpson, Duane B., Stephen Mocas, and Dawn Bradley

2013   *The Archaeological Evaluation of the Newcomb (12CL2) and M. Kraft (12CL935) Sites Located in the Proposed Lewis and Clark Trail Project, Clarksville, Clark County, Indiana.* AMEC Environment and Infrastructure, Louisville, Kentucky.

Simpson, Duane and Nancy A. Ross-Stallings

2017   *RiverPark Place: Documenting 5000 Years of Occupation along the Ohio River through Excavations at Sites 15Jf594, 15Jf596, 15Jf597, 15Jf598 and 15Jf599 Jefferson County, Louisville, Kentucky. Volume 3: Archaeology and Skeletal Biology of Interments.* AMEC Environment and Infrastructure, Louisville, Kentucky.

Simpson, Duane and Nathan Scholl

2014   Geoarchaeology of the Falls of the Ohio River: Quaternary Landforms at the Falls. *Quaternary International* 342:139–48.

Smith, Bruce D.

1989   Origins of Agriculture in Eastern North America. *Science* 264:1566–71.

1992   *Rivers of Change: Essays on Early Agriculture in Eastern North America.* Smithsonian Institution Press, Washington, D.C.

2006   Eastern North America as an Independent Center of Plant Domestication. *Proceedings of the National Academy of Sciences* 103(33):12223-28.

2009   Initial Formation of an Indigenous Crop Complex in Eastern North America at 3800 B.P. *Proceedings of the National Academy of Sciences* 106:6561–66.

2011   The Cultural Context of Plant Domestication in Eastern North America. *Current Anthropology* 52, Supplement 4:S471-S484.

Smith, Dwight L., and Ray Swick (editors)

1997   *A Journey through the West: Thomas Rodney's 1803 Journal from Delaware to the Mississippi Territory.* Ohio University Press, Athens.

Smith, Edward E.

1986   *An Archaeological Assessment of the Swan's Landing Site (12Hr304), Harrison County, Indiana.* Reports of Investigations 86–85. Glenn A. Black Laboratory of Archaeology, Indiana University, Bloomington.

Smith, Edward E., and Stephen T. Mocas

1993   *Archaeological Investigations at the Paddy's West Substation, Floyd County, Indiana.* Reports of Investigations 93–98. Glenn A. Black Laboratory of Archaeology, Indiana University, Bloomington.

1995   *Archaeological Investigations at the Paddy's West Switching Substation, Floyd County, Indiana.* Reports of Investigations 95–94. Glenn A. Black Laboratory of Archaeology, Indiana University, Bloomington.

Smith, Maria O.

1993   A Probable Case of Decapitation at the Late Archaic Robinson Site (40SM4), Smith County, Tennessee. *Tennessee Anthropologist* 18(2):131–42.

1995   Scalping in the Archaic Period: Evidence from the Western Tennessee Valley. *Southeastern Archaeology* 14:60–68.

1997   Osteological Indications of Warfare in the Late Archaic Period of the Western Tennessee Valley. In *Troubled Times: Violence and Warfare in the Past,* edited by Debra L. Martin and David W. Frayer, pp. 241–65. Gordon and Breach Publishers, Amsterdam.

2015   Contextualizing the Precolumbian Postmortem "Life" of Modified Human Remains. In *Transforming the Dead: culturally modified bone in the prehistoric Midwest,* edited by Eve A. Hargrave, Shirley J. Shirmer, Kristin M. Hedman, and Robin M. Lillie, pp. 262–86. University of Alabama Press, Tuscaloosa.

Snow, Clarence

1948   *Indian Knoll Skeletons of Site Oh2, Ohio County, Kentucky.* Reports in Anthropology, Volume 4, Number 3, Part II. Department of Anthropology, University of Kentucky, Lexington.

Springer, Gregory S., D. Matthew White, Harold R. Rowe, Ben Hardt, L. Nivanthi Mihimdukulasooriya, Hai Cheng, and R. Lawrence Edwards

2010   Multiproxy Evidence from Caves of Native Americans Altering the Overlying Landscape during the Late Holocene of East-Central North America. *The Holocene* 20:257–83.

Stafford, C. Russell

1991   Archaic Period Logistical Foraging Strategies in West-Central Illinois. *Midcontinental Journal of Archaeology* 16:212–46.

1994   Structural Changes in Archaic Landscape Use in the Dissected Uplands of Southwestern Indiana. *American Antiquity* 59(2):219–37.

2004   Modeling Soil-Geomorphic Associations and Archaic Stratigraphic Sequences in the Lower Ohio River Valley. *Journal of Archaeological Science* 31:1053–67.

2006   Prather Site Core Descriptions. In *Archaeological Investigations at the Prather Site, Clark County, Indiana: The 2005 Survey and Excavations,* edited by Cheryl Ann Munson, Michael Strezewski, and C. Russell Stafford, pp. 219–27. Reports of Investigations 802. IPFW Archaeological Survey, Fort Wayne, Indiana.

2009   Lithic Tools from the Thebes/St. Charles and Early Side Notched Components at the James Farnsley Site. In *Early Archaic Occupations at the James Farnsley Site, Caesars Archaelogical Project, Harrison County, Indiana,* edited by C. Russell Stafford and Mark E. Cantin, pp. 285–305. Technical Report 39. Indiana State University Archaeology and Quaternary Research Laboratory, Terre Haute.

Stafford, C. Russell, C. Michael Anslinger, Mark E. Cantin, and Robert E. Pace

1988   *An Analysis of Data Center Site Surveys in Southwestern Indiana.* Technical Report 3. Indiana State University Anthropology Laboratory, Terre Haute.

Stafford, C. Russell and Mark E. Cantin

1992   *Test Excavations at Poffey Creek in the Ohio River Valley, Harrison County, Indiana.* Technical Report 11. Indiana State University Anthropology Laboratory, Terre Haute.

1996   *Archaeological Phase I Surface and Subsurface Investigations in the Caesars*

World Development, Harrison County, Indiana. Technical Report 32. Indiana State University Anthropology Laboratory, Terre Haute.

2009a   Archaic Period Chronology in the Hill Country of Southern Indiana. In *Archaic Societies: Diversity and Complexity across the Midcontinent,* edited by Thomas E. Emerson, Dale L. McElrath, and Andrew C. Fortier, pp. 287–313. State University of New York, Albany.

2009b   *Early Archaic Occupations at the James Farnsley Site, Caesars Archaeological Project, Harrison County, Indiana.* Caesars Archaeological Project Vol. 3. Technical Report 38. Indiana State University Archaeology and Quaternary Research Laboratory, Terre Haute.

2010   Archaeological Buried Site Potential of the Duke Energy Gallagher Pipeline, Floyd and Harrison Counties, Indiana and Jefferson County, Kentucky. Submitted to Indiana Division of Historic Preservation and Archaeology. Indiana State University Archaeology and Quaternary Research Laboratory, Indianapolis.

Stafford, C. Russell, Mark Cantin, John Schwegman, and Stephen T. Mocas

2008   Middle Archaic, Late Archaic, and Terminal Archaic Components at the Knob Creek Site (12HR484), Harrison County, Indiana. In *The Middle, Late, and Terminal Archaic Occupations at the Caesars Archaeological Project, Harrison County, Indiana,* edited by C. Russell Stafford and Stephen T. Mocas, pp. 259–849. Caesars Archaeological Project Report Volume 3. Technical Report 38. Indiana State University Archaeology and Quaternary Research Laboratory, Terre Haute.

Stafford, C. Russell and Kathryn G. De Rego

2012   Buried Site Potential, Early Holocene Landforms, and Channel Dynamics in the Lower Ohio River Valley. Paper presented at the Geological Society of America, Charlotte, North Carolina.

Stafford, C. Russell and Stephen T. Mocas (editors)

2008   *The Middle, Late, and Terminal Archaic Occupations at the Caesars Archaeological Project, Harrison County, Indiana.* Caesars Archaeological Project Report Volume 3. Technical Report 38. Indiana State University Archaeology and Quaternary Research Laboratory, Terre Haute.

Stafford, C. Russell, Ronald L. Richards, and C. Michael Anslinger

2000   The Bluegrass Fauna and Changes in Middle Holocene Hunter-Gatherer Foraging in the Southern Midwest. *American Antiquity* 65:317–36.

Staller, John, Robert Tykot, and Bruce Benz

2009   *Histories of Maize: Multidisciplinary Approaches to the Prehistory, Linguistics, Biogeography, Domestication, and Evolution of Maize.* Left Coast Press, Walnut Creek, California.

Stallings, Richard J.

1996   *Analysis of the Lithic Material from the Hedden Site (15McC81), McCracken County, Kentucky.* Cultural Resource Analysts, Lexington, Kentucky.

2001   *Phase III Mitigation of 40WM184 Located along Concord Road, Williamson County, Tennessee.* Cultural Horizons, Harrodsburg, Kentucky.

Stallings, Richard J., Anne Bader, Stephen Mocas, Bridget Mohr, Evan Peacock, Matthew Prybylski, Jack Rossen, David Schatz, Duane Simpson, Nancy Ross-Stallings, and Melinda Wetzel

2008   *Phase III Archaeological Mitigation of the Panther Rock Site (15CL58), Carroll County, Kentucky.* AMEC Earth and Environmental, Louisville, Kentucky.

Stallings, Richard J., Stephen T. Mocas, and Jack Rossen

2013   *Feature Excavations at the KYANG site (15JF267), Jefferson County, Kentucky.* AMEC Environment and Infrastructure, Louisville, Kentucky.

Stallings, Richard J., David W. Schatz, Kim D. Simpson, Stephen T. Mocas, and Michael W. French

2010   Mississippian Period Lithic Analysis. In *Final Report: Intensive Archaeological Investigations at the McAlpine Lock and Dam, Louisville, Kentucky, Volume II: Mississippian Components at the Shippingport Site (15JF702)*, edited by Michael W. French, pp. 221–95. CRM Report 2009–17. AMEC Earth and Environmental, Louisville, Kentucky.

Stinchcomb, Gary E., Timothy C. Messner, Forrest C. Williamson, Steven G. Driese, and Lee C. Nordt

2013   Climatic and Human Controls on Holocene Floodplain Vegetation Changes in Eastern Pennsylvania Based on the Isotopic Composition of Soil Organic Matter. *Quaternary Research* 79:377–90.

Stiner, Mary C., and Steven L. Kuhn

2016   Are We Missing the "Sweet Spot" between Optimality and Niche Construction Theory in Archaeology? *Journal of Anthropological Archaeology* 44:177–84.

Stothers, David M., Timothy J. Abel, and Andrew M. Schneider

2001   Archaic Perspectives in the Western Lake Erie Basin. In *Archaic Transitions in Ohio and Kentucky Prehistory*, edited by Olaf H. Prufer, Sara E. Pedde, and Richard S. Meindl, pp. 233–89. Kent State University Press, Kent, Ohio.

Stuiver, M., P. J. Reimer, and R. W. Reimer

2017   CALIB 7.1 [WWW program] at http://calib.org.

Styles, Bonnie W., and Erin Brand

2008   Appendix C: Faunal Remains from the Knob Creek Site (12HR484), Harrison County, Indiana. In *Early Woodland and Middle Woodland Occupations at the Knob Creek Site (12HR484), Caesars Archaeological Project, Harrison County, Indiana, Volume 2*, edited by Stephen T. Mocas. Technical Report 37. Indiana State University Archaeology and Quaternary Research Laboratory, Terre Haute.

Styles, Thomas R.

1985   *Holocene and Late Pleistocene Geology of the Napoleon Hollow Site in the Lower Illinois Valley.* Kampsville Research Series 5. Center for American Archaeology Press, Kampsville, Illinois.

Sussenbach, Tom

1993   *Agricultural Intensification and Mississippian Developments in the Confluence Region of the Mississippi River Valley.* Unpublished PhD dissertation, Department of Anthropology, University of Illinois, Urbana-Champaign.

Swartz, B. K.

1970   *Adena: Seeking of an Identity.* Ball State University, Muncie, Indiana.

Swihart, Matthew R., and Kevin C. Nolan

2014   *Investigation of Fort Ancient Settlement and Community Patterns: An Archaeo-logical Survey of Dearborn County, Indiana.* Reports of Investigation 83, Vol. 1. Applied Anthropology Laboratories, Department of Anthropology, Ball State University, Muncie, Indiana.

Szabó, Péter

2015   Historical Ecology: Past, Present and Future. *Biological Review of the Cambridge Philosophical Society* 90:997–1014.

Tankersley, Kenneth B.

1985   Mineralogical Properties of Wyandotte Chert as an Aid to Archaeological Fin-gerprinting. *Proceedings of the Lithic Resource Procurement: Proceedings from the Second Conference on Prehistoric Chert Exploitation,* edited by Susan C. Ve-hik, pp. 251–64. Occasional Paper No. 4. Center for Archaeological Investiga-tions, Southern Illinois University, Carbondale.

Taylor, Ralph

1989   Changes in Freshwater Mussel Populations of the Ohio River: 1,000 to Recent Times. *Ohio Journal of Science* 89(5):188–191.

Taylor, S.

1933   Old Louisville Ponds. *Courier-Journal,* April 6, 1933.

Thibadeau, Leonard

1972   Analysis of the Small Mammal Remains of the Old Clarksville site, Clark Coun-ty, Indiana. Manuscript on file, Corn Island Archaeology, Louisville, Kentucky.

Thompson, Victor D.

2010   The Rhythms of Space-Time and the Making of Monuments and Places during the Archaic. In *Trend, Tradition, and Turmoil: What Happened to the Southeast-ern Archaic?,* edited by David H. Thomas and Matthew C. Sanger, pp. 217–28. Anthropological Papers of the American Museum of Natural History No. 93.

2013   Whispers on the Landscape. In *The Archaeology and Historical Ecology of Small Scale Economies,* edited by Victor D. Thompson and James C. Waggoner Jr., pp. 1–13. University Press of Florida, Gainesville.

Thwaites, Reuben Gold (1853–1913) (editor)

1904–7 *Early Western Travels, 1748–1846, Volume 26,* pp. 48–51. Arthur H. Clark, Cleve-land, Ohio.

Trotter, Mildred and Goldine C. Gleser

1958   A Re-evaluation of Estimation of Stature Based on Measurements of Stature Taken during Life and of Long Bones after Death. *American Journal of Physical Anthropology* 16:79–123.

Turnbow, Christopher A., and A. Gwynn Henderson

1992   Ceramic Analysis. In *Fort Ancient Cultural Dynamics in the Middle Ohio Valley,* edited by A. Gwynn Henderson, pp. 113–35. Monographs in World Archaeol-ogy No. 8. Prehistory Press, Madison, Wisconsin.

Turnbow, Christopher A., and William E. Sharp
1988   *Muir (15JS86): An Early Fort Ancient Site in Central Kentucky.* Archaeological Report No. 165. University of Kentucky, Lexington.

Turner, Jocelyn C.
2006   Analysis of Archaeobotanical Remains. In *Archaeological Investigations at the Prather Site, Clark County, Indiana: The 2005 Survey and Excavations,* edited by Cheryl Ann Munson, Michael Strezewski, and C. Russell Stafford, pp. 197–208. Reports of Investigations 802. IPFW Archaeological Survey, Fort Wayne, Indiana.

2011   Appendix II: Analysis of Macrobotanical Remains from Sites 12CL2, 12CL890-U, and 12CL935 in Clark County, Indiana. In *Phase 1 Archaeological Survey of the Lewis and Clark Trail, Town of Clarksville, Indiana,* edited by Cheryl Ann Munson. Department of Anthropology, Indiana University, Bloomington.

2017   Chapter 8: Analysis of the Macrobotanical Remains from Site 15Bu463 in Bullitt County, Kentucky. In *Phase II Archaeological Evaluation and Phase III Mitigation at the Buffalo Run Site (15Bu463) Bullitt County, Kentucky,* edited by Melinda K. Wetzel, Anne Tobbe Bader, and Kathryn J. McGrath. Corn Island Archaeology, Louisville, Kentucky.

Vickery, Kent D.
2008   Archaic Manifestations in Southwestern Ohio and Vicinity. In *Transitions: Archaic and Early Woodland Research in the Ohio Country,* edited by Martha P. Otto and Brian G. Redmond, pp. 1–28. Ohio University Press, Athens, Ohio.

Vickery, Kent D., Theodore S. Sunderhaus, and Robert A. Genheimer
2000   Preliminary Report on Excavations at the Fort Ancient State Line Site, 33 Ha 58, in the Central Ohio Valley. In *Cultures before Contact: The Late Prehistory of Ohio and Surrounding Regions,* edited by Robert A. Genheimer, pp. 272–329. Ohio Archaeological Council, Columbus.

Voegelin, Ermine Wheeler
1944   *Mortuary Customs of the Shawnee and Other Eastern Tribes.* Prehistory Research Series. Indiana Historical Society, Indianapolis.

Voegelin, Kinietz and Ermine W. Voegelin (editors)
1939   *Shawnese Traditions, C.C. Trowbridge's Account.* Occasional Contributions from the Museum of Anthropology of the University of Michigan No. 9. University of Michigan Press, Ann Arbor.

Wagner, Gail E.
1987   *Uses of Plants by the Fort Ancient Indians.* Unpublished PhD dissertation, Department of Anthropology, Washington University, St. Louis, Missouri.

2000   Tobacco in Prehistoric Eastern North America. In *Tobacco Use by Native North Americans: Sacred Smoke and Silent Killer,* edited by Joseph C. Winter, pp. 185–201. University of Oklahoma Press, Norman.

2005   Anthropogenic Changes at the Carlston Annis Site. In *Archaeology of the Middle Green River Region, Kentucky,* edited by William H. Marquardt and Patty Jo Watson, pp. 213–42. University Press of Florida, Gainesville.

Walker, M. J. C., M. Berkelhammer, S. Björk, L. C. Cwynar, D. A. Fischer, A. J. Long, J. J. Lowe, R. M. Newnham, S. O. Rasmussen, and H. Weiss

2012   Formal Subdivision of the Holocene Series/Epoch: A Discussion Paper by a Working Group of Integration of Ice-core, Marine, and Terrestrial Records (IN-TIMATE) and the Subcommission on Quaternary Stratigraphy (SQS) of the International Commission on Stratigraphy (ICS). *Journal of Quaternary Science* 27(7):649–59.

Walker, Phillip L.

2001   A Bioarcheological Perspective on the History of Violence. *Annual Review of Anthropology* 30:573–96.

Webb, William S.

1940   The Wright Mounds, Sites 6 and 7, Montgomery County, Kentucky. *Reports in Anthropology and Archaeology* 5:6–134. University of Kentucky Press, Lexington.

1941   The Morgan Stone Mound, Site 15, Bath County, Kentucky. *Reports in Anthropology and Archaeology* 5(3):233–91. University of Kentucky Press, Lexington.

1946   Indian Knoll Site Oh2 Ohio County, Kentucky. University of Kentucky. *Reports in Anthropology and Archaeology,* Part I, 4(3):115–356. University of Kentucky, Lexington.

1950   The Carlston Annis Mound. *Reports in Anthropology and Archaeology* 7(4):266–354. University of Kentucky, Lexington.

Webb, William S., and David L. DeJarnette

1942   *An Archaeological Survey of Pickwick Basin in the Adjacent Portions of the States of Alabama, Mississippi and Tennessee.* Bulletin Number 129. Smithsonian Institution Bureau of American Ethnology, Washington, D.C.

Webb, William S., and John B. Elliott

1942   The Robbins Mounds, Site Be3 and Be4, Boone County, Kentucky. *Reports in Anthropology and Archaeology* 5(5):377–499. University of Kentucky Press, Lexington.

Webb, William S., and William D. Funkhouser

1932   Archaeological Survey of Kentucky. *Reports in Anthropology and Archaeology.* Volume 2. University of Kentucky Press, Lexington.

Webb, William S., and William G. Haag

1947   The Fisher Site, Fayette County, Kentucky. *Reports in Anthropology and Archaeology* 7(2):49–104. University of Kentucky, Lexington.

Webb, William S., and Charles E. Snow

1945   The Adena People. *Reports in Anthropology and Archaeology.* Volume 6. University of Kentucky, Lexington.

1974   The Crigler Mounds, Sites Be20 and Be27, and the Hartman Mound Site, Be32, Boone County, Kentucky. *Reports in Anthropology and Archaeology* 5:505–79. Reprint of 1945 edition. University of Kentucky, Lexington.

Wells, Joshua J., Craig R. Arnold, and Robert G. McCullough

2008   *Multiple Methods of Landscape and Site Specific Survey in an Archaeological Assessment of Clark County, Indiana.* Reports of Investigations 802. IPFW Archaeological Survey, Fort Wayne, Indiana.

Wetzel, Melinda K., Anne Tobbe Bader, and Kathryn J. McGrath

2017   *Phase II Archaeological Evaluation and Phase III Mitigation at the Buffalo Run Site (15Bu463) Bullitt County, Kentucky.* Corn Island Archaeology, Louisville, Kentucky.

Whallon, Robert

2006   Social Networks and Information: Non-"utilitarian" Mobility among Hunter-Gatherers. *Journal of Anthropological Archaeology* 25:259–70.

White, Andrew A.

2002   *Survey and Excavations in the Nugent East Area, Clark County, Indiana, 1998–1999.* Reports of Investigations 206. IPFW Archaeological Survey, Indiana University-Purdue University, Fort Wayne.

2004   *Excavations at the Clark's Point Site (12-Cl-3), Clark County, Indiana.* Reports of Investigations 302. IPFW Archaeological Survey, Indiana University-Purdue University, Fort Wayne.

Wiant, Michael D., Kenneth B. Farnsworth, and Edwin R. Hajic

2009   The Archaic Period in the Lower Illinois River Basin. In *Archaic Societies: Diversity and Complexity across the Midcontinent,* edited by Thomas D. Emerson, Dale L. McElrath and Andrew C. Fortier, pp. 229–85. State University of New York Press, Albany.

Wilkins, Gary R., Paul A. Delcourt, Hazel R. Delcourt, Frederick W. Harrison, and Manson R. Turner

1991   Paleoecology of Central Kentucky Since the Last Glacial Maximum. *Quaternary Research* 36:224–39.

Willey, P.

1990   *Prehistoric Warfare on the Great Plains: Skeletal Analysis of the Crow Creek Massacre Victims.* Garland Publishing, New York.

Williams, L. A., and Company

1882   *History of the Ohio Falls Cities and Their Counties. Illustrations and Biographical Sketches.* Volume I. Cleveland.

Williams, Sloan R., Kathleen Forgey, and Elizabeth Klarich

2001   An Osteological Study of Nasca Trophy Heads Collected by A. L. Kroeber During the Marshall Field Expeditions to Peru. *Fieldiana* 33:1–137.

Winterhalder, Bruce

1994   Concepts in Historical Ecology: The View from Evolutionary Theory. In *Historical Ecology: Cultural Knowledge and Changing Landscapes,* edited by Carole L. Crumley, pp. 17–42. School of American Research Advanced Seminar Series, Santa Fe, New Mexico.

Winters, Howard D.

1968   Value Systems and Trade Cycles of the Late Archaic in the Midwest. In *New Perspectives in Archaeology,* edited by Sally R. Binford and Lewis R. Binford, pp. 175–221, Aldine Publishers, Chicago.

1969   *The Riverton Culture. Monograph 1. Illinois Archaeological Survey, Urbana.* Reports of Investigations 13. Illinois State Museum, Springfield.

Wobst, H. Martin

1977   Stylistic Behavior and Information Exchange. In *For the Director: Research Es-*

says in Honor of James B. Griffin, edited by Charles E. Cleland, pp. 317–42. Anthropological Papers No. 61. Museum of Anthropology, University of Michigan, Ann Arbor.

Wolf, David J., and Robert L. Brooks
1979   The Prehistoric People of the Rosenberger Site. In *Excavations at Four Archaic Sites in the Lower Ohio Valley Jefferson County, Kentucky, Volume II,* edited by Michael B. Collins, pp. 899–945. Occasional Papers in Anthropology No. 1. Department of Anthropology, University of Kentucky, Lexington.

Young, Biloine Whiting and Melvin L. Fowler
2000   *Cahokia: The Great Native American Metropolis.* University of Illinois Press, Urbana.

Zeanah, David W.
2017   Foraging Models, Niche Construction, and the Eastern Agricultural Complex. *American Antiquity* 82(1):3–24.

Zegwaard, Gerard A.
1959   Headhunting practices of the Asmat of Netherlands New Guinea. *American Anthropologist* 61(6):1020–41.

Contributors

Anne Tobbe Bader is the owner of Corn Island Archaeology in Louisville. Her work over the past forty-five years has focused on native groups that lived in the Falls region. Her research interests include mortuary behavior and ritual, boundaries and frontiers, and intergroup interaction during the late Middle Archaic.

Rick Burdin is retired and now works as an independent researcher. His overall research focus is on how hunting and gathering societies of the Lower Ohio River drainage, including the Falls region, changed over time. He also specializes in the analysis of groundstone tools.

Justin N. Carlson is project director at the Kentucky Archaeological Survey at Western Kentucky University. For his research, he utilizes geoarchaeological methods to examine human-environmental interactions during the Holocene and to identify the origins of anthropogenic environments during the Archaic period.

Michael W. French formerly of senior associate archaeologist at Wood Group. His research focused on Mississippian and Fort Ancient interaction in the Falls region, and Early Archaic hunter-gatherer chert exploitation.

Richard W. Jefferies is professor of anthropology, Department of Anthropology, University of Kentucky. His research focuses on hunter-gatherer societies of the southeastern and midwestern United States; Mississippian settlement and subsistence systems; and the Spanish Mission period in the Southeastern United States. He is the author of *Holocene Hunter-Gatherers of the Lower Ohio River Valley*.

Greg J. Maggard is staff archaeologist with the Oklahoma Department of Transportation. He specializes in the study of Paleoindian and Archaic hunter-gatherers in Peru and the Ohio valley.

Robert G. McCullough is section head and assistant director for special projects for the Illinois State Archaeological Survey, Prairie Research Institute, University of Illinois at Urbana-Champaign. He specializes in the study of Late Prehistoric societies in Indiana, the lower Ohio Valley, and the Falls region, as well as the application of geophysical techniques to archaeological sites.

Stephen T. Mocas is staff archaeologist with Wood. He has spent much of his fifty years in archaeology studying the cultures of the Ohio valley, with an emphasis on the development of Woodland ceramics.

Cheryl Ann Munson is research scientist with the Midwest Archaeology Laboratory, Department of Anthropology, Indiana University. She specializes in the study of Mississippian societies in southern Indiana and Native American use of caves and cave minerals.

David Pollack is director of the Kentucky Archaeological Survey at Western Kentucky University. He specializes in the Mississippian and Fort Ancient societies of the Ohio River valley and has edited numerous professional publications on Kentucky archaeology. He is the author of *Caborn-Welborn: Constructing a New Society after the Angel Chiefdom Collapse*.

Jack Rossen works for the non-profit History Flight, conducting the recovery of MIA marines from the World War II Battle of Tarawa. He is retired professor of anthropology at Ithaca University. He specializes in the analysis of plant remains recovered from archaeological sites in the Ohio valley, New York, and South America.

Christopher W. Schmidt is a bioarchaeologist, professor of anthropology, and director of the Anthropology Graduate Program at the University of Indianapolis. He has engaged in research pertaining to the Early through Late Archaic in Indiana, including the Falls region, for over twenty years. His work has focused on dietary reconstruction, trophy-taking, and cremation.

Claiborne Daniel Sea is a PhD student at University of Alabama. He has conducted research on Fort Ancient occupations in central Kentucky using techniques such as geophysics. He also has an interest in lithic and ceramic technologies.

Duane B. Simpson is senior archaeologist at Cardno in Louisville. He has directed archaeological and geomorphological research on a wide variety of sites over his twenty-five-year professional career, with a particular focus on Late Archaic settlement patterns of the Falls region.

C. Russell Stafford is professor emeritus in the Department of Earth and Environmental Systems at Indiana State University, Terre Haute. His research focuses on the Archaic Period and Holocene landscape reconstruction through soil-geomorphic studies in the Lower Ohio River valley and the Falls region.

Gary E. Stinchcomb is assistant professor in the Watershed Studies Institute and Department of Earth and Environmental Sciences at Murray State University. His research is in soils, paleosoils, quaternary geology, geomorphology, and paleoenvironment.

Jocelyn C. Turner is research associate in the Department of Anthropology at Indiana University Bloomington, specializing in archaeobotany and paleoethnobotany, with research interests in the utilization of plants by the native peoples of Falls region, the lower Ohio River valley, and adjacent regions.

Index

RIPLEY P. BULLEN SERIES

Florida Museum of Natural History

Tacachale: Essays on the Indians of Florida and Southeastern Georgia during the Historic Period, edited by Jerald T. Milanich and Samuel Proctor (1978)

Aboriginal Subsistence Technology on the Southeastern Coastal Plain during the Late Prehistoric Period, by Lewis H. Larson (1980)

Cemochechobee: Archaeology of a Mississippian Ceremonial Center on the Chattahoochee River, by Frank T. Schnell, Vernon J. Knight Jr., and Gail S. Schnell (1981)

Fort Center: An Archaeological Site in the Lake Okeechobee Basin, by William H. Sears, with contributions by Elsie O'R. Sears and Karl T. Steinen (1982)

Perspectives on Gulf Coast Prehistory, edited by Dave D. Davis (1984)

Archaeology of Aboriginal Culture Change in the Interior Southeast: Depopulation during the Early Historic Period, by Marvin T. Smith (1987)

Apalachee: The Land between the Rivers, by John H. Hann (1988)

Key Marco's Buried Treasure: Archaeology and Adventure in the Nineteenth Century, by Marion Spjut Gilliland (1989)

First Encounters: Spanish Explorations in the Caribbean and the United States, 1492–1570, edited by Jerald T. Milanich and Susan Milbrath (1989)

Missions to the Calusa, edited and translated by John H. Hann, with an introduction by William H. Marquardt (1991)

Excavations on the Franciscan Frontier: Archaeology at the Fig Springs Mission, by Brent Richards Weisman (1992)

The People Who Discovered Columbus: The Prehistory of the Bahamas, by William F. Keegan (1992)

Hernando de Soto and the Indians of Florida, by Jerald T. Milanich and Charles Hudson (1992)

Foraging and Farming in the Eastern Woodlands, edited by C. Margaret Scarry (1993)

Puerto Real: The Archaeology of a Sixteenth-Century Spanish Town in Hispaniola, edited by Kathleen Deagan (1995)

Political Structure and Change in the Prehistoric Southeastern United States, edited by John F. Scarry (1996)

Bioarchaeology of Native American Adaptation in the Spanish Borderlands, edited by Brenda J. Baker and Lisa Kealhofer (1996)

A History of the Timucua Indians and Missions, by John H. Hann (1996)

Archaeology of the Mid-Holocene Southeast, edited by Kenneth E. Sassaman and David G. Anderson (1996)

The Indigenous People of the Caribbean, edited by Samuel M. Wilson (1997; first paperback edition, 1999)

Hernando de Soto among the Apalachee: The Archaeology of the First Winter Encampment, by Charles R. Ewen and John H. Hann (1998)

The Timucuan Chiefdoms of Spanish Florida, by John E. Worth: vol. 1, *Assimilation;* vol. 2, *Resistance and Destruction* (1998; first paperback edition, 2020)

Ancient Earthen Enclosures of the Eastern Woodlands, edited by Robert C. Mainfort Jr. and Lynne P. Sullivan (1998)

An Environmental History of Northeast Florida, by James J. Miller (1998)

Precolumbian Architecture in Eastern North America, by William N. Morgan (1999)

Archaeology of Colonial Pensacola, edited by Judith A. Bense (1999)

Grit-Tempered: Early Women Archaeologists in the Southeastern United States, edited by Nancy Marie White, Lynne P. Sullivan, and Rochelle A. Marrinan (1999; first paperback edition, 2001)

Coosa: The Rise and Fall of a Southeastern Mississippian Chiefdom, by Marvin T. Smith (2000)